Gardens, City Life and Culture

Gardens, City Life and Culture

Gardens, City Life and Culture

Gardens, City Life and Culture

Gardens, City Life and Culture

Gardens, City Life and Culture

Dumbarton Oaks Studies in Garden and Landscape History

Acknowledgments

Michel Conan

This edited volume is the offspring of an earlier Dumbarton Oaks working group between Chinese scholars and American sinologists in March 2005, hosted by Xin Wu (Coordinator of Asian Programs) and Michel Conan (Director of Garden and Landscape Studies). Three Chinese scholars: Professors Yang Hongxun from the Chinese Academy of Social Sciences, Chen Wangheng from Wuhan University and Wang Yi from the Chinese Academy of Social Sciences, and three American sinologists: Professors Peter Bol from Harvard University, Martin Powers from the University of Michigan and Stephen West from Arizona State University were invited. At the conclusion of this two-day meeting, the topic "Contributions of Gardens to City Life and Culture" was recommended and Dumbarton Oaks was asked to prepare an edited volume in order to broaden the dialogue between Chinese and Western scholars, and to give scholarly and historical background to the development of parks and garden policies for cities worldwide. A larger group of scholars contacted for the book project responded enthusiastically. After a common agreement was signed between the Director of Dumbarton Oaks and the President of Wuhan University in June 2005, a first manuscript of this volume was translated into Chinese by the Environmental Aesthetics program of Wuhan University and published by Wuhan University Press in October 2006. Meanwhile, Professor Chen Wangheng, with help from Xin Wu at Dumbarton Oaks, organized, in Wuhan, an international conference to disseminate the ideas contained in the book among Chinese specialists and to open the floor to more Chinese authors. The Wuhan University and Dumbarton Oaks joint international conference, *Green Bond: Cities and Gardens,* took place on October 20-22, 2006, with support from the Bureau of Garden and Landscape of the City of Wuhan. The first two days offered a unique opportunity for an exchange between some authors of the book who had been able to come to Wuhan, and a number of scholars from China, Korea, Japan and also Western scholars working in China. The third day was hosted by Zhan Lin, the head of the Bureau of Garden and Landscape of the City of Wuhan. It comprised three keynote speeches and an "International Roundtable" that included twenty-five scholars and experts from Europe, America and China to discuss possible greening policies of the city. Vincent Asselin, Michel Conan and Chen Wangheng were asked to give the keynote speeches. Xin Wu chaired the roundtable, a formidable task to be carried simultaneously in Chinese and English. The audience (primarily city officials) was asked to write down their questions and the panel responded accordingly. It is worth noting that the main questions were related to the participation of citizens to the greening of the city, the possibilities for public-private partnership for the financing of projects and the balance between short term development and long term environment. It resulted in a very interesting discussion with lively interventions by Chinese and international panelists. As a result of this international conference, a few changes were introduced into the book, and this publication is slightly different from the Chinese version published in 2006. It owes much to the authors who have been extremely generous with their time and documents, to the President of the University of Wuhan who has supported the development of a new academic interest for the public environment, to all the Chinese students who helped with the meeting with great eagerness to learn more about landscape approaches in the rest of the world, and to the City of Wuhan a—3000-year old modern metropolis in the center of China.

Gardens, City Life and Culture: A World Tour

Co-edited by Michel Conan and Chen Wangheng

Dumbarton Oaks Research Library and Collection
Washington, D.C.
Distributed by Harvard University Press, 2008.

Published by Dumbarton Oaks Research Library and Collection and
Spacemaker Press. Distributed by Harvard University Press, 2008.

Library of Congress Cataloging-in-Publication Data

Gardens, city life, and culture : a world tour / co-edited by Michel Conan
and Wangheng Chen.
        p. cm.
    ISBN 978-0-88402-328-9
    1. Urban gardens. 2. Urban gardens--Social aspects. 3. City and town
life. I. Conan, Michel, 1939- II. Chen, Wangheng. III. Dumbarton Oaks.
    SB473.G28897 2007
    712.09173'2--dc22

                                    2007039438

Printed in China

Contents

Gardens, City Life and Culture

Gardens, City Life and Culture

Gardens, City Life and Culture

Gardens, City Life and Culture

Gardens, City Life and Culture

Gardens, City Life and Culture

City Gardens, Intercommunication and Culture

Michel Conan and Chen Wangheng

One may regret that most travelers, even when they greatly admired gardens, only paid scant attention to them. Historians are travelers to the past whose efforts are often more systematic, even though they may share some of the limitations of ancient travelers. Like them, they are foreign to the country they visit, and at risk of misunderstanding the perspective on gardens of people who lived in the cities they study. Nevertheless they bring to life aspects of the past that have long been forgotten and they give us the privilege of much more precise descriptions of gardens, their uses, their development and their meanings in several cities for which much information has been conserved up to the present.

The Mysterious Aura of City Gardens

Why do great travelers marvel so much when they find on their path a city embowered in gardens, taking the abundance of gardens in or around a city as a sign of excellence? Is the welfare brought to a city by its gardens mostly economic or aesthetic or do gardens convey a sense of the liveliness of city life to which the travelers intuitively responded? The boat of the great Arab traveler, Ibn Baṭṭûṭa (1304-1368/78?), landed in China in 1344 at a city he called Zaytûn (Quanzhou or Ts'in Kiang in the Fujian province).[1] After noting that this must have been the largest harbor in the world, and that it produced some of the finest damask fabric and satin in China, he makes an unexpected remark: "In this city, as in all other Chinese cities, each inhabitant owns his garden, his field in the middle of which stands his home, as in Sijilmâsa among us. This explains why Chinese cities are so large."[2] And then he notes that Muslims live in a segregated neighborhood. The significance of his remark about the excellence of Chinese city gardens is underscored by the fact that his own interests are focused on Muslim religious activities and history rather than gardens and city life. This is a man who left his city for the hajj, the holy pilgrimage to Mecca in 1325.[3] That he would pay such attention to the comfort of city life as attested by the numerous gardens in which all Chinese city people dwelt is most telling.

He casually repeats similar observations several times in his accounts. "After ten days we arrived near Quanjanfû, large and beautiful city located in a huge plain and surrounded with orchards as in the Ghouta of Damas(…) It is a city surrounded with four bulwark walls(…)Chinese people live within the fourth wall: it is the largest of the four cities(…)As we already said, each inhabitant has his own garden, his field, and his house" (Ibn Baṭṭûṭa 1356/1995, 985). Not too surprisingly, his praise for Yangzhou is even higher "This is the largest city that I have seen on earth: it would take three days to walk through it in its greater length. It is built according to the same principle as all other Chinese cities: each inhabitant owns his orchard and his house"[4] (Ibn Baṭṭûṭa 1356/1995, 987).

That this traveler from Morocco, where extremely large gardens were a source of riches for the Almohad Sultan (as Mohammed El Faiz explains in this volume), could respond to the presence of common gardens in a Chinese city, tells us more, probably, about their significance, rather than their ubiquity. China was under Mongol rule, the Yuan dynasty (1279-1368) at the time of his visit. This also may have led him to exaggerate the praise he could lavish on the country since he was clearly favorably inclined towards the Mongol rulers for religious reasons. Yet it is very interesting that in order to praise the Yuan regime he extolled the life afforded by gardens to common people in all the cities of China!

These are not the only examples of cities in which he admired the gardens. He lavished great praises on the gardens all around Damas (visited in 1326) where inhabitants would go for a delightful walk at the end of the week,[5] and to the rich orchards that he discovered at the end of his trip when visiting Granada in Andalusia in 1352.[6] China, however, is the only country to which he attributes such a lavish presence of city gardens, and it is also the country that he considered the most advanced in many arts and sciences.[7] We can see how city gardens form, in his mind, a symbol of the excellent achievements of a civilization in spite of his dislike of other aspects of the culture, such as their religious practices and beliefs.[8]

Other travelers—from Ruy Gonzalez de Clavijo (?-1412) who admired the rich gardens of Samarkand during his embassy to Timour Leng (1402-06)[9] to Bernal Diaz del Castillo who marveled at the gardens of Tenochtitlan—have expressed bewilderment in front of city gardens that seemed to serve very different purposes, and looked very different from one another. It is also remarkable that their admiration of gardens does not seem to imply a necessary admiration for the political regime or the civilization that made them possible. Ibn Baṭṭûṭa saw gardens as a testimony of the general welfare in China, and admired the gardens but not Chinese culture; Clavijo saw the gardens as part of the extraordinary well-being of the city but cast a cold ambassador's eye on the kingdom, and Diaz del Castillo admired the grandeur of the city gardens but shared his companion's revulsion for Aztec religious practices. It seems that their admiration for gardens transcended the form and function of the gardens, and even the culture from which they proceeded. Thus travelers' enthusiasm for cities with many gardens seems to invite more general attention to the contribution of gardens to city welfare and yet fail to suggest why and how city gardens transformed the economy, the life or the culture of city dwellers.

A Worldwide Historic Perspective

To examine these questions we shall turn to a small number of in depth studies of the contribution of gardens to city life and culture in cities of the world celebrated for their gardens among other things. To avoid privileging a particular perspective the examples range from the ancient Mediterranean world and China in and after the Song dynasty, the Ottoman Empire, the Almohad dynasty in Al Andalus, Baroque Italy and France, to nineteenth century America. It shows that gardens can contribute in many ways to cultural changes, without fulfilling a clear function in the maintenance of the city identity, culture or economy.

This book opens up with the extraordinary example of a city that was destroyed by an eruption of Vesuvius in A.D. 79 and completely covered by lava ashes until the eighteenth century when it was rediscovered. Wilhelmina Jashemski was the first archaeologist to attempt systematic excavations of the open spaces inside and around the ruined constructions. She presents here some of the results of her work that have radically modified the view of cities and gardens in the Roman world. Literary sources gave the impression that gardens had been a recent aspect of the development of luxury life in Roman villas, mostly outside the cities, since the first century B.C. Her study of Pompeii suggested that gardens occupied as much land as public roads and spaces as a whole, or one third of the area covered by all constructions in the entire city. Far from being a marginal phenomenon, gardens contributed to the structure and density of the city. They contributed in different ways to its economy, public and private life, and to the very important metaphysical relationships with the dead. Gardens in their infinite variety of scales, forms and functions appear constitutive of the multifarious fabric of Roman life in Pompeii. Jashemski's study demonstrates that Roman culture developed in the shade of its gardens.

Turning to a distant world, Georges Métailié and Kenneth Hammond, in chapters two and three, demonstrate that in spite of all the differences between the Chinese and the Roman empire, despite the difference in time between the gardens of Pompeii and those of Luoyang, Kaifeng (West 2005, 291-321), and Nanjing, gardens were as varied and as important in city life in China as they had been in the Roman world. More interestingly, however, they show that the contributions of gardens to city life in China are entirely specific to China and that they reflect the historical capacity for change and renewal of its culture. Because the extraordinary development of horticulture in Luoyang is beyond comparison with any previous attempt at plant selection in the Mediterranean world, the cultural life that developed around the display, visit, and aesthetic appreciation of flower collections in Luoyang must be acknowledged as a major invention in terms of world culture. This cultural dynamism seems predicated on horticultural ingenuity as much as conspicuous consumption.

On the other hand, the production of literati gardens as places of withdrawal in the city of Nanjing, studied by Kenneth Hammond, demonstrate other ways in which gardens have contributed to the "vibrant nexus of city life" in China. In Nanjing garden making and garden uses by private families is part and parcel of a process of internal differentiation of the class of commoners. In spite of the obvious differences between the kinds of gardens under discussion, and between the political and economic conditions that prevail in these different cities, we can see that gardens support social changes largely through the establishment of new forms of interaction within and between different groups in Chinese society.

Lauro Magnani and Michel Conan, in chapters four and five, respectively discuss the gardens of the Republic of Genoa one century later and the royal gardens of Paris in the seventeenth and eighteenth centuries. They both show that garden uses led to unsuspected cultural developments in spite of differences in the physical forms and political and economic conditions of garden production in the respective cities. These gardens enabled new forms of social interaction to bring about the emergence of unplanned cultural developments. Similarities are not identities however. The financial aristocracy of Genoa created garden cities and invented commuting. These families lived in a busy competitive world in the center of the city during the day, and withdrew to a world of leisure and aristocratic pursuits in their gardens in the evening, especially when they entertained guests from other countries whom they wanted to impress with the refinement of their lifestyle.

Gardens were built to support the establishment of a banking hegemony of the Genoese finance establishment in Europe, and they became part of the self-representation of the city leaders. As such, they put their imprint upon the image of the city as a whole, but they failed to compensate for the violence exercised by the king of France, and to sustain afterwards a dynamic image of the city.

In the meantime in Paris successive kings opened their gardens to the public, and—somewhat like in Kaifeng (West 2005, 291-321), but five centuries later—a variety of new interactions developed among the crowd of commoners, priests and aristocrats who mingled in these gardens. New mores, new practices, and new cultural identities were forged through ritualized garden encounters during two centuries. These phenomena were totally unplanned and baffled all serious observers throughout the eighteenth century. As in Genoa, garden life greatly contributed to the image of the city and to the liveliness of debates between citizens.

Most significantly, in all of these cases in China and Europe, gardens seem to root the pursuit of new practices in a generally accepted view of nature, and do so because gardens give cultural forms to nature. New gardens provide forms of nature amenable to contesting the legitimacy of certain behavioral and attitudinal experiments between groups of garden users. In these essays, shuttling back and forth between China, Italy, and France sheds a surprising light upon the links between gardens and cultural change in city life. Wherever gardens provide a new domain of social interactions for city dwellers engaged in exploring, negotiating, or contesting cultural shifts, resulting changes linked to well-accepted views of urban nature may become widely accepted. Then gardens become a melting pot of city culture.

In chapters six and seven, Shirine Hamadeh and Robert Rotenberg show how gardens in two very different cultural and political contexts performed precisely in this way—as places where social and cultural changes were explored and contested and linked to new attitudes towards nature. Changes in garden practices in two neighboring cities, Istanbul and Vienna, belonging to empires that had fought one another into a stalemate, extended over the whole of the eighteenth century in Istanbul and the first half of the nineteenth century in Vienna. They are all the more interesting because of the difference in the sources of initiatives leading to garden developments. In Istanbul the Sultan and his court seem to have attempted control of the middle classes by opening or creating public gardens with fountains and coffee houses; alternatively, in Vienna, the middle-class took the initiative, creating private gardens in a new style in an unplanned effort to evade political control by the state in public places. In neither case can it be demonstrated that private or public gardens fulfilled a clear political function. Rather we can see that the cultural contests that they made possible display a common feature: the development of new forms of social interaction and of ritualized practices that enabled the construction of new ways of life and contributed to new forms of social identity. Chapter eight pursues the idea that gardens can be places in a city where important cultural and social changes are explored, with a twist due to the colonial context of Shanghai, where they developed in the second half of the nineteenth century. At first only Western colonizers were allowed to live in the Shanghai concessions. So they wholeheartedly imported Western architecture, objects and ways of life. This is how a Western style public park was established in the 1880s, for the sole use of Westerners. However, by that time, more and more Chinese people were living in the concessions. The racist policy of exclusion of Chinese people from this park spurred Chinese entrepreneurs into creating profit-oriented gardens open to the whole public. Zhou Xian-ping and Chen Zhe-hua tell how these gardens became during the next twenty years the testing ground of Western techniques, ways of life and even political debate for all the inhabitants of Shanghai, thus contributing largely to the development of the Shanghai-style culture, a new hybrid of Chinese and Western cultures. This confirms the role of gardens as accelerators of cultural creativity for large groups of city people.

Parks and the Beginnings of Urban Planning

During the nineteenth century several keen observers of gardens reached a similar conclusion and assumed that it warranted the development of private and public gardens in a well planned manner in order to achieve widespread cultural or social reforms. John Claudius Loudon (1783, 1843) was followed by many reformers in England, Germany and France. Some were more successful than others, and this triggered international emulation.

Chapter nine, the last of the first part devoted to examples prior to the twentieth century, introduces the first clear attempt presented in this volume to create city gardens in planned efforts at municipal development. David Schuyler shows how, in the course of one year, an already well-known American landscape architect offered propositions for a park and garden public policy aimed at solving the most pressing problems of urban life. In 1868, American cities were undergoing a rapid industrial development creating much squalor, health problems, individual stress, traffic problems and social unrest. Frederick Law Olmsted's proposal for a comprehensive network of parks and parkways over a whole metropolitan area, together with suburban communities, has been followed to a large extent by many American cities at the turn of the twentieth century. These problems and the solutions offered are of great interest for all rapidly developing cities in the contemporary world.

They were not the first examples however of public park and garden policies. In fact they were partly inspired, at their beginning at least, by examples in Great Britain, in particular by Joseph Paxton (1801-1865) at Birkenhead near Liverpool in 1843-47, and by the transformation of the city of Paris by Jean-Charles Adolphe Alphand (1817-1891) after the coup of Louis Napoléon in 1852. Since gardens seem to play an important role in the transformation of city life, both in Birkenhead and in Paris, Olmsted believed he could use these examples to improve the general welfare in American cities. This very straightforward idea suffers a number of difficulties which were cleverly explored by a very important English gardener, William Robinson (1838-1935). Based on his travels to France, in 1869 Robinson published in London a very large book devoted to the parks, promenades and gardens of Paris considered in relation to the want of English cities, and of London in particular, of which we planned to republish the introduction in this volume. We did not, but since it is a rather rare book at present, it is worth quoting here some of his introductory remarks. They provide a rationale for urban park planning and for borrowing ideas from foreign cities. They also highlight several difficulties that these still common practices usually raise.

> There is no need to expatiate on the necessity of a thoroughly good system of public gardening in the great cities of a wealthy and civilized race; nor to describe the want of it in our own case – this is painted but too plainly on the faces of thousands in our densely-packed cities, in which the active brain and heart of the country are continually being concentrated. That London is no longer a city, but a nation gathered together in one spot, is a truism: our other great cities are almost keeping pace with it in growth: but in none of them can we see a trace of any attempt to open up their closely peopled quarters in a way that is calculated to produce a really beneficial effect on the lives and health of their workers (Robinson 1869, xcvii-xcviii).

Having asserted the need for public parks, Robinson acknowledged that while there were already parks in London, they failed to serve the whole city population consistently: yet, "The French have their parks and public gardens, and very extensive and well- managed ones, though, like some of our own, embellished in a wasteful and unnecessary manner with costly and tender plants; but their noble tree-planted roads, small public squares and places, are doing more for them than parks and pelargoniums—saving them from pestilential overcrowding, and making their city something besides a place for all to live out of who can afford it" (p. xviii).

This leads to the first problem: the park policy in Paris resulted from the action of an emperor, Napoleon III, who exercised an autocratic government contrary to English traditions and expectations. Thus Robinson calls for Parliament to give the city the power to develop a plan for its parks, gardens and promenades. The political dimension of such park planning is inescapable. It makes landscape planning into an important domain of public debate that should be part of discussions about the allocation of public funds to different aims and projects. This is exactly the end to which Robinson intended his 644-page book. "Is it too much to hope that a portion of our vast expenditure for arsenals, armies fleets, and fortifications may some day be diverted to making such alterations in our cities as will render possible in them the rearing of worthy representatives the English race?" (p. xix). It raises issues of public justice. He knows very well that there are magnificent parks in the very center of London and that they are tended with great care, but he points to the fact that they are only serving a few privileged people, and that their maintenance cost could be appropriated to better serve a larger population. So the city should exercise economic choices in the design, planting, and management of urban parks: "The new avenue gardens in the Regent's Park, with their griffins and artificial stonework have certainly cost as much as would have created an oasis in some pestilential part of the East-end" p. xxi). Yet he insists that a general urban policy should not be limited to the creation of parks, even better distributed over the whole territory of the city. He wants streets to be planted with trees, bringing new amenities to dwellings bordering them and improving the conditions of traffic. Thus he sees the park and promenade policy as an integral part of city planning, not as a subsidiary aspect that can be addressed independently of major issues: "In the creation of tree-planted streets in the more crowded parts both of London proper and the suburbs, they should not as a rule be formed on the site of old and much frequented streets, but, so far as possible, pierced between them, leaving the largest and most populous thoroughfares of the present day to become the secondary ones of the future" (p.xxiii). This was clearly inspired by Hausmann's policy of city renewal in Paris, and we may see in Schuyler's chapter how it was translated for the U.S. cities by Olmsted. Then Robinson goes on to explain that such large schemes demand the establishment of public nurseries and the development of a specialized urban horticulture, which lacks in England in spite of its superior competence in many domains of horticulture such as the production of hybrids and the naturalization of foreign plants. Robinson who has a clear sense of the superiority of English over French horticulture points out that this should not deter Englishmen from learning, in some specialized domain, from a less advanced country.[10] And he concludes with a plea for his countrymen to visit Paris and see for themselves whether gardens contribute to a better life there, opening the first chapter in defiance of their skeptical attitudes: "If not already the brightest, airiest, and most beautiful of all cities, Paris is in a fair way to become so; and the greatest part of her beauty is due to her gardens and her trees" (Robinson 1969, 1).

The Dilemmas of Parks and Garden Planning

The second part of this book is devoted to a large extent to presentations of urban park and promenade policies in different cities and countries during the twentieth century. Some chapters propose examples and discuss their limits with greater care than Robinson when he advocated emulation in England of the questionable policies of Haussman in Paris. Others show that serious questions may be raised by the complete absence of such public policy today in some cities that had once derived their excellence in the past from the remarkable balance of garden and urban activities over an extended territory. It raises interesting questions for policy makers and planners to consider.

In chapter ten, Thorbjörn Andersson presents the remarkable urban park and promenade policy of the city of Stockholm developed and implemented during the middle of the twentieth century. He demonstrates, much better than

Robinson, the extent to which an urban park policy can be a fundamental tool in the implementation of public welfare reform. He shows how issues of park design in social democratic Sweden contributed to a broader policy of cultural development for the whole metropolitan population. He even shows how the parks and promenades of Stockholm were conceived as instruments of the modernization of Swedish culture and mentalities, and how they were meant to help passing from a hierarchical and tradition-ridden, to an egalitarian and progress-oriented society. Yet he also shows the reverse figure of that policy. The promise of a bright future in an egalitarian society allowed the development of authoritarian practices by public managers that eventually proved to be self-defeating. The parks of the city of Stockholm are still very much used and appreciated by the population, but it would be wrong to believe that they achieved their purpose as originally conceived.

The next chapter, by Nicholas Dagen Bloom, about the leading American new towns of the sixties, Columbia (Maryland), Reston (Virginia), and Irvine (California), confirms the strange observation that plans calling upon a new garden and park policy to improve city life seem neither to fail nor to be completely successful. Like the planners of the Stockholm school of public parks, the American landscape planners of the sixties wished to promote cultural changes predicated upon a renewed bond between citizens and wild nature, a sense of accountability to nature. So, cultural goals and landscape methods differed from the Swedes.

The Americans were concerned with the conservation of wildlife as well as agricultural landscape for the sake of developing a new nature ethic among American suburbanites, rather than abstract presentations of an imagined wilderness devoted to the pursuit of egalitarian practices. Bloom observes that long after the cities were completed, and in spite of large tracts of open space devoted to nature preservation and a strong engagement of local associations and cultural centers devoted to an introduction of city dwellers to nature observation, pedestrians are rarer in the open landscapes and footpaths of the city every year. And he makes an enlightening observation: "A society less obsessed with crime, abduction, and juvenile delinquency might find natural areas around the home less threatening."

This is enlightening because it helps us understand the limits of city park planning. It points to a cultural change that governs U.S. citizens' interactions at present and yet could neither be predicted nor modified by city planners. A similar observation applies to the Stockholm case: the social democrat planners could not anticipate that their good willing policies would be denounced for their authoritarianism after their results had been thoroughly enjoyed by large populations. Yet we should see that in both cases these park planners correctly anticipated both the interest for and attitudes towards nature of their future users, which were different in Sweden in the mid century and in the U.S. in the second half of the century. This created favorable conditions for engagement of large groups of citizens interacting in the parks, and these engagements ran a course of their own. Collective interactions and individual choices were mutually reinforcing and contributed to a constant reframing of issues and engagement with nature by city users. For example, we learn that artificial lakes offering much appreciated scenery in the American new towns are not self sustainable. Thus the maintenance of an undefiled nature is subjected to unexpected difficulties that, in turn, have brought many people together. An effort to maintain the quality of water, perceived as a symbol of environmental quality, in turn introduces subtle changes in the view of nature and the nature of interactions between park users. In fact, we can see that the transformation of the whole city into a public garden devoted to the preservation of the presence of wilderness, brings people together in ways that depend as much on changes in the natural and in the cultural and political environment, as from the initial intentions of landscape planners. The partial success of these park policies is a result of the engagement of groups of local inhabitants in mutual interactions in and about the parks. Yet, the same interactions contribute new practices, representations of nature and cultural expectations with respect to city life that lead away from the planners' goals.

Chapter twelve brings a more critical note to our study of gardens and cities, and alert us to the risks of wanton destruction of gardens. Mohammed El Faïz calls attention to the risks for the city of Marrakech, which has enjoyed a rich garden environment for centuries, to ignore and destroy it for the sake of modernization. El Faïz describes the history of the construction and the destruction of this extraordinary garden environment. Given the remarks by Bloom about the fragility of attempts to create sustainable wildernesses in the American new towns, it is all the more interesting to note that an artificial oasis created by Almohad rulers nine hundred years ago had resisted the passage of time until the middle of the twentieth century, allowing the city of Marrakech to enjoy an extraordinary bond with its large palm tree oasis during eight hundred years. El Faïz explains under which political and institutional conditions an artificial oasis was deliberately organized, and created the conditions for the development of the Medina, the traditional center of the city. He also shows how from the beginning of the French protectorate in 1912 to the present a new kind of approach of city planning and economic development allowed immigration into the city and constant encroachment of the Medina on surrounding gardens thus destroying the relationships to nature and the hydraulic system that sustained the oasis. He proposes that the pursuit of a positive relationship between the city and its gardens depends to a large extent upon the role of institutions and political leaders in their search for a new ecological model after the city economy has radically changed.

Yinong Xu in chapter thirteen and Sylvie Brosseau in chapter fourteen precisely address issues of cultural continuity in cities where, as in Marrakech at present, a felicitous relationship between urban dwellers and their gardens has been disrupted. Both of them concur that gardens cannot be defined in the absolute since their contribution to a city culture depend on deep-rooted cultural attitudes towards time and nature shared or debated by local citizens. Xu's study of the conservation of the historic gardens of Suzhou during the last centuries calls into question the orientation towards the continuity of material form that is proposed as a universal rule of conservation by well-meaning Western experts. He shows, moreover, that the continuity of historical gardens in Suzhou has served to maintain both the constant renovation and deepening of a literary culture, and a popular culture of sensuous and horticultural pleasures (to which Métailié had called attention in chapter two).

In parallel fashion Brosseau shows how interactions between local groups of concerned environmentalists and public authorities in Tokyo have led to the development of new forms of urban parks in which ancient cultural practices can be brought up to date in the context of new Japanese ways of life. In both cases garden conservation at the city level implies the creation of new gardens or parks by public authorities, and reinvention of traditional practices at the initiative of individuals, families or groups engaged in social and cultural changes. The encounters of public plans and private groups' initiatives results in unpredictable dynamics and results. Xu sees in Suzhou's historic past what Brosseau sees in present-day Tokyo: garden making and garden practices are instrumental in the pursuit of changes and mediate deep-rooted cultural practices on the one hand, and external pressures for new forms of city life on the other.

After so many chapters in which city gardens have been presented as instruments of cultural experience and change, the last chapter by U.M. Chandrashekara and S. Sankar brings us back to the importance of gardens as economic resources. Very far from Pompeii, they are in Kerala, an Indian region that provides one of the most successful examples of sustainability in the world at the end of the twentieth century. This may serve as a reminder of the possible economic role that common gardens may play in developing economies. Yet, their presentation also describes the contribution of home gardens to the conservation of varieties and species that would be threatened by industrial cultivation. They also show that home garden practices have important cultural implications for the equality of men and women in the family, the integration of women in the work force, and the strengthening of social bonds in residential areas. Yet they also warn that this is a fragile development that is threatened by world trends towards more specialized forms of farming.

Gardens as Sources of Intersubjective Development

Three observations seem to impose themselves as we advance in the reading of this book. First, there is no universal essence of a garden, no feature of gardens that would fulfill some universal function in any city of the world. Second, in an even more surprising manner, studies of very interesting examples of city planning in the twentieth century show that there is no garden policy or garden planning at city level that can guarantee a certain type of city welfare for any length of time. This might deter any attempt at promoting gardens in a city, and yet when we turn to cultures that were not under the sway of the idea of planning as we are, we can see that gardens have sometimes played a very fruitful role in their own development. Third, it should be said that gardens have not always benefited all citizens to the same extent, and yet they allowed very important changes in the culture and identity of some groups who had free access to city parks and gardens. This is an idea that provides an interesting thread for readers to follow throughout the chapters.

It is very interesting to observe that gardens have been instrumental in the development of public life in Paris in the seventeenth and eighteenth centuries, and of Stockholm in the twentieth, of cultural life in Nanjing and Shanghai or in Suzhou at very different periods, of commoners' pleasures and economic situations in Pompeii, Luoyang and Kaifeng (West 2005, 291-321), of aristocrats in Genoa, and the middle class in American new towns. Yet all of these developments run their course as a consequence of the encounters between large numbers of individual initiatives in garden making and practices within the context of a cultural matrix shared by most of them. Not only did these people contribute to a mediation between the culture they inherited from their parents and new forms of urban culture, but as they meet one another at random in their gardens or public parks—as in Istanbul in the eighteenth century—they came to share a deeper sense of their own identity as a group. It is important to note that when sharing pleasures they came to share emotions and to feel more and more alike one another as they engaged in more clearly shared emotional bonds with an invented nature and the ritualized practices it supported. Thus we can see gardens as sources of intersubjective development: processes of production of a shared culture that enables large groups of people—at the scale of a whole city—to engage in emotional communities geared towards collective achievements. These processes contribute to the formation of new forms of social praxis, new systems of judgment, new kinds of intercommunication, new articulations of knowledge, opinion, and metaphysics. It seems that when gardens create a new possibility for many people to engage together in creative interactions they enable them to make a fresh collective sense of their existence, rooting culture into nature in a new way.

BIBLIOGRAPHY

Charles-Dominique, Paule. *Voyageurs arabes*. Paris: Gallimard Bibliothèque de la Pléiade, 1995.

Conan, Michel, Jose Tito Rojo, Luigi Zangheri, eds. *Histories of Garden Conservation. Case Studies and Critical Debates*. Florence: Leo Olschki, 2005.

Conan, Michel, ed. *Baroque Gardens, Emulation, Sublimation, Subversion*. Dumbarton Oaks Colloquium Series in the History of Landscape Architecture (XXV). Washington D.C.: Dumbarton Oaks, 2005

Ibn Battûta. Voyages et Périples, in *Voyageurs arabes* translated and commented by Paule Charles-Dominique, 369-1050. Paris: Gallimard Bibliothèque de la Pléiade, 1995.

Robinson, William. *Parks, Promenades and Gardens of Paris, described and considered in relation to the wants of our own cities and of Public and Private Gardens*. London: John Murray, 1869.

West, Stephen H. "Spectacle, Ritual, and Social relations: The Son of Heaven, Citizens, and Created Space in Imperial Gardens in the Northern Song," in *Baroque Gardens, Emulation, Sublimation, Subversion*, edited by Michel Conan, 291-322. Washington D.C.: Dumbarton Oaks, 2005.

Xu, Yinong. "The Making and Remaking of Cang Lang Ting, Attitudes Towards the Past Evinced in the History of a Garden Site in Suzhou," in *Histories of Garden Conservation. Case Studies and Critical Debates*, edited by Michel Conan, Jose Tito Rojo and Luigi Zangheri, 3-62. Florence: Leo S. Olschki, 2005.

NOTES

[1] It was probably the largest harbor in thirteenth century China. Marco Polo called it Çaiton. Ibn Battûta heard Zaytûn, which is a word meaning olive tree in Arabic, and noted that "After crossing the sea we landed in Zaytûn, the first Chinese city. No olive tree grows there, neither are there olive trees in China or India, so Zaytûn the name of that city has no particular meaning attached to it." (Ibn Battûta1356/1995, 980) It displays an unconscious association between the olive tree, a source of wealth all around the Mediterranean sea, and a Chinese city. Ibn Battûta had heard much about China before he arrived and expected to find a country crossed by a large river comparable to the Nile: "On its banks, there are villages, fields, orchards, market-places as on the banks of the Nile river, with the difference that China is more prosperous. Hydraulic millwheels are quite numerous on this river. China produces much sugar, of equal or even better quality than Egyptian sugar, grapes and plums. I believed that the "uthmânî" plums of Damas were unsurpassed until I tasted Chinese plums…" (Ibn Battûta 1356/1995, 975-976).

[2] Ibn Battûta 1356/1995, 981.

[3] According to Charles-Dominique, in the Eastern world, he was known under the nickname of Shams-ad-dîn, the Sun of Religion. A large part of his travel accounts is devoted to visits to Muslim saints and descriptions of religious or mystical practices (Charles-Dominique 1995, 1131).

[4] He calls the city al-Khansâ. Marco Polo called it Quinsai, and said that it was" the largest city that could be found in the world, where one may enjoy so many pleasures that one feels in paradise." (Charles-Dominique 1995, 1198)

[5] Ibn Baṭṭûṭa 1356/1995, 447.

[6] Ibn Baṭṭûṭa 1356/1995, 1019.

[7] He admires chinaware, the feats of poultry selection, the production of silk, the development of paper money, the exploitation of coal which is a source of wonder for him, the organization of the public tax system applied to commerce by boat, and interestingly the mastery of the arts that extends to perfection in the representation of the human face, a skill which is used to portray and control foreign travelers.(Ibn Baṭṭûṭa 1356/1995, 976-9).

[8] "Even though China is a very beautiful country, I did not enjoy being there because I was vexed by the reigning paganism. When I left my dwelling I was shocked by many unacceptable behaviors, and it vexed me to such an extent that I only went outside my house under absolute necessity." (Ibn Baṭṭûṭa 1356/1995, 986).

[9] "Samarqand stands in a plain, and is surrounded by a rampart or wall of earth, with a very deep ditch. The city itself is rather larger than Seville, but lying outside Samarqand are great numbers of houses which form extensive suburbs. These lie spread on all hands for indeed the township is surrounded by orchards and vineyards, extending in some cases to a league and a half or even two leagues beyond Samarqand which stands in their centre. In between these orchards pass streets with open squares; these all are densely populated, and here all kinds of goods are on sale with bread stuffs and meat. Thus it is that the population without the city is more numerous than the population within the walls. Among these orchards outside Samarqand are found the most noble and beautiful houses, and here Timur has his many palaces and pleasure grounds. Round and about the great men of the government also here have their estates and country houses, each standing within its orchard: and so numerous are these gardens and vineyards surrounding Samarqand that a traveller who approaches the city sees only a great mountainous height of trees and the houses embowered among them remain invisible." Quoted from http://depts.washington.edu/uwch/silkroad/texts/clavijo/cltxt1.html on March 18, 2006.

[10] "I have never asserted. As has been assumed, That the French are our superiors in general horticulture, for I know right well that we are as far before them in horticulture, agriculture, and rural affairs generally, as we are in journalistic and magazine literature; but I do assert that in certain point of fruit and vegetable culture they are equally as far in advance of us. I am convinced, too, that more than one of their modes of culture will prove of far greater value to ourselves than ever they have been to the French." And he adds this amusing remark: "If I were to find in use in the backwoods of America some handy tool or implement effective in saving human labour, should I be wise in refusing to adopt it because the rude inventor had not attained to the simplest luxuries of existence?" (Robinson 1969, xxv).

Gardens, City Life and Culture

Gardens, City Life and Culture

Gardens, City Life and Culture

Gardens, City Life and Culture

Gardens, City Life and Culture

Gardens, City Life and Culture

CHAPTER 1

Gardens and Garden Life in Pompeii in the First Century A.D.

Wilhelmina Jashemski

Pompeii was a small and thriving Roman city located at the foot of Mount Vesuvius, a large volcano, in the year A.D. 79 when it was hit by an eruption of Vesuvius and buried under several meters of lapilli and ashes. It was rediscovered by archaeologists in the eighteenth century. In the early part of the twentieth century, root cavities were reported in five gardens but until the second half of the twentieth century little attention was given to gardens because it was assumed no trace had been left. Contrary to these expectations I have found evidence of many different types of gardens in the city,[1] and it was even possible to compute the percentage of space devoted to gardens as well as to other purposes: buildings occupy 64.7 percent, gardens and cultivated land 17.7 percent, and streets count for another 17.7 percent. Over one-third of the excavated city was open space.[2]

The Variety of Garden Forms and Functions in the City

The unique preservation of Pompeii by the eruption of Vesuvius in A.D. 79 (Fig. 1) permits us, in a way possible in no other city in the Roman Empire, to study the layout of the city – the location of its public buildings, places of business, homes, gardens and open land. Most numerous are the gardens within the houses. There were also temple gardens and sacred groves, parks, gardens connected with baths and palaestras (sport grounds), in gymnasia and schools, vineyards, orchards, commercial flower gardens, and gardens connected with the tombs that lined the roads leading to the city gates.

The city plan of Pompeii utilized the natural topography. The walls were laid out in an irregular oval, following the contours of the old lava stream (Fig. 2). The walls were about three kilometers in circumference and enclosed an area of about sixty-three hectares. The forum (public place) was laid out in the level area on the western edge of the city. The public buildings were located for the most part in three areas of the city, in the so-called triangular forum, around the forum, which was the heart of every Roman town, and at the eastern edge of the city where the amphitheater and large palaestra were built. The only public buildings not located in these areas were the public baths, which were conveniently located at major crossroads in the city, and at the entrance to the city.

Gardens connected with houses

The Pompeian house was a row house. It had an inward orientation with the house enclosing an atrium (courtyard), one or

Fig. 1. Air view of Vesuvius and Pompeii: Courtesy Superintendete di Archeologico, Pompeii.

Fig. 2. Plan of Pompeii: H. Eschebach. When Giuseppe Fiorelli became Director of the excavation in 1880, he divided the city into nine regions. Each region was subdivided into numbered *insulae*, or blocks, and each entrance in each block was assigned a number. Thus each house had an address of three numbers.

several peristyle gardens (Fig. 3) (a garden court completely or partially surrounded by a colonnaded passage). The most elegant houses in Pompeii were built by the Samnites in the second century B.C.[3] There were also courtyard gardens, which had no portico.

There was by no means a typical dwelling, but the one family house was usual, in contrast to the apartment buildings in Rome. The atrium-peristyle house however was not as typical as has been thought. Only about 240 atrium-peristyle houses have been found at Pompeii in the area excavated so far, some with as many as three or four peristyles. There were also many smaller houses of irregular design, the homes of the more humble citizens, which had gardens. The unpretentious house (I.xiv.2) on the Via di Nocera is typical of those occupied by many a humble citizen in the southeastern part of the city. The garden, which I excavated in 1972, obviously supplied much of the family food. A few orchard trees provided a variety of fruit (olive, fig, lemon) and nuts for the family, and shade for the cultivation of vegetables such as fava beans underneath. The vines that shaded the triclinium furnished table grapes. This garden, as so many others at Pompeii, cannot be classified as either a small orchard or a kitchen garden.[4]

Many houses were frankly commercial in character, with living quarters upstairs, to the rear, or to the side of the shop. In shop houses living quarters connected with the shop were usually small, but the shop owner frequently used part of his precious space for a tiny garden. A bit of green, perhaps a small tree or an oleander bush, a few vegetables or flowers, and at times even a fountain, would add immeasurably to the comfort of these small, dark, and stuffy homes. Shop-houses were scattered throughout the city, for Pompeii had no zoning laws. To the north of the Stabian Baths there is a typical two-room shop with living quarters at the rear. We can be sure the owner placed great value on his tiny garden, for he gave it more than half the ground area of his dwelling.

Some shop-houses were too small for even a tiny garden, but the owner managed a tiny plot of green or perhaps a few potted plants in a small light well. The desire for a bit of green seems to have been a basic trait of the Roman character.

Gardens connected with places of business

Scattered throughout the city were gardens connected with other places of business. Many businesses had been set up in houses during the last years of the city. One of the most interesting is the one in a house (I.xii.10) in which the fish sauce industry was carried on. The popularity of the various fish sauces at Pompeii had long been known, but this is the first site connected with this business to be found. The industry had moved to the peristyle garden of this old house, where there were many large *dolia* and *amphoras* which still contained many tiny fish bones and shells, the remains of the fish sauce. There was a beautiful garden painting on each side of the doorway that led to the rear garden. We wouldn't associate garden paintings with such a smelly place of business, but these paintings were made after the house was converted to commercial use. Much to our surprise we found evidence for a garden planted with two fig trees.[5] (Fig. 4) The workers had been sheltered from the hot Campanian sun, and the garden enlivened by the beauty of flowers or herbs. The location of one tree near the latrine that had been built in the corner of the garden for the workers reflects

Fig. 3. Peristyle Garden of House of the Vettii. Photo: Stanley Jashemski.
Fig. 4. Peritsyle Garden in Garum Shop (I.xii.8). Photo: Stanley Jashemski.

the practice still followed in rural areas in south Italy. Not only does the dense shade of the fig furnish privacy; the large leaf of this tree has long served the peasant as a substitute for toilet tissue.

There is plenty of evidence that whenever possible, tradesmen combined gracious living quarters, including a private garden, with their places of business.

Gardens connected with inns and restaurants

Inns and restaurants are found throughout the city, but they tend to be clustered near the city gates, in the forum area, and in the vicinity of the amphitheater. Many inns and restaurants at Pompeii had beautiful gardens in which guests might enjoy the same pleasures proffered in a delightful little poem of unknown authorship, who invites the weary traveler to stop and rest beneath the shady vine and enjoy the various pleasures of an inn. It paints a charming picture of a landscaped garden with vine-covered arbors, and a gurgling brook.[6] The largest hotel in the city (VII.xi.11/14) was located near the forum on a winding street less than two blocks off the busy Via dell'Abbondanza. This hotel, which could accommodate more than fifty guests, had a large secluded garden with three vine covered arbors. The *caupona* of Euxinus, a rather rustic restaurant with rooms to rent, was located in the amphitheater area. Euxinus served food and drink at the counter, in the dining room, and in the garden, to those attending the spectacles in the amphitheater. We found that much of the garden had been planted in a vineyard. At the west end of the garden were two booths where guests might be served, or perhaps at tables set up under the spreading branches of the huge tree at the west edge of the vineyard.

Gardens connected with public buildings

There were also large public green spaces in various parts of the city. It is not surprising to find gardens connected with public architecture in a culture in which so much of daily life took place outdoors. Pompeii affords an excellent opportunity to see the garden in relation to such buildings for they can be seen here in their original setting and not as isolated structures, as at most sites. The great Palaestra, located across from the amphitheater, on the eastern edge of the city, is a good example. The area was enclosed by porticoes on the north, west and south with in the center a pool surrounded on these three sides by a double row of trees as recommended by Vitruvius for palaestras. In the center was a large swimming pool. Such plantings would give these areas the character of a public park, a welcome respite to the throngs coming to Pompeii for the spectacles in the amphitheater.

Gardens were also found in connection with theaters. Vitruvius recommends building a colonnade behind the stage as a place of refuge in case of thunderstorms. He recommends that the open space between the colonnades be laid out in green plots and planted with trees and shrubs, and contain pathways for promenades.

Temple Gardens

The ancient literature speaks often of temples surrounded by a sacred grove. It seems quite probable that the Doric temple was surrounded by a sacred grove, but the temple was excavated between 1767 and 1797 before there was any interest in checking for evidence of root cavities. When Spano was Director of Excavations at Pompeii, in the early twentieth century, he planted a grove of beautiful evergreen oak around the temple. The temple of the Egyptian goddess, Isis, also excavated in the eighteenth century was also probably surrounded by a sacred garden. Two paintings of the Temple of Isis show plants around the temple. Egyptian gardens were often surrounded by a garden. There is some evidence that the temple of Venus had plantings. There is definite archaeological evidence for a garden connected with the temple of Dionysus located outside the city wall not far from the amphitheater.

Gardens connected with public baths

We know from literature that gardens were connected with baths. There is no definite archaeological evidence for gardens in baths at Pompeii, but August Mau, the eminent Pompeianist, believed that the palaestra in the Forum Baths was definitely a garden. Its small size, the fact that it had no swimming pool and dressing rooms, and that the large marble basin in the center of the garden was believed to have been found there, led him to this conclusion.

Gardens for food production

Still other types of gardens were found in
Pompeii. Our excavations revealed various large
and important areas within the city, especially in
the southeast part, that were given over to food
production. Most were attached to small
houses. In addition to the large formally planted
vineyard (*vinea*) in the large insula to the north
of the amphitheater (Fig. 5), we found a good
part of the lower garden in the House of the
Ship Europa was formally planted in vines. The
vineyard in the garden of a Pompeian vinarius
(IX.ix.6-7), the one in the northwest part of
insula vii in Region VI, in the Caupona of the
Gladiators (L.xx.1) at the first entrance on the

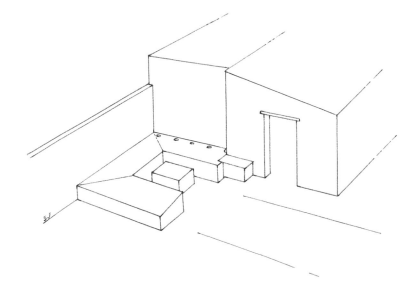

Fig. 5. Masonry triclinium found in a large commercial vineyard. Drawing:
Stanley Jashemski.

left after entering the Porta di Nola, and the shop-house garden (I.xx.5), were less formally planted, often staked and at times
trained on trees in the vineyard.

We found one large commercial orchard (*pomerium.*) An orchard normally had both fruit and nut trees. Home gardens,
as in the Pompeii area today, were often planted with many fruit and nut trees, as the garden at I.xiv.2 on the Via di Nocera.
We also found one large commercial flower garden (II.viii.6) within the city walls of Pompeii.

Gardens for the Dead

The roads leading out of the five city gates at Pompeii were lined with tombs and many of these tombs had gardens. It seems
quite natural that the ancient Romans, for whom gardens were so important in life, should surround their final resting place
with plantings.

The amount of land under cultivation and the amount of open space tell us a great deal about the quality of life in this
ancient city. Ancient Pompeii with its many open green areas – ornamental gardens, kitchen gardens, parks, vineyards,
orchards, and large commercial flower gardens—must have been very beautiful. The planted areas within the city were probably
greater at the time of the eruption than before the earthquake,[7] for we found in several large gardens that we excavated that the
land had been cleared of buildings destroyed by the earthquake. It is difficult to say if this would have substantially altered the
percentage of planted land.

Life in the Garden

In the hundreds of homes that have been preserved by Vesuvius we get an intimate picture of the role of the garden in daily life.[8]
Even the poor, if at all possible, made place in their modest homes for a tiny garden. There were a few houses with no garden,
but it is telling that a neighbor who had a large garden had at times cut a window in the wall that separated the two houses so

that the poor family might enjoy the view of their neighbor's spacious garden.

The garden served as a much-used room in the house, for the clear skies and the warm Campanian sunshine made it possible for much of life to be lived outdoors during a large part of the year. The garden was a place to work and play, to gather for the afternoon meal, to worship the household deities and to share the tranquil joys of the outdoors with relatives and friends.

Outdoor dining and entertaining

The large number of masonry triclinia found in gardens attests to the popularity of eating outdoors, not only in well-known aristocratic homes, but also in those of the more humble inhabitants. The main meal of the day (*cena*) came in the afternoon, after the day's work was done and a visit had been made to the baths. The hour would vary with the season, but for the most part the meal began about three o'clock, and for much of the year, in many homes, it was served in the garden, as it still is in the Pompeii area today. The triclinia (sing. triclinium) found in the gardens of Pompeii are for the most part simple U-shaped structures, consisting of three couches, each of which was large enough to accommodate three people, thus making nine the ideal number for a dinner party (Fig. 5). Originally the Romans sat to eat, but later adopted the Greek custom of reclining at meals. The garden triclinium was usually made of concrete, but traces of decayed wooden triclinia have been found. The hard couches would have been made comfortable with mattresses and pillows, and shaded with a vine-covered arbor or vellum (sheet of linen).

There were three dining rooms in the house of Albucius Celsus (V.ii.i), including a formal banquet hall, but it was in the large secluded garden that the family enjoyed their most delightful summer meals. The garden had a masonry triclinium and a table with a circular white marble top that had an opening in the middle for a jet of water, so that the table served as a fountain when it was not used for meals. A channel near the south couch directed the water into the garden. There was a large rectangular pool in front of the triclinium and water jetted from a low column in the pool, so the family could dine with the cooling sound of water nearby. When the jetting water filled the pool, water spilled over through a large hole near the top of the pool into the garden and was directed to flow through the various little channels found in the garden. This was a kitchen garden planted with both flowers and vegetables, which probably contributed many items to the family meals. No doubt many a guest was entertained in this delightful garden during the long summer months and enjoyed the cooling breezes, the music of the fountain, and the fragrance of the flowers as the dinner hour lengthened into the evening.

A secluded garden, such as that of Albucius Celsus, was a favorite place for outdoor dining, but houses lacking such a garden frequently had an outdoor triclinium in the peristyle garden. The best-preserved outdoor triclinium at Pompeii is in the beautiful garden in the House of the Ephebe (I.vii/10). This house was made by combining several smaller houses and is typical of the homes of the well-to-do commercial class. The masonry triclinium was shaded by a pergola supported by four sturdy columns. The rear wall was decorated with a large animal painting, such as were very popular at Pompeii. The nymphaeum built against this wall held a fountain statue of Pomona holding a shell filled with fruit, from which water fell down four marble steps into a small pool below. From here it was carried further down until it rose in a small jet in the middle of the couches. The furrows in the eastern part of the garden indicated that it was a kitchen garden. A basin at the end of the garden had two openings that could be alternately opened or closed to water either half of the garden. It was not at all unusual in a luxurious

GARDENS AND GARDEN LIFE IN POMPEII IN THE FIRST CENTURY A.D.

20

Fig. 6. Drawing of a destroyed wall painting found in the House of M. Lucretius shows a dancing girl entertaining guests in the garden.

Fig. 7. Drawing of a destroyed wall painting in the house of M. Lucretius shows guests entertained by music.

home to have an elaborate triclinium with a kitchen garden near by.

But the more humble citizens also enjoyed eating in their gardens. The garden at the rear of a modest home (I.xiv.2) on the Via di Nucera tells us much about the little-known people who made up such a large part of the population. In the southeast corner we found a triclinium and two tables: a round table between the couches, and a crudely built rectangular table against the south wall with small, neatly piled pieces of wood to the east of this table probably used as cooking fuel. The triclinium was shaded by a vine-covered arbor, and we even found evidence of the last meal: clam shells (*Venerupis decussata* L.) and the beautiful snail shell (*Murex* [Bolinus] *brandaris* L.)–not considered a table delicacy, but eaten by the poor in this area–were on the menu that evening. There were also a number of large bones–domestic cow (*Bos taurus* L.) and wild boar or pig–which indicated that more desirable food had also been enjoyed. When the debris around the triclinium accumulated, the ancient Pompeian simply tossed the debris into the garden. The inhabitants of this modest home obviously spent much time in their garden. Meals were enjoyed under the vine-covered arbor many months of the year. The household gods would have been worshipped at mealtime. We also found a terra-cotta watering pan for birds or small animals, which attests to the presence of pets in the garden.

Even families that did not have a triclinium in their garden enjoyed eating in the cool of their garden. The family that lived in humble quarters above the shop at I.xx.5 had no triclinium but they obviously spent much time in the open area at the rear of their garden, near the crudely built niche in the west wall. The soil was well-packed, and the objects found are

Fig. 8. Lararium with altar in front in the garden of the copo Euxinus. Photo: Stanley Jashemski.

revealing, showing that meals were cooked and eaten here. We also found a small lamp and a fragment of a very small dish with one handle, such as served as votive offerings and as toys.[10] The discovery of lamps suggests that the family lingered in the garden long after dark. The children may have entertained themselves with their doll dishes and toy lamps, one of which had been dropped on a trip to the back of the garden. It is easy to picture the family gathering here in the cool of the late afternoon and early evening, to escape the heat of their stuffy second-floor dwelling. I found it delightful to work in this area in the shade of the west wall from four o'clock on. In antiquity the shade of the three trees nearby would have made this a pleasant spot much earlier in the day.

The sound of music coming from a garden in the cool of the evening would not have been an unusual one at Pompeii, for musical entertainment was an important part of a dinner party, even at a simple meal with friends. The delights of dining out-of-doors are pictured in two charming, but badly preserved wall paintings found in the house of M. Lucretius. One shows cupids and psyches reclining on a shaded triclinium entertained by a dancing girl accompanied by the strains of a single pipe (Fig. 6), in the second, too, the music of a single pipe added to the joy of the occasion (Fig. 7). In a third, much better preserved painting from the same house, a dancing girl is accompanied by a cithara. The Pompeians frequently pictured cupids and psyches engaged in the activities of everyday life. In the first century A.D. it was not unusual for a well-bred Roman to sing and play an instrument. Wall paintings and mosaics, as well as the discovery of actual musical instruments, attest to the popularity of music in the Pompeii area. The syrinx, or panpipe, made of reeds of different lengths, is frequently pictured in Pompeian art. On the beautiful blue glass cameo vase found at Pompeii, music is furnished by cupids playing a panpipe, a cithera and a double pipe as their companions tread the grapes.

Theatrical performances were also a favored entertainment at dinner parties. Seneca says that nearly every private house had its stage. The lovely peristyle garden of the House of the Golden Cupids (VI.xvi.7) had an unmistakable theatrical quality. Sculptured decorations with theatrical motifs abound.

Religious worship

Worship was an important activity in the garden. The large number of lararia (sing. lararium) (house shrines) and altars found in gardens bear witness to the worship of the household gods. The two essential elements of a lararium are the images of the gods to be worshipped in them and the provisions for sacrifices. There were free standing altars, or tiny altars could be placed in a lararium. Little images of the deities were placed in a lararium, or sometimes representations of them were painted on a nearby wall. The house shrine took various shapes. It could be a simple niche, the niche could be framed by an aedicula (temple-like) façade (Fig. 8) or it could be an aedicula (a small temple-like structure), or a wall painting. Sometimes the wall painting is

GARDENS AND GARDEN LIFE IN POMPEII IN THE FIRST CENTURY A.D.

22

combined with the niche or the aedicula. At times a small room or building (sacellum) was devoted to worship. All these forms are found in various gardens. The care with which shrines in houses destroyed by the disastrous earthquake of A.D. 62 were quickly rebuilt speaks eloquently of the vitality of family religion. Few statuettes have been found in lararia by archaeologists. The fact that the frightened Pompeians stopped long enough to take their household deities with them, when fleeing the wrath of Vesuvius tells much about the importance of these little deities.

At these lararia the members of the household worshipped, with prayer and sacrifice the divine powers on which they depended for the protection of their daily life. Worship took place at the family meal. The head of the family conducted the family worship, although his wife and even the children might participate. The offerings made to the household gods were customarily modest. The ones most often mentioned by the Latin authors are a few cereals and salt, wine and little cakes (*strues*) or oblation cakes (*fertum*) and incense. Remains of burnt offerings – burned dates, figs, pine kernels, cones and nuts – were found in pits containing the refuse from sacrifice in the Temple of Isis at Pompeii. Animals were rarely sacrificed by the family, but on occasion a piglet was sacrificed to the genius of the father. After the gods were given their small portion as a burnt offering, the family enjoyed the rest. Besides the household deities, Venus, the goddess of gardens, Hercules, Diana, and Bacchus were worshipped in these gardens.

Fig. 9. Larger than life size marble statue of Diana found in a Pompeii garden. Photo: Stanley Jashemski.

In Italy Hercules had become the patron deity of merchants, who dedicated a tithe of their profits to him. The impressive shrine and large triclinium in a commercial flower garden makes it seem improbable that they were used only by the occupants of the humble house. This garden was perhaps the center of considerable business activity. The gold coins found near the triclinium may have been dropped by merchants who made this garden their headquarters. Two votive offerings found near the altar, a slender cupid and a small draped female figure were finely made, suggesting that they were the offerings of people of means.

There is also definite evidence for the worship of Diana in the garden (Fig. 9). Diana, too, was an old Italic deity, commonly worshipped in groves in Campania. Her most famous sanctuary was the grove (*nemus*) near modern Nemi, where she first had an altar and later a temple. The Romans were well aware that "trees were once the temples of the deities."

Celebrating mystery cults

The worship of the Greek Dionysus (or Bacchus) was adopted early in south Italy and he would have been especially venerated in the vine-growing region of Vesuvius. The mysteries of Dionysus had become popular in this area after the second Punic

War (218-201 B.C.).[11] At the two large triclinia in front of the temple of Dyionysus, the wine drinking and banqueting connected with the mysteries took place in a vineyard setting. The temple was one of the few temples that had been repaired after the earthquake.

The worship of Sabazius was one of the mystery cults that, along with the mysteries of Dionysus and Isis, we find at Pompeii. It took place in a large peristyle garden that occupied most of the area of a building (II.i.12) in the southeastern part of Pompeii. Upon entering the garden with a row of four trees and an altar there was a banquet room on the left. The altar used in the worship of the Thraco-Phrygian god Sabazius was suitable for offerings of perfume, incense, libations or blood sacrifices. On the night of initiation the initiates sat on the ground on a faun skin and were washed with bran and mud, symbolic of death.[12] They then rose one by one and recited the formula of resurrection. Finally they celebrated the symbolic marriage of the initiate and the god. The banquet that followed anticipated those that the eternally happy would enjoy after death. The discovery of this rustic garden with its shrine room, altar, and banquet hall and the presence of many lamps for the evening rites, enables us to picture the setting for the worship of Sabazius. The mysteries of Sabazius took place in a humble garden in a part of the city inhabited by petty tradesmen and foreigners, who were a considerable part of the population of this port town.

Garlands used in worship

Garlands, made of ivy sprinkled with flowers, played an important part in religious worship. They were hung on the hearth, and prayers were offered to the Lares "on the Kalends, Nones and Ides, and whenever a holy day comes."[13] Painted garlands are found on many lararia, and actual hooks still in place on these shrines and on the large altar of Sabazius indicate where the fresh garlands were hung.

There were elaborate worship services twice each day at the "opening" and the "closing" of the temple of Isis at Pompeii. The temple was excavated too many years ago for any garden evidence to have survived, but two paintings of the temple of Isis found at Herculaneum may picture the afternoon ceremony, which takes place in a garden setting through which ibises wander. It may be significant that the mysteries of Dionysus, Sabazius and Isis, whose devotees looked forward to a life of eternal bliss, were celebrated in a pleasant garden. Isis was a popular deity at Pompeii. In the garden of the House of the Moralist (III.iv.2–3), which was almost as large as the house, there were many large trees. In the middle of the garden on a high pedestal was the marble statuette of the goddess worshipped in the garden, Isis or Isis/Diana. At the foot of the statue was a bronze incense burner in the shape of a woolly lamb; behind the lamb was a column on which rested a receptacle for the incense. Standing about three meters in front of the statue was a cylindrical brazier of bronze and iron for burnt offerings.

Worship when traveling

The innkeeper Euxinus had even made provisions for travelers away from home to worship in the garden of his restaurant (Fig. 8). In addition to the lararium painting in the one room wine shop that served customers at the counter, there were two altars in his garden for the use of the overnight guests. The deities worshipped in the garden of Euxinus would have varied with the guests. A votive offering, a small crudely made terracotta head of a bearded Zeus-type (6.5 cm in length), was found near the altar in front of the lararium. Perhaps the carefully buried pig bone that we found in the garden had been given to the dog after a guest had made a sacrifice and both the deities and man had gotten their share.

Housework

The garden was also a place of work. Much of a woman's work would have been carried into the shade of the garden or portico, if at all possible. The economy of Pompeii was based in good part on wool, and there were probably few households in which the women did not spend some time spinning and perhaps weaving wool. What better place for such activity than the garden or the portico, according to the weather? In every garden that I have excavated I have found loom weights – an indication that weaving was common in the garden. The garden or shaded portico was also a pleasant place for more serious work. Pliny the Younger says that while staying at his Tuscan villa, depending upon the weather, he was accustomed to think through his work and then dictate it either in his garden or in his covered portico.[14]

Children play

The garden was also the place of children. It must have echoed often with their songs as they played. Little girls may have played quietly with their dolls and doll dishes. It is difficult to know if the diminutive dishes, such as the one we excavated in the shop-house garden on the Via di Nocera (I.xx.5) were doll dishes or votive offerings. Children, however, were not permitted to play in all gardens. The fences that enclosed elegantly planted gardens, and those with deep pools may have been designed to protect both the plantings and the young children. But the portico along the garden would be a pleasant place to play and work.

Fig. 10. Painting of a dog found in Pompeii. Photo: Stanley Jashemski.

Caring for animals and pets

The Roman love of animals has long been known and the evidence from Pompeii indicates that Pompeians shared their homes and gardens with their animals. A good watchdog was essential. The mosaic watchdogs that guard the entrances of several homes at Pompeii are well known. I have found the bones of dogs in every large garden that I have excavated at Pompeii. These gardens were planted in valuable vines, fruit and nut trees, so watchdogs would be needed to protect gardens as well as homes. But the watchdog that terrified the thief was also the faithful friend of his master **(Fig. 10).** Small dogs were also kept as pets. There were no doubt pet cats in many gardens, and there is some evidence for turtles.

The rabbits and the ducks so delightfully pictured in Pompeian wall paintings could well have been pets in the garden. Pigs were also more common in ancient cities than is commonly realized, and they were a great favorite with children. Garden paintings attest to the presence of birds in the garden.[15] They can be seen sitting in the branches, flying through the air, and fluttering near the bubbling fountain, or perched on its rim. Wild birds – the golden oriole, song thrush, jay, turtledove, Sardinian warbler (Fig. 11), swallow, black-eared wheatear, gray shrike and European robin are all found. It has been suggested

Fig. 11. Sardinian warbler and roses in a garden painting in the House of the Bracelet at Pompeii. Photo: Sarah Gladden.

that the brackets found on the columns in various peristyles were for birds to perch on, for Varro had used a bracket in this way.

The most spectacular wild birds found in the garden paintings are the beautiful herons and egrets. They are pictured so often that we get the impression that they were a desirable part of the garden scene, and it is possible that when migrating they stopped off in the large villa gardens along the sea.

Among the domesticated birds most frequently pictured in the garden paintings are feral pigeons, also known as rock doves (Fig. 12), which were great favorites of the Romans. The aristocratic peacocks, found in some garden paintings, were no doubt raised by wealthier Romans as a status symbol. Peacocks pictured in the garden paintings, perched high on walls, suggest that the highly vocal peacock was not unappreciated as a "watchdog."

There are more references to pet birds in the Latin authors than to all other kinds of pets together. Such birds were frequently taught tricks of various kinds, and could be taught to speak. Others were valued because of their beautiful song. There is a small bird in a wicker cage in the garden painting at Livia's villa at Prima Porta. The commercial aviary (VII.vii.16)[16] located in the garden in a house behind the Temple of Apollo may have furnished some of the pet birds in Pompeian gardens.

The most desirable of the singing birds was the nightingale. One second-story dweller on the Via dell'Abbondanza had converted his balcony, which extended out over the street, into a little aviary about two meters square. The three windows would have been covered with netting. There were nine complete watering pans for birds on the balcony, as well as fragments of others. Perhaps nothing speaks more eloquently of the Pompeian love of birds than this tiny aviary tucked into an upstairs apartment on a busy thoroughfare.

Raising fish as favorite pets, food or display

Fish were also regarded as pets by the Romans. We read in the ancient authors of fish that answered their master's call or fed from his hand. The Roman orator, Q. Hortensus, who had a fishpond at his villa across the Bay of Naples from Pompeii, wept at the death of his pet eel.[17] Wealthy Romans went to great expense to build artificial fish pools on their estates, for they were considered a definite mark of social status. Fish were also raised in home pools for food. Two pools at Pompeii have rows of round openings, the mouths of small terracotta amphoras built into the sides of the pool, which served as places where the fish could lay their eggs. They were also ideal places for octopuses, eels and other fish to seek shade. The unique covered alcoves at the bottom of the long pool in the garden of Julia Felix (II.iv) served the same purpose. The inclusion of well-stocked fishponds in two garden paintings at Pompeii indicates that a fishpond was considered a desirable part of the garden. There is a well-stocked pool in the center panel of the rear wall of the triangular peristyle in the villa of Diomede, just

Fig. 12. Dove in a garden painting, House of the Bracelet at Pompeii. Photo: Stanley Jashemski.

Fig. 13. Mask on mosaic fountain in the garden of the House of the Great Fountain. Photo: Stanley Jashemski.

outside the Herculaneum Gate. In a modest house (I.ii.10) on the Via Stabiana, a real pool took up most of the space of the small garden. Above the pool was a painting of a well-stocked pool that extended the size of the actual pool. On the side panels were typical garden paintings. The most elaborate painting of sea animals was found in the nymphaeum of the House of the Centenary (IX.viii.3/6), which was decorated to suggest a luxurious garden.

Enjoying the cool at night

Activity in the garden did not cease when the sun went down. The cool of the garden and its porticoes were much more pleasant than hot and stuffy rooms on a warm summer evening. Special provision had been made for night lighting in several gardens. In the house of the Ephebe the owner had converted his valuable and cherished statue of an ephebe into a lamp stand by placing heavy candelabra brackets in the hands of the statue to illuminate the garden. We find various methods of lighting the garden at Pompeii, such as the two handsome masks with wide-open mouths and eyes with pierced pupils that decorated the mosaic aedicula in the garden of the House of the Great Fountain (VI.viii.22/1) appear to have held lamps (Fig. 13). They would have presented a striking appearance as they lighted the fountain on summer nights.

But most gardens did not have such elaborate provisions for lighting. The little lamps found in such large numbers in many gardens would have been placed on garden tables, or put in the small niches frequently found in gardens. Most had only one flame, but occasionally lamps with many flames are found.

These archaeological observations show that gardens did not only occupy as much space in the city of Pompeii as public space, but that they were essential for the pursuit of good family life: they provided places for worship, housework family dinner, children's play , entertainment of guests, and care for wild and domesticated animals. Since they occupied such an important place in family life, it is not really surprising that they also sheltered public life, and several forms of cult including the cult of the dead with whom one could have a dinner in the garden where they rested forever. Gardens seem to have offered ancient Pompeians metaphysical comfort of significance in daily life besides their economic value, and much appreciated climate controls.

BIBLIOGRAPHY

Dobbins, John J. and Pedar W. Foss. *The World of Pompeii*. London and New York: Routledge, 2007.

Jashemski, Wilhelmina Mary Feemster. *The Gardens of Pompeii: Herculaneum and the Villas Destroyed by Vesuvius*. Photographs, drawings, and plans by Stanley A. Jashemski. New Rochelle, N.Y.: Caratzas Brothers, 1979-1993.

Jashemski, Wilhelmina Feemster and Frederick G. Meyer, eds. *The Natural History of Pompeii*. Cambridge; New York: Cambridge University Press, 2002.

MacDougall, Elisabeth B. and Wilhelmina F. Jashemski, eds. *Ancient Roman Gardens*. Dumbarton Oaks Colloquium on the History of Landscape Architecture VII (1979). Washington, D.C.: Dumbarton Oaks Trustees for Harvard University, 1981.

Mau, August. *Pompeii, Its Life and Art*, Translated by Francis W. Kelsey. New Rochelle, New York: Caratzas Brothers, 1982.

Reese, David . "Marine Invertebrates" in *Natural History of Pompeii* Edited by Wilhelmina Feemster Jashemski and Frederick G. Meyer. Cambridge; New York: Cambridge University Press, 2002.

Van Buren, Albert William. "Further Pompeian Studies." *Memoirs of the American Academy in Rome* 10 (1932): 10-13.

NOTES

[1] (Jashemski, 1979-1993), (MacDougall and Jashemski 1981), (Jashemski and Meyer 2002).

[2] We should note that only approximately seventy-five percent of the city has been excavated; the remaining twenty-five percent is thought to have a larger percentage of open space.

[3] This type of house was derived from a Hellenistic model. However, when the Italians added the peristyle to their atrium house, they transformed it by making it into a garden, instead of leaving it as a beaten clay court or paving it with cement, cobblestones, or mosaics as was done in Classical and Hellenistic times.

[4] As a matter of comparison it is interesting to note that this garden is similar to many in the Pompeii area today. The slightly larger garden of one of our workers that we visited also supplied his family needs. We counted thirty-three different species in his densely planted garden, which he showed us with great pride. His orchard trees included the apple, peach, hazelnut, fig, lemon, and walnut, all familiar to the ancient Pompeians, and many vegetables and herbs available in ancient Pompeii were grown under the trees. Six vines trained as an arbor over the little patio furnished table grapes.

[5] When the ancient city was destroyed the roots of plants gradually decayed and lapilli trickled in the cavities. We carefully removed the lapilli with special tools that we made and filled the cavities with cement. After three days when the cement had hardened we carefully removed the surrounding soil and had the cast of the ancient tree. The top of the casts then were painted white and the small roots covered with a white disc.

[6] *Appendix Vergiliana Copa*.

[7] There was a major earthquake that destroyed part of the city in 62 A.D. a few years before the fatal eruption of Vesuvius.

[8] See (Jashemski 1979, chaps.4, 5, 8-10) for a detailed discussion of life in the gardens of the Vesuvian area and the pertinent references.

[9] (Jashemski 1979, 193-194).

[10] A war between Rome and Carthage, near the present city of Tunis in Tunisia, that ended in the complete destruction of Carthage and the progressive conquest of North Africa by the Romans.

[11] According to Clement of Alexandria, born about A.D. 10, and well acquainted with the pagan mysteries before he became a Christian.

[12] Cato *RR*. 143.2.

[13] Pliny, *Letters*, Book 9 Letter 36 to Fuscus.

[14] See George Watson in (Jashemski and Meyer 2002), for a detailed catalogue and discussion of the birds found in the Vesuvian garden paintings..

[15] (Van Buren 1932, 10-13).

[16] See David Reese, "Marine Invertebrates," in (Jashemski and Meyer 2002).

GARDENS AND GARDEN LIFE IN POMPEII IN THE FIRST CENTURY A.D.

28

Gardens, City Life and Culture

Gardens, City Life and Culture

Gardens, City Life and Culture

Gardens, City Life and Culture

Gardens, City Life and Culture

Gardens, City Life and Culture

CHAPTER 2

Gardens of Luoyang: The Refinements of a City Culture

Georges Métailié

The city of Luoyang, the former capital for several dynasties during the Chinese middle age, was already famous for its Buddhist monasteries in the sixth century when a small official, Yang Xianzhi, wrote a book not only about them but also about policy, people, sceneries and gossips in this renowned city. This book, *Luoyang qielan ji* (*Notes on the Buddhist monasteries of Luoyang*) written in 547 and transmitted up to the present is still a precious landmark for historians of social life in ancient China.

The city kept its ancient prestige, and also attracted much attention from scholars throughout the early modern period, for its flowers, and in particular the tree peony. Several monographs were written on both peony and tree peony, but it is also very fortunate that two particularly interesting works of the Northern Song period (960–1127) literature survived. The first one, *Notes on the famous gardens of Luoyang* by Li Gefei, evokes some of the most famous gardens of the town, and the second, *Notes on the trees and flowers of Luoyang* by Zhou Shihou, the botanical diversity in the gardens. Besides these two texts, there is also a fascinating description by the renowned historian and former Prime Minister Sima Guang (1019-1086) of his life in his own "Garden of solitary enjoyment," *Du le yuan.*[1] At the same period other scholars living in the lower Yangzi valley also wrote memoirs about their gardens. We may also easily read later texts that show the importance of garden culture throughout Chinese history.[2] When considering novels, one may for instance remember the garden that the rich merchant Ximen Qing, the main male character of the Ming novel *Jin Ping Mei*, commissioned for his fame and pleasure (*Jin Ping Mei*, chapter 19, book 2). Gardens also play an important part in several short novels of the Ming collection *Jin gu qi guan*, edited by Feng Menglong (1574 – 1646), and, of course it would be impossible to forget that the core of probably the most famous novel in China, the *Hong lou meng*, by Cao Xueqin (? – 1763/64), is a beautiful garden.

Praised for their beauty, sometimes evocating famous landscapes or renowned pictures, gardens also became highly appreciated and valued as pure works of art as Craig Clunas (1996) has shown. Although not a full bibliography about gardens in China, we would like to mention a few helpful documents. Chen Congzhou (1984) provides valuable guidance on how to look at a Chinese garden, as Maggie Keswick's book does in another way. A comprehensive "Guide to Secondary Sources on Chinese Gardens" by Stanislas Fung (1998) offers a golden key to the subject. Two different historical points of view are to be found in the books in Chinese by Zhang Jiaji (1986) and Wang Yi (1990).

Let us turn to Luoyang during the early Song period (960 – 1126). Li Gefei, personal name Wenshu, who was born in Jinan, Shandong province, gives brief descriptions of nineteen gardens in his Notes on the Famous Gadens of Luoyang. This text, written after 1039, was published long after the city had been ransacked by the Jürchen who created the Jin dynasty in 1115 and victoriously attacked the Song empire in 1125, capturing the emperor in his capital Kaifeng the next year. This short text, with a preface dated from the eigth year of Shaoxing reign (1139), evokes at the same time the places visited by its author and the loss of these beauties for the editor and the readers at the time of publication.

Even if every garden is accounted for in a different way—Li Gefei insisting on what he considers as particularly striking or interesting in each one—a few general points of special interest emerge. It is remarkable that these gardens were huge places, since the one hectare garden of Sima Guang was said to be "small, not being able to compete with the others." Li Gefei often quotes the names of various pavilions, terraces, ponds–a reminder of the deep concern for naming by Confucian scholars.[3] He also indicates when a garden originates from a famous old one dating from the Tang dynasty. Then, as a true guide, he insists on the significance of choosing the right places to obtain the best view in or from the gardens. In some cases he even provides a very precise tour guide for making the best of a visit. Generally the reader gets a broad sense of the place with its main structures, ponds, buildings, terraces, masses of plants, like bamboos that were used to create special effects for streams or grottoes. But in other cases, the author may also point to very precise details. In the "Western garden of Mr. Tong," *Tong Shi xi yuan,* he notices the water springing from the petals of a lotus-shaped stone fountain in the middle of a ring of bamboos. Very often the plants are just named as a whole, using the term *huamu,* 'flowers and trees.' When their proper name is given, it is for a particular reason. For instance, in the same "Western garden of Mr. Tong," he mentions a spectacular juniper *gui* [*Sabina chinensis* (L.) Antoine] with a circumference of six armfuls which gives fruit as small as pine kernels but sweeter and more perfumed. He also notices lines of pines and junipers in the "Garden of M. Liu," *Liu Shi yuan*: paulownias, catalpas, junipers and arborvitae [*Biota orientalis* (L.) Endl.] in the "Garden of all Spring times," *Cong chun yuan.* The most noticeable for its flowers is the "Peony garden of the courtyard of the Emperor of Heaven," *Tian Wang yuan huayuanzi.* He writes:

> Many flowers are cultivated in Luoyang but only one is just named as 'the flower,' it is the tree-peony, *mudan.* In every garden peonies are grown but only one is called 'Peony garden,' *Huayuanzi*花園子. Actually, there are no buildings, nor ponds, but only peonies, several hundred thousand. When they blossom all the town comes here. The two most appreciated varieties are 'Yellow of Yao' and 'Purple of Wei.' The price of the second one is a hundred silver ounces, as for 'Yellow of Yao' there is none to sell.

If we want to know what this extraordinary flower looked like, we have just to open the book by Zhou Shihou to find the answer.

> Double yellow flower. Very vivid color. Deep purple heart of the flower. Once opened it can reach 8 to 9 inches. Originally this flower comes from the estate of Mr. Yao, on the Baisima hill, in the lower part of the Beimang Mountains. Today in the famous gardens of Luoyang it is multiplied by grafting. North of the River Huai, though there are plenty, the flowers are simple or double following the years. South of the River the flowers are always double but cannot compete with the flowers from the North. The reason is that since it comes originally from a mountain it is adapted to altitude. Close to towns, the soil is too rich and does not correspond to its nature. It blossoms late, when all other flowers have already faded. Very beautiful color and very pure nature. When it

blossoms it is particularly different from any other peony. It is the reason why the people of Luoyang gave it the name of 'Emperor of flowers.' Only three buds blossom every year.

It is not surprising, as we learn from a monograph *Notes on Luoyang tree peonies* by Ouyang Xiu (1007-1072), that every year a few branches of this most appreciated variety about to bloom, were carefully conditioned in bamboo containers lined with freshly cut cabbage leaves, the stems sealed with wax and sent to the capital in one day and one night, thanks to the horse-stages, to be offered to the emperor.[4]

This private garden was opened to the citizens of Luoyang as the others seem to have been, probably under particular conditions.

Li Gefei describes very briefly the "Garden of Confidence in Humanity," *Gui ren yuan,* which, he says, is the best compared to many large gardens in the region. To the north, there are thousands of two kinds of peonies (*Paeonia albiflora* and *Paeonia suffurticosa*); to the center, more than a hundred *mu* (over six hectares!) of bamboos; to the south, there are peach trees [*P. persica* Batsch.] and prune trees [*P. Prunus salicina* Lindl.] as far as one can see.

The description of the "Garden of Humanity and Prosperity" of Mr. Li, *Li Shi ren feng yuan,* highlights other idiosyncrasies. Not only are the buildings a true marvel, but its collection of plants grows richer in rarities each year. There are dozens of varieties of peach trees, prune trees, Japanese apricots, apricots, lotus, chrysanthemums, and more than a hundred kinds of the two peonies. There are also plants from far away places, such as the 'purple orchid,' *zilan* [*Bletilla striata* Reichb. fil.], the Arabian jasmine, *moli* [*Jasminum sambac* Ait.], the 'neephrite flower,' *qionghua* [*Hydrangea* sp.],[5] and the camellia, *shancha* [*Camellia japonica* L.]. He states that being "particularly difficult to cultivate, they can only be grown in Luoyang," which is supposed to enjoy very exceptional pedological conditions. This remark was probably not without reason, but we believe that the skill of professional floriculturists helped make the best of this natural gift because a much greater number of kinds of plants were cultivated in Luoyang at that time. To know them more precisely, we have to turn to the *Notes on the trees and flowers of Luoyang, Luoyang hua-mu ji,* published some fifty years earlier.

It is a short text of fifty pages with a preface dated 1082. The author, Zhou Shihou,[6] personal name Dunfu, came from Yinxian, in what is today Zhejiang province. He passed the imperial exams and became doctor *jinshi* between 1049 and 1053. He says he had first visited the famous gardens of Luoyang between 1068 and 1077 and returned to this town as a civil servant in 1082. Having a passion for flowers he used his free time to visit gardens. He acknowledges in his preface that he did not succeed in visiting more than ten percent of them and had been able to see only half of the extraordinary flowers. Anyway, the result is fascinating. Zhou Shihou gives the name of some five hundred thirty kinds of flowers which are presented following a taxonomy of his own: *mudan,* tree peony, *shaoyao,* herbaceous peony, *za hua,* various flowers, *guozi hua,* flowers of fruit trees, *ci hua,* thorny flowers, *cao hua,* herbaceous flowers, *shui hua,* aquatic flowers and *man hua,* creeping flowers.

It deserves study in order to show how a culture of gardens can stimulate the talent for innovation. Ouyang Xiu had mentioned twenty-four kinds of tree peonies in 1034, but in 1082 Li Gefei can name one hundred and nine varieties!

They are classified into subgroups following a criterion of appreciation taking into account flower structure and color. 'Double flowers,' literally 'thousand leaves' *qian ye* are the most appreciated. He mentions the 'Double yellow flowers' (ten kinds), 'Double red flowers' (thirty four), 'Double purple flowers' (ten), 'Double pale red' (one), 'Double white flowers' (four). They are followed by the cultivars with 'many leaves' flowers, *duo ye,* in which the transformation of stamens into pseudo petals has not succeeded so well. He quotes thirty-two kinds of red, fourteen of purple, three of yellow and one of white *duo ye*.

For the herbaceous peonies, *shaoyao*, he only mentions forty-one kinds with double flowers, among them sixteen yellow, sixteen red, six purple, two white and one pale red.

Under the eighty-two names of 'various flowers' we can identify, probably in order of appreciation, some fifty botanical species, beginning with two varieties of daphnes (*Daphne odora* Thunb.) *rui xiang*, six kinds of apple trees (*Malus spectabilis* Borkh.) *haitang*, four kinds of Japanese apricot (*Prunus mume* Sieb. et Zucc.) *mei*, one wintersweet (*Chimonathus praecox* K. Koch.) *lamei*, one pomegranate (*Punica granatum* L.) *haishiliu*, three species of magnolias, (*M. liliflora* Desr., *xiyi*, *M. denudata* Desr., *mulan*, *M. amoena* Cheng, *mubi*), three species of jasmine, and various kinds of rhododendrons and azaleas.

The category 'flowers of fruit trees' reveals the diversity reached through selection. It comprises thirty kinds of peach trees, followed by six kinds of Japanese apricots (*Prunus mume* Sieb. et Zucc.) *mei*, sixteen kinds of apricots (*Prunus armeniaca* L.) *xing*, twenty-seven kinds of pears "nashi" (*Pyrus serrotina* Rehder) *li*, twenty-seven kinds of prune trees (*Prunus salicina* Lindl.) *li*, eleven kinds of cherries (*Prunus pseudo-cerasus* Lindl.) *yingtao*, nine of pomegranate (*Punica granatum* L.) *shiliu*, six of apple trees (*Malus prunifolia* Borkh. var. *rinki* Relider.) *linqin*, ten kinds of another apple tree (*Malus* sp.) *nai,* and five kinds of Japanese quinces (*Cydonia lagenaria* Lois.) *mugua*.

There are thirty-seven kinds of thorny flowers, half of them being different species of roses, some with double flowers.

Among the eighty-nine kinds of herbaceous flowers, there are three kinds of *Cymbidium* orchids *lan*, the narcissus (*Narcissus tazetta* L. var. *chinensis* Roem.) *shuixianhua*, twenty-four kinds of chrysanthemums *ju*, eight kinds of daylilies (*Hemerocallis* sp.) *xuan*, six kinds of lycoris (*Lycoris sp.*) *jindeng*, two kinds of carnations *shih-chu*, one opium poppy, two kinds of poppies, one impatiens, one hosta, three kinds of daturas, eight kinds of hollyhocks (*Althea* sp.) with simple and double flowers, and more.

Out of the seventeen kinds of aquatic flowers, there are six kinds of Indian lotus.

The climbing flowers are the least numerous with only six kinds, among them cross vine and morning glory.

There is no doubt that the interest in plants and the existence of gardens had created a very lively market in the city that attracted professionals who greatly increased the variety of choice among the most appreciated fruits and flowers. It is worth noting here that interest in plants was not confined within the limits of aestheticism: at least two gardens mentioned by Li Gefei had a collection of medicinal plants, the Eastern garden of Mr Gonglu without any more precision and the garden of Sima Guang. Although Li Gefei does not elaborate on the topic, Sima Guang fortunately explains how he proceeded with medicinal plants in his essay "Garden of Solitary Enjoyment," *Du le yuan*. They appeared more important for him than ornamental ones, of which he just kept two specimens of each because, as he wrote "Once I have learned their names and characteristics, I don't try to collect anymore." On the contrary, the wild herbs were subject to great attention. He sent servants to pick them in the mountains and had them transplanted in 120 small plots where he could study them at ease, identifying and classifying them. Apparently he also used to sell them on the local market (Métailié 1998, 250). Even though Sima Guang's text does not allow a precise reconstruction of his garden, it yields an understanding of his appreciation and use of plants. Bamboo appears to have been the most versatile building block for landscape architecture. Behind opened windows, they created a moving landscape and brought freshness during the summer; planted on a small surface they gave the sense of presence of a building; as a small circular grove they became a fisherman's hut, and densely planted in a narrow path and covered with medicinal vines they were like a covered corridor. All flowers and medicinal herbs, to the contrary were grown in very regular beds more in keeping with a systematic square in a modern botanic garden than with the received idea of a "Chinese garden." Lastly, medicinal trees were used to fence off different parts of the garden. We are, indeed, far from the sea of peonies in the Courtyard of the Emperor of Heaven!

In the same period and geographical context some very rich people could have huge gardens filled with the most expensive and fashionable flowering plants, while others, like Sima Guang, would use their smaller estate as a place for reading and meditating, as a way of reflection on the nature of plants and eventually a source of a small income (Métailié 1998, 249-50).

Gardens in a city contributed to the development of sociability. This was true in Luoyang, but we have found further evidence in many texts. Gardens introduced a culture of gift and counter-gift that built and strengthened social bonds between givers and receivers, as Marcel Mauss explained (Mauss 1954). A garden was a perfect 'conversation piece' and also a generator of social relationships. Notes on gardens always refer to exchanges of cuttings or scions for grafting. Even in the eighteenth century Pierre le Chéron d'Incarville (1706-1757), a French Jesuit missionary and a good botanist, exchanged seeds received from France against seeds of Chinese plants with the gardener of the imperial gardens, once they had engaged in a friendly relationship.

It is difficult at present to imagine a city like eleventh-century Luoyang, and the feeling its private gardens created for its inhabitants. The modern town which can best suggest this feeling might very well be the city of Kyoto in Japan, a city deeply influenced for centuries by Chinese art, ways of life, garden culture and which borrowed its ancient name from Luoyang. Besides the world famous gardens of the former Imperial palace, rich Buddhist monasteries, or the Golden Pavilion (Fig. 1) there is a great number of smaller gardens in Buddhist sanctuaries and patches of so-called wild vegetation around Shinto shrines. Parts of the city still maintain many small private gardens, sometimes very small (Fig. 2) just in front of the houses (Figs. 3; 4; 5). When invited to enter one of these ancient houses, one meets a second small garden just inside, and sometimes another one before seeing the main inner garden of the house through the sliding doors of the reception room. In some other small walking lanes, residents seem to compete to create green corridors (Figure 6). If local inhabitants are short of time for a leisurely visit to the famous gardens, the proximity of these numerous planted patches brightens their days. When running an errand, one can choose a path along a wall covered by well-tamed vegetation, or beside a more exuberant grove behind a Shinto shrine. This is to say nothing of the olfactory delights caused by small light purple flowers of *Daphne odora* in the spring, orange or white tiny flowers of Osmanthus in the autumn, and probably the most unusual, the mild perfume of winter sweet, or Japanese apricot, in the dead of winter when the earth is under the snow.

Conclusion

It is striking, when considering life beyond purely material interests in ancient China—and not only during the Song dynasty—how crucial the role of plants and gardens in the life of city people was. Of course the texts still extant mostly concern gardens of rich officials or princes, but careful and wide ranging readings reveal that a great interest in plants, economical, medicinal and ornamental, was deeply shared in China from the emperor to common people. Chen Haozi, the author of a treatise, *The Mirror of Flowers* (1688) *Huajing*, influential both in China and Japan, noted that everybody would like to own a

Fig. 1. The size of the garden of the Rokuon-ji, known as the Golden Pavillion, created in the Chinese style, can give an idea of what could have been the large gardens of ancient Luoyang. © G. Métailié.

vast estate in a forested mountain, but given the reality of an exiguous dwelling space in the city, even people of a high rank used to cultivate flowers in pots to create small landscapes.

There is no doubt that tree planting by municipal park services, such as the continuous gardens along the 'Century Avenue' in Pudong, are important for the life of citizens, but they cannot replace the contributions of private gardens–even very small–to cultural development. In Luoyang and later in other cities–the most famous being Hangzhou, Suzhou and Yangzhou–private gardens gave rise to sophisticated botanical culture and advanced horticultural practices, and made possible the blossoming of particularly refined aesthetic cultures. Parts of them were used for researches on medicinal and useful plants. They were places of interest for all city inhabitants to visit. They created special links between people through the exchanges of seeds, grafts and cuttings. Chinese culture has shown an extraordinary capacity to be reborn from its ashes, even after cities had been completely erased and all the ancient gardens destroyed. We hope that the memory of the gardens of Luoyang, emulated during the following dynasties in many cities of China, will contribute to the re-birth of a Chinese urban culture of flowers and other ornamentals in the present century.

Fig. 2. A tiny "garden" on the front of a simple house in a small street nearby the main campus of Kyoto University. © G. Métailié.
Fig. 3. A sophisticated lanscape garden on the side of a small street in Gion, a district of Kyoto where geishas still reside. © G. Métailié.

Fig. 4. A small garden in and out the walls of a private house near the Botanic Garden in Kyoto. © G. Métailié.
Fig. 5. A residential street, near the Botanic Garden in Kyoto. © G. Métailié.
Fig. 6. A small lane close to the main campus of Kyoto University. © G. Métailié.

Bibliography

In Chinese

Chen Congzhou. *On Chinese Gardens*. Shanghai: Tongji University Press, 1984. 陈从周。说园。上海: 同济大学出版社。(with a translation in English)

Chen Congzhou, Qiting Jiang, and Houjun Chao. *Yuan zong*. [Compilation on gardens]. Shanghai: Tongji daxue chubanshe, 2004. 陈从周,蒋启霆,超后均。园综。上海同济大学出版社。

Chen Haozi ji, Yi Qinheng xiaozhu. [Chen Haozi, with notes by Yi Qinheng] *Hua jing* [Mirror of flowers]. Beijing: Nongye chubanshe, 1962. 陈淏子辑,伊欽恒校註.花镜.北京农业出版社.

Chen Zhi, Gongchi Zhang, and Congzhou Chen. *Zhongguo lidai ming yuan ji xuanzhu*. [A selection of memoirs on famous gardens in Chinese history, with notes]. Hefei: Anhui kexue jishu chubanshe, 1983. 陈植，张公弛，陈从周.中国历代名园记选注。合肥 : 安徽科学技术出版社。

Li Gefei. *Luoyang ming yuan ji*. [Notes on the Famous Gardens of Luoyang] *Juan 26*, 4a-11b, *Shuo fu, ju Ming chaoben*, Nanfenlou zangban. 李格非。洛阳明园记。说郛, 卷二十六. 据明钞本南据明钞本淊芬楼藏板.

Wang Yi. *Yuanlin yu Zhongguo wenhua*. [Gardens and Chinese Culture]. Shanghai: Renmin chubanshe, 1990. 王毅。园林与中国文化。上海人民出版社。

Yang Xuanzhi. Zhou Zumo (ed.). *Luoyang qielan ji xiaoshi*. [Memoir on the Buddhist Monastries of Luoyang by Yang Xuanzhi, edited by Zhou Zumo] Beijing: Zhonghua shuju, 1963. 杨衒之撰.周祖谟校释. 洛阳伽蓝记校释. 北京中华书局.

Zhang Jiaji. *Zhongguo zuo yuan shi*. [History of garden creation in China]. Harbin: Heilongjiang renmin chubanshe, 1986. 张家骥。中国造园史。哈尔滨: 黑龙江人民出版社。

Zhou Shihou [Zhou Xu]. *Luoyang huamu ji*. [Notes on the Flowers and trees of Luoyang] *Juan 26*, 11b-27a, *Shuo fu, ju Ming chaoben*, Nanfenlou zangban. 周师厚(周叙)。洛阳花木记。说郛, 卷二十六. 据明钞本南据明钞本淊芬楼藏板.

In Western languages

Clunas, Craig. *Fruitful Sites. Garden Culture in Ming Dynasty China*. London: Reaktion Books Ltd, 1996.

Fung, Stanislaus. "Guide to Secondary Sources on Chinese Gardens," *Studies in the History of Gardens & Designed Landscapes* 18, no. 3 (1998): 269-86.

Keswick, Maggie. *The Chinese Garden*. London: Academy Editions, 1978.

Li, Hui-lin. *The Garden Flowers of China*. New York: The Ronald Press Company, 1959.

Makeham, John. "The Confucian Role of Names in Traditional Chinese Gardens." *Studies in the History of Gardens & Designed Landscapes* 18, no. 3 (1998): 187-210.

Mauss, Marcel. *The Gift, The Form and Reason for Exchange in Archaic Societies*. New York: W.W. Norton, 1954.

Métailié, Georges. "Some Hint on 'Scholar Gardens' and Plants in Traditional China". *Studies in the History of Gardens & Designed Landscapes* 18, no. 3 (1998): 248-56.

Needham, Joseph, Lu Gwei-djen. *Science and Civilisation in China*, Vol. 6: 1, *Botany*. Cambridge: Cambridge University Press, 1986.

Watelet, Claude-Henri. *Essais sur les jardins*. Paris: Prault, 1774. English translation: *Essay on Gardens: A Chapter in the French Picturesque*. Philadelphia, University of Pennsylvania Press, 2003.

Wu, Xin. "Yuelu Academy: Landscape and Gardens of Neo-Confucian Pedagogy." *Studies in the History of Gardens & Designed Landscapes* 25, no. 3 (2005): 156-90.

Notes

[1] It is probably the earliest Chinese text on gardens to have been known outside of China. The text of an approximate translation done probably by a French Jesuit missionary, Pierre Martial Cibot, was published for the first time in 1774 by Watelet (125-36).

[2] A great number of these essays have been recently collected and edited with notes, see, Chen, Zhang, Chen (1983); Chen, Jiang, Chao (2004).

[3] On this subject, see Makeham (1998), Wu (2005).

[4] See Li (1959, 22-36); also, Needham, Lu (1986, 394-09).

[5] See, Needham (1986, 431-33).

[6] Some editions of the text give Zhou Xu as the name of the author.

Gardens, City Life and Culture

Gardens, City Life and Culture

Gardens, City Life and Culture

Gardens, City Life and Culture

Gardens, City Life and Culture

Gardens, City Life and Culture

CHAPTER 3

Urban Gardens in Ming Jiangnan: Insights from the Essays of Wang Shizhen

Kenneth J. Hammond

The Ming dynasty, especially during the sixteenth and early seventeenth centuries, was a period of intense economic and demographic growth in China during which the development of urban centers was particularly significant (Brook 1998; Meskill 1994). The Jiangnan region in southeastern China, the most densely populated and wealthiest part of the empire, was the area most affected by these developments. Cities in the Jiangnan region expanded their roles as centers for economic growth and as venues for the cultural activities of the educated elite, the *shidafu*, or literati (Johnson 1993). The expansion of the commercial economy generated tensions and new developments in Chinese cultural and social life, including broadening literacy among urban populations, increasing opportunities for consumption, and fostering competition for power and status between newly rich merchant families and the traditional literati elite.

This was not a simple binary opposition between a new bourgeoisie and an older, decaying agrarian elite. In economic terms there was extensive investment in commercial ventures by well established land owning families, often in partnership with emergent mercantile interests. At the same time, families amassing wealth through commercial activities devoted much of their new resources to educating their sons in the classical Confucian curriculum in the hope of winning success in the civil examinations, and to engaging in other kinds of acquisitive activities or forms of public philanthropy which allowed them to present themselves socially on par with literary gentlemen (Brook 1998).

Yet despite certain elements of convergence in the economic and cultural spheres, many literati families and individuals were concerned with eroding status boundaries and threats to their hegemonic power in cultural and political life. They sought ways to assert their aesthetic sophistication and social superiority, often through various forms of status display and by emphasizing their unique role as arbiters of taste and consumption (Clunas 1991). The specific forms these activities took were not necessarily new, but rather often consisted of the elaboration of long-established cultural practices which were further reinforced by a continuing discourse of sophistication and connoisseurship.

One highly significant form of literati cultural practice, which expanded dramatically in the middle and later Ming, was the building and possession of gardens. Gardens in China have a long history of their own, dating back at least to the Han dynasty (202 B.C.E.-220 C.E.). By the Tang dynasty (617-907), gardens were well established as part of imperial space, as enclosures within palace grounds, or as separate entities to be visited on excursions (Owen 1995). Officials of the imperial government during the Tang built gardens at their homes in the capital at Chang'an and the secondary capital at Luoyang. These gardens served a range of purposes: as private retreats, as social space, as economic investments, and as modes of status display (Clunas 1996).

In the Song dynasty (960-1279) China's imperial political culture underwent significant transformations, largely linked to the development of the Confucian examination system as a principal means of recruiting men to serve in government administration (Chafee 1985; Elman 2005). The aristocratic social elite which had been dominant from the Han through the Tang was swept away in the chaos of the ninth and tenth centuries, and in its place an elite defined in terms of *learning* assumed the hegemonic center (Bol 1992; Hymes 1986). The literati became a self-conscious social formation with a shared core of cultural theory and practice based in the Confucian examinations, but encompassing aesthetic and material dimensions which further buttressed their sense of common identity. Gardens began to play a more significant role in literati culture during the Song, at the capital in Kaifeng, in Luoyang, and in the flourishing urban centers of Jiangnan. While the imperial palaces and residences of members of the imperial family continued to have gardens associated with them, gardens increasingly came to be seen as characteristic of the cultural milieu of the literati. Individual literati advanced this claim through the literary production of texts about gardens, which included descriptions of particular sites, accounts of journeys to visit famous gardens, and records of an almost inventory-like nature listing the gardens found in cities like Suzhou or Luoyang. The physical and textual construction of gardens as spaces for literati social life and private retreat became a significant dimension of the identity of the elite and their assumption of dominance in the social and political realms.

The thirteenth century Mongol conquest and the establishment of an imperial court which mistrusted Chinese scholar officials brought on a period of marginalization for many literati during which a retreat to private life, and private space, was an attractive choice for men denied the kinds of public careers and status which had been characteristic of the Song. When the alien Mongol dynasty was replaced by the Chinese ruling house of the Ming after 1368, the literati began to resume their central role as the dominant elite in both cultural and political affairs. By the sixteenth century, literati cultural hegemony had been reestablished, but was challenged both by eunuchs based in the imperial household and by merchant families competing for power and prestige through cultural consumption and display. Gardens continued to play a powerful role in the social and cultural life of the literati, especially in Jiangnan, where they proliferated in number and where famous gardens became objects of local pride and national envy. Joanna Handlin Smith writes that "a veritable mania for garden building swept through the centers of prosperity" (Handlin Smith 1992, 57). Literati discourse about gardens likewise expanded, driven both by the general growth of the printing and book selling industries and by the desire of literati to assert both their possession of, and their power to arbitrate the value of, cultural capital and elite status.

To enhance our understanding of the way gardens and their place in the urban landscape of Ming China were perceived and articulated by members of the contemporary literati, I propose to examine writings by the scholar-official Wang Shizhen (1526-1590) concerned with surveying the gardens of two urban centers in Jiangnan (Hammond 1994, 1999). The first of these is Nanjing, the secondary imperial capital, and the second is Taicang, Wang Shizhen's hometown near the important cultural center Suzhou. These texts afford overviews of the famous gardens in each city, providing both capsule descriptions and allowing the reader to situate the gardens in both the urban landscape and their cultural and social nexus, often with detailed information about the current owners and original builders of the gardens. Through these writings, and through an analysis of Wang Shizhen's activities as an arbitrator of literary and cultural values, I will develop a complex view of the position of gardens in the urban life of Ming China.

Wang Shizhen

Wang Shizhen was born in 1526 into a very wealthy and well-established Jiangnan literati family. His father and grandfather both served as imperial officials, his father's career overlapping with his own. Wang became a *jinshi* in 1547, before his twenty-first birthday. He began a promising career with a series of appointments in the capital, but in the early 1550s came into conflict with the powerful grand secretary Yan Song. The enmity between them persisted and ultimately led to the impeachment and execution of Wang's father Wang Yu in 1560. Wang and his younger brother Shimou withdrew from office for the requisite mourning period, and remained in retirement in their hometown of Taicang even after the formal mourning time had ended. Yan Song fell from power in 1562, and in 1567 the Longqing emperor came to the throne, which allowed Wang to resume his official career as many of his friends and allies now rose to high office. Longqing's reign was rather brief, however, and Wang soon found himself in conflict with Zhang Juzheng, the chief grand secretary of the new Wanli emperor in the early 1570s. He once again retreated into retirement at home. He remained in Taicang despite being appointed to a series of offices in Nanjing, until 1588, when he finally accepted the position of Right Vice Minister of the Board of War in Nanjing. In July 1589 he was named Minister of the Board of Punishments in Nanjing, the last official post he held. He retired for the final time in April 1590 and died in December of the same year.

While Wang's official career was often overshadowed by his clashes with powerful political figures at the center of the imperial state, he achieved wide notoriety and respect as a literary leader of the Old Phraseology (*gu wenci*) movement. While this movement was later attacked for promoting a slavish imitation of a narrow range of ancient styles, Wang in fact advocated emulation of a wide range of past worthy models in the writing of poetry and prose. While Qin-Han prose and High Tang poetry are most commonly held up as the ideals of the Old Phraseology movement, Wang also greatly admired the Song dynasty scholar and poet Su Shi and later writers whom he felt manifested the desired qualities of straightforwardness and a proper blending of form and content. Wang opposed writing which he felt subordinated the true expression of feeling to the didactic purposes of the Learning of Principle school of philosophy, a position he associated with the work of scholars such as Tang Shunzhi. Interestingly, Tang was politically linked to Yan Song, uniting Wang's literary and political foes in the "in-group" of the 1550s.

Wang Shizhen viewed the writing of good literature as the duty of the literati, and upheld the ideals of the literary gentleman as personified by figures like Su Shi. His literary views and political career put him into a position of chronic tension with the imperial center in Beijing. For Wang, the role of the great urban complex of Nanjing as a center for literati political culture was embedded both in his own life experience and in his literary discourse. At the same time, because of his repeated and extended periods of residence at home in Taicang due to his withdrawal from active service in the imperial government, he maintained a very active role in the cultural affairs of this smaller city in Jiangnan.

Wang was both an owner of gardens himself and a frequent visitor to the gardens of others. He was widely recognized in the latter decades of the sixteenth century as one of the great arbiters of taste in literati circles, both on the basis of his own patronage and collecting activities and through the circulation of his writings on issues of connoisseurship. His views on gardens were given material form in the several gardens he had built for himself in Taicang, and literary expression in a series of essays he wrote describing the gardens of Taicang and Nanjing. After a few preliminary comments on the historical lineage of Wang's portrayal of the place of gardens in the urban landscape, I will first consider his writings about gardens in Taicang, both his and those of his fellow townsmen, and then turn to his account of the famous gardens of Nanjing.

Historical Antecedents

In writing about these urban centers of the Ming period, Wang lays claim to a place for them as the historical successors to the great capital city of previous dynasties, Luoyang. Luoyang was famed not only as a former capital, but for its central role in the cultural life of the Tang and Song dynasties. Gardens played a prominent role in the image of Luoyang, and Wang refers explicitly to the well known *Record of the Famous Gardens of Luoyang* by Li Gefei[1] which describes nineteen gardens situated in the city at the beginning of the twelfth century (Li 1954). In one of his essays on gardens in his hometown, *A Brief Record of Various Gardens in Taicang*, Wang writes:

> When I was serving in Yunyang I had occasion to make a visit of inquiry to Luoyang. The present city is but
> a quarter the size of the ancient one, and all that can be seen are government offices and marketplaces.
> Outside the walls there are some ten different kinds of orchards and gardens. The Mudan and Shaoyao rivers
> both have shifted their courses and now barely bubble forth. Of the many bamboos along the shore of the
> ponds described by Li Wenshu [Gefei], not a one is left. Thus I have relied on this record [of the old city] to
> seek to disclose the life and sense of the present. One reads it and is still moved to follow in its steps. The
> gardens of our city are mere mounds of earth. In the last dozen years or so it has not been possible to open up
> new land. So I have made these notes merely to record what can be recorded (Wang 1990, 60.15a-17a).

Here Wang deploys a view of present day Luoyang as in a state of decline from the glories of the past. The city has shrunk in size, and the sites referred to by Li Gefei have disappeared. He then refers to the role of Li's written account of the gardens of Luoyang as a way of reconnecting with this lost past. Wang then asserts that his motive for writing his own record of the gardens in Taicang is to create a comparable record of his own hometown, although he is careful to modestly disclaim any direct assertion that Taicang, whose gardens are mere "mounds of earth," is a match for Luoyang. Nonetheless, his note that land has become so scarce in recent years that it was impossible to find new sites to build on, suggests the flourishing urban scene of sixteenth century Jiangnan.

In his essay on the gardens of Nanjing, Wang also invokes the precedent of Song dynasty Luoyang and Li's *Record*:

> Li Wenshu [Gefei] recorded nineteen gardens in Luoyang. Although Luoyang was known as the
> Ancient Capital, in the aftermath of the disorders of the Five Dynasties period it never fully regained its
> former glories. As for the officials who were living there, they were either posted there as magistrates or to
> other positions, or seeking a retreat from the weariness of service. Their homes were mingled with those of
> scholars resting in exile from the capital. If one looked about carefully at what were called gardens and ponds,
> they provided the utmost of lovely views.
>
> Now it has been some sixty years since our August Emperor set up the tripods at Jinling,[2] from where
> two sages led the universe.[2] The form of the city, within and without, comes down from antiquity. As for the

officials and servitors of the imperial capital, where half the imperial bureaucracy is established, with mountains and streams of great beauty and the finest of human talents, how can it not be spoken of as like the ancient capital of the Song?

Could it be only the gardens and ponds which cannot be said to be like those described by Li Wenshu? Does it not in fact excel that age? Now, literati gentlemen do not like to live away from the home districts, so there are few retired gentlemen's residences in Nanjing.[4] But if one goes but a little way around the city, everywhere are the marvels of nature, and Buddhist monasteries scattered all about. If one has just a bit more energy, how can one not encounter gardens and ponds equal to those of old? (Chen 1983, 158-59)

No longer referring to his own hometown, but instead describing the great secondary capital of the Ming, Wang is much less modest in this passage. He claims that Ming Nanjing is not just the equal of Song Luoyang, but "in fact excel[s] that age." And here again gardens are presented as central to the definition of what makes a city glorious.

Wang Shizhen and the Gardens of Taicang

After a promising start to his official career at the imperial capital in Beijing, Wang Shizhen returned to his native city Taicang in 1560 in the wake of his father's execution as a result of political conflict with the leading official Yan Song. During his years of retirement from official life, Wang devoted himself to the literary and cultural life of his hometown and the broader Jiangnan region. He built the first of several gardens at his residence in Taicang, which he called the Garden for Evading Thorns, invoking the dangers of political life which he was seeking to avoid. This was subsequently expanded to become the Yanshan Garden, about which he wrote a series of essays describing the garden in great detail. He also had a small garden built just outside the city walls which he used as a private retreat. Other members of his family also had their own gardens in Taicang, and Wang was intimately familiar with gardens in the city owned by friends like the future Grand Secretary Wang Xijue and other fellow townsmen.[5]

As part of the burgeoning Jiangnan region, Taicang had played an important role in the grain trade since at least the Yuan dynasty, benefiting from the Mongols' decision to ship grain north by sea (Marme 1993, 25-26). It was administratively designated as a guard (*wei*) in 1368, the first year of the Ming dynasty. In 1497 it was redesignated as a subprefecture (*zhou*). At the same time portions of the surrounding districts (*xian*) of Kunshan, Changshu and Jiading were pared away and added to Taicang's territory (*Mingshi* 1986, 4.40: 918-20). The lands of Wang Shizhen's family were part of the area transferred from Kunshan to Taicang (Sato 1988). According to Gui Youguang (1507-1571) this transaction was a net loss to the former:

Of the villages subordinate to Wu, Kunshan was the largest. Then the eastern part of the district was cut away to make a new department. Specifically, the rich soil of the coastal area and the honest and homely people for the most part went to Taicang, and [Kunshan] was impoverished (Gui 1981, 11:261-62).

Both towns, nonetheless, were part of one of the most prosperous and developed prefectures in the empire. Lying in the heart of the Lower Yangzi macroregion,[6] Suzhou prefecture was both economically and culturally rich. According to the geographical treatise in the official *Ming History*, its 1491 population included 535,409 households with a total of 2,048,097 individuals, and in 1578 consisted of 600,755 households totaling 2,011,985 individuals (*Mingshi* 1986, 4.40: 918). Suzhou was one of the most heavily taxed prefectures, and also one of the highest producers of *jinshi*, holders of the highest degree in the imperial civil service examination system. It had long been a center of artistic and literary schools and movements.

Since Song times (960-1279) the Lower Yangzi region had been a major grain production area, but by the middle of the Ming dynasty, grain was becoming less important and production of cash crops for the market was increasing (Sato 1988). Taicang was part of an area where cotton production was developing rapidly (Huang 1990, 45 and 83). Expanding trade and handicraft production also contributed to the growing commercialization and urbanization of Jiangnan in the mid to late sixteenth century already discussed in the previous chapter. This development has been characterized by Michael Marme:

> Ming-Qing Suzhou was at the center of an urban system in which commerce had replaced both taxes and rent as the leading factor. Thus, like other cities which attained this critical mass, Suzhou made over the traditional society which produced it. Given its integration with the late imperial polity and the primacy it afforded commercial capitalism, the strain of modernity it embodied was an alternative to, not a precursor of, an industrial revolution (Marme 1984, 41-42).

Taicang was not as metropolitan as Suzhou, but their close proximity and the economic and cultural interaction between them meant that many of the same forces of change were felt in Taicang as well.

For Wang Shizhen, gardens formed an integral part of the urban landscape of his hometown. In his introductory essay on the Yanshan Garden, Wang begins by situating the garden in the overall context of the city:

> Just south of the Great Bridge is an area of markets. If one goes about a half *li*, then suddenly turns west, one reaches a byway called Iron Cat lane. About three hundred paces along this rather rustic alley, just before it peters out, there is a slight curve to the south, then west again. A bit less than halfway along this new lane is the Longfu temple. In front of the temple is a small pond of about 12 *mou* (3 acres) in area. On either side old orchards press close by, and the water of the pond seems to vaguely receive the misty moon, causing one to think of being in a thicket of trumpet creepers. On the right side of the temple is my Yanshan garden, also called the Yanzhou garden.
>
> Across from the garden is a small clear stream, on the near bank of which are clumps of willow, their shady branches tangled together as if they formed a single tree. On the southern side of the stream are the rich fields of Mr. Zhang, covering many *mou*. When the cold of winter is past, and the sprouts are quickening in the warmth, a yellow mist spreads over the fields, and from time to time the aroma of cakes and dumplings makes one think of the steamed rice buns of Yicheng [Hubei].
>
> West of my garden is the tomb of Mr. Zong, with more than ten ancient pines and cedars growing on the grounds. Also to the west of my garden is the shrine to Marquis Shouting of the Han [Huangfu Gui 105-175]. Clouds unfurl among the lofty peaks of its azure tiles and carved beams. All this adds to the abundance of my garden (Chen 1983, 131).

Here Wang guides the reader along a visualized itinerary through the town, leading him to the gates of the garden and evoking the surrounding sights and smells to enmesh us in the life of the neighborhood. Beginning in the northern part of Taicang with its markets, one moves south and into quieter lanes with orchards and ponds. Wang presents the journey to the garden as a movement away from the bustle of the commercial world and into a quieter and more "rustic" setting. The garden itself is flanked by the Longfu temple and an elaborate tomb compound, with a shrine to a Han dynasty worthy located further on. The impressive architecture engenders associations with antiquity and Buddhist spirituality, it "adds to the abundance" of the garden, again emphasizing the transition from the urban nexus to Wang's private space.

In another essay, the "Brief Record of Various Gardens in Taicang," Wang provides a kind of inventory of the important gardens of his native city:

> The wall around our city runs 18 *li*. This makes us a bit larger than the surrounding towns. The three districts outside the market area all were vacant land, but my elders erected three gardens there. Besides these there were eight others. Two of these were outside the city walls. Two others have disappeared. Those which can be visited [today] are only four.
>
> Nowadays families of wealth and honor (*guifu jia*) store up money until they accumulate tens of thousands. Yet they hide their fame and do not build [grand] residences, or if they build such homes they do not build gardens. Yet there is one among them who first built a garden, then followed it with a rich mansion to complete it. Only I am obsessed with giving priority to the garden, and relegating the residence to second place. This is because a house is adequate for my body, but it is not enough for my eyes and ears. And the personal fulfillment of a garden is not just a matter of one's [own] life, but extends to sons and grandsons.
>
> For a garden's abundance is in lofty trees. But it is not easy to make trees grow tall. It is not like ordering up the materials to build a house in the morning and having the work done by dusk. Because of this my Yan Garden was the first I built, and the first to attain wide fame. And because of this there is nothing about the obsession [with gardens] which is abroad in the world which does not come back to me. I made a record of my garden in order to rank others after it (Wang 1990, juan 60, 9b–10a).

Here again, Wang begins by establishing the larger urban setting for the gardens he will be discussing, and reminding us of the burgeoning commercial economy which is generating wealth for the city's elite. He then rather dramatically lays claim to being the source for the current passion for garden building in the town. He argues that building gardens is necessary to promote the fame of one's family, and to demonstrate the proper qualities, both moral and cultural, which only a member of the literati elite like he is able to fully appreciate and articulate. This is far preferable to the practices of some prominent families who hide away their success. In a time of social flux, as wealth is being built up by newly rising groups as well as the long-established literati elite, it is important for the "wealthy and honorable" to make their inherent worth manifest. Wang uses the term *guifu jia* to refer to the proper leaders of society. While the character *fu* is a straightforward reference to wealth, the term *gui* bears connotations of being people of quality, almost a kind of nobility, not of rank but of character. If the truly elite families do not make their value, and values, known through acts of public display such as building gardens, they will abandon the field to the cultural pretension of the *nouveau riches*.

Having situated the gardens of Taicang within the physical and social landscape of the city, Wang turns his attention in his essays to what lies within their walls. For the most part the thick description he provides is beyond our specific interests in this study, but in taking the reader through a detailed and almost virtual tour of the gardens Wang from time to time makes comments which further illuminate his sense of the garden and its place in urban social life.

In his initial essay on the Yanshan Garden, Wang provides an overview of the kinds of activities he engages in within the garden during the course of the year. For the most part he recounts these as aspects of his life in retreat from the cares of official life in the outside world. On occasion he is compelled to welcome into his garden reminders of that world in the form of visits from prominent men visiting Taicang. He notes that, "[h]aving served among ministers and generals, and obeyed the powerful without rest, to now have to put on formal attire and follow along after them as they shout about the scenery, destroying the tranquil nature [of the garden], or to worry about the food being prepared or the that mats will be set out for a banquet; these are the woes of my garden" (Chen 1983, 132). These social obligations cannot be avoided, and the wider world intrudes into Wang's retreat whether he likes it or not. The ideal of the garden as a place of withdrawal is seriously compromised by Wang's need to maintain his network of relationships even during periods when he is out of official service. But in another passage Wang emphasizes the role his garden plays in local society in a very different tone, "[m]y garden is really quite beautiful. When my neighbors heard of it they daily came to wander about in it, and other friends and strangers come to visit every week. As I think back on it, this has been going on for some five or six years now (Chen 1983, 132–33).

The sense here is once again of the garden as an instrument of cultural power, an objectified accumulation of social and cultural capital as well as the fruit of economic success, to be shown off proudly to friends and neighbors, even strangers. The practice of opening private gardens to public viewing on some regular basis, as Wang suggests here took place on a weekly basis, reinforced the role of the garden as an object of cultural consumption not merely for its owner but for a broader public as well. The blurring of class lines made the display of wealth and sophistication, even to an anonymous audience amounting to early modern tourists, imperative. How many of these strangers had passed through Wang's garden in the "five or six years" he had been opening his gates on a regular basis?

This passage also alludes to the use of gardens as venues for gatherings of like-minded gentlemen, whose discussions were generally articulated in purely literary terms, yet who also used social scenes such as gatherings in gardens to pursue additional agendas. The trope of the literary assemblage and its attendant drinking and composing has ancient origins, and remained the basic façade for social gatherings among literati. Political factionalism and open forms of political association were not acceptable in late imperial political life, yet there were substantive divisions and alliances among groups and individuals who shared common ideas or policy orientations, and who could take advantage of informal assemblies like parties in gardens to discuss their views and formulate plans for advancing their particular positions. In the 1550s and early 1560s the factional conflict centering around the chief grand secretary Yan Song was a major focus for Wang Shizhen's circle of friends and colleagues, and he deployed a range of cultural practices in this cause, including writing and staging dramatic productions in his home. Discussions of these and other political topics would have animated the conversation when he played host in his garden. Later in the Ming, as overt political organizations became briefly more active, groups like the Donglin or the Fushe often met in gardens to discuss their ideas and develop their plans (Xie 1982).

Thus far we have considered Wang Shizhen's writing about literati gardens in his hometown. Wang was more than a local or regional figure, though, and spent much of his later career in the southern capital of Nanjing where he observed a somewhat different complex of urban garden culture.

Nanjing

Nanjing had been a capital city in several earlier periods of Chinese history. During the Three Kingdoms (220-265) and the Northern and Southern dynasties (290-581) period, it had been the seat of the Kingdom of Wu, and the Eastern Jin, Song, Qi, Liang, and Chen dynasties. Though eight centuries had passed since the fall of the Chen, the imperial heritage at Nanjing was still strongly felt, and was given concrete revival when Zhu Yuanzhang made Nanjing the capital of his newly founded dynasty in 1368. The city was rebuilt as an imperial capital, with palaces, altars, tax granaries, and the full complement of government offices and other structures associated with its role as the center of the empire.

Nanjing's reign as the premier city of China did not last long, however, as the third Ming emperor, Zhu Di, who usurped the throne in 1402, moved the capital north to his former princely fief, which became Beijing. The Liao, Jin and Yuan dynasties had all had capitals at this site, and Zhu Di built his new city largely on the infrastructure of the old Mongol city. By 1420 Beijing became the seat of imperial power, and remained so for the rest of the Ming and under the succeeding Manchu Qing dynasty (1644-1912).

Nanjing at first suffered serious eclipse with the shift of the capital to the north, but by the sixteenth century it had become a very dynamic center of literati culture and politics. This was due in part to its proximity to the heartland of literati wealth and power in Jiangnan. Nanjing also provided a useful focal point for scholar-officials who wished to remain engaged with the imperial state, but who sought to avoid the factional politics of Beijing, or who perhaps found themselves in the "out" group in factional conflict. Fritz Mote has noted that, "Nanking, as opposed to Peking, came to represent an attractive alternative course where previously there had existed only a single acceptable course for men of talent and ambition. The rich life of the great city came close to being politically subversive as well as morally scandalous in the late sixteenth and seventeenth centuries" (Mote 1977, 152). Like Luoyang in the Northern Song, Nanjing in the later Ming shared some of the glory of imperial power, but was principally a literati city, where members of the *shi* elite could assert their social and cultural primacy in tension with their requisite loyalty to the dynastic state.

At the end of his official career Wang Shizhen spent two years serving in Nanjing. During this time his official duties were relatively light, and he devoted a considerable amount of time to his cultural activities. He wrote that, "I went about to the famous gardens, such as those of the Prince of Zhongshan. Altogether I visited ten, large and small." He adopted the same mode of exposition as he had used in writing about Taicang, taking the reader through a kind of virtual tour of each garden, and in each case beginning by situating the garden within the larger urban scene, noting the street one traveled to reach the gate, or the buildings to be found in adjacent spaces. As noted above, Wang saw Ming Nanjing as inheriting, and exceeding, the glories of Song Luoyang, and his record of these gardens was meant to redeploy that glory in the contemporary era, and to transmit the achievements of the Ming to later generations. Nanjing was both a great aristocratic city, as suited the secondary capital of the empire, and a center of literati cultural life. Gardens were integral components of the city and served as the venues for many of the most important aesthetic, social and political activities of literati life. As Wang wrote, "when I was lucky enough to have the chance to visit them, how could I not undertake to record them?" (Chen 1983, 158)

Conclusion

The urban world of middle and late Ming Jiangnan was a dynamic and complex place, with the long-established hegemony of the literati elite being challenged by rising commercial wealth and the ensuing competition for status and conspicuous consumption. Within the vibrant nexus of city life, the gardens of individual literati served as places of withdrawal, but also as objects to be displayed as part of the contest for prestige. Gardens were also gathering places for like-minded gentlemen, and from time to time, even scenes open to the public for their edification and awe.

Wang Shizhen, from his position as one of the leading literary figures of the age and as member of a prominent Jiangnan literati family, was both a connoisseur of gardens and a voice which articulated their proper place in social and cultural life. In writing about his hometown of Taicang or the southern capital at Nanjing, Wang described the many uses of gardens, the physical beauties to be seen within them, and their incorporation into the larger social landscape. As with his comments about Li Gefei's record of Song Luoyang, we must note that the gardens of Ming Jiangnan have largely disappeared. We are fortunate to have Wang's essays to remind us of what has been lost.

Bibliography

Bol, Peter K. *This Culture of Ours: Intellectual Transitions in T'ang and Sung China.* Stanford: Stanford University Press, 1992.

Brook, Timothy. *The Confusions of Pleasure: Commerce and Culture in Ming China.* Berkeley: University of California Press, 1998.

Chaffee, John. *The Thorny Gates of Learning in Sung China.* Cambridge: Cambridge University Press, 1985.

Chen Zhi et al., compilers. *Zhongguo lidai mingyuan ji xuanzhu* (Selected texts on famous gardens in Chinese dynasties). Hefei: Anhui kexue jishu chubanshe, 1983.

Clunas, Craig. *Superfluous Things: Material Culture and Social Status in Early Modern China.* Bloomington: Indiana University Press, 1991.

———. *Fruitful Sites: Garden Culture in Ming Dynasty China.* Durham: Duke University Press, 1996.

Gui Youguang. "Ceng siyi Tang Jun xu" (Preface for ceremonial official Tang Jun). *Zhenchuan xiansheng ji* (Collected writings of Mr. Zhenchuan). Shanghai: Guji chubanshe, 1981, 11:261-62.

Hammond, Kenneth J. "History and Literati Consciousness: Towards an Intellectual Biography of Wang Shizhen." Ph.D. thesis, Harvard University, 1994.

———. "Wang Shizhen's Yanshan Garden Essays: Narrating a Literati Landscape." *Studies in the History of Gardens and Designed Landscapes.* 19 3/4 (1999): 276-87.

Handlin Smith, Joanna. "Gardens in Ch'i Piao-chia's Social World." *Journal of Asian Studies* LI:1 (1992): 55-81.

Huang, Philip C.C. *The Peasant Family and Rural Development in the Yangzi Delta, 1350-1988.* Stanford: Stanford University Press, 1990.

Hymes, Robert. *Statesmen and Gentlemen: The Elite of Fu-chou, Chiang-his, in Northern and Southern Sung.* Cambridge: Cambridge University Press, 1986.

Johnson, Linda Cooke. *Cities in Ming-Qing Jiangnan.* Albany: State University of New York Press, 1993.

Legge, James. *The Chinese Classics VII.* Reprint, Taibei: 1990.

Li Gefei. *Luoyang Mingyuan ji* (Record of the famous gardens of Luoyang). Beijing: Wenxue guji kan, 1954.

Little, Daniel. *Understanding Peasant China.* New Haven: Yale University Press, 1989.

Marme, Michael. "Population and Possibility in Ming Suzhou: A Quantitative Model." *Ming Studies* 12 (1984).

———. "Heaven and Earth: The Rise of Suzhou, 1127-1550." *Cities in Ming-Qing Jiangnan.* Edited by Linda Cooke Johnson. Albany: State University of New York Press, 1993.

Mingshi (History of the Ming). Beijing: Zhonghua shuju, 1986.

Mote, Frederick W. "The Transformation of Nanking." *The City in Late Imperial China.* Edited by G. William Skinner, 101-53. Stanford: Stanford University Press, 1977.

Owen, Stephen. "The Formation of the Tang Estates Poem." *Harvard Journal of Asiatic Studies* LV.1 (1995): 39-59.

Sato Ichiro. "Dokyonin Ki Yuko to O Seitei" (Fellow townsmen Gui Youguang and Wang Shizhen). *Chugoku bunshorun.* Tokyo: 1988.

Skinner, G. William. "Regional Urbanization in Nineteenth Century China." *The City in Late Imperial China.* Edited by G. William Skinner, 211-49. Stanford: Stanford University Press, 1977.

Songshi (History of the Song). Beijing: Zhonghua shuju, 1990.

Wang Shizhen. *Yanzhou shanren xugao* (Supplemental collected works of the Yanzhou recluse). Shanghai: Guji chubanshe, 1990.

Wyatt, Don. *The Recluse of Luoyang*. Honolulu: University of Hawaii Press, 1996.

Xie Guozhcn. *Ming Qing zhiji dangshe yundong kao* (Examination of factional activities in the Ming Qing transition). Beijing: Zhonghua shuju, 1982.

Notes

[1.] For a biographical note on Li see *Songshi* 1990, 13121.

[2.] Setting up the tripods represents the founding of a dynasty. The term derives from the early Zhou, when the founding kings supposedly possessed a set of ritual bronzes which legitimized their rule. Cf *Zuozhuan*, Duke Xuan, year 3 (Legge 1990, VII): 292-93.

[3.] The two sages refer to the Hongwu and Yongle emperors. Wang does not include here the second Ming ruler, the Jianwen emperor, though by the time of the composition of this essay the legitimacy of the Jianwen reign was being reestablished.

[4.] This contrasts with the large number of retired officials settled in Luoyang during the Northern Song, as described by Li Gefei. For insight into the role of Song Luoyang as a venue of literati retreat see Wyatt 1996.

[5.] For information on the Wang family gardens, and for her many insights into Wang Shizhen's activities in the realm of gardens, I am greatly indebted to Allison Hardie, especially for her paper "'Massive Structure' or 'Spacious Naturalness'?: Aesthetic Choices in the Gardens of the Wang Family in Taicang" presented at the conference *The World of Wang Shizhen: Cultural Politics and Political Culture in 16th Century China* at the International Institute for Asian Studies, Leiden, The Netherlands, June 13-14, 2003.

[6.] For the model of macroregions in late Imperial China, see Skinner 1977, 211-49. For a discussion of the theoretical debate surrounding Skinner's model, see Little 1989, 68-104. Although Skinner's model is based on data for the later Qing period, its general applicability for the late Ming, particularly for the Lower Yangzi area, seems reasonable. Nonetheless, in this thesis I will refer to the region including Wang Shizhen's hometown of Taicang, the cultural center of Suzhou, and the surrounding area by the traditional term of Jiangnan, as this is the term Wang Shizhen himself used.

CHAPTER 4

Genoese Gardens:
Between Pleasure and Politics

Lauro Magnani

One aim of the governing class of the Republic of Genoa, the aristocracy of one of the most active centers of European finance between the sixteenth and seventeenth centuries, was to project an image of international prestige.[1] With this purpose, they became generous patrons of the arts investing heavily in the building of grand mansions and in the gathering of magnificent collections.[2] Within this context, the garden became endowed with special significance and developed into an integral component of the villa way of life, a testimony to the quality of its dwellers' life and noble condition.[3] This widely shared understanding spread among the ruling class in the second half of the sixteenth century and led to the building of a multitude of monumental domains. These suburban villas and their gardens emerged as one of the most significant images of the city, familiar to the Genoese and acknowledged by foreign visitors.[4] These images resulted from the city's pleasant climate and unique landscape located between sea and mountain; ease of botanical reproduction; and the capacity to transform the landscape according to current fashion. This capacity originated from the extraordinary financial strength of the Genoese aristocracy, and was promulgated as an image of success to be advertised to the ruling class' international financial networks and trading partners. Villas and gardens were an "ideal" projection of the city: whereas the city itself was somewhat enclosed within its walls, the villas' territory opened to the landscape and contributed to its Edenic character (Fig. 1). The space of the villas and their gardens was recognized as "other," separate from the space of *negotium* (business) in the urban center. It was continuously enjoyed by people making the daily commute between city dwelling and suburban villa, a precursor to a modern "middle class" lifestyle.

The development of the villa/garden phenomenon—already significant in the Middle Ages—resulted from attempts by the Fieschi and Doria families to impose their preeminence in local politics during the first half of the sixteenth century. These families, whose residences were embellished with remarkable gardens, occupied areas immediately neighboring the city. The Fieschis were located on the eastern hill of Carignano, and the Dorias on the western part, an even more strategic location on the way to the urban center.[5] In both cases, the residences implied through size, decorative repertoire, and complexity of their gardens a claim by their owner to the role of "lord" of the city, whether or not this was actually true. The Fieschis' defeat brought the destruction—the overall deletion of their palace and gardens—by the Dorias, while the failure of the Doria's dynastic ambition resulted in the isolation of the "magnificent" model proposed by Andrea Doria, Carlo V's admiral, and by his successor Giovanni Andrea I (Fig. 2a). Therefore, the development of the model of suburban villa with garden spread to the whole oligarchy of the Republic as an affirmation of the identity and political role of that class, and thus implicitly became a

Fig. 1. Jan Massys, *Flora (or Venus) with gardens and a view of Genoa in the background* (1561), oil on canvas, Stockholm, Nationalmuseum.

gesture of refusal of, and possibly defiance to, the supremacy of a unique "lord."

In the clearest fashion since the middle of the sixteenth century, the development of the villa with garden appears as a driving force of local city planning. A city of an 'other' kind gradually asserted itself, expanding in particular to portions of the *Levante* (Eastern) and the *Ponente* (Western) rivieras, as opposed to the city, which resulted from a centuries-old development within urban walls. It promoted a parallel residential world in which to organize public and private life. The union of the urban center and villa territories offered visitors the image of an incredibly large 'modern' town: "They build…elegant villas and they wonderfully embellish them with woods of healthy trees, cedars, and green garden parterres decorated with flowers. The villas are so numerous, around a four-mile area, that those who sail towards the harbor…have the impression of seeing one uninterrupted and huge town" (Giovanni Maria Cattaneo, 1514).

This impression was even emphasized by the Genoese Giustiniani, who declared that it has a "splendid perspective view…twenty or twenty-five miles long, and I doubt a view like this exists somewhere else in Europe." (Agostino Giustiniani, 1547) To the west, villas and gardens were lined up along the small flat strip parallel to the shore (Fig. 3), whilst to the east they were built in a landscape of small creeks running down the steep mountain slope to the sea (Fig. 4). There, the urban fabric of palaces with gardens was organized along roads that ran along hill ridges and formed narrow ways enclosed between property walls.

Halfway through the century, Galeazzo Alessi[6]—a Perugia-born architect with up-to-date knowledge of the most recent Roman innovations, familiar with the modern reinterpretation of classical texts and Vitruvio's treatise in particular[7]—was given the opportunity to intervene in this context in perfect mutual understanding with Luca Giustiniani, one of the most prominent personalities of the Genoese ruling class. The architect, in accordance with his patron's will, developed a new architectural model making the villa into a huge cubic building (Fig. 5).[8] The incisive character of this architectural intervention was a perfect match for the outstanding landscape where mountain and sea engaged one another. Alessi organized the building around a central axis with a porch opening to the south prospect and a loggia to the north. When viewed from the interior of the palace, the landscape was framed by the architecture and became a garden space,

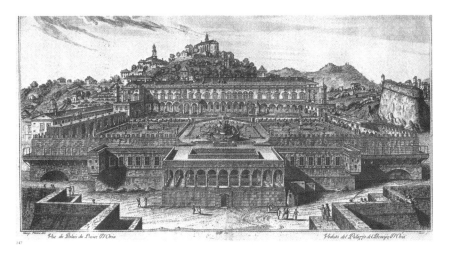

Fig. 2. (Top) A. Giolfi, G. Riviera, L. Guidotti, *View of the Villa of Prince Doria*, 1769, engraving.

Fig. 3. (Above) Sampierdarena's beach and villas as seen from the hill of the "Lanterna" (Lighthouse) in Genoa, detail from Henry Parker, *View of Genoa from the hill of St Benigno* (1822), watercolor, Collezione della Cassa di Risparmio di Genova e Imperia, Genoa.

Fig. 4. Carlo Antonio Tavella (1668-1738), *Landscape with villas in Albaro, from the hill of S. Maria del Prato to the sea*, Genoa, Palazzo Rosso, Gabinetto Disegni e Stampe, inv. no. 2948, drawing.

Fig. 5. Villa Giustiniani Cambiaso (1548-1552), south façade (author's photo).
Fig. 6. Villa Giustiniani Cambiaso, view from the main hall toward the sea (author's photo).

Fig. 7. Villa Giustiniani Cambiaso, view from the north façade's loggia (author's photo).
Fig. 8. The grotto in the garden of Villa Pallavicini delle Peschiere (about 1562), Genoa (Photo: Archivio Natura e Artificio, U. Morelli).

captured rather than borrowed to the satisfaction of the patron's ambition. The windows of the palace main room opened to a small valley that flowed down to the sea (Fig. 6), featuring, like the neighboring landscape overlooking the sea, a combination of kitchen and pleasure gardens. The monumental loggia on the northern side, incorporating a wealth of elements from the classical past—arches held by double columns, a coffered dome vault, and ancient Roman statues—offered a wide mountain view (Fig. 7), in all absolutely opposed to the character of the southern prospect. Both perspectives belonged together in the relatively small portion of property enclosed in the garden as if they were its natural development. It made clear the exceptional

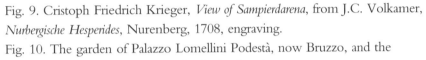

Fig. 9. Cristoph Friedrich Krieger, *View of Sampierdarena*, from J.C. Volkamer, *Nurbergische Hesperides*, Nurenberg, 1708, engraving.
Fig. 10. The garden of Palazzo Lomellini Podestà, now Bruzzo, and the palaces of Strada Nuova, Genoa (author's photo).

features of the landscape while defining the garden as a space architecturally ordered around a visual axis.

At the same time, other instances of a similar, fruitful cooperation between patrons and artists resulted in the creation of artificial grottoes (Fig. 8),[9] the very precocious Genoese version of a fashion that later spread to the whole of Europe. It also led to the creation of other artificial landscape features, such as fishponds or small lakes,[10] typical of aristocratic gardens aimed at "capturing" elements of nature in the controlled space of the garden itself. The conformation of the Ligurian landscape led, in the most significant cases,[11] to the building of gardens articulated in a succession of levels, often terraced. This architectural model was later followed and coherently adapted to other villas according to their site first by Alessi himself, and subsequently by the architect assistants who had previously collaborated on his Genoa projects.

Villas proved to be the testing ground of a new way of developing the city, allowing interlacing and permeability between urban and suburban spaces. The new architectural model created for the suburban villas was readily adopted mid-century in the already mentioned renovation of urban spaces in the aristocratic neighborhood of Strada Nuova.[12] From there, it was again transferred to the villas of Sampierdarena. Indeed, the *lustgarten* (pleasure gardens) of Sampierdarena provide an emblematic example (Fig. 9): the suburban area of pleasure villas to the west of the city adopted the Alessian villa type while incorporating the new dwelling pattern introduced by the ruling aristocracy in the urban neighborhood of Strada Nuova. As a result, Sampierdarena villas came to be organized around an axial road for the exclusive use of aristocratic residences, just like the palaces of Strada Nuova (Fig. 10), yet the villas were enriched by the more conspicuous presence of large gardens in direct communication with the seashore to the front and mountains to the back, rather than contiguous with the urban fabric as in the city center. This typology was also adopted in the contiguous neighborhoods of the 'villa with garden-city' in the Ponente, extending through the boroughs of Cornigliano, Sestri Ponente, Pra, Pegli, and Voltri, with a slowly decreasing building density and growing extension of parks and villas as distance to the city center grew. These areas were later exploited for new and prestigious settlements by the ruling aristocracy until the eighteenth and early nineteenth century.[13]

Rubens, the great Flemish artist of the Baroque age and an international diplomat, acknowledged these villas and the new urban palaces as testimony to the originality and modernity of a cultivated elite of private gentlemen not enslaved by compulsory imitation of "courtly" standards.[14] This recognition by a high profile representative of the seventeenth century European intellectual elite underlines the emblematic value of the dwelling model adopted by the Genoese aristocracy. In this context, the garden qualifies as a most significant sign of self display in a strategy directed internally towards the local oligarchy and externally towards the European power elite.

On the domestic stage, the choice of monumental villa settlements fueled the clashes between supporters of traditional trading practices and the emerging upper strata of the oligarchy, the so-called Eminences (*Eminenti*), involved more in purely financial activities. Although the aristocracy as a whole adopted the villa fashion, the creation of the most significant villa complexes was initiated by a most powerful group of noblemen. They were united by their engagement in the same financial investment and loan activity, even though they either belonged to the old (of ancient origin) or to the new (of popular origin) part of the oligarchy. The opposition, composed of aristocrats who supported the ancient trade (rather than financial) vocation of the city,[15] indulged in a radically different idea of the garden. Their position is documented by the writings of Oberto and Paolo Foglietta, two brothers belonging to the "new" (i.e. of recent date) aristocracy. Oberto condemned the 'spectacular enrichment' of financiers and the immobilization of capital invested in luxurious villas: "let's have less villas and more galleys," he exhorted his fellow citizens. Paolo opposed the use of vast resources in the establishment of new villas with gardens, and supported a completely urban view of the garden. He objected to the private appropriation of parts of the Genoese territory, and instead called for a thoroughly ideal 'possession' of the view:

> I've found a villa so close to Genoa that I can live without having a mule (i.e. without having to move between town and the suburb)…and this villa is in Piazza Nuova (i.e. right in the city center, next to the Palace which was the headquarters of the Doge), my lawn is in Carignano (the first hill on the eastern part of town), my fountain is the sea and my orchard the Bisagno plain (the Bisagno is the stream that flows on the eastern side of town). …Without leaving Genoa…we have villas on the roofs (i.e. from the top of our city palaces we enjoy the same view we have in the villas) and we can say we are in the villa and at home at the same time. And I have a terrace which is *in* Genoa and *in* the villa, which has cultivated land, gardens, woods and lawns, a fountain and a water-trough.[16]

This idealized return to within the city limits, this urban-centered vision focused on the city harbor, investments, and trade risks, contrasted with the coeval expansion of villa territories and simultaneous investment in an urban palace as well as a villa and its garden. The most sumptuous examples of this wealth and luxury impressed the representatives of international circles of power, namely the visiting members of court aristocracies. Their admiration was often mingled with a perception of excessive tendencies by the Genoese aristocracy, which was not suitable for the ruling class of a Republic that welcomed feudal aristocracy and popular nobility, and whose members were often "compromised"—from the old blood aristocracy's point of view—by their engagement in trading and making loans, sometimes bordering on usury. This feeling emerged in the mid-sixteenth century in the contradictory impressions reported by a gentleman of the Farnese house. He was fascinated by the way the new villas' owners and their ladies welcomed him (he mentions the Pallavicino and Giustiniani villas in particular), but he also noticed the "too superb" and excessive wealth "with gardens so wonderful as to make me fall in love with them...."[17] A tougher, more lucid opinion, less moved by mundane seductions, was expressed some decades later by a clergyman, the Apostolic Visitor Monsignor Bossio, who described these complexes as "overpassing Christian modesty and somehow even the good health of a well ruled Republic."[18] Similar opinions about the importance of the gardens can be found during this time in reports from visiting court emissaries, such as the Farneses, the Gonzagas, or the Medicis. Letters sent by Genoese aristocrats, often written in the villas themselves,[19] are kept in the same archives. The

Fig. 11. The grotto in the garden of villa Pavese Doria in Genoa-Sampierdarena (about 1594) (Photo: Archivio Natura e Artificio, U. Morelli).

Genoese often underlined, with a lovely nonchalance, that gifts such as rare plants, particular stones, tartars, corals—which they sent to the European princes they were in contact with—came from their gardens. Therefore, local noblemen saw themselves as genuine producers of luxury artworks and creators of the latest trends and unique models, and not simply as conspicuous consumers of the European aristocracy.

This is why, at the beginning of the seventeenth century, Rubens—a man accustomed to courts yet also a *bourgeois* from Antwerp who had personal experience with the Genoese way of life—recognized the villa/garden for its "modernity" and chose it as a possible model for the Catholic ruling class of Flanders.[20] By that time, the 'town palace and suburban villa' way of life was fully established. The combination of gardens, urban residences adorned with great frescoed interior decoration, rich collections, and the aulic portraiture that Rubens himself and Van Dyck[21] produced for the Genoese (which displayed characters similar to the portraits made for the great European Houses), played a significant role in creating the image that Genoese aristocrats wished to project.

Clearly, even in the urban palace the owner used all the seductions of his well-funded 'magnificence,' but they built upon the possibility offered by the villa and its garden to present an ideal version of the town; purified from the social contrasts and distanced from the cares of business which could ruin their effort towards an aristocratic "presentation of self."

This trait was exemplified when Francesco Gonzaga, Duke of Mantua, paid a private visit to Genoa accompanied by his court and Rubens. The days spent at the villa by the aristocratic guest, and the entertaining activities organized by his generous hosts, were immediately reported: "Everybody showed signs of incredible joyfulness at this visit and at the familiarity

Fig. 12. Workshop of Domenico Fiasella, *The Imperiale family with the garden of their Sampierdarena villa in the background (detail)* (1642), oil on canvas, Genoa, Musei di Strada Nuova.

Fig. 13. *Genoa with its new walls and its surroundings* (about 1635), fresco, Roma, Palazzi Vaticani, Loggia delle Carte Geografiche.

with which His Highness related to the others in his conversation…This sweetness is actually caused by the domestic *ambience* of the villa."[22]

The "other city," the city of pleasure gardens, offered the stage on which this behavior was possible: a "representation" of the aristocracy against the "heroic" backdrop of villa façades next to each other, and also against the "satiric" backdrop of the garden[23] with its wonders of humanized nature. The importance of fashionable garden elements such as grottoes,[24] which in Genoa reached the greatest decorative wealth through the use of a variety of precious materials, was highlighted in the garden. Gonzaga was entertained by a seductive dance 'of beautiful nymphs' in front of the Pavese garden's grotto[25]—miraculously, it is still preserved today—whereas inside he could see characters taken from Ovid's *Metamorphosis* represented in rich mosaics made from different materials such as corals, crystals, majolica, shells and glass-paste tesserae, among water effects (Fig. 11). The garden became the place where social rites were more easily celebrated in an idealized form: the foreign aristocrat guest, seduced by the 'quality' of the ambience, would abandon the rigidity of courtly etiquette so the host could indulge in the luxury of a more familiar attitude.

Even as the garden became a sign of the quality of life shared by the ruling class, the exceptional splendor of some of the villas-with-garden underlined their owners' position in the social hierarchy and on the map of local power. But the image of the city was predicated upon the gardens as a whole, first in the late Renaissance and later in the Baroque Age. In the villa neighborhoods, any single garden enjoyed the effects of the presence of adjacent gardens and benefited from the reassuring dimension of a humanized space. Of course the gardens differed by their extension and character, but all contributed to the uniqueness of this Edenic landscape. Inside, traditional garden types and innovative models co-existed: from the small pleasure garden attached to the house with its organized green space divided into simple geometries, flower beds, espaliers, and pergola walks; to more complex landscaping with extended terraced gardens (Fig. 12). During the second half of the sixteenth century, the latter emerged as a transition from the building to the landscape, from humanized nature to "wilderness." It became a conquest of eminent viewpoints from which the exceptional qualities of the landscape could be appreciated as well as, often, the city background and its landmarks such as the lighthouse and the city walls.

The 'sweetness' of the city of gardens that surrounded the urban perimeter and the 'dreadfulness' of the new grand wall circuit from harbor top to hills realized in the 1630s, were strictly coeval images of alternative power strategies etched into the landscape (Fig. 13). Both images were used by the Senate of the Republic to promote the role of the State among the other European powers.

Of the two expressions of power, the wall circuit versus the crown of gardens and villas, the latter emerged as the most effective

Fig. 14. Villa Balbi (later owned by the Durazzo and Castelbarco families) and its garden, Genoa (Photo: Enrico Polidori, Genoa).

Fig. 15. Gregorio De Ferrari, *Spring*, 1689, fresco on the ceiling of a room, Genoa, Palazzo Brignole (now Palazzo Rosso) in Strada Nuova (Photo: Frederick Clarke, Genoa).

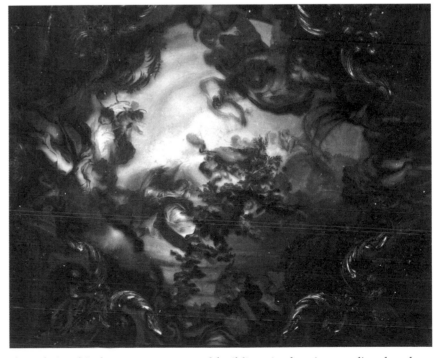

and enduring emblem of power. The admiration for the relationship between nature and buildings in the city, mediated and asserted by the close "fabric" of gardens, was upheld throughout the seventeenth century and confirmed by travelers performing the Grand Tour [26] until the early nineteenth century. In 1684 the humiliation of the bombardment of Genoa by

Fig. 16. The temple of Diana and the artificial lake in the park of the Villa Pallavicini (1840–1856), Pegli, Genoa (author's photo).

Fig. 17. Villa Saluzzo, known as "Paradise" (end of the 16th century), among the modern palaces of the Albaro neighbourhood, Genoa (aerial view) (Photo: Photo Shop, Genoa).

the Sun King's fleet showed the frailty and the lack of real usefulness of the powerful walls which surrounded the town.[27] By the end of the seventeenth century, great changes were taking place: the idea of an internationally significant political role for the Republic of Genoa was showing weakness. Since then, even though the forceful image of the villa owner as a patron of the arts survived, it only contributed to an image of collective power as an accumulation of different private villas and gardens, but not as a significant "state" entity.

Nevertheless, the idea of a garden maintained its vitality and function of cultural stimulus throughout the seventeenth century. Gardens were not only perceived as limited domains on the territory, but as worthy of being described by men of letter who responded to the exceptional qualities of these places of seduction set in the bosom of a remarkable landscape (Fig. 14). Dwelling in the "timeless" space of the garden made it possible to engage in both familiar and ironic practices of mythical space, to construct and deconstruct the scene of the classical Gods' fables as Chiabrera did.[28] One could see the fables take place in the reality of the garden, and then uncover their deceptive nature.

Familiarity with the garden as a place made the architecture of a "garden of words" possible in the poetry of Gio. Vincenzo Imperiale, an aristocrat and politician admired as a collector of paintings and a man of letters. He described his magnificent garden in Sampierdarena, which is the actual protagonist of his poem *Lo Stato Rustico (The Rustic State)*, with an amazing, baroque inventiveness (Fig.12).[29]

The creation by Domenico Piola and Gregorio De Ferrari of large painted decorations that gave the illusion of opening the interiors of Genoese residences toward spaces of nature and gardens provided a visual testimony of reaction to a period of political crisis. This decoration became one of the salient features of the idea of domestic space in the Baroque era.

Sensitivity to the elements of nature turned into interior decoration, visible in the works of Filippo Parodi and his son Domenico. They created a unity of space that involved painting, sculpture and stuccoes, and made reference, even when the decorations were inside city palaces, to objects intimately known in the space of the garden (Fig. 15).[30]

Obviously, at this time, Genoese designs could not match the great gardens created to hold a mirror to the power of European monarchs. Attempts to update and enlarge their gardens by certain families who defended the significance of their international financial role did not go beyond individual displays of magnificence.[31] On the other hand,

Fig. 18. The sea garden of Villa Doria del Principe after the recent conservation work (aerial view), Photo: Archivio Arti Doria Pamphilij, Genoa.

the shared sensitivity illuminated by the specific nature of the Ligurian landscape, which could easily be translated into the two-dimensional illusion of painting or into sculpture and plastic decoration, proved more original.

However, the comprehensive and Edenic image of the Republic, preserved for many centuries by cautious management of the territory, showed its intrinsic weakness. It collapsed as a result of a new organization of power and of the transformations of a society that, in the last century of the *ancien régime,* was not really able to renovate itself. And yet surprisingly, at the end of the eighteenth century, the garden was the field of a last renovation attempt of city culture by the most energetic and eminent members of the ruling class. They took a personal stance, like the philosopher Doge Agostino Lomellini who renovated his garden according to the latest Anglo-Chinois ideas,[32] in favor of a cultural renewal responsive to new ideas, and in deep protest against the political management of the Republic.

After the advent of the Savoy monarchy in 1815, new factors came into play, such as heavy industrialization followed by the first phase of large urban expansion and the renovation of the communication system. Until the mid-nineteenth century, the ruling class—who had by this time adapted itself to the new political context—was able to conceive and commission impressive gardens in the fashionable Romantic style (Fig.16),[33] but in the meantime the fabric of *ancien régime* gardens neighboring the city suffered the consequences of these novelties. It revealed its fragility and it progressively surrendered to a process of deep change that would end, with devastating effects, more than a century later with the post-war chaotic urban development. The transformation and consumption of land occurred at an accelerated pace throughout the Italian 'economic miracle' years. It is still going on today, despite recessive features of an economy engaged in a de-industrialization process.[34]

A few garden spaces, rarely as large as the original, are still attached to the villas surrounded by a mostly residential city fabric (Fig. 17). Among a few rare domains that remain in private hands, there are a large number of historic gardens, turned into public parks, which have suffered through the transformation into recreational green space.[35]

Today, many ancient gardens survive only as fragments. The political community is committed, at least formally, to preserve and protect these pieces of history. From the 1992 fifth century anniversary of the discovery of America by the Genoese Christopher Columbus, until 2004 when the city was nominated the European Capital of Culture, the city of Genoa debated important town planning interventions and urban restorations as a way of improving its own image to boost economic growth.[36]

Gardens play a very important role for the historical image of the city, however, there currently exists a contradiction between the perceptions of scholars and those of the majority of the people, including most suburban dwellers living close to the site of the ancient gardens. Some scholars with specific knowledge of the past can still visualize the Edenic landscape, and are able to recognize in the remainders of a historic garden surrounded by modern buildings the idea of a garden offering an opening towards the landscape, and to experience the "direct access" to nature in surviving sixteenth-century grottoes. People lacking that knowledge, particularly those who live in alienating conditions in the city outskirts where the fragments of the gardens survive in the middle of the recent chaotic urban development, cannot recognize the ancient traces that synthesized city, garden and landscape.

It is easier to neglect those fragments and to instead use available funds for the restoration of the few parks and gardens still extant today as complete entities (Fig. 18).[37] The result is certainly more immediately rewarding, and yet it does not bring back to life the ancient image of a city of gardens, nor does it meet the need to stitch the surviving parts of the historic gardens back into the fabric of the modern city.

Bibliography

Anon, *Synodi Diocesanae et Provinciales editae atque ineditae*, Genova: 1833.

Anon, *Città. Urban Regeneration*, exhibition catalogue. Genova Alinea: Firenze, 2004.

Anon, *Galeazzo Alessi e l'architettura del Cinquecento, Atti del Convegno internazionale di studi, Genova 1974*. Genova: Sagep, 1975.

Barns, Susan J., Piero Boccardo, Clario Di Fabio, and Laura Tagliaferro. *Van Dyck a Genova. Grande pittura e collezionismo*, Genova exhibition catalogue. Milano: Electa, 1997.

Bianchi, Fulvio and Claudio Russo. *La scelta della misura. Gabriello Chiabrera l'altro fuoco del barocco italiano*. Genova: Costa & Nolan, 1997.

Boccardo, Piero and Clario Di Fabio. *El siglo de los genoveses e una lunga storia di Arte e Splendore nel Palazzo dei Dogi*, Genoa exhibition catalogue, Milano: Electa, 1999.

Boccardo, Piero. *L'età di Rubens Dimore, committenti e collezionisti genovesi*, Genova exhibition catalogue, Milano: Skira, 2004.

Braudel, Ferdinand. *La Mediterranée et le monde méditerranéen à l'époque de Philippe II*. Paris: Colin, 1966.

Brejon de Lavergnée, Arnauld. *Rubens*. Paris: Editions de la Réunion des musées nationaux, 2004.

Cattaneo, Giovanni Maria. *Genua (1514)*, edited by Giuseppe Bertolotto, *Atti della Società Ligure di Storia Patria*, XXIV, 2, 191.

Cazzato, Vincenzo. *La memoria, il tempo, la storia nel giardino italiano tra '800 e '900*. Roma: Istituto Poligrafico e Zecca dello Stato, 1999.

Cazzato, Vincenzo, Marcello Fagiolo and Maria Adriana Giusti. *Atlante delle grotte, e dei ninfei in Italia*, I, *Toscana, Lazio, Italia*

Meridionale e Isole. Milano: Electa, 2001.

Cazzato, Vincenzo, Marcello Fagiolo and Maria Adriana Giusti. *Atlante delle grotte, e dei ninfei in Italia,* II, *Italia settentrionale, Umbria e Marche.* Milano: Electa 2002.

Ciardi, Roberto Paolo. *Gian Paolo Lomazzo. Scritti sulle arti.* Firenze: Edizione Centro Di 1974.

Conan, Michel, ed. *Bourgeois and Aristocratic Cultural Encounters in Garden Art, 1550-1850.* Washington, D.C.: Dumbarton Oaks, 2002.

Costantini, Claudio. *La Repubblica di Genova nell'età moderna.* Torino: UTET, 1978.

Costantini, Claudio. *Dimore, committenti e collezionisti genovesi,* Genova exhibition catalogue. Milano: Skira, 2004.

De Maddalena, Aldo and Hermann Kellebenz. *La Repubblica internazionale del denaro tra XV e XVII secolo,* Bologna: Il Mulino, 1986.

De Seta, Cesare. L'Italia nello specchio del "Grand Tour", *Storia dell'arte italiana,* vol. I, *Questioni e metodi.* Torino: Einaudi, 1979.

Doria Giorgio. "Conoscenza del mercato e sistema informativo: il 'know – how' dei mercanti finanzieri genovesi nei secoli XVI – XVII" in *La Repubblica internazionale del denaro tra XV e XVII secolo.* Edited by Aldo De Maddalena and Hermann Kellebenz, Bologna: Il Mulino, 1986.

Foglietta, Oberto. *La Repubblica di Genova.* Roma 1559.

Foglietta, Paolo. *Rime diverse in lingua genovese.* Pavia: Gerolamo Bartoli, 1583.

Francesco, Vescovo di Novara, visitatore appostolico, al Serenissimo Duce, all'Illustrissima Signoria, al Clero et Popolo di Genova, Milano 4 dicembre 1582, published in *Synodi Diocesanae et Provinciales editae atque ineditae,* Genova 1833.

Ghigino, Silvana. "Un'esperienza di restauro: il Parco Durazzo Pallavicini a Pegli e il Parco Serra a Comago" in *Parchi e giardini storici, Parchi letterari. Conoscenza tutela valorizzazione, Atti del II Convegno Nazionale.* Monza: Ministero per i Beni Culturali e Ambientali, 1992.

Giustiniani, Agostino. *Castigatissimi Annali con la loro copiosa Tavola della Eccelsa et Illustrissima Repubblica di Genova.* Genova: A. Bellone, 1537.

Goldthwaite, Richard A. *L'economia del collezionismo,* in *L'età di Rubens. Dimore, committenti e collezionisti genovesi.* Edited by Piero Boccardo. Genova exhibition catalogue. Milano: Skira, 2004.

Gavazza, Ezia and Lauro Magnani. *Pittura e decorazione a Genova nel Settecento.* Genova: Sagep, 2000.

Gorse, George L. "Genoese Renaissance Villas. A Tipological Introduction." *Journal of Garden History,* 4, 1983.

Gorse, George L. "A Classical Stage for the Old Nobility. The Strada Nuova and Sixteenth-Century Genoa." *Art Bulletin,* June 1997.

Imperiale, Gio Vincenzo. *Lo Stato rustico.* Genova: Giuseppe Pavoni, 1611.

Lapi Ballerini, Isabella and Litta Medri. *Artifici d'acque e giardini. La cultura delle grotte in Italia e in Europa Atti del V Convegno internazionale su Parchi e Giardini Storici, Firenze - Lucca 1998.* Firenze: Centro Di Firenze, 1999.

Leoncini, Luca. *Da Tintoretto a Rubens. Capolavori della Collezione Durazzo.* Genova exhibition catalogue. Milano: Skira, 2004.

Lomazzo, Gio Paolo. *Trattato dell'Arte de la Pittura.* Milano: G. Ponzio, 1584.

Magnani, Lauro. "Struttura e tecnica decorativa della grotta artificiale a Genova: la grotta del giardino di villa Pavese." *Studi di storia delle arti*, 3, 1980.

Magnani, Lauro. "Committenza e arte sacra dopo il Concilio di Trento: materiali di ricerca." *Studi di storia delle arti*, 5, 1983-1985.

Magnani, Lauro. "'L'uso d'ornare i fonti'. Galeazzo Alessi and the construction of grottoes in Genoese Gardens." *Journal of Garden History*, 2, 1985.

Magnani, Lauro. "Residenze di villa e immagini di giardino tra realtà e mito" in *La scelta della misura. Gabriello Chiabrera l'altro fuoco del barocco italiano*. Edited by Fulvio Bianchi and Claudio Russo. Genova: Costa & Nolan, 1997.

Magnani, Lauro. "Natura e artificio decorativo" in Ezia Gavazza and Lauro Magnani, *Pittura e decorazione a Genova nel Settecento*. Genova: Sagep, 2000.

Magnani, Lauro, *Il tempio di Venere. Giardino e villa nella cultura genovese*. Genova: Sagep 1987; revised edition Genova: Sagep, 2005.

Magnani, Lauro. *The Rise and Fall of Garden in the Republic of Genova, 1528 – 1797, Bourgeois and Aristocratic Cultural Encounters in Garden Art, 1550-1850*. Edited by Michel Conan. Washington, D.C.: Dumbarton Oaks, 2002.

Magnani, Lauro. "Fortuna e continuità di una immagine della natura: grotte in Liguria tra la seconda metà del Cinquecento e il primo Seicento" in *Artifici d'acque e giardini*. Edited by Isabella Lapi Ballerini and Litta Medri, 308–320. Firenze: Edizione Centro Di, 1999.

Magnani, Lauro. "Storia di un giardino." *Ricerche di storia dell'arte*, 82-83, 2004.

Maltese, Corrado. *Galeazzo Alessi e l'architettura del Cinquecento, Atti del Convegno internazionale di studi, Genova 1974*. Genova: Sagep 1975.

Maniglio Calcagno, Annalisa. *Giardini parchi e paesaggio nella Genova dell'Ottocento*. Genova: Sagep, 1984.

Martinoni, Renato, *Gian Vincenzo Imperiale politico, letterato e collezionista genovese del Seicento*. Padova: Antenore, 1983.

Oeschlin, Werner. "La dimensione europea dell'Alessi" in *Galeazzo Alessi e l'architettura del Cinquecento, Atti del Convegno internazionale di studi, Genova 1974*. Edited by Corrado Maltese, 19-34. Genova: Sagep, 1975.

Olcese Spingardi, Caterina. "La cultura del giardino a Genova tra le due guerre" in *La memoria, il tempo, la storia nel giardino italiano tra '800 e '900*. Edited by Vincenzo Cazzato. Roma: Istituto Poligrafico e Zecca dello Stato, 1999.

Pacini, Arturo. *La Genova di Andrea Doria nell'Impero di Carlo V*. Firenze: Leo Olschki, 1999.

Pagliara, Pier Nicola. "Vitruvio da testo a canone," *Memoria dell'antico nell'arte italiana, Dalla tradizione all'archeologia*. III Einaudi: Torino, 1986.

Poleggi, Ennio. *Strada Nuova, una lottizzazione del Cinquecento a Genova*. Genova: Sagep, 1972.

Poleggi Ennio-Cevini, Paolo, *Genova*. Bari: Laterza, 1981.

Poleggi, Ennio and Fiorella Caraceni. "Genova e Strada Nuova," in *Storia dell'arte italiana*, XII, *Momenti di architettura*. Torino: Einaudi, 1983.

Poleggi Ennio. *L'invenzione dei rolli. Genova città di Palazzi*, Genova exhibition catalogue. Milano: Skira, 2004.

Rotta, Salvatore. "Genova e il Re Sole" in *El siglo de los genoveses e una lunga storia di Arte e Splendore nel Palazzo dei Dogi*. Edited by Piero Boccardo and Clario Di Fabio. Genova exhibition catalogue, 15-21. Milano: Electa, 1999.

Savelli Rodolfo. *Il rovescio e il diritto. Immagini e problemi della storia di Genova in età moderna*, in *El siglo de los genoveses e una lunga storia di Arte e Splendore nel Palazzo dei Dogi.* Edited by Piero Boccardo and Clario Di Fabio. Genova exhibition catalogue. Milano: Electa, 1999.

Stagno, Laura. *Palazzo del Principe. Villa di Andrea Doria.Genova.* Genova: Sagep, 2005.

Turchi, Marcello. *Opere di Gabriello Chiabrera e lirici del classicismo barocco.* Torino: UTET, 1984.

Vazzoler, Franco. Letterature dialettali e manierismo in Italia, in *Manierismo e letteratura, Atti del Convegno.* Torino: A. Meynier, 1983.

Zorzi, Ludovico. *Il teatro e la città. Saggi sulla scena teatrale italiana.* Torino: Einaudi, 1977

+*Città. Urban Regeneration.* Genova exhibition catalogue. Firenze: Alinea, 2004.

Notes

[1] In the fifties the expression "century of the Genovese" was coined to define the period of international supremacy of Genoese businessmen, partly based on their privileged financial relations with the Habsburgic monarchies, between the sixteenth and the seventeenth centuries. Since the coinage of that definition by F.C. Spooner in 1956, the theme has been the subject of many studies and publications (such as Braudel 1966, 454; Doria 1986, 57-122; more recently Pacini 1999). A number of essays published in the catalogues of exhibitions on Genoese history and art (such as Savelli 1999, 15-21) offer a synthetic overview of recent research on the subject.

[2] Among the latest contributions on the link between economy and art in sixteenth- and seventeenth- century Genoa, (Goldthwaite 2004, 13-20). On the subject (with special reference to the building of palaces), (Gorse 1997, 301-327).

[3] Magnani 2002, 43-76.

[4] This image is frequently cited, for instance by the great poet Francesco Petrarca, who visited Genoa at the beginning of the fourteenth century, and by Piccolomini and Giovio, both protagonists of Renaissance literary circles, but also by "Grand Tour" travellers (see note 26) and nineteenth century visitors.

[5] On the development of Genoese villas, starting from the Doria and Fieschi residences, see (Gorse 1983, 43-76) and (Magnani 1987).

[6] On Galeazzo Alessi (Perugia 1512-1572).

[7] On late Renaissance and Mannerist interpretations of Vitruvius' treatise, (Pagliara 1986, 3- 85). The "modernity" in the European context of the architectural models elaborated by Alessi for the Genoese ruling class has been noted by several scholars (Oechslin 1975; Poleggi 2004). Significantly, the adjective "modern" is used in the title of the second edition of Rubens' book (I palazzi moderni di Genova). In Vasari's Vite (Vasari 1568), the same expression is used, with an even more definite and precise meaning: the writer defines the Genoese palaces as "disegnati alla moderna" or "designed in the modern way." The German architects Schickhardt (1599) and Furttenbach (1627) also emphasize this aspect in their writings, citing the modernity of materials, techniques and comforts typical of the Genoese aristocracy's palaces.

[8] On the relationship between this villa (built in 1548, as contemporary documents show) and the landscape, as well as on other aspects of Alessi's activity as an architect of villas, see (Magnani 1987, 59-80).

[9] Cf. (Magnani 1985, 135-153). The bibliography on artificial grottoes in Genovese gardens is now large. As Giovan Paolo Lomazzo, author of an important treatise on art, noted at the end of the sixteenth century, Genoa was one of the centers from which this new fashion spread to the rest of Europe (Ciardi 1974, II, 300) Among the latest contributions on the subject: (Cazzato, Fagiolo, Giusti, 2001 and 2002), with previous bibliography.

[10] Giorgio Vasari, in the 1568 edition of his *Vite* (a collection of biographies of artists), quotes the small lake in Adam Centurione's villa in Pegli, later Villa Doria, which survives to this day albeit in very bad condition see (Magnani 1987, 125).

[11] Here reference is made, in particular, to the well known gardens of Andrea Doria's villa, completed at the beginning of the seventeeth century by Andrea's successor (Magnani 1987, 114-124), and to the terraced gardens of Villa Imperiale (later Scassi) in Sampierdarena, originally organized around a vertical axis about one kilometer long, parts of which still survive (ibidem, 125).

[12] On the building of the urban neighbourhood of Strada Nuova, where a new dwelling pattern for the aristocracy was first established in accordance with the will of the oligarchy's governing bodies (Poleggi 1972; Poleggi and Caraceni 1983, 301-361).

[13] Among the most remarkable examples of mid and late eighteenth century villas are the Villa Durazzo in Cornigliano, the structure of which is based on French models (Magnani, 1987,199-208), the Villa Lomellini in Pegli (see note n.32), and the Villa Brignole or "Duchessa di Galliera" in Voltri, endowed with a very large park where traces of the up-to-date "romantic" plan created by architect Andrea Tagliafichi in 1804 still survive in the late nineteenth century layout (Magnani 1987, 222).

[14.] The first edition of Peter Paul Rubens' *Palaces of Genoa*, published in Antwerpen, dates back to 1622. On the great artist (Siegen 1577-Antwerpen 1640), see the catalogue of the recent exhibition in Lille (Brejon de Lavergnée 2004) on his activity in relation to Genoa, see (Boccardo 2004). On Genoese palaces in general, among the latest contributions see (Poleggi 2004).

[15.] On political debate and clashes of ideas in the Republic of Genoa, cf. (1978, 65-73, 232-244) where the polemic between supporters of finance and supporters of maritime trade as main vocation of the Republic is followed to its seventeenth century developments.

[16.] See, in particular, (Foglietta 1559), and (Foglietta 1583), from which all passages are quoted in the Italian translation by F. Vazzoler (the original version is in the Genoese dialect). On Paolo Foglietta cf. (Vazzoler 1983, 233-245).

[17.] Letter from Jerolamo Ceruli to the Duke of Parma, dated September 13, 1557, in *Fondo Farnese*, Parma, Archivio di Stato, quoted in (Magnani 1987, 104).

[18.] Francesco, Vescovo di Novara, visitatore appostolico, al Serenissimo Duce, all'Illustrissima Signoria, al Clero et Popolo di Genova, Milano 4 dicembre 1582, published in Synodi Diocesanae et Provinciales editae atque ineditae, Genova 1833. On Bossio's visit, his opinions and the reaction of the Genoese aristocracy, cf. (Magnani 1983-1985, 136-143).

[19.] Letters sent by Luca Giustiniani and Francesco Pallavicini from their villas in Albaro and Multedo are to be found in the *Fondo Farnese* of the Archivio di Stato in Parma; other letters are in Mantua, Archivio di Stato, *AG Busta 777*, with reports from the Sampierdarena villas. A remarkable testimony to the relations of the Genoese aristocracy with the Medici is the report by Luca Martini, a gentleman belonging to Cosimo I's *entourage*, describing the villa of Adam Centurione, one of Charles V's great financiers, who commissioned Galeazzo Alessi to design an artificial lake for his villa in Pegli (cf. L. Magnani, *Il tempio di Venere*, 61 e 68 n.16).

[20.] Cfr. note no.14.

[21.] On the activity in Genoa between 1621 and 1628 of the other great Flemish artist besides Rubens, Anthony Van Dyck (Antwerp 1599- London 1641), cf. (Barns, Boccardo, Di Fabio and Tagliaferro 1997).

[22.] Letter from Annibale Fleschi to the Duchess of Mantua, dated July 8, 1607, in Archivio di Stato, Mantua, *AG Busta 77*.

[23.] The villa being seen as the perfect setting for a "representation" of the aristocracy's ideal life, the conventions of the Renaissance theatre become relevant here. The garden is the place which shares the elements typical of the "satiric" scene, i.e. the backdrop in use for the representation of pastoral and mythical fables set in the natural world, whereas the noble façades of the palaces – for instance, Villa Imperiale, Villa Lercari and Villa Grimaldi adjoining each other – with their aulic decorations in the classical orders provide the kind of backdrop required for the "tragic" scene, typical of the historic and heroic drama. In these same years, Serlio, the author of a largely influential treatise on architecture, codified in his writings the architectonic characters of Renaissance scenery, according to the subdivision of all theatrical performances in the three genres - the comic, the tragic, the satiric – derived from Vitruvius and from classical tradition. On this subject, see (Zorzi 1977).

[24.] In addition to the bibliography cited in note no.9 cf. also (Lapi Ballerini and Medri 1999). On the grottoes in Genoa, see in the same volume (Magnani 1999, 308-320).

[25.] Magnani 1980, 77-97.

[26.] Genoa is one of the places usually visited during the so called "Grand Tour", that is the long journey through European capitals and art cities which in the seventeenth and eighteenth centuries was considered to be an essential part of the education of young gentlemen and of those intellectuals who could afford it. In the seventeenth century the Italian itinerary normally focused on the cities in the north and in the center of the country, with Rome as the last and most meridional destination. Later the south of Italy was "discovered" and included in the journey, while only in the Neoclassical age did travellers pursuing the knowledge of classical art add Greece to their itinerary. Cf. (De Seta 1979).

[27.] On the project and building of the New Walls between 1626 and 1632, related to the war waged against the Republic by the Duke of Savoy with French support, as well as on the 1684 bombardment of Genoa ordered by Louis XIV and executed by the large naval squad commanded by the Marquis of Seignelay: cf. (Costantini 2004, 245-299 and 335-354) (Rotta 1999, 286-291).

[28.] Most works by Gabriello Chiabrera (Savona 1552-1638), a classicist poet of the Baroque age well known at the courts of Florence, Turin and Manta, are published in (Turchi 1984). For the frequent references to the Ligurian villas and gardens in Chiabrera's *oeuvre* – the poet preferred to live there and often chose them as sources of his inspiration - cf. (Magnani 1997, 467-486).

[29.] On Gio. Vincenzo Imperiale's villa (Villa Imperiale, later Scassi), see note no 11. Imperiale's poem was published in 1611 (Giuseppe Pavoni: Genoa).

[30.] Domenico Piola (Genova 1627 - 1703) and Gregorio De Ferrari (Porto Maurizio 1647 - Genova 1726), both painters, and sculptor Filippo Parodi (Genova 1630 - 1702) are the protagonists of the late phase of the Genovese Baroque art in the last decades of the seventeenth century. On the special relation between interior and exterior spaces which characterizes their art in the conclusive years of their careers, at the very end of the century, see (Magnani 2000, 137-206).

[31.] In the first decades of the twentieth century, while the urban landscape was being radically changed with the consequent loss of many monumental domains, a new interest for historic gardens developed, which brought on a policy of acquisition by local authorities (Olcese Spingardi 1999, 31-42).

[32.] Agostino Lomellini - a correspondent of Montesquieu and D'Alembert (who dedicated his *Recherches sur la précession des Esquinoxes* to him and whose *Discours* he translated) and a friend of Claude Henri Watelet, the author of a famous treatise on gardens – became *doge* (the head of state in the Republic of Genoa) in 1760. Cf. (Magnani 1987, 209-216).

[33.] Maniglio Calcagno 1984.

[34.] For a study of the inner dynamic of urban development in Genoa between historic heritage and nineteenth and twentieth centuries expansion, cf. (Poleggi and Cevini 1981).

[35.] The new interest for historic gardens and the policy of acquisition by local authorities in the first decades of the twentieth century are the subject of (Olcese Spingardi 1999, 31-42).

[36.] The policy of the Genoese local authorities with regard to town planning is partly illustrated in (Anon 2004).

[37.] This kind of approach is evident in the restorations carried out in 1992 by local authorities for the celebration of the fifth centenary of the discovery of America, under the supervision of the Soprintendenza per i Beni Architettonici ed il Paesaggio della Liguria (i.e. the State office for the protection of Ligurian Landscape and Architectures), in Villa Durazzo – Pallavicini in Pegli and Villa Serra in Comago (Ghigino 1992, 501-508). These two villas in the outskirts of the city have large parks designed in the mid nineteenth century by scene designer Michele Canzio and architect Carlo Cusani respectively. More recently (1998-2000), the garden of villa Doria Pamphilij was restored by its private owners (Fig. 18): in this case, a modern reinterpretation of the late sixteenth century outlay – defined through historic research and a specific archaeological campaign – was carried out in a garden which had undergone many complex changes, bombardments in 1944 and a long period of lack of care (Magnani 2004; Stagno 2005, 107-122). The most recent conservation work regards the garden of villa Imperiale Scassi in Sampierdarena (2003): commissioned and paid for by the Municipal Authority and realised under the supervision of the already mentioned Soprintendenza, this restoration modified neither the arrangements of plants and trees nor the architectural structures of a garden which, albeit preserving its sixteenth century layout, was transformed into a public park in the 1920s. Rather, restorations were aimed only at consolidating extant structures and repairing single objects, such as statues, fountains and grottoes.

Gardens, City Life and
Culture

Gardens, City Life and
Culture

Gardens, City Life and
Culture

Gardens, City Life and
Culture

Gardens, City Life and
Culture

Gardens, City Life and
Culture

CHAPTER 5

Royal Gardens and City Life in Paris (1643–1789)

Michel Conan

The opening of a few large royal gardens to the well-do-do people of Paris in the early seventeenth century allowed the development of several new forms of social practices and encounters. This chapter will propose an interpretation of the role of garden space in processes of cultural transformation that extended over more than a century, between 1643, the beginning of the Regency of Ann of Austria, and 1789, the French Revolution. The examples will stress the activities that contributed important cultural changes to city life, leaving out a large number of casual uses of the gardens. The examples will mostly be drawn from the Tuileries gardens—the first ones to be opened to the public—even though most changes developed at the same time in several Paris gardens and public promenades[1] (Fig. 1).

The Garden Setting

Three major changes impacted Parisian life at the beginning of the seventeenth century: the irresistible growth in the number of carriages, gardens, and conversation circles in the city. These three domains of practical changes were related. Carriages allowed wealthy nobles to pay a daily visit to the Tuileries, attracting the curiosity of the bourgeoisie that flocked to the royal garden. It resulted in the development of new forms of city life that provided endless topics of conversation throughout the city, as we shall see. The construction of the *Cours La Reine,* near the Tuileries gardens, by Queen Marie de Medicis also attracted a daily venue of bourgeois who came to watch a conspicuous display of riches by aristocrats in their carriages. At the same time a growing number of wealthy Parisian noblemen, churchmen, bourgeois and *robins* (the recently ennobled bourgeoisie that grew rapidly at the turn of the sixteenth and seventeenth centuries) became frequent users of several royal gardens: the Tuileries, Luxembourg, and Arsenal gardens, and sometime later the Palais Cardinal gardens (built in 1624). In each of these gardens people would walk up and down the alleys, then some would sit on the benches or the lawn or lean along a balustrade, and watch the strollers. This prompted the development of the promenade, a new form of social intercourse and of some voyeuristic rituals. Garden visits became a major aspect of city life in Paris during the regency period separating the death of Louis XIII (1643) from the political coup by Louis XIV in 1661, which ushered in the second phase of absolutism in France. An ever growing number of daily visitors would crowd the Tuileries as well as the Cours La Reine, Luxembourg, Cours de l'Arsenal, the Jardin du Roi where the royal botanical collections were kept, or private gardens opened to the public by their owners, such as the gardens of the Prince de Soubise planted with dense horse-chestnut trees and with a gallery in the shape of a demi-lune,[2] or the gardens of la Folie-Rambouillet, and the garden of the Convent of Celestine monks. The cloister

Fig. 1. Reception of the Polish ambassadors by Catherine de Médicis on Sept. 14, 1573 Tapisserie de la suite des fêtes des Valois in Bresc Bautier Jardins du Carrousel et des Tuileries (p. 19)

of the Cordeliers was a later promenade, built in 1683. In a city where it was difficult to walk because streets were filthy and made dangerous by the passage of horses, carts and carriages these gardens offered wonderfully convenient places for a walk in a clean and pleasant setting. At the beginning of the seventeenth century the alleys of the Tuileries were rather narrow, but Colbert ordered a transformation of the whole garden in 1664. Le Nôtre created a garden with three lateral alleys on both sides of a major alley, the Grande Allée, where even a large crowd of visitors could most conveniently walk back and forth.[3] This was the common pattern. Two young Dutchmen described the gardens of the convent of Celestine monks in 1657: "The near-by garden was behind the convent. One found vine-covered arbors first, and then large alleys bordered with beech trees neatly trimmed. There were small beds of rare flowers and artificial grottoes with statues of painted wood."[4] The gardens of the Arsenal offered a long walk (approximately 670 m), all the way on the city wall from the Bastille to the Seine River.

Inventing New Mores

We may count daily walks in a public place, new demeanors, new gender relationships, conspicuous consumption of clothes and fashion development, new forms of sociability, and the development of newsmongers and public opinion among the numerous cultural transformations of city life in Paris to which ritualized practices in the Tuileries contributed. Emergent practices were gleefully pursued without any other purpose than enjoying the pleasure of unfettered social encounters. The gardens had not been designed to encourage free exploration of innovations in public life, they simply made it possible, and it gave rise to unheard of collective behaviors. A Sicilian

Fig. 2. La grande alleé au 18e siècle in Bresc Bautier, Jardins du Carrousel et des Tuileries (1945).

visitor wrote in 1692, "In this most charming place, one jests, one banters, one talks of love, of news, of public affairs and of the war. People make decisions, criticize, argue strenuously, cheat one another, and with all of that every one takes much pleasure."[5]

New Demeanors

During the day, at the Tuileries, it was common for some visitors to walk in a group along the *allées* and for others to watch them. The great *allée* was not as wide as it is now, since it was a double alley, meaning that on each side of the main alley there was a side-alley (*contre-allée*) lined with trees on both sides that were casting shade over the two sides and the larger central alley. "Six to seven rows of chairs on each side presented all the women belonging to Paris with the most charming faces and the most refined clothes. The center was only for strollers who brought life and even more beauty to this picture by the display of taste and richness of their clothing"[6] (Fig. 2). Learning how to dance and to walk, take a bow, give a nod in passing, or a salute with the hat were part of courtiers' training and gave them a distinctive demeanor.[7] Since bourgeois and courtiers mingled and vied for attention in the garden, new ways of walking, laughing, casting the eyes aside, or answering the salutations of other passers-by developed among women of all ages, and new modes of self presentation developed among male bourgeois and *robins*. Noble ladies started going to the Tuileries in the 1630s for the sake of finding some freedom from the demands of social life and interaction with all other members of their households. They would abandon themselves to their dreams, and feel free to exchange their feelings with a chosen lady companion. This apparently innocent craving for freedom was then a breach of convention. A noble lady and her husband were expected to "act according to their rank,"[8] that is to show a public face throughout their lives, either receiving or showing deference to others.

New Gender Relationships

The years passed by producing surprising changes. We learn for instance from a comedy of 1709, the *Ambigu d'Auteuil*, that it became utterly ridiculous for a husband and his wife to walk together in the Tuileries.[9] (Bordelon 1709) A young lady could come for a stroll with a servant, her mother, or other young girls and their respective mothers. In the latter case the girls would walk together ahead of their mothers at some good distance that enabled them to chat and giggle at leisure and offer themselves to the admiration of young men they met in chance encounters as they proceeded through the garden. The male admirers were expected to catch their attention by bowing, casting amorous glances, and delivering flattering poems to the group of girls. So each girl would pretend that it was addressed to the others and engage gleefully in infinite games of platonic flirtation. Again this may seem to be quite innocent, and yet we should see that these behaviors were unheard of, and unthinkable outside the Tuileries. Young maidens were not likely to meet young men to whom they had not been formally introduced in their parents' house, and chance encounters at church did not allow any of the giggling and chuckling with girl companions, or the pursuit of a joking relationship with a flirtatious suitor that became commonplace in the garden.

As more and more people visited the Tuileries it became normal for adults, men and women alike, to engage in conversation without being introduced or to join at will with any group standing or walking in the garden, and break into their conversations.[10] This new habit made it possible for women to address men walking in the garden. This was undoubtedly a breach of etiquette. In particular it allowed for small groups of women to engage in all sorts of games of make-believe. Feigning love at first sight with strangers passing by, they would encourage them to join in conversation by some skillful compliments, and fool them into treating their group to a "*collation*" (a light meal) to quench their thirst and exercise their sweet tooth at one of the little restaurants in the garden. The freedom to join any group in conversation in the garden even gave rise to a new urban character, christened "*le fâcheux*" (" a male interloper who ruthlessly imposed his presence and conversation on others), after the title of a comedy by Molière (1661) showing a lover harassed by a succession of such characters in a garden where he waits for his beloved.

Class Cross-dressing

Persons in uniform were not allowed in the Tuileries garden and any male visitor had to wear a sword. So, military officers had to come in courtly attire, and church people and magistrates had to slip from official into courtly dress. Bourgeois vying for public admiration with members of the nobility would don sumptuous clothes. "After noon hour one could only enter dressed up in the Tuileries."[11] (Philippon-La-Madelaine 1797) These games did not suppress differences of rank, but contributed to blurring social distinctions, in outright contradiction with the ideal of a society where everyone should behave according to his birth rank and never pretend to belong to a higher one. This was a more serious breach of social norms than we can readily imagine. Yet it was very common, and it extended its consequences into somewhat offensive behaviors in some encounters. Abbeys or low ranking secular church officials would flirt with elegant women in definite transgression of church rules. When this befell an aristocratic lady she would enjoy humiliating the churchman by pretending to follow him outside the garden. She would lead him to the garden door where her servants, wearing a uniform that declared her rank, would surround her and take her to her carriage, spurning her would-be suitors. A character in the Ambigu d'Auteuil, (Bordelon 1709), declared:

> The sun has never gazed upon such a century as ours:
> One half of the world ponders how to cheat the other.[12]

The blurring of social differences also led to the development of another urban type, the "*petit-maître*,"[13] a character who bears some resemblance to the snob in his efforts to ape aristocratic courtiers. They utterly failed. Courtiers belonged to the sword nobility, *petits-maîtres* to the robe nobility or the rich bourgeoisie. Whereas young courtiers tried to hide their misbehavior under the appearance of an orderly life, the *petits-maîtres* who aped them tried hard to give the impression that their life was even more unruly than it was. Courtiers pondered deeply what they said before speaking, while *petits-maîtres* spoke without thinking. In a word the *petits-maîtres* offered a comical parody of the courtiers they emulated. This could create delusion only among bourgeois visitors in the garden. We see how transgression of social difference in an ascriptive status society led to the construction of a new status as much craved for by some individuals as it was ridiculed by others.

Conspicuous Consumption of Fashionable Dress

Petits-maîtres were mocked for their long hats that fell upon their ears, their solemn coats, red-heeled shoes, and slovenly appearance, but women were an even easier target when discussing conspicuous display of dress, hair, and millinery. Ladies competed for the most magnificent attire, of dress, jewels, and cloths of silver and gold, and for the extravagance of their hairdos towering above their heads.[14] Du Fresny called them pleasant birds that can change feathers two or three times a day.[15] (Du Fresny 1702) The Grande Allée was a showcase of constantly renewed elegance of dress that invited ceaseless criticism from the rows of people sitting in the side-alleys. Most surprisingly for garden visitors they discovered that as soon as they were in the garden, and against their own sense of proper behavior in public, they all felt compelled to criticize the behavior and appearance of others and became in turn the object of the others' mockeries and criticisms.[16] Yet we should not be misled by these exchanges of mockeries. Most contemporary visitors to the garden were delighted by the display of fashionable dress that was offered by the promenade in the Tuileries, and especially by the sight of women's hats best enjoyed in the evening when everyone rose from the seats and walked to a dinner outside. Then the flow of ribbons and hats looked like a flower parterre in motion.[17] (Mercier 1979) It encouraged the development of fashion and conspicuous consumption in spite of the sumptuary laws that every bourgeois was supposed to follow. Offering light meals and flowers to a lady was common practice and more or less conspicuous depending upon circumstances, but the gift of music played by a band of musicians and singers at night was certainly meant to call the attention of a large audience besides the lady herself, and a fairly expensive consumption when she turned a deaf ear. All of these practices contradicted the principles of restraint in public consumption that the sumptuary laws were supposed to enforce, but they also contributed to the growth of a market economy, and in that respect they may be considered a very significant contribution of the ritualization of fashionable display in public walks toward the development of a capitalist economy in France.

Public Scrutiny and Public Opinion

One would search in vain for the birth date of an emergent social phenomenon, since a new form of agency grows out of a large number of unrelated practices, and makes sense in a way that was not intended *a priori*. Since 1563 all publications in France fell under the control of a Royal jurisdiction that grew more and more rigorous and punitive as time passed.[18] It had been strictly forbidden to distribute poems or songs libeling the regent queen, Marie de Médicis, or her favorite Concini, under the threat of being jailed for an indeterminate length of time if caught by the royal police. At the Tuileries garden there was, at that time (1610s), a circular wall that formed a distinctive echo. It repeated the last words of any sentence spoken in a loud voice in its center, and was very much used for this reason by singers to present their songs, and by lovers to publicize their feelings and honor the lady they wooed, as well as by poets who wanted a criticism of the government to be heard, even though they could claim they had never pronounced it. We may take this as an example of the political gossip already taking place in the early seventeenth century, when the garden had been opened to the public for less than fifteen years. This was certainly not the only type of gossip that went on, but we lack written evidence about other forms until the emergence of the newsmen, the '*nouvellistes*' as they would call themselves. It became common in several gardens, among them the Tuileries, to gather around a man or a small group of men who could dispatch news of some unusual nature. High society gossip, news from the literary world—the Parnassus as it came to be called in Paris—or from the war at the borders, internal political strife, or the actions of the government were the most prominent.

Self-stated information leaders found out very quickly that it was useful to specialize in order to provide fresh and interesting news that caught the attention of the garden public; and they also discovered that some amount of internal criticism helped protect themselves from contradiction by members of the public. So they formed small groups called *peloton*, that gathered together to form a *compagnie* with a secretary, or a committee presided by the *coq* who directed a joint discussion of the daily news before they would disperse to present them in the garden. This last phase was currently known as the *caquetage*, the cackle. This is a most extraordinary social movement, since it gave rise to formal organizations deriving only from the entrepreneurship of a few idle men, and fueled by the unbounded source of energy provided by the conjunction of vanity and curiosity among many of their contemporaries. It allowed a ritualization of public opinion debates, in a way that is historically significant, and yet cannot be accounted for in teleological terms. To make a long discussion short, this is a construction of public opinion that is not geared towards the establishment of democratic debate or communicative action. It is acting out wild impulses, some voyeuristic, some paranoid, most of them expressing some vain pursuit in search of egotistic pleasures derived from standing at the center of attention of a small group of well-to-do people. It was an emergent social movement, which derived its authority only from the attention the public freely warranted to it.

Newsmongers specialized along five lines: the "rehashers of news" (*regrattiers de nouvelles*) who read foreign publications for news published during the preceding six months and repeated them as if they were recent, the "state affairs *nouvellistes*" (*nouvellistes d'Etat*) who discussed government affairs and the secrets of government, the "Parnassus *nouvellistes*" (*nouvellistes de Parnasse*) who disseminated the latest poem, literary discussion or dispute in the fashionable salons of Paris and provided a public criticism of public architecture, the "song baggers" (*coureurs de chansons*) who repeated the new songs they heard, and the "playful nouvellistes" (*nouvellistes enjouez*) who amused their audience with all sorts of pleasant stories.[19] (Donneau de Vizé 1663) They were already attracting much attention in the Tuileries garden in 1663, and it never abated until the revolution. At the end of the eighteenth century the Tuileries garden was buzzing with public discussions of governmental reform, even though it was strictly forbidden to publish or disseminate any news about the king's secrets, which included his personal life as well as all affairs regarding the government and its projects.[20] Louis-Sébastien Mercier—skillfully dissociating himself from the speakers whose ideas he reports in the last chapter of his book, the *Conversations in the Tuileries (1782-1788)*—outlines a critical utopia meant to show the ridicule of a monarchic regime. (Mercier 1979). At the Tuileries, a man whispers in the author's ear that he has the solution to all problems of social organization in the kingdom. He proposes that the Prince be made the sole owner of everything in the kingdom and in exchange procure food, garment, work, housing, and health services to all his subjects according to their rank. He makes a long description of all the consequences this measure would entail even going into hilarious details about the catering system that he proposes with a hierarchy of different menus being served at home according to the rank and status of each family head.[21]

Emplacements and Public Space

The Tuileries stimulated all sorts of new activities, and provided a hub dispatching them throughout the city in royal gardens, convents and other promenades. Each of these activities concentrated in some part of the gardens, thus allowing a large number of very different activities, including casual activities that did not contribute any cultural change in the life of the inhabitants of Paris, to take place at the same time in the gardens. The new activities only claimed one or a few emplacements[22] in any garden while they extended themselves into several gardens.

At the Tuileries each company of newsmonger had its own meeting place either on the Terrace along the Seine, along the large circular basin, the *rond d'eau* or on the Feuillant Terrace where they would meet every evening after six o'clock standing or sitting on chairs forming a circle and surrounded by eager listeners. At the Luxembourg, the newsmongers used to walk surrounded by their listeners under the elms of the quincunx or along two alleys (*Allée des Soupirs* and *Allée des Carmes*), or they stood under the very large yew tree in the garden. At the Palais Royal the major meeting place was also under a tree, a very large horse-chestnut tree. The news circulated from one garden to the next, since some listeners in a garden would play the role of newsmonger in another one. News was never repeated verbatim, but to the contrary it was always adapted by each story teller, according to his own opinions and to suit the leanings of the crowd of visitors in each particular garden, making it interesting to walk from one garden to the next for the sake of hearing how the prattle and babble of the city was echoed there. The news traveled from garden to garden, and from gardens into private houses. There, more people—those who did not have a chance to go to the garden—were appraised of the most recent news, and would discuss and repeat them in turn. Any news presented in the Tuileries thus would go through the whole city and come back to the garden in less than three days.

The fashionable promenade, informal courting between young people, illicit sexual activities, dissemination of news, each of these activities followed an unwritten script, and repeated itself in an infinite series of daily variations in the same places within the different gardens. The particular audiences of these ritualized activities created, at specific hours, their own emplacements in the gardens. A place used by children for playing group games in the early afternoon, could be used by newsmongers later in the day, and become a place for sentimental pursuits during the night. Emplacements are temporary territories where a group of people pursue a domain of activity that it has brought into the garden. In this way the emplacements became symbols of the existence of certain groups of city dwellers during the few hours when they pursued their activity in a garden. Yet each kind of activity was engendered by a group of inhabitants who circulated from one garden emplacement to the next disseminating new practices, attitudes and opinions, and thus linking many emplacements belonging to different gardens into a single network that was covering the public gardens and beyond, extending its influence over the whole of the city. The group of newsmongers, for instance, formed a social movement, and even if it was internally differentiated it asserted the right of all citizens to be informed of public affairs, and contributed to the development of public opinions.

Social Movements and Institutions

The groups that produced innovative activities were very different from one another and shared only a limited sense of their own identity as a group, as did the *nouvellistes*. To a large extent they were built from informal groups of people who engaged in similar ritualized practices in the garden and contributed to the dissemination of their practices and of the new cultural attitudes they entailed in the city. These social movements engaged in a dialectical process of transforming existing institutions: their action strived towards instituting new practices and new attitudes—such as freely debating public opinions—against the prevailing institutions that restricted such practices and attitudes. To do so they established control over a network of emplacements that they appropriated within the gardens or the convents, availing themselves of lands belonging to the King's house and to religious orders. In order to fully appreciate the importance of garden space, or space in general, in this process we should see that each space in the city was expressive of at least one particular institution, if we agree to call institution the set or principles ruling a specific domain of social activities that are endorsed by the ruling political power.[23] Any institution creates and maintains its own space. These spaces are made of the material organizations and forms with their respective functionalities necessary for the institution's operation and ordering of its constituency. This is easily understood if one thinks of the dwelling as the space of the family, or the court and the prison as the spaces of law, or the cathedral and the convent as two of the spaces of the church institution. These spaces exercise a control over the activities that they make possible. They also allocate each of their visitors or users to a particular position with respect to the institution, specifying the kinds of attitudes and activities expected from anyone who enters the institutional space. Christians entering a church immediately feel that they should lower their voice and cross themselves, Muslims entering a mosque feel that they are called to performing their ablutions and walking barefooted into the prayer room. Each institutional space involves its members, its users, and its visitors in a world of action, meaning and feeling that escapes all foreigners to the institution. This space with its wealth of memories, demands, and shared sentiments is called a place. It implies a horizon of understanding of individual or collective action that may be more or less constraining: some actions are absolutely imposed or prohibited, while many actions call upon the imagination of and the improvisation by members of the institution. We can see that institutions do not simply appropriate some parts of the city, claiming them as their own space, but they create spaces that imply an institutional sense of agency. Space embodies institutional agency.

This understanding of space runs counter to the empiricist view of space that developed during the Renaissance and was encoded in Descartes description of all human space as geometrical space. It enables an understanding of the role of social movements in the transformation of institutional space, and of their role in the dialectics of innovation and control that enables a society to invent a new culture. The royal gardens belonged to the domain of leisure of the king and his court. They incorporated dreams of Arcadian freedom in a pastoral world entertained by the aristocracy, and very well known and understood by the literate members of the Parisian society. This was not a very constraining institutional space, to say the least. The social movements that invaded them found themselves protected from more repressive institutions like the city police or the church, and could appropriate emplacements where they proposed and elaborated new ideas of the common good: the freedom of encounters between young maidens and young men, the freedom of conversation between men and women, the right to take pleasure in consuming rich garments and displaying them publicly, the right to debate publicly of all affairs of common interest to the inhabitants of the city. These new ideas ran contrary to principles defended outside the garden by the church, the family, the police, and the government. Had the institutions prevailed throughout the city these ideas would have had great difficulty developing and spreading throughout the population. The networks of garden emplacement allowed their collective exploration by the public over more than one century, and eventually their partial transformation into some of the tenets of the institutions after the Revolution, leading to the appearance of new social movements and new forms of cultural change.

Changing Mores

Let me recapitulate a few things we have learned from this survey of cultural innovations in the royal gardens. First, as emerging practices became ritualized in a public garden in the seventeenth and eighteenth centuries, they preferentially took place in particular emplacements endowed with a specific sense of agency: the great *allée* in the Tuileries invited parading and spreading frivolous and gallant news, and the next parallel *allées* lined with benches for gossiping and mocking the people who walked there, and many emplacements seemed to invite discussion of public affairs as Mercier noted.[24] In the Tuileries the benches in the shade around the great *rond d'eau*, the round basin, as well as the ramps towards the terraces, and a very long bench at the head of the *Boulingrin* seemed to call for gatherings around novelists, while the next parallel alley, which was very dark, looked perfectly fit for love affairs.[25] These places had not been designed to that effect, and they derived their sense of place from the kinds of practices they sheltered. This demonstrates that the sense of place results neither from physical appearance, nor from patrons' or designers' intentions, but first and foremost from the activities experienced there: sense of place is a concept that describes landscape reception rather than production. Newcomers soon discovered that they were expected to conform to local habits, and in this sense each emplacement in the garden demanded a particular type of personal behavior. It is fascinating to see how easily newcomers would accept engaging in very unusual behaviors as soon as they entered the garden because its setting and users urged the adoption, or at least the acceptance, of unusual behaviors. Thus emerging practices, at great variance with ordinary practices in other institutional surroundings, would grow into well established practices in the garden. This process fostered norms of behavior attached to particular places in the garden, as if instituting them in the absence of any embodiment of authority that pronounced or promoted them.

Second, we observe that innovative practices were not followed by everyone in the garden. They could even be sneered at or frowned upon in the garden itself, ridiculed in comedies or verses, or even restrained by force by some witnesses. In the same place where some people made a show of themselves, others would enjoy the intimacy of conversing with bosom friends; close by the libertine, young girls would learn social skills demanding modesty and self-restraint. There were many activities, such as bowling games, in the garden that would have looked perfectly innocuous to the strictest censor. Current garden practices instituted a horizon of interpretation of the garden, rather than introduced a world of meaning as does a text, or to a world of rules as does an institution.[26] Thus emplacements in the garden, and the garden as a whole, became imbued with innate senses of agency that could not be ignored by coeval visitors, and that gave rise to confrontations of traditional and innovative practices, which invited further discussion outside of the garden itself. In particular some emplacements became imbued with an urge for innovation in matters of fashion, and stimulated heated debates about the moral significance of conspicuous consumption of clothes in and out of the garden. These public gardens did not direct or impose, but rather introduced an ambiguous sense of agency,[27] and this may be a reason why they deserve much attention as works of art of particular significance for cultural development during the seventeenth and eighteenth centuries: they stimulated creative responses by the public as a social group united beyond its internal divisions.

Third, we have observed that the Tuileries as a whole did not constitute a pertinent unit for the analysis of the role of gardens in the development of cultural changes in Paris. A detailed analysis of the activities in the garden revealed the heterogeneity of its space made of a mosaic of emplacements that addressed different constituencies and exercised different forms of agency; and a comprehensive view of the actors engaged in a particular activity within the city of Paris revealed the interdependence of many emplacements in different gardens. This invites focusing attention upon garden activities in order to discover how, where, and why they engender garden emplacements, and how these garden emplacements are linked to one another in various gardens and relate to other places in throughout the city.

Fourth, as soon as nature was thought of as an embodiment of ideas of liberty, gardens open to the public could become interworlds[28] that mediated between contending cultural groups and offered the possibility of confronting different behavioral uses of human freedom. Gardens could harbor several emplacements, each urging ambiguous directions of agency, because the garden as a whole was perceived as an embodiment of an ideal nature in which harmony prevails in the absence of social constraints. Thus gardens were quite different from the rural countryside, or the hunting forest where some rules imposed by custom or law prevailed whatever actions the visitors took.[29] So, in order to embody an ideal nature, gardens had to be distinguishable from nature as it was ordinarily encountered outside cities. Royal gardens in Paris displayed design with nature made clear by alleys, basins, canals, grottoes, arbours, garden buildings, and shady walks. I want to stress here that design was more important than it would seem if paying heed only to the little interest visitors took in it. Garden design imbued the place with an out-worldly quality, it bespoke the leisurely world of high society and the imaginary freedom from social constraints of the king, to which ordinary visitors were introduced. Design qualified casual nature, and this civilized nature welcomed its visitors in a new interworld that developed against the horizon of leisurely aristocratic life, since the garden features it borrowed were known by visitors to be the hallmark of princely gardens. I want to stress the difference between the discussion of gardens as text, as places that conveyed meaning to their visitors, and the discussion I propose of gardens as interworlds that open a domain of collective agency. The second reading may help us understand how gardens contributed significantly to cultural change, while the first one sees them as mere imprints of a culture that develops outside in the world of language, or eventually painting. This is to say after Merleau Ponty that "space is (derived from) existence."[30] (Merleau-Ponty 1945)

Fifth, this liberated play of urbane civility and wilderness engendered three types of consequences over the years: a condemnation by moralists who developed a nostalgic description of the past, development of repressive institutions, and further transgression of established norms which compounded the two previous responses. A very graphic example of these linkages is provided by Louis Sébastien Mercier (1740-1814) in his *Pictures of Paris*,[31] where he describes the development of new behavior of prostitutes in the Tuileries at the end of the eighteenth century. His tone is clearly moralistic. He deplores loudly that prostitution is no longer what it used to be, when it was duly performed after dusk, whereas at the time of writing, prostitutes clad in a lady's attire would sit on chairs in the garden, wait for some visitor to respond to their glances, and invite him for lunch. Several prostitutes would join forces sometimes to form what has been called ever since a "*partie carrée*," a "four-sided party," thus giving the most immoral examples to young ladies who trained their eyes upon their needlework on nearby chairs.[32] It yields a most interesting insight into the role of gardens in the dynamic of cultural change. The garden appears as a place of encounter between cultural conservatism and innovation that stimulates a public debate about ethics or civility, as a place where the repressed or forbidden urges lurking in urbane minds could surface and force public debate, as long as there were no better means of expression. The public gardens of the baroque age engaged the public, rather than individuals, in experimental praxis through which the existing norms of civility were challenged by the social forces they repressed. Yet, the outcome was not a new ethically reconciled society, but rather a society divided in a new way around different issues of public behavior.

Conclusion

The royal gardens in Paris contributed to the development of public spaces of communication because they attracted very different groups of people, in a place where behaviors did not fall under the *a priori* rules of a repressive institution, but rather allowed different groups to experiment freely with new public attitudes and behaviors. These unplanned experiments developed in specific emplacements in many royal and convent gardens forming a network of activities attracting a varied and ever-changing constituency. Thus conflicting attitudes were acted out in public, and provoked public debate. The large gardens opened to the public in Paris created the possibility for a collective use of a relative freedom of action and of thought. The contribution of gardens to this development was two-fold: they presented a realm of imaginary freedom where all citizens were freed from the constraints of city and family life, and they allowed the formation of emplacements where social movements could explore and present to everybody's appreciation new public attitudes and behaviors. All of this disappeared or radically changed after the 1789 Revolution. This history does not invite any attempt at reproducing such a city phenomenon, but simply to remember that gardens may offer the necessary space for a free pursuit of cultural innovations. "It concerns the possibility to introduce into human relationships and history the radical sense of freedom that denies that humanity is a given at the same time that it calls for creating a new humanity."[33]

Bibliography

Anon. *Nouveau Traité de la Civilité qui se pratique en France parmi les Honnestes Gens.* Paris: Chez Helie Josset, 1673.

Berthoz, Alain and Roland Recht, eds. *Les Espaces de l'homme.* Paris: Odile Jacob, 2005.

Blythe, Richard, ed. *Wild Cities/Urbane Wilderness.* Launceston, Tasmania: School of Architecture at Launceston, 2002.

Bordelon, Abbé Laurent. *L'Ambigu d'Auteuil, ou Veritez historiques; composées du Joueur. De l'Inconnu. Du Nouveliste. Du Sincere. Du Financier. Du Subtil. Du Critique. De l'Hypocrite. Et de plusieurs autres personnages de differens caracteres.* Paris: Chez la veuve de Courbe, 1709.

Brillon, Pierre Jacques. *Le Théophraste moderne, ou Nouveaux caractères des moeurs.* Paris: M. Brunet, 1701.

Dezallier d'Argenville, Antoine-Jospeh. *La théorie et la pratique du jardinage.* Paris: Pierre-Jean Mariette, 1747.

Donneau de Vizé, Jean. *Nouvelles nouvelles.* Paris: P. Bienfaict, 1663.

Du Fresny, Charles. *Entretiens ou Amusemens serieux et comiques.* Amsterdam: chez Estienne Roger, 1702.

Foucault, Michel. *Aesthetics, Method and Epistemology.* Edited by James D. Faubion. New York: The New Press, 1998.

Franc-Nohain (Maurice Etienne Legrand). "Les Promenades de Paris" in *La Vie Parisienne au XVIIIe siècle,* conférences du musée Carnavalet. Paris: Payot, 1928.

Funck-Brentano, Frantz. *Les Nouvellistes.* Paris: Hachette, 1905.

Gell, Alfred. *Art and Agency: An Anthropological Theory.* Oxford and New York: Clarendon Press, 1998.

Hermant, Abel and Frantz Funck-Brentano, et al. *La Vie Parisienne au XVIIIe siècle.* Paris: Payot, 1928.

Mercier, Louis Sébastien. *Tableau de Paris* Originally published in Amsterdam: 1782-1788. Genève: Slatkine Reprints, 1979.

Merleau-Ponty, Maurice. *Phénoménologie de la Perception.* Paris: Gallimard, 1945.

Merleau-Ponty, Maurice. *Sens et Non-sens.* Paris: Gallimard, 1996.

Molière, *Les Fâcheux.* Paris: 1662.

Mongin, Monsieur. *Les Promenades de Paris.* Paris: Hôtel de Bourgogne, 10 juin 1695.

Rustin, Jacques. *Le Vice à la mode, étude sur le roman francais du XVIIIé siècle de Manon Lescaut à l'apparition de la Nouvelle Héloise (1731-1761).* Paris: Ophrys, 1979.

Philipon-La-Madelaine, Louis. *Manuel ou nouveau Guide du promeneur aux Tuileries.* Paris: Hautbout-Dumoulin, 1797.

Poëte, Marcel. *Au Jardin des Tuileries.* Paris: Auguste Picard, 1924.

Notes

1. This presentation builds upon several previous texts that I wrote about public gardens of the seventeenth and eighteenth century in Paris, bringing together ideas that were not yet completely integrated. See in particular: Michel Conan, "A Tale of Two Gardens: Urbane Wilderness in the Tuileries Gardens and Saint-James Park," in (Blythe 2002, 12-20), and "L'espace actant des jardins royaux à Paris au XVIIe et XVIIIe siècle à Paris," in (Berthoz and Recht 2005, 291-307).

2. Funck-Brentano 1905, 140.

3. Garden designers took note of this phenomenon and paid increased attention to the establishment of a main alley as flat as possible in an aristocratic garden; the longer it was the larger the crowd it could attract, and henceforth the wider it had to be, as can be read in (Dezallier d'Argenville 1747).

4. Funck-Brentano 1905, 133-134. From 1608 to 1611, Antonio Perez, a former minister of Philippe II, was the very successful chair of a circle of novelists. (Funck-Brentano 1905, 136).

5. Funck-Brentano 1905, 172-173.

6. Philipon-La-Madelaine 1797, 68-69.

7. When walking with a member of the high society it was recommended to walk slightly behind her, and to mark deference in various ways. "If this happens in a garden, one should walk to the left of the person, and make sure to regain this position without any affectation when she would turn upon her heels to walk back in the *allée*. When there are three people who walk together the central position is the most honorable one, and as a matter of consequence the place to be reserved for the most qualified person." (Anon. 1673, Chap. X).

8. In French, "*tenir son rang*." This was of course an expression of neo-stoic ethics all aristocrats were expected to follow.

9. Abbé Laurent Bordelon (1653-1730) in (Poëte 1924, 299).

10. "This is the only place in the universe where people so easily address one another without being introduced. A lady of the highest position when being there would gladly enter into conversation with a perfect stranger." (Mercier 1979, 39).

11. "The fashion of presenting oneself in these carelessly informal attires, known under the name of frock- or tail-coat, arrived in France from England only a few years before the revolution. The prince of Chinon, the grandson of the Duke of Richelieu, arrived once in this attire at his grandfather's just as a large and elegant company was passing to table. —Son, where are you coming from, asked the Duke? — Well... papa... from Versailles. — Behind which carriage?" (implying he was dressed like lackeys walking behind a nobleman's carriage) (Philipon-La-Madelaine, 1797, 69 and note).

12. Poëte, *Au Jardin des Tuileries,* 300.

13. The "petit-maître" originated at the time of the Fronde led by Condé. Young men of the sword nobility who paraded in very affected manners, came to be called "petit-maîtres." They were imitated by men of the robe nobility in the most affected and ridiculous fashion (Rustin 1979, 93-98).

14. In a comedy Arlequin explains to another servant upon entering the Great Allée in the Tuileries: "This is the riding of high society, this is where in sumptuous trappings when the sun goes to bed (the phrase alludes to the king's bedding ceremony), the Dark- and the Fair-haired lady make an exhibition of themselves, this is where one puts on display one's laces, cloth, and ribbons." (Mongin 1695, 140).

15. (Du Fresny, 1702) quoted in (Poëte 1924, 286).

16. Since the beginning of the eighteenth century authors have repeatedly noted that visitors to the gardens felt compelled to engage in activities they did not approve or intend as soon as they stood in some part of the Tuileries. See for instance (Brillon 1701, 15) and (Mercier 1979, 19-20).

17. (Mercier 1979, 19-20).

18. Funck-Brentano, *Les Nouvellistes*, 8-9.

19. Jean Donneau de Vizé was the publisher of the *Mercure Galant*, an authorized periodical publication, who felt some competition from the newsmongers. So his descriptions might have been unfavorably biased, yet they provide most valuable information about the institution of news making by the nouvellistes (Donneau de Vizé 1663, 318-329).

20. Mercier shows in his book how this prohibition could be turned by accounting for discussions of public affairs in the Tuileries, in a book that claimed only to describe events taking place in the garden. "There is no empire, no society, no family where reform are not necessary, said in grave tone two scholarly men, when I joined their company. They were walking along the allees of the Tuileries, as they pursued this discourse, and I found them full of wit and very gentle. The general conversation (in the garden) turned on questions of (social) reforms and I could not refrain from broaching on the subject, like everyone else." (Mercier 1979, 3-4).

21. (Mercier 1979, 204-210).

22. This is a word I borrow from Michel Foucault. See Michel Foucault, "Different Spaces" text of a lecture given in March 1967 in (Foucault 1998, 175-186).

23. In seventeenth century Paris such institutions as the church, the family, the law, the hierarchy of social orders, the police were put to a test by some of the garden movements of innovators.

24. See note 20. Also (Mongin 1695, 143-144).

25. (Funck-Brentano, *Les Nouvellistes*, 178).

26. I want to stress that they contributed to, rather than produced, the conditions for public debate about some issues of public behavior or expression.

27. Alfred Gell has proposed a very interesting anthropological approach to the arts, suggesting that when studied in a cross-cultural perspective, artworks should not be approached from an aesthetic perspective, or from the point of view of the Western art world, but rather as artifacts imbued with a sense of agency that have a specific domain of efficiency within the culture where they are produced. He even shows how the Western art world collects works of art in such a way that it may completely alter their cultural significance because it turns a deaf ear to their original sense of agency. I am suggesting here that visitors experienced very strongly the embodiment of various senses of agency in these public gardens, and yet that these senses of agency were not designed

a priori, and were ambiguous since they were amenable to different interpretations of the proper behavior to be adopted in response to each place in the garden. I do not think that this contradicts Gell's perspective, but rather points to the garden as a collective work of art, in a sense an "open art work." (Gell 1998).

28 An interworld is a domain of shared understanding that allows men belonging to the same culture to engage in communication with one another according to conventions of which they are not aware and that they acquire as they grow up during their childhood. Language, bodily gesture, vision, taste are examples of interworlds in which we are immersed.

29. These private actions could amount to praise or defacement, but left the sense of agency embodied in the place untouched.

30. "We said that space is existential. We might have said that existence is spatial…" (Merleau-Ponty 1945, 348-349). The whole chapter about "space" from which this passage is quoted could be commented to introduce to the shift of perspective adopted in this paper. It criticizes the idea that the geometrical description of the objects in the world accounts for the space we are living in, and that our perceptions are simply attaching meanings to the features that we perceive in it. It opposes to such objectivation of the life-world that there is no perception which does not appear on a background, and that any perception presupposes a perceiving subject with a history of his own. So, our acknowledgement of objects in the world rests upon a more secret mental action depending upon our way of conceiving the situation to which we participate. (Merleau Ponty 1945, 325-6). Instead of asking for either a material description of a garden, or for its meaning, we have to understand from which perspective it was perceived, and how this perception came into being, if we are to make sense of observations by their visitors, users, or designers.

31. "These creatures (the prostitutes) should be ordered to wait in the shadow and the darkness, as they did hitherto, to avoid the scandalous disorder that puts a Royal garden to shame, and urges family mothers to rush out of certain allée, and prevents them from sitting on certain benches." (Mercier 1778) quoted by (Franc-Nohain 1928, 64).

32. These "four sided parties" (*parties carrées*) became an unspoken part of the way of life of the Parisian bourgeoisie. They had never been celebrated by the arts until Edouard Manet painted them in 1863 under the famous title "*Le Déjeuner sur l'Herbe*" (Lunch on the Grass) which created a scandal and introduced at the same time in the cultural heritage of the city of Paris the image of a deviant practice the origins of which can be traced back to the Tuileries. Mercier's moral condemnation of such practices calls implicitly for repression: "This impudent behavior so obviously visible under the gaze of the sun, in the middle of a garden, where honest bourgeois are forced to turn away the eyes, such a deliberate show of scorn for public decorum is what is most repugnant to defenders of public decency." In (Franc-Nohain 1928, 64).

33 (Merleau-Ponty 1996, 58).

CHAPTER 6

Garden Sociability in Eighteenth-Century Ottoman Istanbul

Shirine Hamadeh

As a social, cultural, and topographical phenomenon, public gardens have become, in the distant context of European cities, deeply implicated in the rise of a middle class and in the march toward modernity. In the Ottoman capital in the eighteenth century, public gardens represented an important dimension of change as well because there too, they disturbed an established social order. They provided a major arena in which newly emergent social and recreational practices were enacted; and these practices, in turn, partook of the process of reshaping the city's social and physical map. How they emerged as a distinctive feature of Istanbul's physical and social landscape is what this essay sets out to examine. Pictorial images of gardens like those of Kağıthane and Küçüksu (Figs. 1 and 2), endlessly reproduced in books and postcards, leave us today with a sustained impression that these gardens did really exist. How they actually happened is a question that has seldom been discussed.[1] How these gardens became loci of sociability and everyday venues in which new forms of distinction were tested are other issues that I will address.

Of course, public gardens were not new to the landscape of Istanbul. In his account of the city, the famous seventeenth-century Ottoman traveler, Evliya Çelebi, had described the garden of Kağıthane as an unrivaled space of recreation that was mostly frequented on holidays (Evliya 1993, fols 18b-19a, 120a-146b passim, 171a, 188a). His contemporary, the Armenian chronicler Eremya Çelebi, remarked that the shores of the Bosphorus and the Golden Horn offered agreeable walks that were popular across all segments of Istanbuli society, particularly during the spring season (Kömürciyan 1988, 50-1, 54). But by the eighteenth century, "public" gardens, or to be more precise, gardens for the public, penetrated cultural expression in ways unseen before that evoked a new intensity in Ottoman urban life. In the textual and visual records of painters, poets, chroniclers and travelers, they stood out as the most vibrant venue of social and leisure life that catered to a wide range of social classes, ranks, and ages and in which women and children, seldom visible in the mostly male recreational universe of taverns and coffeehouses, became a noticeable presence (Figs. 1 and 2). Strikingly full of movement, pictorial images captured live shots of the activities and pleasures of ordinary people. They differed markedly from earlier garden scenes, which centered exclusively on courtly sociability and conveyed a sense of a nearly codified entertainment ceremonial (Fig. 3). In poetry too, the garden as

Fig. 1. Outdoor recreation at Kağıthane, by Thomas Allom.

Fig. 2. View of the promenade and fountain of Küçüksu, by William Bartlett.

Fig 3. Princely entertainment in garden, anonymous, from an illustrated copy of Alī Şir Neva'i's *Divan*.

a social experience and public hangout began to predominate. Unlike the classical poetry of the sixteenth and the seventeenth century that focused on the enclosed and exclusive garden and on the cultivation of private enjoyments through elite culture and sociability the new poetic discourse on gardens accommodated a broad social, professional, and cultural spectrum and a new range of sensibilities and expectations (Hamadeh, forthcoming).

At some level, one might argue that public gardens (and outdoor public spaces, generally) were the "natural" extension of a burgeoning urban culture of coffeehouses, taverns, shadow theater, and story-telling street performances that had been in place since the latter half of the sixteenth century (Tietze 1977, Kafadar, forthcoming, Kırlı 2000, 18-66). The difference, however, is that urban life was now resisted and propelled forward at one and the same time. In the eighteenth century, public gardens managed to negotiate new territory and become part of mainstream urban culture, in part, because the state elite encouraged them to expand and proliferate. In this essay, I will contend that their emergence in the early decades of the eighteenth century intersected with three concurrent developments: the building patronage of a ruling class aspiring to restore its recently sullied image; changing rituals of sociability and recreation among the middle classes; and state concerns about public order. In other words, while public life was kept in check through constant law enforcement it was, paradoxically, continuously nurtured by the creation of new spaces by the state elite in which it could prosper, most notably by the opening of older imperial gardens to public access.

Architectural Patronage of the Ottoman Ruling Elite

The return, in 1703, of the court of Sultan Ahmed III from Edirne to Istanbul after long periods of absence had ushered in one of the most explosive periods of architectural patronage in the history of the Ottoman capital. It was mostly concentrated in the extra-muros city, along the suburban banks of the Bosphorus and the Golden Horn. Perhaps its most conspicuous aspect was the dozens of new and lavish palatial gardens that were being erected along these shores by sultans, grand-viziers, and members of the court and palace entourage.[2] Without any doubt, the construction frenzy, just like the unusually flamboyant decorative style that the new buildings displayed, was meant to reflect an illusion of renewed state glory at a time when the image of Ottoman sovereignty had fallen into an all-time low. This quest for a fresh image was partly a response to the heavy military blow the empire had recently suffered at the hands of European powers, most notably in Vienna in 1699; but it also answered to the pressure of internal transformations, namely, the gradual erosion of a system of social hierarchies. In Istanbul, much energy was directed towards affirming the renewed presence of the court. Shows of power and authority and displays of imperial magnificence went hand in hand. The new palaces and palatial gardens that dotted the suburban shores were integral to this process. Partly as a result of this extensive palatial patronage, however, numerous old suburban imperial gardens (ḥāṣṣ bāġçe) gradually lost their appeal as foci of court life. While many were renovated, some fell into disuse and others aged to the point of disrepair. Yet others turned into gardens for the wider public.

The exact details of these developments remain relatively obscure. Nor do we always know, from the fragments of evidence at our disposition in the local histories and chronicles and in foreign travel accounts, the exact circumstances in which they took place. In several cases, we have clear indication that efforts by a monarch or a grand-vizier to restore an old and dilapidated imperial suburban garden resulted in the opening of a portion of the garden to public access. The decision to refurbish an imperial garden often entailed its conversion into a imperial endowment (waqf). Typically, the monarch or a member of the ruling elite built a new mosque along with a complex of commercial and recreational facilities that served as the mosque's endowment. The patron parceled and leased out part of the land, which eventually grew into a "village," renovated extant pavilions, and in certain cases opened the surrounding gardens to public access. The imperial garden of Kandilli, for example, built in the late sixteenth century on the Anatolian shore of the Bosphorus, followed exactly this trajectory. Renovated in 1718, but neglected thereafter, it survived as a ruin until 1749. In that year, sultan Mahmud I annexed the land to the royal endowments, added a mosque, a bath, a few shops, and leased out as much of the land as was requested. He restored the ruined pavilion to its former glory, turning the place, as contemporary observers intimate, into a public showcase of royal magnificence and a new sightseeing attraction for the leisured and the curious among the people of Istanbul (Şemdanizade 1976-1980, 1:162; İncicyan 1831, 257-8; 1976, 129-300; İzzi 1784, fols 272-3; Raşid 1867, 5:160).

Not far from Kandilli, downstream on the Asian shore, the town of İncirliköyü had developed, sometime in the latter part of the seventeenth century, on plots of land located inland from the century-old imperial pavilion and garden of İncirli Bağçesi and leased by the state to high-ranking officials. As a courtier of Mustafa III refurbished the town in the 1760s, he also expa nded it to the shore, reaching down to the cape. The old garden, which had long disappeared from the imperial garden

Fig. 4. The garden, coffeehouses, and fountain of Emirgan, by William Bartlett after an engraving by J. Cousen.

registers,[3] was in all likelihood absorbed in this process, and part of it opened to public access. Indeed, the town now boasted a public promenade whose name, Burun Bahçesi, or Cape Garden, suggests that it wrapped around the little cape on the waterfront, running along a segment of the former imperial estate. Considered a fashionable spot among the city's residents for some twenty years, it later became increasingly subjected to the Chief Imperial Gardener's harsh security measures on account of repeated mischief and improper behavior among the garden's visitors. By the time the Armenian chronicler İncicyan wrote his chronicle of the city at the end of the century, Burun Bahçesi had been abandoned and "its old joy was forgotten" (Incicyan 1976, 127; 2000, 171-2).

In another account of Istanbul, İncicyan described the imperial gardens of Sultaniye at Paşabahçe, south and uphill from İncirliköyü, as a "place of public recreation" ("*luogo di pubblico divertimento*") (İncicyan 1831, 269). By the late sixteenth century this old suburban retreat, attributed to Sultan Bayezid II and celebrated as one of Süleyman's favorite spots, had been abandoned. In 1763-64, in an effort to revitalize the suburban town of Paşabahçe, Mustafa III endowed it with a mosque, a bath, a boys' school, an outdoor prayer place or *namazgah,* and a *meydan* fountain (a large, ornate cubical fountain of a type distinctive of the eighteenth century) (Ayvansarayî 1864, 2:155). Contemporary accounts are not specific about the exact

Fig. 5. *Meydan* fountain of Abdülhamid I in Emirgan.

location of the new imperial complex. But archeological evidence indicate that the project extended into the garden of Sultaniye. Indeed, traces of the lost imperial garden were recorded around the *meydan* fountain and the *namazgah* (Eldem 1976, 14-9; Gökbilgin, 685; Gökyay, 8), the area which, one can surmise from numerous precedents in eighteenth-century Istanbul (Hamadeh 2002, 135-44), had become the very locus of public recreation described by İncicyan.

The "hand-over," so to speak, of Ottoman imperial estates to the public domain since the eighteenth century illustrated a broader phenomenon that extended beyond imperial property and well into *mīrī*, or state land. The most celebrated, if little understood, example of state land being converted to the public domain was the formerly restricted forest of Belgrad, an extensive tract of state-owned land located in the southern outskirts of the capital and made famous by Lady Montagu in her letter to Alexander Pope, dated June 1717. Like several pictorial representations of the forest her descriptions confirm that by that time, Belgrad was a truly public forest and one of the most fashionable recreational spots in Istanbul:

The heats of Constantinople have driven me to this place, which perfectly answers the description of the Elysian fields. I am in the middle of a wood, consisting chiefly of fruit trees, watered by a vast number of fountains famous for the

excellency of their water, and divided into many shady walks upon short grass, that seems to me artificial but I am assured is the pure work of nature, within view of the Black Sea, from whence we perpetually enjoy the refreshment of cool breezes that makes us insensible of the heat of the summer (Montagu 1993, 102-6).

Likewise, the hugely popular garden of Emirgan, located on the European side of the Bosphorus and immortalized in a famous engraving by William Bartlett (Fig. 4), developed on a plot of state land in the last quarter of the eighteenth century. According to Ayvansarayî, author of the encyclopedic *The Garden of Mosques,* the land had been formerly granted as gift to a *şeyhülislam,* or head of the religious elite, but was reclaimed by Sultan Abdülhamid in 1779 as the religious man fell from royal grace. The practices of confiscation and recall of state property were severely enforced around this time. Two years later, in 1781, the sultan erected on the property a mosque, a bath, several shops, and a public fountain — which still stands today (Fig. 5) (Ayvansarayî 1864, 2:137-8, 286-7; Gökbilgin, 679; Demirsar, *DBIA* 3:169-70). Like other *meydan* fountains, the fountain of Abdülhamid must have provided, from the moment it was built, a focal point around which all activities converged. By the time the British traveler Julia Pardoe journeyed in the city, around the beginning of the nineteenth century, a vast public garden had spread around the fountain, which she described in the following words:

> A long street, terminating at the water's edge, stretches far into the distance, its center being occupied by a Moorish fountain of white marble, overshadowed by limes and acacias, beneath which are coffee terraces, constantly thronged with Turks, sitting gravely in groups upon low stools not more than half a foot from the ground, and occupied with their chibouks and mocha (Pardoe 1838, 111; 1837, 2:167).

Although the coffeehouses of Emirgan are not mentioned in *The Gardens of Mosques* (which Ayvansarayî was completing the year construction of the imperial complex began), they were most probably planned for from the very start as part of the income-generating shops to which the author does refer.

As in Paris, London, Berlin, and Vienna (although for different reasons and in different circumstances) the history of Ottoman public gardens unfolded slowly, and not always in a progressive, linear fashion. To be sure, it had begun long before the creation, in the 1860s, of the first "modern" (western) municipal public parks of Taksim and Büyük Çamlıca.[4] If we consider the rapidity with which one imperial garden after another was abandoned in the course of the eighteenth century and the zeal with which they were refurbished from the 1700s on, it would be safe to assume that other gardens followed the same course as those of Emirgân, Kandilli, Incirili, and Sultaniye.[5]

Changing Rituals of Sociability and the Question of "Public" Space
Whether or not the development of state land and the refurbishment of old imperial gardens were merely a step towards the revitalization of the city's waterfront suburbs they were, undeniably, consequential to the emergence of new public spaces. Clearly, the new public gardens were also, to a great extent, a response to new needs and desires of urban society. While the passage from courtly to urban, and "private" to "public" was no doubt initiated by urban interventions from above, what happened later around a new fountain, or under the watchful eye of the gardeners, was the result of how these interventions

intersected with social demands and public rituals. The prominence of public gardens in the eyes of contemporary observers was in itself an indication that noticeable changes had occurred in the sphere of leisure and recreation. These were not sudden changes, however. Gradual mobility among professional groups, emerging social and financial aspirations, and changing habits of consumption all lay at the crux of these developments. They were the outward manifestations of more than a century of transformation in the economic and social structure, and of an eroding system of hierarchies that for many Ottoman intellectuals, at the time, also meant the breakdown of order and stability.[6] If these developments were more palpable and visible in eighteenth-century Istanbul than at other times and places, it was because of a particular juncture in the histories of the city and the empire during which the image of state sovereignty was being actively and thoroughly refashioned.

While it is impossible to engage, based on the available sources, in a thorough discussion about eighteenth-century Ottoman rituals of recreation and sociability, one can nonetheless point to a few signs that revealed certain changes in the way men and women conceived of their social and public lives. There is little doubt, for example, that the widespread integration of fountains and coffeehouses in the gardens and squares of Istanbul was a sign of growing

Fig. 6. *Meydan* fountain of Mahmud I at Tophane.
Fig. 7. *Meydan* fountain of Ahmed III at Bab-ı Hümayun.

recreational demands among urban society. In the eighteenth century, fountains graduated from their former status as minor edifices, tucked into the wall of a mosque courtyard, to become objects for public consumption as well as monuments of public spaces. While this development was mainly a function of their magnified scale and flamboyant style, it was also a result of their physical and institutional detachment from the religious institutions to which they had traditionally been connected (Figs. 6 and 7). They were

Fif. 8. View of the fountain of Mahmud I at Tophane by Antoine-Ignace Melling.

now prominently located in open meadows, gardens, marketplaces, squares and public promenades, as a dominant element in the eighteenth-century city strongly associated with the rituals of public life (Hamadeh 2002): "Here we gather at fountains," the French Countess de la Ferté-Meun observed, "like in France at the Tuileries or at the Boulevard de Gand; on Saturday it is at Kalinder [Kalender], on Monday at Kerelek Bournou [Kireç Burnu?]. In this country they say: This is the day of Kerelek Burnu, we should not miss it" (Ferté-Meun 1821, 100-1).

Much of the popularity of the Square of Tophane, located on the European shore of the Bosphorus and centered around a large marble fountain built by Mahmud I in 1732, must have derived from the services it offered. Its imposing fountain, covered in fine stucco engraving in the idiom of the time, and its rows of coffeehouses shaded by dense plane trees, all brought to the world of outdoor sociability the comfort and pleasures of fresh water, shade, coffee, and water pipes (Fig. 8). Coffeehouses and fountains, attendants serving water, bands of musicians, candy vendors, and ambulant sellers of refreshment, pastry, and fruit juice became the sort of frills one expected to find at places like Tophane and Emirgan, and they enlivened an increasingly rich leisure ritual (İncicyan 1976, 95, 112; Allom and Walsh 1838, 1:8, 17, 21; Pertusier 1815, 2:7, 328-31). By the late eighteenth century, especially, and particularly under Abdülhamid, coffeehouses, like fountains, were becoming an integral feature of gardens and squares and a commonplace of new imperial pious endowments. In the first years of his reign,

Fig. 9. Anonymous garden scene at Sa'dabad, from a copy of Enderunlu Fazıl's *Ḥūbānnāme ve Zenānnāme*.

for example, the monarch had coffeehouses and "other shops" built across from the sixteenth-century Defterdar Mosque located in the town of Eyüp, by the Defterdar landing dock on the Golden Horn, as income generators for the upkeep of the mosque. The new facilities were lined up on either side of the landing dock, neighboring the mosque, thus creating a new sense of enclosure out of which a public square emerged. The quarter soon took on the character of a marketplace (Ayvansarayî 1864, 286-7; 2000, 305 n2354). It is likely that the coffeehouse terraces that still flourish on the Beylerbeyi, Bebek, and Ortaköy waterfronts, on either side of the Bosphorus and side by side with mosques, had also begun to take shape at that time.

Another sign of change in the conduct of public life and one of the most remarkable features of eighteenth-century accounts of gardens is the degree to which many new imperial palatial gardens like Sa'dabad, on the Golden Horn, Bebek, or Feyzabad, along the Bosphorus, were becoming associated with the lives and the diversions of ordinary people. While these gardens were hailed by some as symbols of courtly splendor and architectural magnificence, they were glorified by others as icons of public pleasures. In these places that we have been accustomed to regard as imperial and exclusive, many Ottoman and foreign contemporaries saw wonderful arenas of urban life, leaving us uncertain as to how notions of "private" and "public" were elucidated. Although this question is impossible to pursue here, implicated as it is in much larger legal, social, and even linguistic issues, one can raise further questions. Did the word *ḥāṣṣ*, in *ḥāṣṣ bāġçe* (imperial garden), already carry the meaning of private in the eighteenth century, or did it refer only to matters pertaining to the court or the elite (as used in the common idiom, *"ḥāṣṣ uāmm"*)? Meninski's famous lexicon suggests that the former meaning was already in place by the seventeenth century.[7] But were there any legal, or paralegal mechanisms that defined and negotiated the boundaries between private and

Fig. 10. Engraving by l'Espinasse of the imperial palace of Sa'dabad and the garden of Kağıthane.

public space? And did a binary opposition exist, in eighteenth-century minds, between private and public space outside the legal Sharia sphere of harem and domestic space (Murphey 1990, 126)?

While some contemporary accounts clearly testify to a keen understanding of newly built imperial gardens as "private" domains (Raşid 5:165-6), one must also remember that the preference of the court, in the eighteenth century, to implant its palatial gardens right in the midst of already populated neighborhoods and along the most public gateway of the city (the Bosphorus), is in itself indicative that concepts of privacy and exclusiveness in these gardens was very relative. This ambiguity transpires clearly in the exhibitionist nature of palatine architecture in this time, in their unusual openness and transparency (Hamadeh, forthcoming). Nor did public gardens flourish on the margins of hermetically-enclosed gardens intended for elite recreation. On the contrary, physical and visual proximity between the two was sometimes essential to their growth and vitality. The popularity of the old public promenade of Kağıthane grew leaps and bounds after the imperial garden of Sa'dabad was constructed, right in the depths of it, by Ahmed III's grand-vizier in 1721 (Figs. 1 and 9). View of the magnificent palace, its landscape, and the glittering domes of the small garden pavilions that Mahmud I added some twenty years later, was something anyone strolling in the adjacent promenade could afford and that many remarked upon. The detailed engraving pro-duced by l'Espinasse for d'Ohsson's *Tableau de l'empire othoman* (Fig. 10) intimates that people wandered in and out of the royal garden enclosure as they pleased, and many a traveler made this point abundantly clear (d'Ohsson 1788-1824, 4:185; Ferté-Meun, 63).

That imperial gardens in the eighteenth century were partly intended for public visual consumption should not be dismissed. The self-appointed historian Şemdanizade's acerbic diatribes about the frequent feasts that Ahmed III's grand-vizier, Damad Ibrahim Pasha, hosted in the imperial gardens of Sa'dabad, Çubuklu, Bebek, Dolmabahçe, Göksu, Beykoz, and Üsküdar, reveal that these events included the high and the low (Şemdanizade, 1:3-4). Madeline Zilfi's observation, that the participation of the plebe in imperial festivities was a first in the history of Ottoman court life, cannot be more stressed (Zilfi 1996, 297-8). While the embittered Şemdanizade was probably right in remarking that such events were meant as uplifting distractions from the deteriorating affairs of the empire, surely such avuncular displays were also intended for the benefit of the court's public image; as spectacles that confirmed to the people of Istanbul the empire's unwavering power and opulence.

Public Space and Public Order

One important question that emerges from our contemporary accounts concerns the nature of the role of the state in the evolution of public spaces. Should we understand the active engagement of the ruling elite in the making of public spaces (whether directly or unwittingly) to be a sign of its "endorsement" of a flourishing public sphere, at a time when, as some historians have suggested, fears of the breakdown of order seemed to have relatively waned? I will argue that this active involvement was sought as a precaution against the possible implications of changing social practices; and it signaled, somewhat paradoxically, an attempt by the state to contain public life. What the opening of state and imperial property to the public provided were "official," controllable venues of recreation, and a well-delineated physical sphere in which urban life could be realized. I am not suggesting that public life was, at any point, a site of confrontation between state and society. What I am saying is that in the eighteenth century, issues of public life and concern for public order never ceased to overlap.

One of the most telling aspects of this relationship was the administrative redefinition of the role of Chief Imperial Gardener *(bostancıbaşı)* — a development about which we have limited knowledge. Whereas until the late seventeenth century, it had been confined to the upkeep of imperial gardens in the old city and the suburbs, by the following century, it extended to the maintenance of order in all the public gardens and forests and meadows that were located in the extra-muros city, along the Bosphorus, the Golden Horn, the Sea of Marmara, and the Princes' Islands. It is likely that these changes were instituted during the periods of absence of the court from Istanbul in the seventeenth century, but it is difficult to determine whether they occurred at one particular point in time or as the result of a series of gradual developments. In effect, by the beginning of the eighteenth century, imperial gardeners were serving as a police and a moral police. They could, at their own discretion, restrict access to a particular garden; or grant it in another pending sometimes on a suitable tip. Moreover, they inflicted punishment on anyone they considered infringed on the limits of normative public behavior (Uzunçarşılı, *Isl.A.* 2: 338-9, 736-8; *EI2* 1:1277-9; Koçu, *IA* 39-90; Sakaoğlu, *DBIA* 2:305-7; Mantran 1962, 129, 149; Erdoğan, 149-82 passim; Evyapan, 14-52 passim). They also played an active role in the process of opening some formerly imperial gardens to public access. Indeed, contemporary chroniclers suggest that the opening of an imperial garden to the public was sometimes sought by the state as a solution to repeated instances of public disorder. This was the case of the two gardens of Küçüksu, on the Anatolian bank of the Bosphorus, and Kalender, on the European shore. By the 1740s, these sites had become favored hangouts for the city's riffraff. In both cases, imperial order was given to the Chief Imperial Gardener (by Mahmud I and Mustafa III, respectively) to construct, in these gardens, barracks for the corps of imperial gardeners. Soon after, we are told, sections of the gardens were opened to the general public. This development was amply confirmed in the case of the garden of Küçüksu, by later pictorial images (Fig. 2) (Ayvansarayî 1864, 163; Şemdanizade, 1:162; Izzi, fol 272-3; Küçük Çelebi-zâde 1865, 377; Incicyan 1831, 257-8; 1976, 129-300; Raşid, 5:160).

It was also to the Chief Gardener (among other police officials and legislative authorities) that imperial edicts regarding the enforcement of sumptuary laws on matters of public outing and behavior were usually addressed. Just as in early modern France, England, China, Italy, or Japan, the essential concern of these laws lay in the maintenance of pre-existing social and religious structures, and even more important, in the preservation of visible marks of hierarchy and distinction. Insofar as these regulations controlled order in the city, they also defined the normative sphere within which public life was to be carried out. Sumptuary laws dated from at least the second half of the sixteenth century, and were rooted in Sharia law and ancient rules governing the public behavior of *zimmī* (non-Muslims). Promulgated in the form of imperial or grand-vizierial edicts, they had often pertained to matters of public life and public places like baths, taverns, and coffeehouses (Ahmet Refik 1931, 38-41, 141-

2). Coffeehouses, in particular, had become a major target from the moment they were introduced in the capital, in 1551, for the state authorities perceived them as focal points of social unrest, rumors, indecent discourses, political gossip, and critique. In Istanbul, the attack was often couched in a puritanical discourse that reacted both against coffee, as a nefarious innovation, and against its public consumption. In the seventeenth century, the state prohibited or shut down coffeehouses repeatedly, especially in periods of brewing discontent and mutiny (Desmet-Grégoire 1997, 13-24; Saraçgil 1997, 25-38; Hattox 1985, 91, 102; Zilfi 1988, 135-44; Terzioğlu 1998, 190-208; Kafadar, forthcoming, 6, 12-3; Kırlı, 18-66).

But even if compared with earlier moments of turbulence, in the eighteenth century the rate of enforcement of sumptuary rules seemed particularly high. One could certainly argue that as the sphere of sociability expanded, its regulation intensified. But more importantly, the locus of controversy seems to have expanded beyond the coffeehouse and into the garden; that is to say, beyond those places that were deemed to foster social and political unrest and into spaces where age, gender, social and professional groups mixed relatively too freely and could threaten to erode established hierarchies. This is not to say that social heterogeneity was the exclusive mark of gardens. In the fifty years that followed their introduction to the capital coffeehouses had attracted a mixed clientele that cut across social, professional, and religious lines and was regarded by the ruling class as a menace to the stability of the social order. But the persistent vilification of these venues by the state eventually led to the eclipse of their elite customers and their domination by the lower ranks. Moreover, throughout the centuries, it was the perception of coffeehouses as dangerous sites of political rumor and critique that remained the chief reason behind the state's discourse against them and the different methods it adopted to punish, control, or monitor them (Kırlı, 18-66). By the eighteenth century, the nature of the controversy had thus changed. Sumptuary laws more pointedly targeted those public arenas in which signs of fluidity and instability in the social structure were being exhibited. Their two new areas of focus became public attire and garden recreation.

Repeatedly throughout the century, the terms by which garden recreation could take place were dictated and enforced. Bans were occasionally imposed on specific types of activities, like carriage rides, or boat excursions. Some regulations barred certain groups from visiting specific gardens, while others addressed the issue of gender segregation in gardens. In a 1751 edict prohibited women's visits to a number of suburban gardens in the areas of Üsküdar and Beykoz, on the Anatolian shore of the Bosphorus. During the festivities held in 1758 to celebrate the birth of a princess, daughter of Mustafa III, women were again subjected to bans on visits to gardens, promenades, and marketplaces. Specific stipulations addressed the issue of gender segregation in gardens and mandated the allocation of specific areas, times of the day, or days of the week exclusively to women (Ahmet Refik 1988, 131-2, 170, 174-5; Şemdanizade, 1:21; Mehmed Hakim, fols 423, 482; Çeşmî-zâde 1993, 25; d'Ohsson, 4:79-81). According to the French traveler Pertusier, "[Fridays], as well as Tuesdays, are allocated to women for their [social] visits, promenades, or visits to the bath, depending on their wishes" (Pertusier, 2:7). Travelers continued to observe that "when parties proceed to those pic-nics, even the members of a family never mix together … The women assemble on one side round the fountain, and the men on the other, under the trees" (Allom and Walsh, 1:33-4); while Ottoman authorities actively worked to ensure that such segregation remained in place. In the closing lines of a wonderful poem in which the garden of Kağthane is equated to a lover's heart so big it could contain all the young lads of Istanbul, the late eighteenth-century poet Sürüri may have been applauding, or perhaps deferentially protesting against, those legal measures that prescribed the terms, time and space in which different forms of sociability could take place in a public garden:

Fig. 11. Portraits by Levni (ca. 1720s).

> I fell in love with a handsome ink-seller; if he answers my prayers
>
> I'll write him a missive, an invitation to Kağıthane…
>
> If all the boys of Istanbul gathered there, they would fit
>
> [For] Kağıthane is as spacious as a lover's heart
>
> Oh! Süruri, what if it's forbidden to women
>
> We will hold converse with young boys at Kağıthane (Süruri n.d., 3:45)

As the regulation of public recreation continued, matters of clothing in the specific context of fashionable gardens became a serious source of concern. The state began enforcing previously existing sartorial laws and repeatedly decreed new clothing regulations. From 1702 until 1748, and time and again under Osman III, Mustafa III and Selim III, imperial edicts asserted the necessity and obligation of certain groups — most notably women, and Jewish and Christian minorities — to abide by the Ottoman dress code. Such edicts as well as those who commented on the changing sartorial landscape in the capital appealed not only to moral and financial considerations, but also invoked the need to maintain visible marks of distinctions, whether vis-à-vis other social or minority groups, or with respect to the residents of foreign countries. In 1758 a new sartorial law sought to check the growing inclination of minority groups to adopt the "Frankish-style" of dressing and to wear yellow shoes, which were customarily reserved to Muslims. Two years earlier, an imperial edict condemned those "shameless [Muslim] women" who paraded about luxuriously adorned in innovative dresses that emulated the fashion of Christian women and those clad in provocative outfits that "stirred the nerve of desire" (Ahmet Refik 1988, 86-8, 182-3; Şemdanizade, 1:26; Sadreddîn-zâde 1973, 2:521,523; Pertusier, 2:89; Koçu 1958, 63; Özkaya 1985, 145-57 passim; Umur 1988, 206-7; Çağman 1993 (1), 258; Binswänger 1977, 160-93; Quataert 1997, 403-25). Innovative fashion, be it in the color of a shoe, the style, cut, or design of a dress, or the length and width of a collar (all of which were sometimes mentioned and described with great precision in the edicts) blurred established boundaries between social, professional, ethnic, and religious groups.

Such preoccupations with clothing regulations certainly predated the eighteenth century (Ahmet Refik 1931, 51-2; Tietze 1982, 580-1). In this period, though, the issue of innovative dress acquired a new significance. After two centuries of almost unaltered dress, noticeable changes were suddenly occurring in both women's and men's outdoor clothing. The writings of foreign merchants and travelers attest to a rising fashion consciousness among Istanbul's middle classes and describe new tastes in fabrics and colors (Flachat 1766, 1:434-4; d'Ohsson, 2:147-50; 4:152; Pertusier, 2:192-3; Çağman 1993 (2), 256-87; Scarce 1976, 199-219; Jirousek 1994, 201-41). Contemporary portraits by Levni and Buhari featured remarkable innovations in women's fashion such as their increasing *décolletage,* broad collars, transparent and loosely worn veils, extravagant headdresses, and hair worn loose (Fig. 11). Such innovations never failed to attract attention: "No woman covers her breast," wrote Mouradgea d'Ohsson, "especially in the summer, except with a blouse that is usually [made] of thin gauze" (d'Ohsson, 4:152). If the state became more diligent about enforcing sartorial regulations, it was partly because changing consumption patterns had brought about new tastes, and partly because these tastes were being paraded in public more conspicuously than ever before. Such displays took the form of new styles, colors, hats, and hairdos that deviated considerably from traditional dress codes. The persistent reiteration of these regulations suggests that dissolving social, professional, ethnic, and religious distinctions may have had far-reaching ramifications. The rising fashion consciousness among Istanbul's middle classes and the implicit relation between clothing, on one hand, and self-image and public display, on the other, come across very frequently in both Ottoman and foreign visual and textual representations. They are captured beautifully by the poet Endcrunlu Fazıl, in the Preface of his long narrative verse, the *Book of Women (Zenānnāme),* that he wrote toward the end of the eighteenth century.

> And if you wish, oh spirit of life
> That to you all manner of women be drawn
> God be praised, [that] the Lord gifted you
> With the attractive power of beauty
> In the season of roses go for a pleasure trip
> Especially around [the garden of] Kağıthane
> Rub the scented oil of its shrubs on your brows
> Cover your head with a Lahore shaw…
> Wear a coral-red vest, a gold embroidered robe
> Let the dagger at your waist be choice…
> Drink one or two cups of wine

[So] that your eyes might look bloodshot

Toward whatever assembly women gather

Walk, oh! swaying cypress

Don't go stumbling along like an old man

Make your every stride like a lion's...

Reveal a lock of hair from under the fez

Show them a build like Rüstem's...

They are attracted to the most handsome

They'd sacrifice their heart for his sake

Here and there, tip that *fes* coyly

Scatter ambergris from your locks, my lovely...

That one laughs from behind the veil

That one looks at the ground, blushing modestly

Those chuckles, that flirting, that glance

When she looks at you out of the corner of her eye, oh my!

One of them starts to sing a song

So they might work their arts on you

One hastens to entice you

[Her] mantle falls from her back

At times, a swing is set up in a cypress

Two of them sit in it, casually clad

One alluringly rocks the swing

The other recites lovely songs

As she swings her gown falls open

Showing every bit of her to you

To you she lets her trouser-tie be seen

To you, perhaps, her secret treasure (Fazıl, fols 79-80)

Fazıl's Preface was a highly popular poem in its own time about the most popular public garden in suburban Istanbul, the garden of Kağıthane. It must have read like a manual of public garden behavior, in which every detail of clothing, demeanor, social and courtship skill and faux-pas was carefully outlined. Although the poem does not claim to be more than an imagined scenario, it is significant that Fazıl should chose a public space to set up an encounter between young men and women, when a more clandestine setting in which such intercourse could be construed more appropriately within the realm of the private, would have equally served his purpose. But Fazıl's poem is, in large part, a counseling guide on the principles of seduction between men and women as they pertained specifically to the context of public gardens. It belongs to a new generation of poems in which the garden no longer appears as an orderly and isolated world meant for the cultivation of courtly sociability. In this respect, it may be viewed as a poetical illustration of an evanescent world order that the Ottoman state aspired to restore. Pointing indirectly to the inability of the state to fully contain public life, it portrays the garden as an urban reality in which potent manifestations of lifestyles, clothing fashions, and recreational practices in currency at the time challenged the notion of urban order; and as a forum where emerging forms of distinction could, eventually, bring about new kinds of group identities. Last but not least, it captures the simplicity with which a complete collapse of gender boundaries could be triggered by a frivolous gaze, or by the location of a swing.

Bibliography

Abou el-Haj, Rifa'at Ali. *The Formation of the Modern State: The Ottoman Empire, Sixteenth to Eighteenth Century*. Albany: State University of New York Press, 1991.

Ahmet Refik. *Hicrî On Ikinci Asfrda Istanbul Hayatı 1100-1200*. Third edition.Istanbul: Istanbul Kitaplığı, 1988.

———. *Hicrî On Birinci Asırda Istanbul Hayatı 1000-1100*. Istanbul: Devlet Matbaası,1931.

Aksan, Virginia. *An Ottoman Statesman in War and Peace: Ahmed Resmi Efendi 1700 - 1783*. New York, Leiden and Köln: E. J. Brill, 1995.

———. "Ottoman Political Writing, 1768-1808." *International Journal of Middle East Studies* 25 (1993): 53-69.

Allom, Thomas and Robert Walsh. *Constantinople and the Scenery of the Seven Churches of Asia Minor* (Illustrated in a Series of Drawings from Nature by Thomas Allom With a Historical Account of Constantinople... by the Rev. Robert Walsh, LL.D. Chaplain to the British Embassy at the Ottoman Porte). 2 vols. London: Fisher, Son, & Co., 1838.

Ayvansarayî, Hafiz Hüseyin. *Ḥadīḳat ul-Cevāmi'*. 2 vols. Istanbul: Matbaa-i. Âmire, 1281 (1864).

———. *The Garden of the Mosques: Hafiz Hüseyin al-Ayvansarayî's Guide to the Muslim Monuments of Ottoman Istanbul*. (Supplement to *Muqarnas*). Edited by Howard Crane. Leiden, Boston and Köln: E. J. Brill, 2000.

Binswänger, Karl. *Untersuchungen zum Status der Nichtmuslime im Osmanischen Reich des 16. Jahrhunderts: mit einer Neudefinition des Besgriffes "Ḏimma."* Münich: R. Trofenik, 1977.

Cerasi, Maurizio. *La città del Levante: Civiltà urbana e architettura sotto gli Ottomani nei secoli XVIII-XIX*. Milan: Jaca Book, 1986.

———. "Il giardino ottomano attraverso l'immagine del Bosforo." In *Il giardino islamico: Architettura, natura, paesaggio,* edited by Attilio Petruccioli, pp. 217-36. Milan: Electa, 1994.

———. "Open Space, Water and Trees in Ottoman Urban Culture in the XVIII-XIXth Centuries." *Environmental Design* 2 (1985): 36-49.

Çağman, Filiz. "Family Life." In *Woman in Anatolia: 9000 Years of the Anatolian Woman*. Exh. Cat., Topkapı Palace Museum, 29 November 1993 - 28 February 1994, edited by Günsel Renda, pp. 202-5. Istanbul: Turkish Republic Ministry of Culture, General Directorate of Monuments and Museums, 1993.

———. "Women's Clothing." In *Woman in Anatolia: 9000 Years of the Anatolian Woman*. Exh. Cat., Topkapı Palace Museum, 29 November 1993 - 28 February 1994, edited by Günsel Renda, pp. 260-87. Istanbul: Turkish Republic Ministry of Culture, General Directorate of Monuments and Museums, 1993.

Çelik, Zeynep. *The Remaking of Istanbul: Portrait of an Ottoman City in the Nineteenth Century*. Seattle: University of

Washington Press, 1986.

Çeşmî-zâde Mustafa Reşid. *Çeşmî-zâde Tarihi*. Edited by Bekir Kütükoğlu. İstanbul: Istanbul Fetih Cemiyeti, 1993.

Dallaway, James. *Constantinople Ancient and Modern With Excursions to the Shores and Islands of the Archipelago*. London: T. Cadell, Junr. & W. Davies, 1797.

Demirsar, Belgin. "Emirgân Camii," *Dünden Bugüne İstanbul Ansiklopedisi [DBİA] 3*: 169-70.

Desmet-Grégoire, Hélène. "Introduction." In *Cafés d'Orient revisités,* edited by Hélène Desmet-Grégoire and François Georgeon, pp. 13-24. Paris: Editions du CNRS, 1997.

D'Ohsson, Mouradgea. *Tableau général de l'empire othoman divisé en deux parties, dont l'une comprend la Législation Mahométane; l'autre, l'Histoire de l'Empire Othoman*. 7 vols. Paris: Firmin Didot, 1788 - 1824.

Eldem, Sedad Hakkı. *Türk Bahçeleri*. Istanbul: Kültür Bakanlığı, Devlet Kitapları Müdürlüğü, 1976.

Erdoğan, Muzaffer. "Osmanlı Devrinde İstanbul Bahçeleri." *Vakıflar Dergisi* 4 (1958): 149-82.

Evliya Çelebi. *The Seyahatname of Evliya Çelebi. Book One: Istanbul* (Fascimile of *Topkapı Sarayı Bağdad 304*). *Turkish Sources* 9: Part 1: Folios 1-106a; 17: Part 2: Folios 106b-217b. Edited by Şinasi Tekin and Gönül A. Tekin. Cambridge, Mass.: Harvard Universtiy Press, 1993.

Evyapan, Gönül A. *Eski Türk Bahçeleri ve Özellikle Eski İstanbul Bahçeleri*. Ankara: Orta Doğu Teknik Üniversitesi, 1972.

Faroqhi, Suraiya. "Crisis and Change, 1590-1699." In *An Economic and Social History of the Ottoman Empire, vol.2: 1600 - 1914,* edited by Suraiya Faroqhi et al., pp. 413-636. Cambridge and New York: Cambridge University Press, 1994.

Fazıl Bey Enderûnî. *Hūbānnāme ve Zenānnāme*. MS. Istanbul Üniversitesi Kütüphanesi [IÜK], Ty 5502.

Ferté-Meun (Comtesse de la). *Lettres sur le Bosphore, ou relation d'un voyage en différentes parties de l'Orient pendant les années 1816 à 1819*. Paris: Domère, 1821.

Flachat, Jean-Claude. *Observations sur le commerce et sur les arts d'une partie de l'Europe, de l'Asie, de l'Afrique, et même des Indes Orientales*. 2 vols. Paris: Jacquenod Père & Rusand, 1766.

Gökbilgin, M. Tayyib. "Tarihte Boğaziçi." *Islam Ansiklopedisi [Isl.A.]* 2: 671-92.

Gökyay, Orhan Şaik. "Bağçeler." *Topkapı Sarayı Müzesi Yıllığı* 4 (1990): 7-20.

Hakim, Seyyid Mehmed. *Vekāyi'-nāme*. MS. Topkapı Sarayı Müzesi Kütüphanesi [TSK], B. 231, B. 233.

Hamadeh, Shirine. "Splash and Spectacle: The Obsession With Fountains in Eighteenth-Century Istanbul." *Muqarnas* 19 (October 2002): 123-48.

———. *The City's Pleasures: Istanbul in the Eighteenth Century* (forthcoming with the University of Washington Press).

Hattox, Ralph. *Coffee and Coffeehouses*. Seattle: University of Washington Press, 1985.

İnalcık, Halil. "Centralization and Decentralization in Ottoman Administration." In *Studies in Eighteenth-Century Islamic History,* edited by Thomas Naff and Roger Owen, pp. 27-52. Chicago: University of Chicago Press, 1977.

———. "Military and Fiscal Transformation in the Ottoman Empire, 1600 – 1700." *Archivum Ottomanicum* 6 (1980): 283-337.

İncicyan, P. Ğ. (İnciciyan, G. V.). *Boğaziçi Sayfiyeleri*. Translated from the Armenian by the Priest of the Armenian Church of Kandilli. Edited and annotated by Orhan Duru. Istanbul: Eren, 2000.

———. *18. Asırda İstanbul*. Edited and translated from Armenian by Hrand D. Andreasyan. (Including excerpts from *Istanbul Topografyası* by Balatlı Sargis Sarraf-Hovannesyan). Istanbul: Baha Matbaası, 1976.

———. "Bostandji-Bashi." *EI2*. 1: 1279.

Zilfi, Madeline. *The Politics of Piety: The Ottoman Ulema in the Postclassical Age (1600-1800).* Minneapolis: Bibliotheca Islamica, 1988.

———. "Women and Society in the Tulip Era, 1718-1730." In *Women, the Family, and Divorce Laws in Islamic History,* edited by Amira El Azhary Sonbol, pp. 290-303. Syracuse: Syracuse University Press, 1996.

———. "The Kadızadelis: Discordant Revivalism in Seventeenth-Century Istanbul." *Journal of Near Eastern Studies* 45, no. 4 (1986): 251-69.

NOTES

I would like to thank the Director of Landscape Studies at Dumbarton Oaks, Michel Conan, for inviting me to participate in this volume and for the intellectual generosity he showed during my fellowship year at Dumbarton Oaks, in 1999 – 2000, in which part of this research was done. Numerous colleagues and friends have offered their insights on aspects of this article, that I had begun exploring in my dissertation. I am deeply grateful to all of them.

[1] Cerasi, 1994; 1986; 1985, are to my knowledge the only attempts at examining the development of public spaces in eighteenth-century Istanbul. These works, however, rely almost exclusively on western sources.

[2] For the early history of suburban imperial gardens, see Necipoğlu 1997; Erdoğan 1958; Evyapan 1972; Gökyay 1990; and Gökbilgin, *Isl.A.*

[3] According to Erdoğan, the last royal garden register in which the garden appears is dated 1679, Erdoğan 1958.

[4] The Taksim public park, completed in 1869, was designed in collaboration with German and French urban planners, architects, and engineers and conceived along Beaux-arts guidelines, Çelik 1987, 46, 64, 69-70; Evyapan, 72.

[5] A thorough examination of the endowment deeds *(waqfiyyas)* of the new projects is likely to shed more light on this question. This is the subject of a separate project I am beginning this year.

[6] For sixteenth- to eighteenth-century social transformations and revisionist interpretations of the paradigm of decline in Ottoman history, see İnalcık 1977, 27-52; 1980, 283-337; Kafadar 1993, 37-48; 1994, 613-5; Abou el-Haj 1991; Itzkowitz 1962, 73-94; 1977, 15-26; Aksan 1995; 1993, 53-69; Zilfi 1988; Faroqhi 1994, 413-636; Salzmann 2004; 1993, 393-424; Quataert 2000 (1), 37-53.

[7] In Meninski's seventeenth-century multilingual thesaurus ḫa̤ṣṣ is translated as (in Latin) *proprius, privates, peculiaris,* (in Italian) *proprio, privato, particolare* and (in French) *propre, privé, particulier;* Meninski 2000. By the latter half of the nineteenth century *"ḫāṣṣ"* meant "special, particular;" special to the state or sovereign," as well as "private, individual;" see Redhouse 1890; Orhonlu *[EI2]* 4:1094-100; and Pakalın 1946, 1:750-2.

Gardens, City Life and Culture

Gardens, City Life and Culture

Gardens, City Life and Culture

Gardens, City Life and Culture

Gardens, City Life and Culture

Gardens, City Life and Culture

Biedermeier Gardens in Vienna and the Self-fashioning of Middle-Class Identities

Robert Rotenberg

The turn of the nineteenth century in Vienna, Austria witnessed the emergence of a new class of urbanites. Drawn from the pre-existing merchant class, military and bureaucracy of the Austro-Hungarian Empire, these people contested with the aristocracy to influence and direct the emergence of an urban identity for Vienna that could compete with Paris, London and Rome. Imitating features from these three existing metropoles, Vienna would eventually offer its own special arena for exhibiting class, the villa garden. While palace gardens had occupied the time and fortunes of the aristocracy for the previous century, the villa gardens offered a smaller canvas upon which to represent the values of the emerging class—property, domesticity and intellectual sophistication. I propose to describe the garden tradition that resulted from this movement, referred to in the Viennese literature as the Biedermeier garden.

Historians have long recognized the Biedermeier Garden as a specific style of garden architecture. It refers to both a period (from the Congress of Vienna, 1812 to the Revolutions of 1848) and to a design template (colorful and varied blooms, curved beds, frivolous ornaments, enclosed by high hedgerows in close proximity to the house). The style contrasted with the two existing gardens templates employed in aristocratic gardens, the Baroque and the English, as well as the utility gardens of the small householders and artisans. The style was spread by nursery owners, who created model gardens of great beauty in the inner districts of the city. People could easily visit these model gardens. They treated them as they would a park, strolling through the lanes, observing the variety of flowers and shrubs. They would then contract with the nursery to deliver plants for their home gardens, arranging them in the same patterns they had observed in the model gardens. This was the first effort at marketing of landscape products to the new middle class in the city. By the end of the period, pattern books and gardening magazines would take the place of model gardens and the nurseries moved further away to the outer suburbs. This chapter provides an analysis of how the identity of the emergent middle class can be identified with the garden style by themselves and their class antagonists.

Who was Who in Nineteenth Century Vienna

The terms bourgeois and aristocratic are not very coherent. As a shorthand description for the social organization of elite groups in post-1700 Europe, they are too coarse a distinction to make. In this period of rapid social change, the average length of an aristocratic family's hold on an estate was three generations. New families were raised to replace the old and new titles were established. The bourgeoisie, too, was in transition from its role as the organizer of long- and short-distance trade to its new role as the owner of the not yet dominant means of producing wealth, the manufacturing system. This transition took over a hundred years to accomplish in Vienna. For much of the period, the people who identified themselves (and were identified by others) as bourgeois engaged in a variety of livelihoods and often had competing interests. For them, the issue was not so much what made them different from the nobility as it was what made them different from the artisan classes.

Class membership involved different levels of property tax obligations (Boyer 1981). Who got what taxable property was determined by imperial grant, transfers through inheritance, transfers at the time of marriage, and occasionally, outright purchase. There were hereditary nobles and life baronets. Hereditary nobles paid taxes to the crown in kind (a ritual transfer that bore little relation to what the noble estates actually produced for the market), in service (military, but also government services were involved), and in cash. Cash was the new form of tax. All nobles had been obligated to provide cash to the emperor for the maintenance of the standing army since the Diet of Worms in 1592. The bourgeoisie paid property taxes too, but did so on a different basis, and in this period, always in cash. Property involved not only real estate, but also the value of inventories in warehouses. The bourgeoisie was required to keep these careful inventories and imperial tax agents were often assigned full-time as accountants to the largest trading houses. Financial and ultimately social success for both classes was measured by increases in their tax bills. Until 1848, the artisan classes paid no taxes and had no voice in public affairs.

Moreover, the aristocratic and bourgeois classes were internally fragmented. The aristocracy made a clear distinction between hereditary and life nobility. Even within the hereditary segment, the length of the family's control of its primary estate, the size of its holdings, the military accomplishments of its ancestors, and its marriage relations with the imperial family were features that promoted families in the aristocratic hierarchy. In this period there was a rapid growth of hereditary and non-hereditary titles to members of the bourgeoisie who had excelled in creating wealth (and who had lent large portions of it to the crown), or who had given extraordinary military or government service to the crown. These were concentrated in the capital cities while the countryside remained the preserve of the old landed families, most of whom had held their titles for many generations.

All bourgeois owned some kind of property. This could take the form of land, factories and warehouses, or inventories. The most financially successful of these were awarded baronet titles. These were non-hereditary, but did afford the bourgeois some rights and privileges reserved for the aristocrats, the most important of which was land ownership. Social deference and honors came with the title, along with higher taxes. Nevertheless, the non-titled bourgeoisie aspired to these baronets. There were other criteria by which they took each other's measure: the number of generations of a family's control of its commercial operations (the older the better); the extent to which the operations were wholly controlled by the family (positive) or publicly traded (negative), the family's possession of an imperial patent and aristocratic patronage (a sign of quality goods), the number and rank of family members accepted into government service or the officer corps of the military, and finally, whether the family used their own in-house bank to move transactions long distances (the highest status), traded long distance without banking, short-distance trade, or manufacturing (the lowest status). Families with various combinations of these qualities in their commercial operations formed a bourgeois social hierarchy, the upper reaches of which owned land and were indistinguishable in their consumption power from the aristocracy, while the lower tiers were bereft of property and no better off materially than the artisans.

Finally, to mount a garden on an estate in Vienna required land. Most of the land surrounding Vienna before 1683 was owned by the crown for military defense purposes or by religious orders to support their communities (Bobek and Lichtenberger 1978). The non-noble Viennese, bourgeoisie and artisan alike, lived in rented houses or lofts within the city walls, or in townhouses and cottages in the small suburban clusters at the foot of the Vienna Woods. Very few bourgeoisie owned enough land for anything more than a kitchen garden. Nobles lived in religious or military accommodations when they visited the Palace, until the emperor ordered them, in 1683, to establish permanent homes in the city and participate in government affairs. Thus, the period discussed here is for all practical purposes the time during which garden art arrived in Vienna as a commodity for both the aristocrats and the bourgeoisie. As the two hundred years unfolded, more land became available for building gardens. These two groups were inventing the garden art traditions of the metropolis as they themselves were evolving into new public, economic, and cultural roles. The aristocratic and bourgeois interactions around garden art in this period correspond to an active dialogue between the landowning elements of both classes.

Encounters in the Garden

In Vienna, the choice by the bourgeoisie to invest in garden art was a mixture of civic politics, of attitudes toward domesticity, and of fashion. As civic politics, the garden represented a model of the relationship of the patron, first to his class and ultimately, to the broader society. To invest in a garden was to make a statement about one's political allegiances and ideals. When we begin to ask questions about what those statements are, we abruptly enter the local design environment. It was in this space that the encounter on garden art between the aristocrat and bourgeois in Vienna took place.

Viennese-specific garden forms were available to help the patron align himself right, left or center. Absolutist aristocrats of the eighteenth century used the design features of the Baroque ensemble to represent their specific views. Enlightened aristocrats and some wealthy bourgeoisie replicate this political use of garden art in the later eighteenth century. It appears again in the early nineteenth century in the gardens of the emergent liberal bourgeoisie, and still again in the gardens of the "new class" industrial elite in the latter half of the nineteenth century. The use of garden art as the language of politics also continues in the twentieth century, but that is beyond the scope of this discussion.

The encounter between aristocrat and bourgeois in garden art always remains a class interaction. The bourgeoisie appropriated aristocratic forms in distinctive ways. Some forms, such as the aristocratic military banners, are inverted into colorful, but meaningless flags enjoyed for their playful dance in the wind, rather than the memory of past battles. Mirror balls on pedestals and swings on four-legged frames derive from the heroic memorials and jousting pitches, but the aristocratic references have been stripped away. Other elements are transformed into ensembles. Full-scale constructions of Swiss villages or the hermit's hut are miniaturized, mass produced and suitable for placement in even the smallest flower bed. The garden dwarf, originally based on the peasant costumes of servants at the aristocratic *ermitage*, begins to appear as a carved wooden garden ornament with a whimsical facial expression. The bourgeoisie then redirected these aristocratic forms toward the symbolic fulfillment of greater class visibility, property and domestic comfort. The cosmopolitanism of the geometrical ground plan of the aristocrat becomes the organic-shaped beds of provincialism among the bourgeois. The selection of imported plant species by aristocrats inverts to the preference for native plants by the bourgeois. The bourgeois transforms the permanent character of the evergreen in the absolutist garden into the effervescence of flowering annuals.

The seventeenth-century Counter-Reformation in Austria created a social and cultural gulf between landed aristocracy and urban merchants. Strict sumptuary and property regulations, not to mention religious differences, had discouraged interactions between the classes. After the lifting of the Turkish siege in 1683, there was a building boom in Vienna. In reconstructing the empire, the Emperor Leopold I (1658–1705) demanded more involvement by the nobility in the imperial government. He decreed that they must establish permanent residence in Vienna. Palaces began to be built outside the walls of the city. At the time, there was a politically tinged competition between advocates of Italian and German styles. This competition would dominate the next century in the architecture and landscape design in Vienna. In the face of this artistic war, the imperial family chose to associate itself with a third style, that of the French, for its gardens. They used this style at a number of their estates: the summer palace at Schönbrunn (1704), the Augarten palace (1705) and the Prater pleasure grounds. As a result, Andre Le Nôtre's (1613–1700) design for Versailles (1660) came to dominate local aristocratic garden tastes. Between 1683 and 1720, 863 noble estates were built in the suburbs of the city (Bermann 1881).

During this aristocratic building boom, bourgeois building remained restricted to the outlying areas of the suburbs. There are no reliable counts, but the amount of building must have been considerable. Between 1683 and 1720 the total population of the city doubled. The aristocratic families and their retinues cannot account for this increase alone. The small cottages of the bourgeois rarely employed Baroque landscape patterns. There was too little space.

The aristocratic class began to change in the mid-eighteenth century. The tensions created by the growth of markets and the volatility in agricultural prices changed the way the nobility ran their estates. These changes had political implications as well. "New" or enlightened aristocrats, the ones who had begun to see themselves as agricultural producers on a continental scale, chafed under economic restrictions and the political inertia that enforced them. Many of the reforms promulgated by emperors Maria Theresa (1717–1780) and Joseph II (1741–1790) were aimed at freeing up labor and capital for this segment of activist aristocrats. Other aristocrats saw these changes as threatening to their way of life and retrenched. Factions on the extremes of both camps became increasingly politicized. Among the activists, progressive social philosophies, especially the works of Jean Jacques Rousseau (1712–1778), were read and discussed. So-called "enlightened" aristocrats attempted to distance themselves from the conservative segments of their class by changing their palace gardens to reflect more English parkscape designs. Moritz Count Lacy (1725–1801), the man who would build the most influential English garden in the city, was a member of the "Salon of the Five Princes," a group of philosophically well-read aristocrats.

According to Hennebo, Vienna was not far behind other German cities in adopting the free-flowing form and naturalist rhetoric of the English style in noble estates. He places their first appearance in Northern German estates around 1760 (Hennebo 1980, 15-41). The English garden design canon in Vienna was based on estates built by two military commanders, the aristocratic Count Lacy, who rebuilt Neuwaldegg in this style in 1766, and the bourgeois Baron Gideon von Loudon (1716-1790), who rebuilt his estate at Hadersdorf-Weidlingau in 1789. It was their military prowess and personal friendship with Joseph II, factors that put their commitment to crown and empire beyond reproach that enabled them to break the hold of Le Nôtre's designs.

The new English gardens differed from their French predecessors in the way that they relied on visual perspective. Instead of an absolute center defined by a clear geometry, the new type of garden offered artistic and spiritual culmination points arrived at through the freedom of fantasy. These culmination points included outlooks and views of the countryside, but also fabriques: Gothic ruins, Palladian temples, Chinese bridges and temples, grottos, fishing huts, log cabins, mausoleums, monuments and memorials. So popular were these constructions that entire magazines devoted to distributing the latest designs, such as LeRouge's *Les jardins anglo-chinois* (1787) and Grohmann's *Ideemagazin* (1796-1802), had very wide circulation. Each fabrique placed in the garden became part of the garden's narrative. Often only the garden owner and his salon knew the connection between fabrique and text. In other cases, the objects partook of more widely recognized references (Mosser 1990).

In the meantime, the wealthy bourgeoisie was beginning to adorn their new estates with English garden design elements as well. With the growth of trade under the reform administrations of Maria Theresa and Joseph II, more money was available among the wealthy of this class to build larger estates and larger gardens. Now, however, there was a choice of styles that signaled primacy in class: the absolutist Baroque and the republican English. First in a trickle, and then by 1820 in a rushing stream, the bourgeoisie adopted the English.

The Geymueller banking family played a similar role among the bourgeoisie that Count Lacy had played among the Enlightenment aristocrats a generation earlier. They established a thirty-three-hectare English garden in Pötzleinsdorf in 1799. Konrad Rosenthal, together with Franz Illner, the palace gardener of Neuwaldegg, executed it. It was a very popular park among the wealthy bourgeoisie in the first half of the nineteenth century and was described by contemporaries as a garden of towering arbors, flowerbeds in full bloom, and quietly winding paths. It continues to be a popular park today. It features a number of segments with small fabriques that can still be seen today. Among these were Greek style statuary, a temple, a grotto, and a pedestal urn.

Geza Hajós has researched the fabriques placed in the gardens surrounding Vienna in this period and found a sizeable number with common references. The Chinese bridges, pagodas and temples were an homage of respect for the Confucian, philosophical basis of the Central Kingdom. This Chinese vogue began in England and quickly spread to centers of enlightened learning on the Continent. The round Palladian temples were named "Temple of the Night," or Temple of Knowledge." They were closely linked to the Freemason lodges and the Illuminati networks to which many of these aristocratic and wealthy bourgeoisie belonged, and symbolized the Temple of Solomon, the only earthly building for which God himself was the designer. The grottos were shadowy and filled with Freemason inspired statuary of Egyptian deities. The Gothic ruins were preferred over Greek ruins because the Gothic reminded the viewer of the perfection of the spirit through the passage of time, while the Greek ruins reminded one of the victories of the barbarians over the first enlightened European civilization. Similarly, Roman ruins were philosophically appropriate as objects of melancholic mediation on the ultimate death of all great things. The fishing huts, log cabins, and grottos were also hermitages, retreats from the world of military, commercial, and civic affairs through which the garden patrons gain their power. The patron was no hermit however. The hermitage was a social statement in sharp contradiction to the utter worldliness of the Baroque palace. The hermitage was given greater prominence in the garden design than the palace residence. The message of the hermitage was that the patron was a true nature lover, an

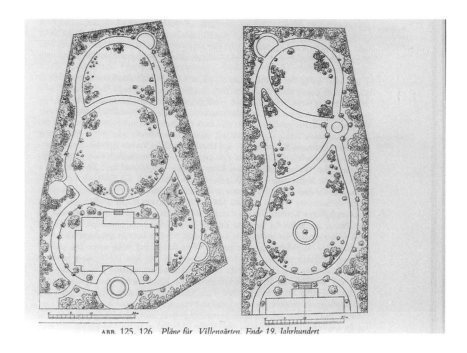

ABB. 125. 126 *Pläne für Villengärten. Ende 19. Jahrhundert*

Fig. 2. Neo-romantic villa gardens at the end of the nineteenth century recorded by Hampel in 1902 (Cf. endnote 5). The plans reflect the domestic designs that dominated the second half of the nineteenth century. The French curve paths and open central bed are typical of *Hausdenken* landscapes that patrons preferred for making their estates attractive to the widest possible market, ensuring a stable investment (Cf. endnote 6). (Source: Hampel, Carl. *Die Deutsche Gartenkunst*. Leipzig: H. Voigt. 1902. Illustration is in the Public Domain.).

Friedrich Fischer emphasizes the role of four private nurseries as the driving force behind the widespread acceptance of these novel design ideas (Fischer 1971). One of Lacy's gardeners from Neuwaldegg, Rosenbaum, built a nursery and public garden in 1820 on the grounds of the former palace of the princely Strahemberg family in the 5th district. Rosenbaum was originally from an artisan family. This was followed by three other model gardens attached to nurseries: Baron von Hügel's Garden in the Hietzing (1824), an outlying bourgeois residential district; Dr. J. P. Rupprecht's Garden in Gumpendorf near Rosenbaum's on the site of another Baroque palace (1822); and Baron Müller-Pronay's Garden in Hetzendorf, another outlying bourgeois residential district near Schönbrunn (1817). Ludwig von Beethoven resided at the villa in this garden while finishing his Ninth Symphony in 1821 (Fig. 1).

The Biedermeier type did present something that was essentially new. Owners of smaller house gardens slowly redesigned them to follow the fashionable new ground plan. In the 1830s and 40s, the core areas for new garden development were the new suburbs of Döbling, Heiligenstadt, Hohe Warte, and especially Hietzing. The succession in garden styles is clearly visible in the lithographic plans from the period. The 1820 lithographic *franziszeische Katasterplan* reveals highly varied garden designs, some resembling the irregular shaped beds of Rosenbaum and Rupprecht, while others used the older perpendicular crossing paths pattern with four or more rectangular beds, often with round beds in the intersections. These older garden types begin in the Middle Ages, but are typical of no specific epoch. Private gardens merely repeat these established bed designs in smaller form, without much innovation. With the Biedermeier, the variety of garden forms suddenly multiplies. The inspiration for this profusion stems from imitating the ground plans of other bourgeois gardens as a representation of class identity. The imitators would then add idiosyncratic elements to give the garden a unique identity.

As the Biedermeier developed, and certainly by the 1840s, new estates had begun to be built in large numbers. These had the advantage of starting from Biedermeier models for the ground plans of their gardens. These plans exhibit a striking commitment to curved paths, both near and away from the house.[5] The paths, however, are regular, and fit the French Curve device of the commercial gardener. The free curving paths of Neuwaldegg, Pötzleinsdorf, and the Rosenbaum gardens have disappeared from the ensemble (Fig. 2).

Having established the garden as a separate preserve, the Biedermeier Viennese then filled them with the small elements borrowed from the model Biedermeier gardens of the early 1800s. Such elements as Chinese bridges, Roman ruins and Gothic castles were gone. In their place, garden patrons erected striped canvas pavilions, statuaries, mirror balls on pedestals, swings, miniature fishponds, and hundreds of species of flowers. These elements convey many layers of meaning, beginning with the playful, the childlike and the disinterested. The choice to follow the English taste over the Classical favored by the aristocrats is a not-so-subtle statement of affiliation with Republican ideals. The flowers are a novel element. They set the Biedermeier apart and nominate it as a third stylistic force in the unfolding of future Viennese gardens, alongside the Baroque and the English.

The reactionary forces set in motion by Metternich define the interactions between aristocrat and bourgeois through the upheavals of 1848. Following the revolution, a voting franchise is extended to the bourgeoisie for the first time. Liberal political victories of the 1870s and 80s give them control of the municipal government. As the bourgeois role in determining the shape of political relations in the city increases, so, too, does a mechanical, functional garden art begin to take hold in the city. Within fifty years of the high point of the Biedermeier in the early 1840s, the only element that was left of the English style that so firmly gripped bourgeois consciousness was the perfunctory rose garden. Now located in a thoroughly functionalist design, the roses no longer evoke an olfactory mood or Biedermeier sentimentality. Instead, they serve as what one contemporary gardener I spoke with called "living wallpaper for an outdoor space" in which specific social activities can take place.

Conclusion: Producing Garden Knowledge

Gardens were built by the bourgeois to signal their feelings of social parity with the aristocracy. While it would be easy to surmise that in such conditions any bourgeois would build a garden that proclaimed the aspirations of their class, the gardens that were actually built displayed a range of styles from the most sycophantic of formal designs to the most radical of English parkscapes. Many factors may have influenced the design of specific gardens. The presence of large bourgeoisie-owned gardening firms account for the dispersal of specific designs in districts with a high concentration of new estates. The rapid increase in the number of landowners brought new demand into the landscape industries. The newly rich also reflected higher levels of anxiety about protecting their wealth. The land surrounding the house was designed to retain and enhance its value rather than serve as an object of value in its own right. It soon fell to the technical specialists to devise and model fashionable designs for the new bourgeois consumers.

I now return to a point I brought up in the introduction about the dialogic nature of consumption. Michel De Certeau reminds us that consumption is a productive process (De Certeau 1984). The mounting of a garden produces changes in the patron, the garden, and the producers of the design regime and its elements. Garden art changes the patron by imposing a representation of himself on his property that is narrower than he might wish, but that offers him the opportunity for identifying with a movement. The patron changes into a movement activist by virtue of mounting the garden. The mounting of a garden changes the design elements by forcing them to conform to a site for which they may never have been intended.

This recontextualization of design elements creates both a satisfying sense of originality, but also a dangerous expansion of the meanings of the elements in the design regime. Every subsequent installation of a design regime undermines the originality of the first installation. The mounting of a garden changes the design regime in large ways, such as the routinization of design, and in small ways, such as the mass production of fabriques. The rules for maintaining the design's integrity slowly evolve into a canon, and finally into the invisibility of the familiar.

There are times when the bourgeoisie, in whole or in part, seem to be following the aristocratic taste in garden art, and other times when the two classes appear to be following quite different stylistic paths. The key element is the interaction between the community's view of the style as a reference to the group or individual, and the patron's view of the style as associated with political views that coincide with his own. The design ensemble had to be seen as speaking on behalf of the patron. The ensemble must address the patron. Something had to convince the patron that he was the sort of person who invests in garden art of this style and has the material and cultural means to sustain the physical and representational weight of the ensemble. No matter how attractive the ensemble might appear to the occasional visitor to the garden, if the patron could not see themselves in the representative qualities of the ensemble, they would be less likely to invest in the installation (DuGay et al. 1997). Garden art patrons in the period had to first identify themselves as members of particular segments of their class in order to see the representational weight of a particular garden style as something to which they were willing to commit themselves.

The fluidity of this social and economic environment eroded the traditional boundary in the consumption styles of aristocrat and bourgeois, even as the political repression at the beginning of the nineteenth century sought to strengthen it. Each family was affected differently by this contradictory movement. Those bourgeois families that had the means to mount a symbolic resistance could do so through the poetics of the Biedermeier gardens. Other families signaled their identification with more conciliatory faux Baroque garden layouts. Still others sought to avoid all momentary political identifications by scrupulously maintaining pre-Baroque garden designs. The material condition of life determined how families located themselves with this social matrix. Those with newly made fortunes were forced into greater exposure. The suburbs were under greater surveillance than the older inner city districts. These different locations, in turn, opened people up or closed them off to a willingness to patronize Biedermeier garden art.

Bibliography

Althöfer, Heinz. *Der Biedermeiergarten*. Ph.D. dissertation. University of Munich, 1956.

Anonymous. *Neues Allgemeine Gartenmagazine* 2(1826): 25.

Auböck, Maria. *Die Gärten der Wiener*. Vienna: Jugend and Volk, 1975.

Bermann, Moritz. *Maria Theresa and Josef II: In Ihrem Leben und Wirken*. Vienna: n.p. 1881.

Bobek, Hans and Elizabeth Lichtenberger. *Wien: Bauliche Gestalt und Entwicklung seit der Mitte des 19. Jahrhunderts*. Graz-Köln: Verlag Böhlau, 1978.

Boyer, John. *Political Radicalism in Late Imperial Vienna*. Chicago, IL: University of Chicago Press, 1981.

Bürgerstein, A. *Die K. u. K. Gartenbaugesellschaft in Wien (1837-1907)*. Vienna: n.p., 1907.

De Certeau, Michel. *The Practice of Everyday Life*. Berkeley, CA: University of California Press, 1984.

Du Gay, Paul., Stuart Hall, et al. *Doing Cultural Studies: The Story of the Sony Walkman*. London: Sage Publications, 1997.

Fischer, Friedrich. *Die Grünflächenpolitik Wiens bis zum Ende des ersten Weltkriegs*. Vienna: Springer Verlag, 1971.

Gaheis, Ferdinand. *Spazierfahren in der Gegenden um Wien*. Vienna: n.p., 1794.

Hajos, Geza. *Romantische Gärten der Aufklärung: Englischer Landschaftskultur des 18. Jahrhunderts in und um Wien*. Vienna: Böhlau, 1989.

Hampel, Carl. *Die Deutsche Gartenkunst*. Leipzig: H. Voigt, 1902.

Hennebo, Dieter. "Gartenkünstlerische Tendenzen in Deutschland um Mitte des 18. Jahrhunderts." In M. Auböck, et al. *Historische Gärten in Donauraum in Geschichte und Gegenwart*. Vienna: Institut für Landschaftsplanung und Gartenkunst. 1 (1980): 15-41.

Hösl, Wolfgang and Gottfried Pirhofer. *Wohnen Wien, 1848-1938: Studien zur Konstitutionen des Massenwohnens*. Vienna: Franz Deuticke, 1988.

Johnston, William M. *The Austria Mind*. Berkeley, CA: University of California Press, 1972.

Kluckholm, Paul. "Biedermeier als literarische Epochenzeichnung." *Deutsche Vierteljahresschrift für Literaturwissenschaft und Geistesgeschichte* 13 (1935): 1-43.

Mosser, Monique. "Paradox in the Garden: A Brief Account of Fabriques." In M. Mosser and. G. Teyssot, *The Architecture of Western Gardens: A Design History from the Renaissance to the Present Day*. Cambridge, MA: MIT Press, 1990.

Oehler, Johann. *Panorama von Wien*. Vienna: n.p., 1807.

Pezzl, Johann *Neueste Beschreibungen von Wien*. Vienna: n.p., 1823.

Weidmann, Josef. *Die Rosenbaum'sche Gartenanlage*. Vienna: Strauss, 1824.

Widemann, Johann. *Malerische Streifzüge durch die interesantesten Gegenden um Wien*. Vienna: n.p., 1805.

Notes

[1] According to William M. Johnston, the application of the name "Biedermeier" was first applied to the period by the Swabian humorist Ludwig Eichrodt. He created the character of pious apolitical schoolmaster named Gottlieb Biedermeier in 1850. The name came to be associated with a design regime of the period from 1812 to 1848 in Vienna during a 1906 exhibition in Vienna of furniture design from that period (Johnston 1972). It was then applied to the literary style of the period by Paul Kluckholm (1923, 1-43).

[2] All of the translations in this chapter are by the author.

[3] The Biedermeier was a time of flower-mania (Cf. Auböck 1975). Many spoke their feelings through flowers, and not only through flower beds in gardens. Paintings of flowers commanded high prices and made the reputations of painters like Johann Knapp (1778-1833) and Franz Xavier Gruber (1801-1862), who specialized in flower painting. Flowers were the favorite motif on porcelain, glass, jewelry, furniture and wallpaper. This decoration permitted a closer integration of garden exterior and house interior.

[4] The Gurk lithographs were published together with an 1824 memoir (Weidmann 1824). These are among the most important documents of Biedermeier gardens in existence.

[5] A reproduction of plans shows how these ground plans were developed to fit any scale (Hampel 1902).

[6] Hösl and Pirhofer call this Hausdenken, 'house thinking', viewing the house as an interest-bearing capital in the form of goods (Hösl and Pirhofer 1988). Maintaining the quality of the building and its grounds protected the investment. The garden had to develop to beautify the land, but it also had to frame the house and display its charms in the best possible light.

風箏會

CHAPTER 8

Shanghai Gardens in Transition from the Concessions to the Present

Zhou Xiang-pin and Chen Zhe-hua
Translated from the Chinese and annotated by Stephen H. West

Introduction: The Opening of Private Gardens

As soon as Western colonial powers forcibly opened up its gates as one of the first treaty ports, early modern Shanghai was on the fast track to Westernization.[1] The foreign concession areas, miniatures of Western society, ceaselessly imported Western civilization and lifestyles into Shanghai. In the 1880s, on the heels of the first garden opened in Shanghai, the Public Flower Garden, a large number of private, for-profit gardens subsequently opened to the public. The first were two gardens opened on the west side of the bustling market at Jing'an 静安: the Shen Garden 申园, opened in 1881–81 (Fig. 1), and the Western Garden 西园 (opened 1884). These were followed by the Zhang Garden 张园 (1885), the Xu Garden 徐园 (1886–87), and the Yu Garden 愚园 (1890, Fig. 2).

These privately owned for-profit public gardens were constructed on the foundations of classical private gardens, and their layout and design features were exactly the same as traditional Kiangnan gardens. The three *mou* of the Xu Garden were filled with luxuriant trees and flowers and were dotted with pavilions and terraces at every turn. The Zhang Garden copied the Lion Forest 狮子林 and Fisherman Gardens 网狮园 of Suzhou, with fragrant grass spreading like embroidery within its walls. The Half Wusong Garden 半吴淞园 took its name from Du Fus famous couplet, 焉得并州 快剪刀，剪取吴淞半江水，"Where can I find a pair of sharp Bingzhou scissors, / To snip off half of Wusong River?"[2] Set in the bustling

Fig. 1. Shen Garden on Dianshizhai Pictorial in the latter part of the Qing Dynasty

Fig. 7. Bird's view of Public Park
Fig. 8. New International Garden

shift from "living apart" to a mixed pattern of Chinese-foreign residence. The superiority of modern Western civilization began to be clearly limned out in the architecture of the concession areas and the establishment of a city government. Compared to the narrow inner-city streets and the reeking polluted water of the city moat in the neighboring South City district, the concession area appeared clean and orderly (Fig. 6). The shock of recognition of this vast difference struck deep chords of both envy and shame in the hearts of people in Shanghai. Because of the complex weave of a paradoxical attitude toward those differences, the scope of Shanghai residents' material life underwent a dramatic change which was paralleled in the transformation of their spiritual life. One classic example was the way in which mass entertainment and leisure activity went well beyond their traditional scope.[8]

Following the explosion of population and the high concentration of merchants and traders in the concession areas, making a living in modern Shanghai became much more innovative and free. After advancements such as gas and electric light were introduced into Shanghai and then became widespread, the concession areas began to enjoy the reputation of a "city without night." People's schedules of activity and rest no longer were limited by the presence of natural light, and they shrugged off the ingrained agricultural work habits of "working with the sunrise, resting at sunset." Instead they borrowed the Western schedule of an eight-hour work day as well as "resting on the Sabbath."[9] They advocated a work ethic of being diligent and earnest during work hours, striving for efficiency, but then relaxing during a day off, pursuing entertainment to one's heart's content. In addition, the standard of living increased. Most Chinese had a cash salary and had enough spare change in their hands that they could spend freely—these factors accelerated the social necessity of leisure entertainment as well as pushed the slow development of a particular style of leisure.

Following the completion of a race track and dog course, foreigners imported public gardens into Shanghai that were meant to be open for the pleasure of everyone. In 1868, the Municipal Council built the first public garden (the Public Flower Garden 公共花园) along the banks of the Bund in the concession area (Fig. 7). Its fresh Western style, so different than that of the traditional Chinese garden, caused a stir among the people of Shanghai. But in the 1870's the famous sign, "No dogs or Chinese allowed"[10] elicited countless bitter lamentations over the injustice.[11] Honorable men sent up various letters to the Municipal Council, raising the question of negotiating over the issue of public parks. It was only in 1890, when the plan for "Separate Chinese and Western Gardens" was implemented that the Chinese had a garden that belonged to them alone, The New Garden 新公园 (Fig. 8). But it was only one-fifth of the size of the Public Flower Garden, and this little offering simply was incapable of fulfilling the dreams of the Shanghai commoner for a suitable garden in which to roam. In the beginning of the 1880's some of the gardens constructed by or belonging to private individuals turned, at some level, toward becoming more of an open public entertainment space. Even though this incorporated a paradoxical mental state which carried both a consensual hatred of the West (expressed as a desire to cleanse away the shame of colonization) as well as the desire to emulate Western success, from an indirect point of view it also reflected the slow historical process by which the general public's concept of public entertainment moved from adaptation, to acceptance, to viewing it as a substantial part of their lives. One can also see how this is reflected on the level of practicality.

Evolution: The Melding of China and the West

In addition to such external factors as a naturally superior geographical environment, highly developed commerce and trade, and a historical significance as an early port city, the evolution of private gardens in late Shanghai was also driven by intrinsic factors as well.

Like the majority of South China gardens, the source of which can be found in the culture of the traditional literati, the traditional Shanghai garden could be classified as a "garden where literati can express their lyrical nature." The private garden, situated in the busy metropolis, was "heaven in a pot," a miniature simulacrum of the mountains and rivers of nature itself and was a place where the owner of the garden could find momentary respite in the bustling city. Thus, its special features were its closed, carefully crafted arrangement, and its potential for providing a place for meditation and contemplation.

After Shanghai became an open port, Western learning gradually filtered into China and the old feudal system of China disintegrated a little more every day. In the environment of this new economy, the literati class was transformed and replaced by a new kind of landlord, comprador, and merchant class that was born from a prosperous urban commerce. The turbulent changes in social environment and structure transformed the users of gardens as well. The traditional Chinese garden, a product of a thousand years of slow development, was destabilized by the powerful shock of modern Western garden culture, and the boundary between the traditional garden and the outside world gradually eroded.

In addition, Shanghai had, before the late Qing, been situated in a remote corner of the empire, far outside the reach of politics, and the particular characteristics of the people there—their marginal, different, and tolerant nature—meant that the cultural frame of Shanghai classical gardens was never as densely textured as in other South China gardens. The inter-melding of multiple cultures in early modern Shanghai hastened the creation of a distinctly urban "Shanghai style culture," and the openness to the world that it displayed became obvious in the transformation of the private garden. Traditional and imported

Fig. 9. Zhang Garden in the latter part of the Qing Dynasty
Fig. 10. Arcadia Hall in Zhang Garden

cultures freely mixed in garden space, forcing the public nature of modern entertainment space to replace the closed and private systems of the traditional private garden. No matter whether in terms of general arrangement, the use of garden features, or the creation of aesthetic space, this newly evolving complex and heterogeneous shape was completely different than that of the traditional private garden.

The Heterogeneous Sino-Western Style

Traditional Chinese gardens had long been infused with the Confucian concept of "venerating righteousness and disesteeming personal benefit," and therefore clearly manifested a tendency toward a purely spiritual function, disassociated with any thought of profit, and they lacked any practical knowledge of the economic relationship between a "sense of pleasure" and "benefit" in the larger sense. Although the construction of the private garden implied a sense of recuperative pleasure, most were still only sites where literati could be introspective or experience a personal spiritual satisfaction. Material function had never truly been a guiding factor in the traditional garden. Moreover, taking its principles from nature, the traditional garden was good at creating a closed environment through its spatial arrangement in which there was an alternation between binaries of light and dark, open and enclosed, break and continuity. Through the techniques of "borrowing scenery" 借景, "opposing scenery" 对景, and "separating scenery" 隔景, they were able to unite the beauty of nature and the beauty of art.

Following the rise of parks in the concession areas, a completely new pattern in public entertainment space influenced both the concepts and the modes of activity in private gardens. The openness and public nature of activity of these sites—both in the conceptual sense and in material execution—were imported into for-profit private gardens. In order to satisfy the needs of the search for novelty and the complicated nature of urban life, the function of a pleasurable activity that was both dynamic and participatory emerged in the for-profit garden, where it accelerated and strengthened.

Completely open spaces of activity and the creation of large-scale architectural forms broke open the inwardly-oriented secluded and preciously wrought spatial arrangement of the classical garden, and turned it into a display of mixed Chinese-Western arrangement. For instance, in the Yuyuan Garden, there are both traditional scenes of small meandering paths and isolated secluded spaces, but also a western-style ambiance dominated by a large foreign building capable of holding five or six hundred people. In a description of the Zhang Garden found in a section of *The Beguiling Charms of Old Shanghai*, we can see the special nature of the English natural garden, with its leafy trees and bushes oriented toward the outside right alongside the meandering layout of the traditional garden, redolent with an ancient feeling (Fig. 9).[12]

Searching for the New and Novel: Elements of Garden Design

For-profit private gardens broke with the fluid flexibility of classical garden design that was planned, but non-structured, that is, both meandering and fragmented into locally meaningful units of space. To provide for the possibility of large gatherings and mass entertainment, they turned their backs on the most prominent architectural forms of the traditional garden—small kiosks, terraces, and pavilions—and brought large-scale Western-style structures into the garden as visual centerpieces. Concrete examples in the Zhang Garden were Arcadia Hall, which could hold more than a thousand people in its main hall (Fig. 10) and the Glorious Site of Sea and Sky, which could be used both for a playhouse and an exhibition hall. The large Western structure Dunya Hall in Yuyuan Garden, which was formerly called the Tower of Flying Clouds, while not as large as Arcadia Hall, could also hold five or six hundred sightseers.

The rock hills and streams created inside for-profit gardens were also influenced by Shanghai culture, and differed remarkably from those special elements of the classical garden. For instance, in addition to the imitations of natural ponds in their water views, garden visitors also loved the formal artificial water features imported from the West in which the use of fountains and other innovations provided an atmosphere of fashionable entertainment. In the same manner, the creation of rockeries seemed an appropriate method by which to compensate for the even terrain of the area. The thoughtful consideration of the function of such rockeries tended to supercede the surface aesthetics of the "layered mountain" structure of the classical garden.

From the standpoint of plant landscaping, the late Qing for-profit garden was influenced enough by western culture to pay more attention to the skillful use of colors in a variety of plant forms than to an intentionally implied signification of design that was perceivable only by those trained to see it. That is, the plum, the cymbidia, the bamboo, and the chrysanthemum, long the companion of the literati and poet in the classical garden, lost their status as the primary plants, like lead actors who had to share their roles now with exotic plants and rare flowers transplanted from the West. Additionally, western style lawns supplied a feeling of expansiveness to gardens, and the creation of appropriate green spaces, both dense and scattered, also had a practical function.

Take the Zhang Garden as an example: its superb transformations of land into green space and the beauty of its lawns were praised as the best of all of Shanghai. The owner, Zhang Shuhe employed horticulturalists to make his garden bloom nonstop through all four seasons: spring cymbidia, fall chrysanthemums, summer lotus, and winter plum. Zhang invited foreigners to the flower shows he held regularly in his garden, and their participation and interest in learning from each other

Fig. 11. Cymbidium Fair in Yuyuan Garden
Fig. 12. Kite Fair in Zhang Garden in the latter part of the Qing Dynasty

led to a wonderful advancement in the techniques of cultivation. In the Pan-national Chrysanthemum Fair once held in the Garden, no matter whether valuable specimens that were "completely white with two-finger wide petals" or grafted flowers "that opened up into the four colors of yellow, white, red, and purple, as though grafted but without any trace of being so,"[13] all were rare specimens.

Moreover, flowers and trees as created shapes were no longer limited to *bonsai*, but under the influence of the West, one could often see various forms of topiary, including every form of human and animal, wrought out of a variety of plants. "Such novel forms and wonderful fences are completely unique, not only in China but in the entire world."[14] At the same time, the Xu Garden and the Yuyuan Garden both held annual festivals for judging cymbidia (Fig. 11). In the for-profit private garden, the confluence of Chinese and western culture was given form in the marvelous and variegated forms of plants and flowers raised there, and this boosted contemporary knowledge of the techniques of plant cultivation.

The Weakening of the Aesthetic World of the Garden
From the third century onward, the fashion of eremetism had begun to slowly spread among gentry, literati, and officials. For them the garden became a place upon which they could rely to express their feelings or dispel sentiments of sorrow or disappointment. Therefore, when constructing the garden, the owner translated subjective emotions through each single plant,

each tree, each mountain or rock into external aesthetic objects. By this process, the garden could elicit the same emotional state again and again through the production of feeling as each visitor to the garden encountered one of those objects. Thus everything that was observed had a meaning: flowing water held deep signification, every bush and tree was a specific emotion. From each single foot of garden space, one could envision a thousand miles of distant landscape that led each person to be able to sense "image beyond the image itself, and sound beyond the string that produces it." This is what is meant by the "potential embodied in the aesthetic world."

In the early modern period, the meteoric fall of the literati class led directly to the dismissal of any process in the construction of private gardens that evoked the ideal of "escaping the political world and cutting off contact with the vulgar realm." A liberal and positive state of mind in this new space replaced that of eremitic withdrawal found in the classical literati garden. In the new Shanghai, a city overwhelmingly infused with a commercial atmosphere, the rhythms of a life of high efficiency changed the expression of sentiments from circumlocutive reticence to open and direct expression. Sparked by a Shanghai style consciousness that sought the new and practical, the establishment of novel garden vistas in for-profit private gardens indirectly reflected the state of mind of an owner that had discerning modern taste and a desire for the unconventional. Pool halls, soccer fields, ice rinks and other amusements were found throughout the park, and Yu Garden and Grand Flower Garden 大花园 had even once set off a small corner of their enclosures to house a menagerie. The original desire to make a profit was exemplified in the fact that seeking a momentary stimulus to the sense organs was more important than the calculation of any aesthetic sense.

Of course the habits of appreciation of the garden were not completely westernized. The aesthetic world of the for-profit garden maintained its inherent values, but these more or less had been tinged by the spirit of the West. For instance, name plaques were still mounted on lintels and there were still poetic couplets on the pillars, but their execution had new supplemental features. The name of the foreign-style hall in Zhang Garden, Arcadia Hall, was taken from a Greek pastoral paradise, but its name seems a perfect match for the original name of the Garden, Weichun 味莼 [A Taste that Evokes Feelings of Home], an unintended match, for sure. All other kiosks, pavilions, and towers in the park all had English names. In the paradoxical world of the Sino-western garden, the incorporation of western name plaques not only evoked the interest and powers of the visitors to make linguistic associations, but it also catered to the air of fashionable modernity of early modern Shanghai.

Influences: Social Benefits

Spurring Development of the Public Entertainment Industry
The opening of private gardens in late Qing Shanghai catered to the expectations that Shanghai residents held toward public entertainment, but it also kept commercial profit clearly in sight. As a new arena of public entertainment in the city, for-profit private gardens bore the imprint of "commerce" from the very beginning. A low ticket price to enter the garden as well as flexible price differentials for entertainments inside made consumption a matter of money rather than status, and anyone of any social level in the city who could at least make ends meet was able to use the garden in their leisure time and enjoy the pleasures of public entertainment. As leisure entertainment moved from an essentially agricultural focus on seasonal festivals to weekly or daily recuperative activity, the for-profit garden also hastened the transformation of its space from a localized

Fig. 13. Scenic Railway in Zhang Garden built by a foreign circus
Fig. 14. Picture of Lamp boats in Zhang Garden

phenomenon marked by class hierarchy and centered on the family to an open public space that, as a part of modern urban life, was dominated by market consumption.

At the same time as the success of the entertainment industry accelerated the competition between guilds, it also created a special awareness of the unique features of each for-profit garden. And because of these particular qualities, loyal and fixed clientele eventually formed around each place. The Xu Garden, with its cultured and elegant air, attracted large numbers of literati to compose poetry, to paint, or to gather to view the chrysanthemums. The grand and spacious Zhang Garden was widely appreciated by Chinese and foreign merchants as well as well-known figures from other social circles. Zhang Garden was a popular place to hold various social activities: banquets, meetings with friends, birthday parties, and weddings (Fig. 12). There has long been a popular saying in Shanghai, "West Garden is a comfortable paradise for students, Xu Garden is for famous people, Yu Garden and Zhang Garden are for the powerful and for prostitutes."[15] The production of particular groups of consumers for each of the for-profit gardens can be seen as an effective strategy of commercial competition, and it efficiently moved forward the cultural enterprise of public entertainment in early modern Shanghai.

The Medium for Importation of Western Culture

Since Shanghai was at the vanguard of westernization, after 1860 every Chinese and foreign commodity was brought together there. For-profit gardens, influenced more and more by the West, exhausted every kind of entertainment venue they could think of to entice consumers, always with an eye on profit and a desire to present the new. In addition to holding traditional Chinese venues for flower and moon viewing or composing poetry and painting, as they always had, they added on events that urbanites loved to hear and see—billiards, dancing, magic, and circuses. These entertaining activities were new and stimulating as well as delightful to the eye and mind and they opened up the eyes of Shanghai folk to a variety of new things (Fig. 13). Western goods that were just imported into Shanghai became both well known and popular through presentation in the for-profit garden, which became an important medium for the display of foreign rarities. Take electric lights, for instance. In 1882, this novelty, still new to the West, was imported into Shanghai where it attracted a packed house at its demonstration; but because electricity was unknown in China, people claimed that ". . .they were about to be struck by lightening; everyone became upset and panicky, and could not be controlled."[16] So there was no way that electricity could be used widely at first. But, in 1886 the Fengtai Foreign Trade Company used Zhang Garden, the most popular garden, as a site to experiment with new indoor lighting, and when the lights shone on that first night, people in every corner of the well-lit garden all sang its praises (Fig. 14). This event finally spurred the fast spread of electric lights in the city. Or, take cinema for example. In 1896, before the establishment of the first cinema house in Shanghai,[17] films were shown in Xu Garden, which was the first screening in Shanghai. Likewise, the Zhang Garden also had shadow play theater in which the light source was from gas lighting. In addition, although photography had been common among westerners in China since 1843, it was still regarded as a fashionable event until the twentieth century. The Photography Studio in the Gallery of Light Breezes and Clear Moon in the Zhang Garden was popular with visitors for its otherwise rarely seen outdoor photography, which utilized the garden's scenic sites for souvenir photographs (Fig. 15). The frequent introduction of various forms of western mechanical novelties made for-profit gardens a place bruited about in early modern Shanghai as symbols of modernity. And, for the people of Shanghai, it became both an important site to encounter the multi-cultural West and a window on early modern urban civilization.

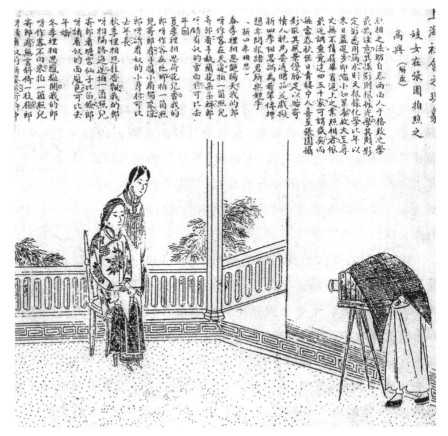

Fig. 15. Photos in Zhang Garden

Fig. 16. Members of South Society in Yu Garden
Fig. 17. Literators' meeting in Xu Garden

Hastening the Integration of Civic Consciousness

In the early 1860's Shanghai stepped onto the initial track of urbanization and was flooded with immigrants. However the special administrative structure of tripartite governance in a single city had kept the citizens of Shanghai from developing an integrated consciousness of belonging to Shanghai as a place. Neither did this structure allow for transitional stages from an identity conscious only of a regional district to one that was complex enough to allow a person to possess both a regional and a Shanghai identity. Following the inevitable growth in the complexity of social interactions between regional associations, for-profit gardens were able to escape negative limitations imposed by regional consciousness; the localization of public space, guilds and other confining spaces; and, through open space and orderly management of such, bring the Chinese society of Shanghai together as a whole. By reflecting the common voice of the collective group that used them, the gardens were able to forge from these disparate regional associations a common language, a common method of behavior, and a common cultural psychology.

As a place outside of the control of the Qing court, the concession areas were under the control of the Western colonial powers and were not subject to the prohibitions of either the Qing court or the Shanghai county government. The differences between Western and Chinese cultures seen in the gap between Chinese Shanghai and the concession areas allowed for-profit gardens to become sites of special public gatherings and public speeches. In 1900 the historically renowned "Congress of China" was held in the Yu Garden. The following year the Anti-Russian Congress was held in Zhang Garden. In 1903 the Shanghai Municipal Council passed new regulations about independent law enforcement in the British and American concession areas.[18] These regulations strengthened the for-profit gardens' ability to create a foothold for mass public meetings. In the same year there were three public meetings in the Xu

Garden to call for merchants to reject American commodities. Natural human rights and the freedom of speech, which were advocated by the West, found expression in the for-profit private garden, and some of these gardens slowly evolved into public fora for the intelligensia of Shanghai to freely express their opinions. Even the Yuyuan Garden, located in the center of the city, witnessed a meeting of thousands, authorized by the Qing government, to spell out the harm of opium. All of the public activities—planning organizations, gatherings for public lectures, or discussions of self-rule—allowed for-profit gardens to function as a site that both assured the modern western democratic right of assembly as well as helped to form a conscious awareness on the part of urban residents that they were "citizens of Shanghai" (Fig 16, Fig 17).

The Embodiment of "Shanghai Culture"

The flood of war refugees as well as awareness of the disparity between Chinese Shanghai and the concession areas produced the diverse characteristics of "everyone from everywhere living together." Later, under the creeping influence of Europe and America this developed into a multi-faceted culture formed by both traditional and imported ideas that, in the public entertainment space in Shanghai, burst forth with a new vitality. In literature it produced the Mandarin Duck and Butterfly Literature,[19] as well as the New Saturday Literature;[20] in painting it spun off the Shanghai style painting school; and the competition between the Shanghai and Beijing Schools of theater stirred up the whole age. These eventually delineated a phenomenon of an urban culture that was enjoyed simultaneously by the vulgar and the refined—Shanghai style culture. The receptive, all-encompassing, incorporative spirit with which it initiated all new fashions has been critiqued by countless scholars. Perhaps the most canonical statement was that from the pen of Lu Xun, "Those in the capital are closer to officials, those who made their way to Shanghai are closer to merchants." This vividly points out how the Shanghai school of culture, through first concerns for constructing a relationship with the market, simultaneously glorified both culture and commodity.

As a catalyst for Shanghai style culture, for-profit gardens, under the influence of a modern consumer market, became part of the daily lives of the urban dweller along with such public spaces as the street, district, and shops, and hence became an important site for daily communication among Shanghai folk. Each word and each line of the short articles, "On Ten Pleasures of Roaming in Zhang Garden" and "An Account of Night Roamings in Mr. Zhang's Garden That Recalls Home," found in the *Record of Sights and Sounds of Thirty Years in Old Shanghai*,[21] clearly show how much Shanghai folk enjoyed roaming in gardens where they had daily encounters with their neighbors. Simultaneous with finding pleasure and repose in roaming through gardens, Shanghai residents also learned of the rich pleasures of consumption of modern urban entertainments. This knowledge pushed consumer habits toward incorporating a multiplicity of pleasures which had the positive effect of generalizing and stabilizing the shared culture of Shanghai urbanites. For-profit private gardens were a product of the increasing movement of Western knowledge to the East. Not only did they appropriate that knowledge to create their own special features, but conversely because of resultant heterogeneous nature they became an important public space that drove the creation of this new urban cultural form known as Shanghai culture—both transforming the physical face of the city but also deeply affecting the state of mind of its citizens.

Peripheral Benefits of the Urban Green Space

Public gardens, in the true Western sense of that term, were born from the pollution, congestion, and turbulence that accompanied the Industrial Revolution in the latter part of the nineteenth century. From that time Western scholars were aware of the necessary function of the public garden in improving the quality of urban environments.

The development of urbanization in Shanghai in the late Qing also brought enormous changes to the physical aspect of the city. Broad streets, bustling traffic flows, merchants' shops set cheek by jowl, and tall buildings standing like a concrete forest: these became the canonical images of early modern Shanghai. But, on the negative side, all the hustle and bustle along the ten mile stretch of "Foreigners Boulevard" that ran the length of the concession areas—particularly construction and urban improvements—also brought a certain number of environmental problems. Therefore the grassy expanses and sweet smelling flowers of the for-profit gardens that appeared in Shanghai compensated its citizens with a green space that was open to the public. One could say, in fact, "Suddenly finding this little clean world in the middle of bustling, dusty Shanghai creates a place people are happy to roam and rest in."[22] Garden construction was no longer for a small number of owners and their friends, a place to possess for their own and their friends' enjoyment, but a place for Shanghai urban dwellers to relax body and mind and ease everyday anxieties. "No matter whether male or female, Chinese or Western, one can chase after another in the evening mists and sunsets of day's end."[23] Although for-profit gardens were based on considerations of making money, to look at their practical function in retrospect, they had an entirely positive influence on the urban environment of early modern Shanghai, even though it was probably unintended. Following the acceleration of urbanization, for-profit gardens with their expansive views, green lawns, and luxuriant trees and shrubs, became indispensable oases in the middle of early modern urban life. Their use and value followed the development of urban expansion: they expanded to the periphery, revealing themselves as urban forests, the "green lungs of Shanghai," the first places to function as modern urban parks.

Decline: The End of an Age

Being guided by a population that was motivated by commercial profit and was increasingly under the sway of "the popular," Shanghai culture became ever more conscious of what was new, and its tastes more and more manifest in "the mutation of the new and novel" and the "race for what was in vogue." For-profit gardens, appearing one after the other with each new tide, began and ceased in time with the vicissitudes of the commercial world. On the heels of the Shen Garden and the Western Jing'an Garden, a new generation of for-profit gardens appeared onstage fully made up in a completely Western way and their new and stimulating entertainment facilities assured that the older gardens would be deserted in the blink of an eye, with nothing to do but fold up and disappear. Later, the enticements of the spacious Zhang Garden stood out among all others, and its dazzling entertainments precisely matched the taste of Shanghai folk who were entranced by the new. This garden dominated all others. Although other new for-profit gardens opened up sporadically during this time, they usually had to shut down and close within the space of a few days.

As public entertainment areas, for-profit gardens had developed a few regulations about garden use over a long period of time, but the basic essence of these private gardens was quite different from those under the control of the Municipal Council in the concession areas. The privately owned gardens often changed ownership, so their planning and administration always remained unstable. As an early modern offspring of the classical private garden, for-profit gardens clearly showed a transitory form and, although they possessed certain markers of modernity, they could not completely escape the limitations of their traditional past. In Shanghai at the turn of the twentieth century, many sites that completely lacked any characteristics of a garden rode on this swelling tide of novelty and hung out their own shingle as "such-and-such Garden." Public entertainment sites like the "Night Flower Market" became places of profligacy and lust where rich merchants and idle gentry could let their passions loose; this caused a certain worsening of social behavior. Add to this the fact that for-profit gardens did not undergo the comprehensive planning that marked Western gardens so they expanded willy-nilly until they simply ran out of room. Some gardens, because they were in remote places, took a lot of travel time by boat or carriage. These symptoms of deficiency and instability predicted that the existence of these open private gardens was a transitory phenomenon limited by temporal circumstance. After the opening of "The Great World" amusement park in 1917, the three great for-profit gardens—Zhang Garden, Xu Garden, and Yu Garden—drew ever closer to their ends; the bustling scenes of the old days were gone forever, and the golden age of the for-profit garden was soon to bid adieu.

After 1917 several for-profit gardens opened sequentially: the Half Wusong Garden in 1918, the Rio Rita in 1930, and the Ye Family Flower Garden in 1931. Located in the southern part of the city, Half Wusong Garden with its scattered arrangement of kiosks and pavilions and towers stirred the feeling of being the perfect place to relax. The Ye Family Flower Garden was of the same ilk, its various rockeries and twisting and turning streams giving one the sensation of paradisiacal seclusion. And Rio Rita Village, constructed by the Russian Golnov (or by some accounts the Spaniard Fernandez), set off by beautiful slow music, exuded the flavor of a rustic European villa. In the last period of the for-profit private garden, those gardens listed here were never able to reproduce either the rich entertainment venues of the past or the milling, noisy feel of public activity. The role that for-profit gardens played before the advent of the comprehensive amusement parks like "The Great World," disappeared and they once again returned to the simple tranquility of the original classical garden. In the end, no matter whether a Chinese or Western garden, the simple fulfillment of this original desire to provide people the joys of visiting them carried the seeds that assured they would never usurp the importance of those sites that were for pure amusement.

After this, as the gardens created by Chinese multiplied, for-profit private gardens began to decline rapidly. One of the earliest gardens, the Shen Garden, as well as the somewhat later Xu Garden were both taken over by housing during the Republican era and the Anti-Japanese war respectively. The Half Wusong Garden was quickly taken over by machine factories and by an electric generating plant that served the southern part of the city. Even something so illustrious as the Zhang Garden could not avoid this fate, and its original site is now a residential neighborhood. The for-profit garden, a product of a transitional nature, basically vanished, winnowed out of history. The only one left, except for the Ye Family Flower Garden, which is now attached to the 1st Shanghai Tuberculosis Prevention Clinic, is the Yuyuan Garden in the center of the old city. Having endured violent turmoil and heartless wars, the Yuyuan Garden was restored and expanded between 1950–1960, becoming one of the most important historical and tourist sites in Shanghai.

Epilogue: The Harbinger of the Shanghai Style

Because of its special regional characteristics, early modern Shanghai became a cradle that was capable of nurturing multiple cultures in a mixed Chinese and foreign living environment. The for-profit garden that was given birth at this particular moment in time was only a transitional link in a developmental process that moved from concession area gardens to Chinese public parks. Whether it was the openness of their spaces, the public nature of their activities, or the public access to their facilities, from the start these for-profit gardens possessed a spirit of public sociality and entertainment that would later be found in modern urban parks. Newly added construction for performances, exercise, and teaching put education, entertainment, and leisure all within the single confines of the for-profit garden. Its special ability to cloak didacticism in pleasure was carried on to some degree in the post-1949 Soviet model of the garden as a place of "cultural relaxation."

If we follow the vicissitudes of the for-profit gardens, they are an indirect indicator of the difficulty the entertainment industry faced in its transition from late Qing Shanghai to the modern age. Simultaneously, as a new form of public entertainment space the gardens had a positive role to play in the development of urbanization and in the integration and production of a distinctly Shanghai style urban consciousness. As the modern fledglings of the classical garden, for-profit private plots were the first in a series of steps that led to the construction of parks by Shanghai city. After the municipality of Shanghai was established in 1927, the appropriate bureaus of the municipal government continued to establish city-owned parks, zoological gardens, arboreta, and the Number One Public Garden. This systematic creation of parks directly reflects the fact that a concept of "public park" was something that had become indispensable in the daily life of Shanghai residents.

In terms of planning and executing the for-profit garden, the melding of different elements of Chinese and Western style garden design, the cultivation of rare flowers and strange plants—even though one could not escape the feeling that there was overkill and too much diversity—could never reach the principles of design or the aesthetic feelings of the traditional garden. But the experimental methods used in the for-profit garden, like the initial use of expansive lawns, the incorporation of large architectural forms, the establishing of Western water courses, and exchanging of specimens and horticultural techniques, far superceded the older classical traditions and directly contributed to the spirit of a "Shanghai Style" that strove to be the first in all things. Not only was the for-profit garden something completely new for Shanghai, it also provided a positive example for the development of the "Shanghai Style" garden at a later time. After unceasing practical experimentation, important elements of structure and design plucked piecemeal from Western gardens soon went beyond their original symbolism as something new and rare, and instead continue to exist as important representative aesthetic and functional structures in contemporary Shanghai gardens. The special nature of the late Qing Shanghai for-profit garden, which was "brave enough to change for the better," and "worked to emulate the best of others," was tempered through the ages, particularly through the new reforms, openness, and more complex international exchanges of the 1980s, until it was no longer a simple mixture of Western and Chinese, but something that was and still is recognized in the modern world as distinctly "Shanghai style."

Notes

[1] On the history of modern Shanghai, see particularly Leo Oufan Lee, *Shanghai Modern: The Flowering of a New Urban Culture in Shanghai 1930–1945* (Cambridge: Harvard University Press, 1999). In the notes that follow, Professor Zhou uses the traditional Chinese citation system, which does not indicate exact page numbers. In the translation I have let these notes stand. Notes that I have introduced for the reader will be concluded by [shw]; I bear sole responsibility for the accuracy of those notes.

[2] The poem is entitled, "A Poem Playfully Inscribing Wang Zai's Landscape," (戏体王宰画山水图歌). The couplet artfully quotes the lines from a previous source about a painting by the famous artist Gu Kaizhi. The rough import of the lines is that the poet wishes he had a sharp pair of scissors to snip off the part of Gu Kaizhi's painting of Wusong Creek. Du Fu, of course, wrote this poem in Chengdu, far away from the area of Shanghai, and about another painting of a different watercourse. Du Fu's intent is to extol Wang Zai's skill as the equal of the most famous early painter [shw].

[3] Zhou Weiquan 周维权, *Zhongguo gudian yuanlin shi* 中国古典园林史. 2nd Ed. Beijing: Qinghua University Press, 1999, p. 452.

⁴ See Xiong Yuezhi 熊月之, "A Rich Commodity in a Rare Age: The Value of Research on the History of Social Life of Shanghai," 稀世富矿：上海城市社会生活史研究的价值, Shanghai Academy of Social Sciences, E-Web http://www.sass.org.cn/eWebEditor/UploadFile/ 20060321132337418.pdf [shw].

⁵ Although Shanghai prefecture had begun to establish parks that were directly under its control during the last part of the Qing, it was not until 1927, when Shanghai was established as a municipality that the establishment of Chinese parks really began to develop in a systematic way.

⁶ See Frederic Wakeman, Jr., "Policing Modern Shanghai," *The China Quarterly* 115 (1988): 410. The Small Sword Society joined the Taiping Rebellion in an attempt to overthrow the Qing government. They established their headquarters in the Yuyuan Garden. When they were routed, the colonial powers tore down the walls that surrounded the old city [shw].

⁷ The population of Shanghai nearly tripled in twenty years: from 1,289,000 in 1910 to 3,145,000 in 1930, see Zhang Kaimin 张开敏, ed. *Shanghai renkou qianyi yanjiu* 上海人口迁移研究 *Shanghai Population Migration* (Shanghai: Shanghai kexueyuan, 1989), p. 28 [shw].

⁸ Frederic Wakeman, "Licensing Leisure: The Chinese Nationalists' Attempts to Regulate Shanghai, 1927–49," *The Journal of Asian Studies* 54.1 (1995): 19–42 [shw].

⁹ See Yeh, Wen-hsin, "Corporate Space, Communal Time: Everyday Life in Shanghai's Bank of China," *The American Historical Review* 100.1 (1995): 97–122 [shw].

¹⁰ In 1914 the regulations for the Public Flower Garden stated, "1. No bicycles or dogs allowed. . . . 4. Except for servants of Westerners, no Chinese are allowed to enter." These were conflated by the citizens into the line, "no dogs or Chinese allowed" (华人与狗不得进内), which was supposedly posted on a wooden plaque at the entrance to the garden. It is a fact that the concession areas tried hard to keep ordinary Chinese citizens out of its environs, but as scholars have pointed out, it is not a certain fact that any such sign was ever posted at the garden's entrance.

¹¹ The regulations actually went through several revisions from 1894 until 1917; the regulation Professor Zhou cites above is the latest revision. All, however, carried the same import. See Robert A. Bickers and Jeffrey N. Wasserstrom, "Shanghai's 'Dogs and Chinese Not Admitted' Sign: Legend, History, and Contemporary Symbol," *The China Quarterly* 142 (1995): 446 [shw].

¹² Lu Qiguo 陆其国, *Lao Shanghai miren fengqing lu* 老上海迷人风情录 (Shanghai: Zhongguo fulishe, 2004), p. 46.

¹³ Anon. "Rare Flowers Display Their Fragrance" 奇花呈芳, *Youxi bao* 游戏报 11.9.1897.

¹⁴ Ibid., 10.30.1897

¹⁵ "Shanghai baimian zhi guan" 上海白面之观 (The Hundred Faces of Shanghai), *Minli bao* 民立报 (Min Li Bao) 12.27.1910.

¹⁶ *Dianhua qi diandeng* 电话器电灯 (Telephones and Electric Lights), vol. 12 *Qing bailei chao* 请稗类钞 (Beijing: Zhonghua shuju, 1986), p. 6038.

¹⁷ By a Spaniard named A. Ramos in 1908.

¹⁸ The concrete stipulations of this code were: 1. No Chinese or foreigner within the concession area may be apprehended or removed from the concession area without the clear authorization of the Mixed Court of the International Settlement; 2. No deputy from outside the concession area can enter the concession area on their own to apprehend a person; 3) Arrest warrants from Chinese officials outside of the concession area must first be sent to the Mixed Court of the International Settlement for authorization, at which time someone will be sent from the concession area to participate in the apprehension.

¹⁹ See Perry Link, *Mandarin Ducks and Butterflies: Popular Fiction in Early Twentieth Century Chinese Cities* (Los Angeles: University of California Press, 1981) [shw].

²⁰ See Timothy C. Wong, *Stories for Saturday: Twentieth-Century Chinese Popular Fiction* (Honolulu: University of Hawaii Press, 2006) [shw].

²¹ Chen Wuwo 陈无我, *Lao Shanghai sanshinian jianwen lu* 老上海三十年见闻录 (Shanghai: Shanghai Shudian, 1997).

²² Ibid., p. 87.

²³ "Shu shengdi naliang hou" 书胜地纳凉后 (Writing after taking the breeze in spectacular spots), *Shenbao* 申报 8.15.1878.

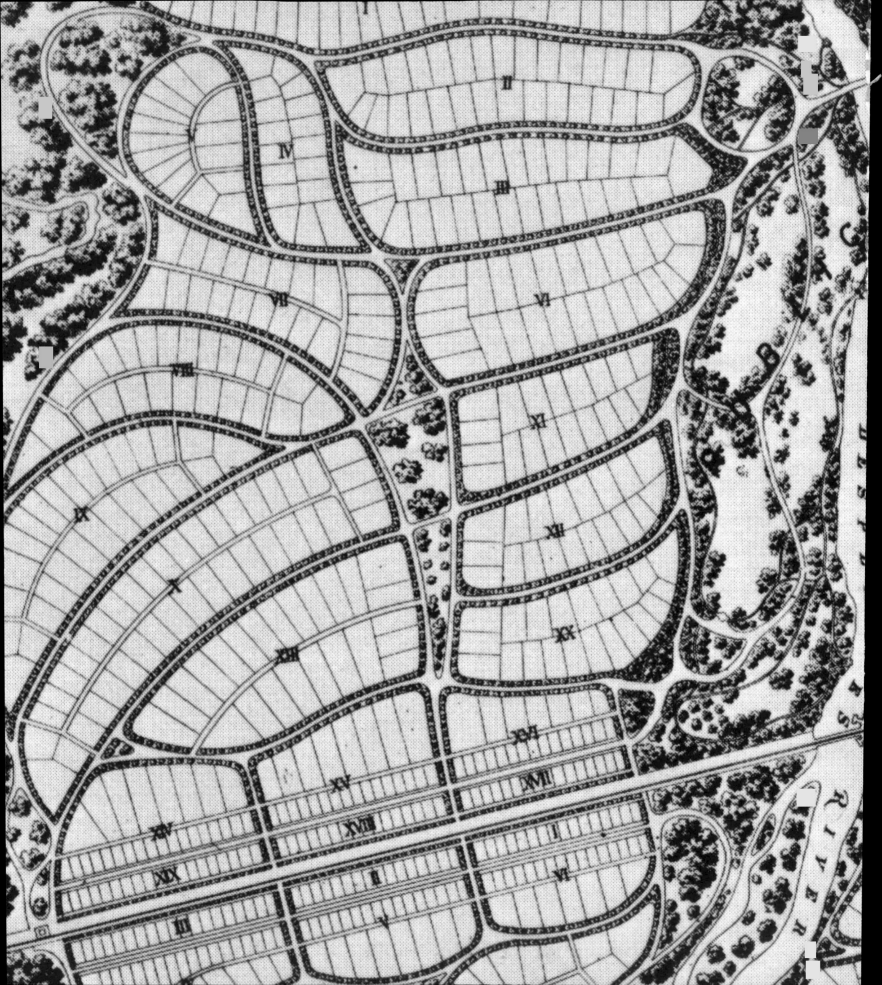

CHAPTER 9

Parks, Parkways, and Suburban Communities: Frederick Law Olmsted and the Modern Metropolis

David Schuyler

During 1868, Frederick Law Olmsted prepared a series of plans that sketched his conception of the modern metropolis. In a remarkably brief period of time, Olmsted articulated a vision of the city characterized by spacious parks, linked to distant recreational areas and residential neighborhoods by wide, tree-lined parkways that structured the direction of urban growth. Essential to his conception of the metropolis was the suburb, a residential neighborhood linked to the city by transportation technologies and infrastructure. Olmsted presented the framework for this new urban form in three principal reports he wrote in 1868. Although signed by the firm, Olmsted, Vaux & Company, they were written wholly or largely by Olmsted and represent his vision of a metropolitan area that served diverse functions yet was divided into discrete areas that incorporated the varying purposes—residence, commerce, manufacturing, culture—essential to urban life. In his reports to the Brooklyn and Buffalo park commissions and to the Riverside Improvement Company Olmsted established the foundations for comprehensive metropolitan planning and the role of the landscape architect as the form giver for the modern city.[1]

The Brooklyn Parks and Parkways

Olmsted and his partner Calvert Vaux shared authorship of the design for Prospect Park, the centerpiece of the Brooklyn, New York park system. Indeed, Vaux had persuaded James S. T. Stranahan, president of the Prospect Park commission, to set aside an earlier plan for the park prepared by Egbert L. Viele, and to seek a new design for a much enlarged tract of land. He also obtained the commission to design the park and invited Olmsted to return east from California and collaborate in the creation of a Brooklyn park. Two months after Olmsted arrived in New York, he and Vaux completed a remarkable report that sketched the outlines of Prospect Park (Fig. 1). Their January 1866 report drew extensively on Vaux's earlier report on park boundaries, which had cogently argued for the acquisition of land south and west of the original park, which became the site of the lake, the hilly area known as the Lookout, and the southern end of the Long Meadow, the sweeping expanse of lawn that is the park's most distinctive landscape feature. Vaux had also urged the commissioners to create a dramatic entrance at the intersection of Flatbush, Vanderbilt, and Ninth avenues, with an oval plaza to direct traffic into or around the park. Still other parts of the 1866 report paraphrase Vaux's earlier document. Clearly, Vaux was responsible for gaining the commission to plan Prospect Park and for the redrawing of its boundaries, which proved to be far more advantageous for park development than the site of Central Park in New York City. He also convinced Olmsted to set aside deep misgivings and pursue a career in

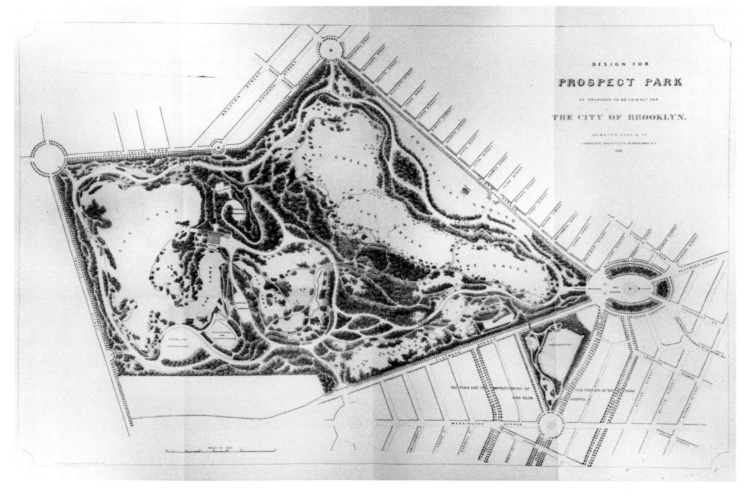

Fig. 1. Olmsted, Vaux & Company, plan of Prospect Park, Brooklyn, New York, 1866-67 (National Park Service, Frederick Law Olmsted National Historic Site, Brookline, Mass.).

landscape architecture.[2]

Crucial though Vaux's efforts were in securing the commission, his role was quickly eclipsed by his partner. When construction of Prospect Park began in July 1866, Olmsted became superintendent and Vaux began designing bridges and structures. Within the month Olmsted had four hundred men at work on the park. During the summer of 1867 as many as 1800 men were employed in construction, most of which was confined to the northern and eastern parts of the park because the lands to the south and west were not yet in the possession of the park commission.[3]

That same year the Prospect Park commission assumed responsibility for other park spaces in Brooklyn, and gave Olmsted and Vaux the opportunity to plan a system of parks that served different functions in distant parts of the city. The first commission was for Washington Park, which occupied the site of Fort Greene, a Revolutionary War redoubt. In their report and plan, Olmsted and Vaux proposed uses that they considered essential for residents of a city but which they considered inappropriate in Prospect Park, including an elaborate memorial over the remains of approximately 11,000 Americans who died in British prison ships during the Revolutionary War, a large space for public meetings, a saluting ground, and athletic fields for boys and girls from the densely-populated working-class neighborhood. When the Brooklyn Park commission acquired land for a Parade Ground located to the south of Prospect Park, Olmsted dedicated the site to the kinds of athletic events and military displays he did not want in the park proper. Other smaller spaces they designed included Carroll Park, a public square bounded by Smith, Court, Carroll, and President streets, where Olmsted and Vaux provided play space for children, walks and benches and other furnishings, and small lodges for the convenience of park users. More innovative was their design for Tompkins Park, a two block site bounded by Greene, Lafayette, Marcy, and Tompkins avenues. Turning the time-honored public square inside out, Olmsted and Vaux proposed planting the center of the space with large trees, framed by an elegantly planted ornamental garden between the trees and the street. Such a design would create a small but handsome park, a place for promenades and gregarious recreation, increase the safety to the square, especially at night, and enhance the attractiveness of the residential neighborhood.[4]

Together, Prospect Park, the Parade Ground, Washington and Carroll parks, and Tompkins Square constituted the beginnings of a comprehensive park system, the first of many such park systems Olmsted would create. The most innovative aspect of Olmsted and Vaux's work in Brooklyn was the system of parkways designed to extend the benefits of parks to distant areas of the city and to structure residential growth in developing parts of Brooklyn.

The Brooklyn park and parkway system was a remarkably imaginative response to the city's sustained urban growth in the nineteenth century. At the beginning of the century Brooklyn had been a small village of 2,378 residents whose merchants provided goods and services to the surrounding agricultural hinterland. But Brooklyn grew exponentially, at a faster rate than New York City throughout the remainder of the century. Following annexation of Williamsburg and Flatbush in 1855, it had become a large, populous city that lacked a coordinated street system. Each town had been laid out in a rectangular grid oriented toward the East River, but its irregular shoreline caused the streets of one town to intersect with those of adjoining municipalities at awkward angles.[5]

When the Brooklyn park commission asked Olmsted and Vaux to study approaches to Prospect Park, Olmsted perceived the opportunity not simply to create a few wider streets but to use park and parkway development to structure the modern metropolis. He had first explored the possibility of extending the benefits of parks through the construction of broad, tree-lined boulevards in his report advocating development of a park in San Francisco. In 1866 Olmsted and Vaux had sketched the outlines of a system of roads extending south and east from Prospect Park, while their 1867 report again urged the construction of a linear extension of the park, a wide shaded pleasure drive extending east from the park to a reservoir in Ridgewood. A gently curving drive following the contours of the countryside would "practically extend the Park to the rear of Williamsburg," a once-distant village that had become part of Brooklyn in 1855.[6]

The January 1868 report to the Prospect Park commission was Olmsted's first comprehensive explication of the importance of a system of parks and parkways to the structuring of urban growth. Brooklyn's street system, like that of most cities and towns, was a rectangular grid. Despite its "apparent simplicity on paper," Olmsted believed that the grid was an unfortunate choice for a city plan, as it necessitated grading and filling that drove up the cost of development or caused traffic congestion and other inconveniences that detracted from the quality of urban life. The grid was a legacy of the past, an anachronism no longer suited to the needs of the modern city; so was density of building, an inheritance from the time when cities were surrounded by walls. Olmsted associated this earlier urban form with military or political despotism, which was

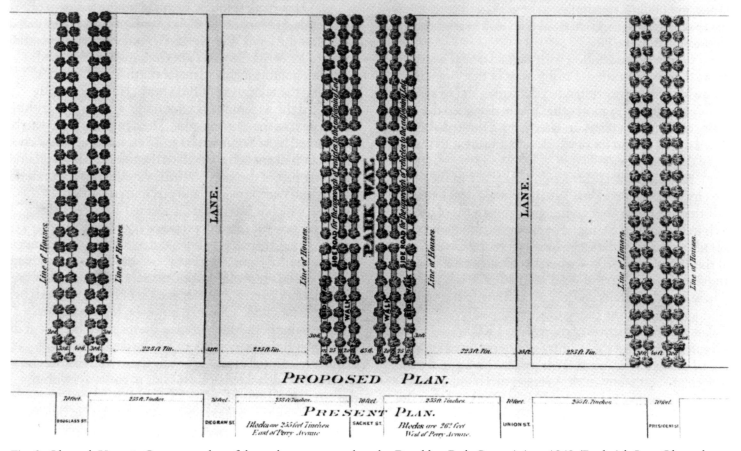

Fig. 2. Olmsted, Vaux & Company, plan of the parkway proposed to the Brooklyn Park Commission, 1868 (Frederick Law Olmsted Papers).

predicated upon the "excessive suppression of personal independence and individual inclinations" and which clearly had no place in the American republic.[7]

In succeeding paragraphs Olmsted traced the evolution of street plans from the middle ages through the nineteenth century. As urban populations increased, streets and sidewalks became more and more crowded: what had been "serviceable foot ways" in medieval towns had evolved into "unserviceable wagon ways" that continued to plague urban life. Fortunately, several important roads on the European continent suggested alternatives to urban congestion, especially the Avenue de l'Imperatrice in Paris and the Unter den Linden in Berlin. The Avenue de l'Imperatrice, which extends from the Arc de Triomphe to the Bois de Boulogne, had been constructed as part of the transformation of Paris under Baron Haussmann. Its central passageway was a carriage drive flanked by a walk on one side and a bridle path on the other. On either side was a wide median planted with grass and trees, then a service road, then another, more heavily planted median. The avenue was 460 feet in width and functioned as an "intermediate pleasure-ground" rather than as a "part of the general street system." The Unter den Linden, which extends between the Emperor's palace and the Thiergarten, had a central carriage drive between four rows of trees.[8]

Olmsted argued that a new system of wider, safer urban roads was imperative because streets were essential to the health and welfare of cities. And one certainty was the continuing growth of urban areas. He was not alarmed by this, because in terms of public health, social order, and educational and cultural institutions, the "larger each town has grown, the greater, on an average, has been the gain." Particularly important was the development of a new spatial pattern, the separation of dwelling from place of work, which Olmsted anticipated would lead to the creation of distinct areas of the city defined by function.[9]

The appropriate urban form of the expanding American city, one that built upon the examples of European boulevards, was the parkway (Fig. 2). Olmsted urged the Brooklyn park commissioners to create a "series of ways designed with express reference to the pleasure with which they may be used for walking, riding, and the driving of carriages; for rest, recreation, refreshment, and social intercourse." The parkway marked the newest stage in the evolution of urban form: it would consolidate the recent gains in public health and welfare, establish the spine of new residential neighborhoods, and extend the benefits of parks throughout the city.[10]

Olmsted and Vaux proposed that Brooklyn's parkways be 260 feet wide, with a central carriage drive, separated from a walk on each side by a row of trees. Another row of trees separated the walks from side roads that provided service access to homes in the neighborhood. Here was a new street system that established different ways for vehicular and pedestrian traffic, created shaded walks and drives, and increased the attractiveness of adjacent blocks for middle-class houses. Olmsted and Vaux established the routes for two major parkways in Brooklyn: Ocean Parkway, which extended south from Prospect Park to Coney Island; and Eastern Parkway, which extended from Grand Army Plaza toward East New York. The route of Ocean Parkways extended beyond the corporate limits of Brooklyn and thus represents a tentative beginning for metropolitan planning: the city had to seek authorization from the state legislature to acquire some of the land for Ocean Parkway, and Eastern Parkway extended to the border of Queens County, where it linked with another road. Clearly, Olmsted had begun to conceive of the need to plan comprehensively for the metropolitan area.[11]

The Buffalo Park System

The Brooklyn park system evolved as a series of pieces. The parks served different functions, to be sure, and when completed the parkways defined a graceful cityscape and brought open space to the neighborhoods through which they passed. But the elements of the park system were not initially conceived as an integrated park system. In August 1868 Olmsted traveled to Buffalo and for the first time had the opportunity to create a comprehensive park system. Following a hasty preliminary survey of three potential sites, on 25 August he addressed a public meeting to present his recommendations for park development. The *Buffalo Commercial Advertiser* reported that the landscape architect:

> suggested that, commencing with the base ball lot and grounds in the vicinity, a small auxiliary Park might be constructed, giving a beautiful river front; from this a Boulevard could be laid out, with roads for business and pleasure

travel, leading to the land on either side north of Delaware street north of the cemetery, where the Central Park would be located. Thence, by another roadway or Boulevard similar to the one first mentioned, to the elevated land in the neighborhood of High and Jefferson streets, where another small Park of thirty acres, more or less, for the accommodation of citizens in that vicinity, might be established, and in which, if the city carried out the plan of enlarging the Water Works, the tower could be erected.

Thus during his initial visits Olmsted established the main outlines of the Buffalo park system: a large, naturalistic park, a parade, and a promenade and civic ground at the Front, adjacent to Lake Erie, all of which would be connected by parkways and wide boulevards[12] (Fig. 3).

Upon his return to New York, Olmsted prepared a report explicating in greater detail the remarks he had presented orally. The purpose of a park, he asserted, is "to establish conditions which will exert the most healthful, recreative action upon the people who are expected to resort to it." Given the density of building, especially in newer parts of the city, he explained that Buffalo's park must offer residents "a character diverse from the ordinary conditions of their lives in the most radical degree which is consistent with ease of access." The most appropriate site for a park was one in which "natural conditions, as opposed to town conditions, shall have every possible advantage," as well as desirable topographical features and overall spaciousness. Almost by definition the only available sites conforming to these prerequisites would be some distance from the built area of the city—in the lands annexed to Buffalo in 1853. The most suitable areas for park development should be acquired immediately, Olmsted advised, before urban growth and speculation drove up the cost.[13]

As the principal site for park development Olmsted then recommended a 350 acre tract adjacent to Forest Lawn Cemetery. This large area had extensive meadows and handsome stands of old trees, while Scajaquada Creek, which meandered

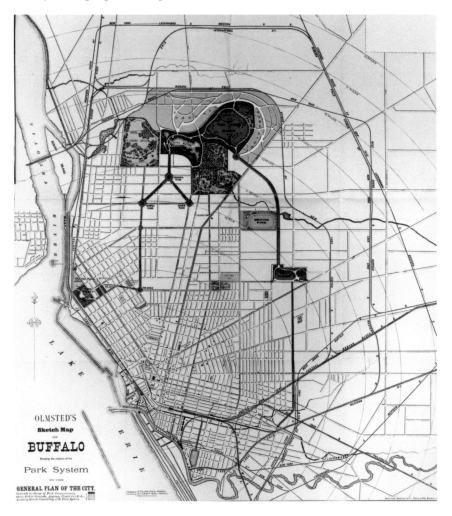

Fig. 3. Olmsted, Vaux & Company, plan of the park system for Buffalo, New York. 1876 map showing parks and parkways in relationship to the street system of the city (Frederick Law Olmsted Papers).

through it, could be dammed and formed into a lake. Here was an opportunity to create parklike or pastoral scenery, which in their 1866 report to the Prospect Park commission Olmsted and Vaux had described as "combinations of trees, standing singly or in groups, and casting their shadows over broad stretches of turf, or repeating their beauty by reflection upon the calm surface of pools, and the predominant associations are in the highest degree tranquilizing and grateful, as expressed by the Hebrew poet: 'He maketh me to lie down in green pastures; He leadeth me beside the still waters.'" Together, these water, lawn and forest features could be shaped into a landscape that was an open, tranquil alternative to the straight lines and congestion that otherwise characterized the city.[14]

Based on his experiences in park development in New York and Brooklyn, Olmsted realized that a naturalistic park, however large, should not be the only recreational ground within a growing city. Such a park provided for "recreation of a decided character, involving an absence of some hours from ordinary pursuits," and thus could not meet the needs of most workers except on Sundays or holidays, or of residents of distant parts of the city. Buffalo also needed smaller, more accessible parks in different neighborhoods "to which many can resort for a short stroll, airing and diversion, and where they can at once enjoy a decided change of scene from that which is associated with their regular occupation."[15]

As facilities for these other types of recreation Olmsted recommended acquisition of two additional sites, the Front, a thirty-two acre tract on elevated ground overlooking the Niagara River and Lake Erie, and the Parade, a fifty-six acre space near the eastern periphery of the city. The Front had long been a popular promenade, and when developed Olmsted predicted that it would "have a character of magnificence admirably adapted to be associated with stately ceremonies, the entertainment of public guests and other occasions of civic display." The Parade occupied the highest ground in the city. This predominantly German working-class neighborhood was especially advantageous for park development because it was "nearer to the more densely populated parts of the city than any other site having distinctive natural advantages." Olmsted undoubtedly also intended that the Parade be a facility for active recreation as well as military display.[16]

In addition to proposing three park sites, Olmsted outlined ways of linking them with each other and with the built areas of the city. In this he drew upon his and Vaux's earlier reports that urged the construction of parkways, which he grafted to the radiating streets of Joseph Ellicott's original plan for Buffalo. From the southeast and southwest corners of the park he proposed extending broad, 200 feet wide tree-lined avenues "adapted exclusively for pleasure travel." One would follow the course of existing streets southwest to connect with the proposed park at the Front, while the other would curve to the southeast to link with the Parade. Other principal thoroughfares, especially Main Street and Delaware Avenue, could be widened and embellished with ornamental circles that would be "suitable positions for fountains, statues, trophies and public monuments." These radiating avenues were more advantageous for parkway development than grid streets because of their greater width and the more direct access they provided to the parks. The result would be a new kind of cityscape, one in which parkways added a sylvan quality to residential areas and served as a spine along which new development would take shape as the process of urban decentralization continued.[17]

Following acquisition of the properties Olmsted recommended, in May 1870 the Buffalo Park Commissioners appointed Olmsted, Vaux & Company landscape architects, and the firm quickly provided preliminary plans for development of the park. As work progressed, the architects who were members of the firm—Vaux and Frederick C. Withers—prepared designs for the numerous buildings that would be erected in the various parks, including a massive Refectory at the Parade, a summerhouse, refectory, boathouse, and other structures for the Park, and a terrace and shelter for visitors at the Front. During the 1870s Olmsted also submitted plans for replanting Niagara Square and other public areas placed under the control of the park commissioners. The parkways too followed the general framework Olmsted had suggested in August 1868, as did the widening of streets that connected the older city to the new improvements.[18]

As the parks and parkways took shape, owners of land on the northern and eastern borders of the Park commissioned Olmsted to plan a residential subdivision. This must have been a welcome opportunity: at least since his 1850 visit to Birkenhead, a suburb of Liverpool, Olmsted had recognized the stimulus park development could give to the value of adjacent property, and his experiences at Central and Prospect parks confirmed that belief. However, "Parkside" was Olmsted's first opportunity to create a residential neighborhood that would complement the naturalistic landscape of a park. He platted curving, tree-lined streets and divided the area into large lots. In thus combining openness in building, proximity to the park, and convenient access to downtown, Parkside would develop as a suburban subdivision within the city.[19]

The Suburban Village at Riverside Near Chicago

During August 1868 Olmsted also traveled to Chicago to assess the suitability of a tract of land for development as a residential suburb, and the report he wrote became his first complete articulation of the components of the suburban community. The property was 1600 acres in extent, most of which had been known as Riverside Farm, that straddled the Des Plaines River about nine miles west of Chicago. In July 1868 Emery E. Childs had purchased the land, presumably on behalf of a group of investors, though the Riverside Improvement Company was not incorporated until 11 March 1869. The act of incorporation created a stockholding company and gave it authority to lay out and develop the Riverside property and to build a parkway between Riverside and Chicago.[20]

Olmsted toured the Riverside property on or about 20 August 1868. His first impression of the land was guardedly optimistic. "The motive is like this," he informed Mary Perkins Olmsted:

> Chic. is on a dead flat. The nearest point having the slightest natural attractions is one about 9 miles straight back— West. It is a river (Aux Plaines) or creek 200 feet wide, flowing slowly on limestone bottom, banks generally sandy & somewhat elevated above the prairie level & about 10 ft above low water with sandy slopes & under water a little limestone debris. As a river not very attractive, but clean water 2 or 3 ft deep, banks & slopes rather ruggard & forlorn in minor detail but bearing tolerable trees—some very nice elms but generally oaks mostly dwarf. The sandy, tree-bearing land extends back irregularly, so that there is a good deal of rough grove land—very beautiful in contrast with the prairie and attractive. 1600 acres of land including a fair amount of this grove but yet mainly rich flat prairie have been secured, & the proprietors are now secretly securing land in a strip all the way to Chicago—for a continuous street approach—park-way. I propose to make the groves & river bank mainly public ground, by carrying a road with walks along it and to plan village streets with "parks" & little openings to include the few scattered motes on the open ground. An excellent R.R. passes through it & a street R.R. parallel with the park way is projected.

Upon his return to New York Olmsted must have worked furiously to prepare the firm's *Preliminary Report upon the Proposed*

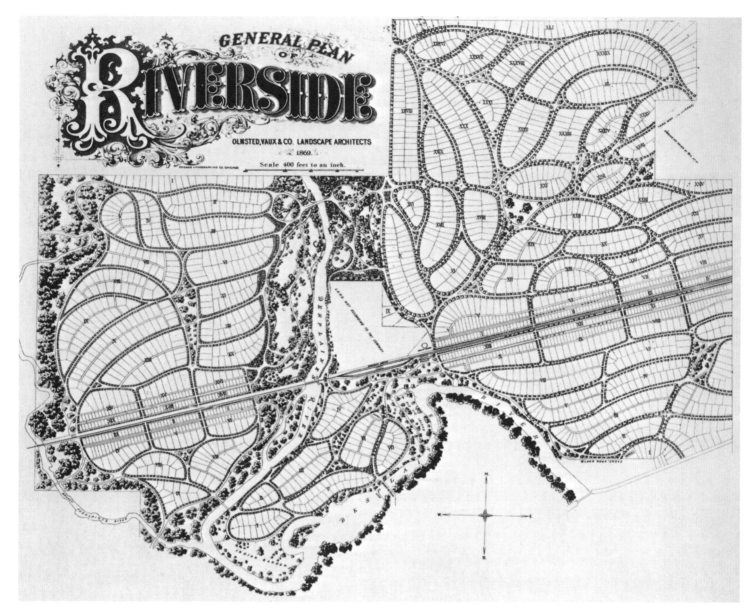

Fig. 4. Olmsted, Vaux & Company, plan of Riverside, Illinois, 1868 (National Park Service, Frederick Law Olmsted National Historic Site, Brookline, Mass.).

Suburban Village at Riverside, Near Chicago, which bears the date 1 September 1868 and which was signed Olmsted, Vaux & Company.[21]

      Olmsted's conceptualization of the design of Riverside incorporated ideas he had first formulated in his two prior ventures in community design. In 1860, he and Vaux had been appointed "landscape architects & designers" to the commission appointed to locate streets and roads in Manhattan north of 155th Street. In the fragmentary documents that survive from that project Olmsted articulated the importance of transportation routes as a means of directing and controlling an area's development. In 1865–66, when preparing plans for the grounds of the College of California at Berkeley, Olmsted established a clear line of demarcation between public spaces within the community—roadsides, parks, and communal

facilities—and the private, domestic landscape. The third element of the Riverside plan that drew upon Olmsted's previous work in landscape design was the parkway.[22]

Although these earlier experiences contributed to the design of Riverside (Fig. 4), Olmsted's report to the Riverside Improvement Company was his first comprehensive statement about the modern suburb, a carefully designed space in which "urban and rural advantages are agreeably combined." Like the parkways he envisioned for Brooklyn and Buffalo, the suburb was part of the evolving metropolitan landscape, another element in the "counter-tide of migration" from city to the urban periphery. Olmsted eagerly greeted the technological advances in transportation that made possible the separation of workplace and residence and thus promoted an openly built city. He predicted that a suburb such as Riverside, if properly constructed, would exemplify "the most attractive, the most refined and the most soundly wholesome forms of domestic life, and the best application of the arts of civilization to which mankind has yet attained."[23]

Olmsted's Riverside report emphasized the importance of developing a modern infrastructure, or what he termed the creation of "abundant artificial conveniences." He deemed the construction of well-engineered roads most vital. Even with efficient rail transportation to Chicago, excellent (and expensive) roads would be essential to the success both of the Riverside Improvement Company and the community itself. Infrastructure development also included the provision of a supply of clean water, thoroughly drained walks, and construction of such communal facilities as a nondenominational chapel and a business block, both designed by architect Frederick C. Withers.[24]

The streets and roads Olmsted designed at Riverside defined and structured the community, just as he had suggested to the commissioners who were platting streets in Northern Manhattan eight years earlier. First, he proposed an approach road, a strip of land ranging in width from 200 to 600 feet extending from Chicago to the suburb. This parkway would be an invaluable second link to the city, but Olmsted realized that such an approach road could confer other benefits as well: it would provide for the separation of commercial and carriage traffic as well as include paths for equestrians and pedestrians. The carriage road would be suitable for pleasure driving, and along its route Olmsted proposed places for "sheltered seats and watering places." As a promenade, the parkway would function as an "open-air gathering for the purpose of easy, friendly, unceremonious greetings, for the enjoyment of change of scene, of cheerful and exhilarating sights and sounds, and of various good cheer, to which the people of a town, of all classes, harmoniously resort on equal terms, as to a common property." Together with the railroad, the proposed parkway would enable residents of Riverside to enjoy the "essential, intellectual, artistic, and social privileges which specially pertain to a metropolitan condition of society." By 1871, seven miles of parkway with dimensions similar to those Olmsted recommended were being constructed.[25]

Within the suburb the streets would be characterized by spaciousness and gentle curves, thus differing from those of the city, where rectangular uniformity symbolized an "eagerness to press forward." Olmsted believed that suburban roads should "suggest and imply leisure, contemplativeness and happy tranquility." Like the parkways, the street system within the suburb would also contribute to the residents' sense of community. Between the roads Olmsted placed a series of open public spaces having the "character of informal village-greens, commons and play-grounds," with fountains, sheltered seats, and facilities for active recreation. In urging yet another provision for neighborly recreation, Olmsted suggested that land adjacent to the Des Plaines River be set aside as a park, and that rustic boat landings, pavilions, and terraces be built to enhance the attractiveness of the riverfront.[26]

Important as these communal spaces were, Olmsted also believed that the "essential qualification of a suburb is domesticity," and he clearly established a distinction between park and community. In their design for the Long Meadow at Prospect Park, for example, Olmsted and Vaux had created a sweeping lawn, visually endless in extent and surrounded by trees and pools of water. The function of park space was to convey to visitors a sense of spaciousness, of range, of rural tranquility not otherwise obtainable in a large city. By contrast, a suburb such as Riverside should provide for domestic seclusion. Families, Olmsted asserted, should be able to enjoy privacy both indoors and out. Shortly after reading Edward Everett Hale's *Sybaris and Other Homes* (1869), a series of fictional stories that idealized the communal aspects of suburban life, Olmsted gently protested that the author's ideas went so far as to place neighborliness above domesticity: "no house is [a] fit place for a family," he informed Hale, "that has not both public & *private outside apartments*," the latter defined by a fence, which Olmsted considered a "sort of outer wall of the house.[27]

A final element of the Riverside plan, evident on the plat but not mentioned in the *Preliminary Report*, was the provision of very small house lots adjacent to the train station. In an 1871 report he prepared for a company developing a suburb at Tarrytown Heights, New York, Olmsted termed similar spaces village lots. These he intended for homes for people of modest means who wanted to live in a suburban environment but who could not afford the expense of keeping a carriage. In both designs Olmsted located small parks near the village lots.[28]

Providing smaller lots within Riverside and Tarrytown Heights was important to Olmsted. He was acutely aware that most of the people who would benefit from suburban amenities would be the wealthy, who could afford the cost of transportation to and from the city as well as to purchase a spacious lot and house. Even though his professional obligations led him to work principally for the rich, he hoped to be able to extend the benefits of a suburban way of life to all classes. For example, at about the time he was formulating his ideas on Riverside, he tried to gain support for suburban subdivisions for families of the working class. Both his writings and his designs, Olmsted informed Edward Everett Hale in 1869, "urge principles, plans & measures tending to the ruralizing of *all* our urban population." His ultimate goal was the "suburbanizing of the residence parts of large towns, elbow room about a house without going into the country, without sacrifice of butchers, bakers & theatres." Thus Olmsted's prototype for the suburban community envisioned the same degree of inclusiveness he hoped his parks would provide for the people of the city. At Central and Prospect Parks, Olmsted wrote in "Public Parks and the Enlargement of Towns," "all classes [are] largely represented, with a common purpose, not at all intellectual, competitive with none, disposing to jealousy and spiritual or intellectual pride toward none, each individual adding by his mere presence to the pleasure of all others, all helping to the greater happiness of each. You may thus often see vast numbers of persons brought closely together, poor and rich, young and old, Jew and Gentile."[29]

Olmsted's plan for Riverside sketched an idealized community, a handsome landscape with public spaces yet also with secluded lots for dwellings. But the transition from plan to construction proved fraught with problems. By the fall of 1869 Olmsted concluded that Riverside was indeed a "regular flyaway speculation." As their disagreements with the speculative developers intensified, the designers were left with little recourse: on 30 October 1870 the firm negotiated a release from its agreement with the Riverside Improvement Company. In time, however, virtually all the residential streets in Olmsted's plan for the Riverside property east of the Des Plaines River—approximately one thousand acres—were laid out according to the plan, and Riverside became the successful suburb Olmsted had envisioned. Today, long since engulfed by the expanding metropolis,

Riverside's tree-lined, curvilinear streets stand amid a sprawling gridiron, its physical form a testament to the nineteenth-century suburban ideal.[30]

Public Parks and the Enlargement of Towns (1870)

Olmsted's 1868 reports advocating the construction of parkways, park systems, and suburban communities represented an ambitious, coherent attempt to control the direction of metropolitan growth. His vision transcended municipal boundaries to embrace the metropolis as a totality; city and suburb were interdependent entities, each essential to the continuing vitality of the other.

Olmsted synthesized these ideas in his February 1870 address at the Lowell Institute in Boston, which was published by the American Social Science Association under the title "Public Parks and the Enlargement of Towns." He had been invited to Boston by proponents of a public park there, and much of his speech drew upon his experiences in park development in other cities. Explaining the need to plan a park that would serve future generations as well as present needs, he advised the audience about what he considered the distinguishing element of a public park, a landscape that provided the "greatest possible contrast with the streets and the shops and the rooms of the town." This Olmsted described in terms of a broad expanse of turf that would convey to visitors a sense of the breadth of scenery, as well as woods and heavily planted boundaries to shut out the sights and sounds of the city. The park was a consciously designed though seemingly natural landscape that would meet the psychological and social needs of residents of the city.[31]

What was most distinctive about Olmsted's remarks, however, was the context in which he placed the parks movement: the assertion that Central and Prospect parks were, in essence, creative responses to urbanization. In the first half of "Public Parks and the Enlargement of Towns" Olmsted described the tremendous growth of cities as a global phenomenon and explained why he was certain that the rapid growth of cities and the "withdrawal of people from rural conditions of living" were fundamental, irreversible changes. Indeed, he recognized that the "further progress of civilization" was dependent upon the "influences by which men's minds and characters will be affected while living in large towns." But while many of his contemporaries found the prospect of great cities worrisome, Olmsted was optimistic: the urban population would surely continue to increase, he asserted, because cities provided access to educational and cultural institutions that were simply not available in small towns and villages. Moreover, the new urban infrastructure—transportation technologies as well as sewer and water service and other innovations that enhanced public health—increased the "comparative advantages of a residence in towns, and especially the more open town suburbs." Taken together, "enterprise and the progress of invention" were sure to "add rapidly to the economy and convenience of town life, and thus increase its comparative attractions."[32]

Olmsted demonstrated this by pointing to Boston and its environs. "It is practically certain that the Boston of to-day is the mere nucleus of the Boston that is to be," he assured his audience. "It is practically certain that it is to extend over many miles of country now thoroughly rural in character." Even as Olmsted spoke, farmers were straightening roads and speculators were platting village streets in a "manner of planning" that was sure to detract from the quality of life in suburban Boston in the years to come. The solution Olmsted advocated required a different kind of planning that embraced the metropolitan area as a totality. The modern city he envisioned incorporated the separation of workplace and dwelling, which was made possible as the network of railroads, ferries, and street railways extended the limits of the walking city. The metropolis would consist of a densely-built commercial center as well as urban and suburban residential areas with space around the house for trees and gardens. Parkways would extend the benefits of parks throughout the city, serve as the spine around which new residential neighborhoods would take shape, and link suburban communities with the city. The new realities of urban life made possible an exciting range of intellectual, social, and cultural experiences, but Olmsted effectively argued that these would not come to fruition if cities continued to grow as they had in the past. Only planning on a metropolitan scale would ensure that citizens be able to enjoy the advantages of living in a modern metropolis.[33]

Bibliography

Beveridge, Charles E. "The California Origins of Olmsted's Landscape Design Principles for the Semiarid American West," in Ranney 1990, 449-73.

Beveridge, Charles E., and Carolyn F. Hoffman, eds. *The Papers of Frederick Law Olmsted, Supplementary Series 1: Writings on Public Parks, Parkways, and Park Systems*. Baltimore: Johns Hopkins University Press, 1997.

Beveridge, Charles E., and David Schuyler, eds. *The Papers of Frederick Law Olmsted, vol. 3: Creating Central Park, 1857-1861*. Baltimore: Johns Hopkins University Press, 1983.

Brooklyn Park Commissioners, *Annual Reports, 1861-1873*. Brooklyn: Brooklyn Park Commission, 1873.

Buffalo Commercial Advertiser, Aug. 26, 1868.

Buffalo Park Commissioners, *First Annual Report of the Buffalo Park Commissioners, January 1871* (Buffalo, 1871).

Hammack, David. "Comprehensive Planning Before the Comprehensive Plan," in Daniel Schaffer, ed. *Two Centuries of American Planning*. Baltimore: Johns Hopkins University Press, 1988.

Jackson, Kenneth T. *Crabgrass Frontier: The Suburbanization of the United States*. (New York: Oxford University Press, 1985.

Kowsky, Francis R., ed. *The Best Planned City: The Olmsted Legacy in Buffalo*. Buffalo: Burchfield Art Center, 1992.

Kowsky, Francis R. *The Architecture and Life of Frederick Clarke Withers*. Middletown, Conn: Wesleyan University Press, 1980.

Kowsky, Francis R. "Municipal Parks and City Planning: Frederick Law Olmsted's Buffalo Park and Parkway System," *Journal of the Society of Architectural Historians* 46 (Mar. 1987): 49-64.

Olmsted, Frederick Law, "The Future of New York," *New-York Tribune*, 31 Dec. 1879.

Peterson, Jon A. *The Birth of City Planning in the United States, 1840-1917*. Baltimore: Johns Hopkins University Press, 2003.

Ranney, Victoria Post et al., eds. *The Papers of Frederick Law Olmsted, vol. 5: The California Frontier, 1863-1865*. Baltimore: Johns Hopkins University Press, 1990.

Riverside in 1871, with a Description of Its Improvements. Together with Some Engravings of Views and Buildings. Chicago: D. & C.H. Blakely, 1871.

Schultz, Stanley K. *Constructing City Culture: American Cities and City Planning, 1800-1920*. Philadelphia: Temple University Press, 1989.

Schuyler, David. *The New Urban Landscape: The Redefinition of City Form in Nineteenth-Century America*. Baltimore: Johns Hopkins University Press, 1986.

Schuyler, David, and Jane Turner Censer, eds. *The Papers of Frederick Law Olmsted, vol. 6: The Years of Olmsted, Vaux & Company, 1865-1874*. Baltimore: Johns Hopkins University Press, 1992.

Vaux, Calvert. "Preliminary Report on Boundaries," Feb. 1865, in Brooklyn Park Commissioners, *Annual Reports of the Brooklyn Park Commissioners, 1861-1873*. Brooklyn: Brooklyn Park Commission, 1873.

Notes

[1] Schuyler and Censer 1992, 18-27, 29-32. Historians continue to debate the origins of city planning. Stanley Schultz, for example, argues that as early as the 1820s, attorneys, engineers, physicians and public health officials, and others anticipated the need for comprehensive planning long before the emergence of the profession of planning. David C. Hammack focuses on the career of Andrew H. Green to make a similar argument. By contrast, Jon A. Peterson traces the origins of city planning to 1840, in the work of sanitary reformers, landscape architects, and engineers, but interprets these as antecedents to comprehensive planning. See Schultz 1989, Hammack 1988, and Peterson 2003.

[2] Vaux 1865, 80-84; Beveridge and Hoffman 1997, 80-106; Schuyler and Censer 1992, 18-21.

[3] Schuyler and Censer 1992, 21-22, 99-100.

[4] Brooklyn Park Commissioners, *Annual Reports 1861-1873*, 165-67, 229-31, 235-39; Schuyler and Censer 1992, 202-08, 309-12, 333-34, 339, 395-99.

[5] Jackson 1985, 25-32.

[6] Ranney 1990, 536-42; Beveridge and Hoffman 1997, 105-6, 114-41; Schuyler and Censer 1992, 157-59.

[7] Beveridge and Hoffman 1997, 12-14, 112-46; Schuyler 1986, 169-71, 174-75.

[8] Beveridge and Hoffman 1997, 117-24, 134 Beveridge and Schuyler 1983, 348-49.

[9] Beveridge and Hoffman 1997, 124-30.

[10] Beveridge and Hoffman 1997, 130-32.

[11] Beveridge and Hoffman 1997, 134-40.

[12] Schuyler and Censer 1992, 266-73; *Buffalo Commercial Advertizer*, 26 Aug. 1868, 3.

[13] Beveridge and Hoffman 1997, 160-61. Although he wrote the report on behalf of the firm of Olmsted, Vaux & Company, Olmsted was the sole author: Vaux was in England at the time of the Buffalo visit and the writing of the report.

[14] Beveridge and Hoffman 1997, 162-66, 90-91.

[15] Beveridge and Hoffman 1997, 164, 161.

[16] Beveridge and Hoffman 1997, 162.

[17] Beveridge and Hoffman 1997, 165-66; Buffalo Park Commissioners 1871, 5-12, 20. See also the essays by David Schuyler, Charles E. Beveridge, and Francis R. Kowsky in Kowsky 1992.

[18] Kowsky 1987, 56-58; Beveridge and Hoffman, 170n18.

[19] Kowsky 1987, 62-63.

[20] Schuyler and Censer 1992, 266-73, 289n1; Olmsted to E. C. Larned, 10 Nov. 1868 and Frederick C. Withers to Olmsted, 16 Nov. 1868, both in Frederick Law Olmsted Papers, Manuscript Division, Library of Congress, Washington, D.C.

[21] Schuyler and Censer 1992, 266-67, 289nn. Again, Olmsted was sole author of the report, and probably of the plan as well, as Vaux was in Europe.

[22] Schuyler and Censer 1992, 266-73; Beveridge and Schuyler 1983, 259-69; Beveridge 1990, 449-73; Ranney 1990, 546-73.

[23] Schuyler and Censer 1992, 273-75.

[24] Schuyler and Censer 1992, 273, 280-86; Kowsky 1980, 94-96.

[25] Beveridge and Schuyler 1983, 259-69; Schuyler and Censer 1992, 277-78; *Riverside in 1871* 1871, 19-20.

[26] Schuyler and Censer 1992, 280, 288.

[27] Beveridge and Hoffman 1997, 287; Schuyler and Censer 1992, 277-78; Schuyler 1986, 162-63.

[28] Schuyler and Censer 1992, 503-22; Olmsted to Calvert Vaux, n. d. [1871], Olmsted Papers.

[29] Schuyler and Censer 1992, 346-49; Beveridge and Hoffman 1997, 186.

30. Schuyler and Censer, 31-32, 291-93, 343-50; Vaux to Olmsted, 11 Apr. 1870, Olmsted Papers; Schuyler 1986, 165.
31. Beveridge and Hoffman 1997, 189-90.
32. Beveridge and Hoffman 1997, 179, 177.
33. Beveridge and Hoffman 1997, 181-82, passim.

CHAPTER 10

Swedish Mid-Century Utopia: Park Design as a Tool for Societal Improvements

Thorbjörn Andersson

Stockholm hosted the International Federation of Landscape Architects (IFLA) World Congress for the first and hitherto only time in 1952 (Fig. 1). On that occasion, Holger Blom, the director of the Stockholm Park Department—not without pride—could present the results of his work: the city with the world's most progressive park policy. Blom was foremost among the design professionals who had led Swedish landscape architecture into a new era and changed the form as well as the function of the parks. In their form, the parks now comprised a network that infiltrated the city; green space had become an integral and symbiotic part of the urban fabric. Earlier ideals had seen the parks as lush oasis, contained spaces that were secular to the city, serving as antidotes to the city surroundings. To the contrary, the parks now served as outdoor living rooms for everyday life, a critical complement to apartment living. In the 1950s, these new roles for the parks had matured and reached their fulfilment, now allowing harvesting efforts that had begun in the early 1930s. One reason for the parks' success was the part they played in a comprehensive program propelling ideological change for the entire society, a mid-century Utopia developing along the ideology of modernism. This general ambition for society has to be explained at some length because it provided the framework for the era's achievements in many different fields, including landscape architecture.

An Utopia Aiming at Deep and Intimate Changes

During the decades bracketing the middle of the twentieth century, Sweden demonstrated how political ideas could be successfully implemented within a society using landscape architecture, architecture, and urban planning as important vehicles. Over a period of forty years, from the early 1930s to the 1970s, a shared vision of a new, modern society of the future brought politicians and civil servants, ideologists, and experts in a close collegial cooperation. Their efforts resulted in what can be called a new national identity. This ambitious experiment in social and political reform was eventually christened the *Swedish model*, a model that showed a middle way between market and planned economy.[1]

This development was triggered by close to disastrous conditions. In the 1930s, the country was paralyzed by a strong economic recession. Machines in the factories stood inactive, and outside the closed industry gates fired workers flocked, now without jobs. Where factories and workshops were still in business, wages were pressed down to ten to twenty percent from former levels. Women were generally preferred as labor since they demanded less pay, and men often had to take governmental

Fig. 1. Urban designers during the modernist era saw the parks as integrated parts of the city. Norr Mälarstrand. Photo C.G. Rosenberg.

Fig. 2. The new parks emphazised use for all ages. Playground at Norr Mälarstrand. Photo C.G. Rosenberg.

work through the so-called unemployment commission, which meant road construction labor in the northern parts of the country, located a long way from home. It was certainly not a favorable time to grow and raise a family.

As a logical consequence, very few children were born in Sweden. The birth rate was among the lowest in Europe. In addition, an estimated one-third of the children in the country suffered from malnutrition. The death rate among infants was among the highest in Europe. The political rightwing feared that the Swedish population would be wiped out, leaving the country without any assets for production. They saw the birth rate deficit as a sign of declining morality, or in clear language a sign that people used contraceptives.

The political left adopted a quite different explanation. The social democrat party claimed that the low birth rate originated in the bad economic and social condition of the working class in the country. They stressed the importance of social reforms: free health care to all children, free school lunches, free schools, and free childcare during working hours were among the demands. The fact that, on the labor market, women were more attractive than men meant that they spent more time away from home, making childcare even harder.

Big strikes occurred in the decade of the 1930s. In 1932, two million strike days were counted, in 1933 more than five million days. In 1932, the Social Democrats won the parliamentary election and came to political power under the leadership of Prime Minister Per Albin Hansson. A number of stately commissions were started: the Social Housing Commission in 1933 and the so-called Population Commission 1935. The commissions had to investigate living conditions in the country and find in-depth answers to the important questions: Why were so few children born in Sweden? And how could that be changed?[2]

Poor physical health of the people was one key factor. Sun, light and fresh air were pointed out as important assets in the struggle against tuberculosis, which had especially plagued the capital Stockholm since the 1890s. The 1930s was the decade of the soap and the broom. The housing situation also was crucial. The Social Democrat movement started several property owning organizations with the purpose to construct quality housing for the working class. The building construction industry was also used as a political tool to raise the employment figures and get the country economically back on its feet.[3]

In the summer of 1930 a new type of architecture was presented at the so-called Stockholm Exhibition. The buildings on display featured extensive windows to let the sun in, open terraces to permit direct contact with fresh air, and generous contacts with the garden and landscape. The buildings resembled white boxes stacked on top of each other. There were no embellishments on the facades that might have collected germs, the color used was predominately a sanitary white, and the interiors also gave an impression of cleanliness and hygienic control. The exhibition was accompanied by a written manifesto, a book called *Acceptera* (Accept) (Fig. 2).

During the 1930s the first housing areas around Stockholm showing signs of the new ideology were built. The houses were slim in volume to permit free flowing air and sunlight from two sides, the roofs were flat to allow for roof terraces open to the sun and the breeze. The day-care centers were located on the top floor to access the terraces.[4] Free day-care centers for children were established in the public parks where they could participate in different activities under the surveillance of educated staff. The service was without charge and this social day-care activity spread over time to most city parks in Stockholm.

The education of the new generation constituted another important family issue. It was clearly class related. The upper class had been in political as well as economic control. Its members owned the factories and their children were consequently educated to carry on their legacy. The working class, lacking political as well as economic power, sold labor to factory owners. It also entertained different ideals: universal suffrage, mass education, and a democratic society. Little by little three cornerstones —the value of labor, the power of knowledge and a collective spirit—stood out in the Social Democrats vision of how to bring up the new generation.[5]

Many results of the governmental commissions about family, children and childcare were spread through "The Laborers Education Organization" ABF (*Arbetarnas Bildningsförbund*). In the beginning information revolved around sanitary issues and physical health. But psychological aspects were soon added. The predominant genetic school of psychology, which among other places grew rapidly in Nazi Germany, put forward that genes directed human behavior. The newly founded psychoanalysis was regarded as politically radical. In 1931, ABF started a study group in child psychology. The instructor was Alva Myrdal (1902–1986). She was a young and ambitious Social Democrat, who from the very beginning opposed the genetic school.[6]

Alva Myrdal saw the woman of the future as a person with her own professional career and in control of her own economy. New principles for child raising should release housewives from domestic burdens and give them opportunities for paid work rather than childcare. She advocated that children should be left alone part of the day to experience a "healthy solitude". Children should be trained to be independent, said Alva Myrdal, lest they suffer bad consequences later in life. Alva Myrdal became one of the leading Social Democrat ideologists and was a cabinet minister in the Swedish government during 1966-73.[7]

The attempt to create a modern life for women, an early edition of what is today called the gender system or the gender hierarchy, was a strong driving force behind Swedish welfare politics. In agricultural society, man and woman shared

responsibility in the household, mutually contributing to work in integrated fashion.[8] The industrialization process had ruined this gender balance between husband and wife. Now the husband took a higher responsibility to support the whole family and the wife was tied to the home, creating a situation where the wife became economically dependent on her husband.[9] In Sweden, this became one of the most important political issues (Fig. 3).

Social Democrats pursuing a large shift in Swedish society faced up to the challenge of bridging the gap between utopian blueprints and programs on one side and the construction of a welfare state on the other. They put a clear emphasis on the "little life," the everyday conditions of the common man, thus

Fig. 3. Declining birth rates triggered modernist ideology in Sweden. Norr Mälarstrand. Photo C.G. Rosenberg.

differentiating the Swedish version of socialism from other contemporary examples.[10]

Prime Minister Per Albin Hansson coined a term—*folkhemmet*—the people's home—that greatly contributed to its methods and goals. The people's home is a metaphor for the nation, seen as an expanded image of the intimate family and its happy life in a home constructed for that purpose.

Industrial Europe had given birth not only to the working class but also to the bourgeoisie.[11] And tensions between factory owners and labor gave rise to class societies everywhere. Swedish social democracy, however, transformed a "factory"-oriented society into a "home"-oriented one with surprising speed. The factory is a central imaginary place in Marxist writings and later in the discourse of international socialism that links political issues with the male world and with "public" as opposed to "private" activities. The Home (house) as an imaginary reference for political interest breaks away from traditional gender hierarchies and also turns upside down the left/right political agenda. Socialism in the Swedish version was directed at the female (since the woman took care of the home) and to the private (since the domestic sphere was private as opposed to the public arena of the factory). From the conservative point of view, private life should be excluded from any government intervention, since the state has to leave initiative and freedom to individuals for directing their own lives. In the 1930s, however, the fate of a majority of Swedish families was simply not acceptable to Social Democrats, and issues concerning nucleus family everyday life consequently became central to their action. From a historical perspective, domestic issues and all issues of privacy had always been the home ground of the conservative ideology of individualism. Social Democrats' political interventions moved into this private world and filled it with a radically new content.[12]

Sweden had a standard of housing considerably lower than other industrialized countries in Europe, especially Germany and Great Britain. These conditions left an open field to be exploited politically by the leftist movement, and may have encouraged the choice of an alternate way towards socialism.[13] Building "the house" as the strategy for Swedish social democracy reverberated on all aspects of the Swedish welfare state; Alva Myrdal often used the word "house" to describe her utopian model of society, large housing neighborhoods were built, and quality regulations for the building industry were established on the basis of research on family life and social matters.[14] And, as we shall see, governmental initiatives started advocating new ways of conducting family life.

Alva and her husband Gunnar Myrdal (1898—1987) were intellectual, radical and "modern," typical features of social engineers active during this almost heroic era of reform. In a letter from Alva Myrdal to family friends, Eve and Arthur Byrnes, we find the self-portrait of this distinctive group: "young people who want to be free to criticise anything (—-) keeping together as a group because they want to be constructive. They are all expert in different fields and all enjoy prestige in their fields, but they are at the same time all friends and probably the most unspoken group in this country (—-) I am warming up on the subject but I simply love these people. Especially our architect friends (—-) They form in Sweden the avant-garde of constructive social radicalism and are very far from sterile aesthetics (…)[15] Later in this letter, Alva Myrdal states in bold letters: "And I am building a house."

This metaphor was even turned into reality. In the same letter Alva Myrdal writes: "We (Alva Myrdal and Sven Markelius) came up with the idea of building a "kollektivhus" (collective house), an ideal family hotel with a cooperative organization taking care of all your material needs and also taking responsibility for your offspring, having a central kitchen with food elevators, restaurant, library, rooms for physical exercise, for clubs and parties, a typewriting bureau, cooperative laundry, and sunbathing on the roof. The children in nurseries in another wing, tennis courts in the park—(—-) in short everything you can dream of, and in Stockholm, and for a rent price that will save us about half of our costs for the household. The whole thing is conceived in the terms of a working mother and wife, but the job is driving the idea home to those most in need of such a house instead of a miniature apartment."[16,17]

The working symbiosis of economists and architects contributed to the Swedish model implementation throughout the nation. It introduced a kinship between political management, economy and technology that proved to be as unusual as it was powerful (Fig. 4). Health and democratic measures of the previous political system had fallen short of solving the acute social problems at hand, and thus were obsolete. Social engineering meant new connections between economy, technology, science and political management. It created a belief in a possible change of society, even of the nation.[18] This very promising view of life was formulated in what may be the Myrdal couple's most influential book, *Kris i befolkningsfrågan (Crises in the population issue)*, which became a political best seller. The book was published in late Fall 1934. Just a few weeks later, Alva Myrdal gave birth to a baby. A friend commented in a letter: "I think it is a splendid idea, to produce a book and a baby at the same time."[19]

Following up on recommendations of the 1935 Population Commission, in 1936 the government started an investigation of the most intimate family issue; namely sexuality (Public investigation no 1936:59). In the investigation report Gunnar Myrdal excels in transporting his dry economic language into the most private area of family planning.[20] At times, a polemic voice can be heard advocating for a secular moral code on questions that earlier belonged only to the church.[21] The report describes how according to scientific research, marriage without children tends to be emotionally poor and less satisfying, and also why the one child family should be avoided since a single child often shows "emotional instability, bodily unease, hyper activity, egocentricism, narcissism etc."[22]

Fig. 4. The parks were designed to host recreation and a varied social use. Norr Mälarstrand. Photo C.G. Rosenberg.

A series of reforms ensued. They were linked to each other in an effort to reconstruct the family institution on an economic basis concerning all stages of family life: marriage, child birth, and education. Housing made it easier to establish a family, free hospital care stimulated reproduction, monthly child allowance and free school lunches were thought to compensate for the economic burden of child rearing. But these "gifts" came with a price. Gunnar Myrdal repeatedly stressed that modern individuals had to adopt a new lifestyle, and that Swedish people had to be taught how to live, love, eat, dress and above all, bring up their children.[23]

The Myrdal's book, *Kris i befolkningsfrågan* targeted the turn around of birth decline, but the ultimate goal was a complete overhaul of society. Both production and reproduction had to be integrated into a new model that made human life more effective. "Social planning under rational control" was the motto.[24] The new type of citizen, as expressed in the previously mentioned manifesto *Acceptera*, should spend a lot of his/her time in open society and its public places, such as restaurants, cinema theaters, parks, concert halls, and departments stores.[25] Children should preferably be raised at boarding schools to avoid hindering their parents from using free time for individual recreation and additional work.[26]

The Myrdals gave intellectual lustre to the Social Democratic Party. Both Gunnar and Alva received the Nobel prize; Alva the Peace prize in 1982, and Gunnar the award in 1974 for his work in economics. His thesis was, in short, that government should use strong public finance interventions to prevent recession in the national economy. Using the building industry as an economic balance instrument, Swedish society had, by the time he received his award, utilized Gunnar Myrdal's ideas for about forty years.

The Myrdal family lived in Bromma, a suburb some six kilometers west of central Stockholm, in a house designed by Sven Markelius (1889-1972), a personal friend and a noted modernist architect. Markelius was one of the co-authors of the manifesto *Acceptera* and also served as Director of Urban Planning for Stockholm, from 1944 to 1954. Markelius and the Myrdals actually collaborated on the scheme for the house, using their respective knowledge of architecture and social science to shape the living space of a modern family living a modern life. Alva and Gunnar Myrdal's close collaboration with Markelius was typical of a society that did not acknowledge constraining borders between professionals and politicians. At that time scientist and politician sat on the same side of the table, the very same side where also sat the architect. The Myrdals have been termed two of the most important "architects" of the Swedish welfare model, suggesting that the title of architect applied equally to those who created social or economic schemes as well as those who designed buildings, and, as we shall see, parks and gardens.

Fig. 5. The natural landscape was used as a motif to form the modernist park. Norr Mälarstrand. Photo C.G. Rosenberg.

Utopia into Nature: Public Parks and Promenades in Stockholm

During the late 1940s, few countries in the world equalled Sweden's engagement with modern social ideas and their architectural counterparts. The past, it was held, meant nothing and there was little to learn from it. Advocates of this brand of modernity in Sweden operated under the conviction that every new day was a little bit better than the one that just passed. And the restructuring of the country and the capital was not only the result of a vision; it was also the response to a strong social need. Time and ideology struck a perfect chord. The mid-century afforded Sweden the necessary conditions for this giant undertaking. The country had been spared from destruction by the two world wars and had been able to establish political stability and economic prosperity. Its citizens shared a prevalent belief in the prospects of a bright future and engaged into innovation with an open mind. This was true for all walks of society, including landscape architecture.[27]

Swedish landscape designers explored and refined the explicit use of a natural landscape as a garden or a park, abandoning any reference to picturesque or formal idioms of landscape architecture (Fig. 5). Again, this distinct change in direction for Swedish landscape architecture was predicated upon the health crisis in the cities. Fresh air and exercise were the best-known cures. To address new policy demands, park design veered away from turn-of-the-century forms to embrace forms based on more contemporary ideas. Now the healing powers of nature were considered more important than bourgeois strolling pleasures, which seemed as stiff in form as rigid in content and social use. The new parks turned to nature as the source of their form, and emphasized recreational use of lawns and plantings that were only decorative in earlier times. Play, physical exercise, and social use became keywords for the coming-of-age park movement. The rich landscape around Lake Mälaren and Stockholm contained enough variation and valuable components to offer prototypes for a new type of landscape design. For the first time in the Swedish history of landscape architecture, ways of thinking did not arrive from the continent or result from international fashion, but derived from the local landscape and a uniquely Swedish idea.

Fig. 6. Swedish modernism was influenced by the purity of the local landscape. Villa Markelius, Kevinge. Photo Architectural Museum, Stockholm.

Stockholm is built on the archipelago formed by the estuary of Lake Mälaren as it flows into the Baltic. The expressive glacially polished crags and scars, semi-closed clearings, open meadows and extensive lake shores, dark forest tarns and aromatic pinewoods are of the many defining features of the landscape around Lake Mälaren. The aesthetic program of the Stockholm School was built upon these premises. Thus fragments of the local landscape were artistically interpreted and reshaped into a condensed form as gardens and parks in the Stockholm area.[28]

Sven Markelius' house in Kevinge, built in 1945 after the architect had moved from Bromma where the Myrdal couple also lived, presented such a fragment of nature (Fig. 6). One photograph of Markelius' villa in particular had a great influence on Swedish landscape architecture of the time. Here the garden in its traditional form has vanished and a

Fig. 7. The children's pond in Fredhäll. Photo K.W. Gullers.

new conception has taken its place. In this image the house does not dominate the place, the home environment, as is often the case. Instead, the house serves as a background for the garden. A few forest trees, birches, imply that the garden is unbounded and continues behind the photographer – or, alternately, that there is no garden. Given its central position in the picture the little pool appears merely as a storm water puddle that has collected in a rock crevice. The young girl is turned away from us. She does not pose but finds her place naturally in this very special garden. She belongs to the first generation that will live a completely modern life. She stands in a landscape that looks more like a clearing in a forest than a designed garden. In this new concept of a garden a historic remnant remains. The picture testifies to an unbroken tradition of a certain perception of nature in the Swedish landscape: where humans have a place in the wild, living in a meaningful relation with nature.[29]

The photo of Sven Markelius' villa in Kevinge in which the young girl stretches her arms towards nature and towards the bright future that belongs to her and to the Swedish modernist garden had a strong propagandistic effect. A second image by the photographer K.W. Gullers, showing the children's pond in Stockholm's Fredhäll Park, was equally influential (Fig. 7). Here we see a peaceful environment, with children playing in what could be a natural lake inlet or stream. Old oak and ash trees, growing freely, their branches reaching out over pastureland, frame the picture. If it were not for the presence of apartment buildings at the back of the photo the scene could have been somewhere in the Swedish countryside: the landscape

Fig. 8. Parks were seen and designed as extensions of the living rooms in the apartments. Norr Mälarstrand. Photo by Thorbjörn Andersson.

Fig. 9. Holger Bloms park program, condensed into one image, had a strong propagandistic effect. Sketch by Kalle Lodén.

and the atmosphere are about the same in both settings.

But Fredhäll is located in the middle of central Stockholm and the lake inlet is a children's pool cast in concrete. The Fredhäll Park was yet another influential representative of the new attitude in Swedish landscape design. The municipal Park Department designed so many parks in this style, with such consistently high quality, that they were later grouped together and labelled the Stockholm School of Landscape Design.

This school took the regional landscape around Lake Mälaren as an aesthetic program and a point of departure for the creation of landscape forms, purifying, distilling and stylizing the site's natural assets, or at times, creating them in places that lacked natural advantages.[30] Yet, not only the design but also the program of the new municipal parks set them apart from the old ones. Parks were now regarded as active and constitutive urban amenities rather than merely green reservations. Parks were seen as integral to social housing, on the same level of necessity as flush toilets, balconies, and hot and cold running water (Fig. 8). For the first time in history, landscapes were planned for active use, for the general public to walk on the grass, bathe in the sun, share a picnic lunch. All this happened despite the fact that for the first time a person had been appointed Director of Parks in Stockholm who knew almost nothing about making gardens.

The man was Holger Blom (1906–1996). He served in office over three decades, from 1938 to 1971. He was trained as an urban planner and had practiced with Lars Israel Wahlman in Stockholm, with Krüger & Toll in Amsterdam, and with

Fig. 10. Norr Mälarstrand creates a transition between the built environment and the natural landscape. Photo by Thorbjörn Andersson.

Fig. 11. To be able to enjoy the presence of the lake and the view are important ingredients in the park concept. Norr Mälarstrand. Photo by Thorbjörn Andersson.

Le Corbusier in Paris. Blom's training in urban design gave him the necessary knowledge to transform park strategy into a meaningful component of the *Folkhemmet* vision, the Peoples Home program. Blom's contribution was twofold: first he established a park program, displaying a strong, strategic mind devoted to questions of park policy; second he implemented it, realizing a system of parks that penetrated almost all areas of the inner city.[31]

Blom's park program was simple, tersely worded, and striking in effect (Fig. 9). It comprised several levels, each developed with a different degree of detail, that could be condensed into a single effective picture, repeatedly used in conversation with politicians, colleagues and the general public. The four main points were:

1. The park relieves the city. (The urban planning aspect)
2. The park provides space for outdoor recreation. (The sanitary and general health aspect)
3. The park offers space for public gatherings. (The social aspect)
4. The park preserves nature and culture. (The ecological aspect)[32]

Norr Mälarstrand and its extensions, built in 1941–43, possibly best exemplify the Stockholm concept of a natural urban landscape combined with recreational facilities. The park is a narrow green finger—three kilometers long and in most parts only twenty meters wide—extending along the north shore of Lake Mälaren on the island of Kungsholmen (Fig. 10). The park cuts through the entire inner city, starting at its center in front of the city hall and ending at the very outskirts of the town. Nowadays, Stockholmers generally believe that Norr Mälarstrand is an area of preserved nature of particular beauty, when as a matter of fact it is a thoroughly constructed environment. Before landscaping, this land was a desolate strip of marshes dotted with accidental storage sheds with no visual or physical amenities. The architect for most of the parks in Stockholm during the

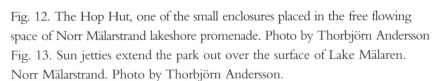

Fig. 12. The Hop Hut, one of the small enclosures placed in the free flowing space of Norr Mälarstrand lakeshore promenade. Photo by Thorbjörn Andersson Fig. 13. Sun jetties extend the park out over the surface of Lake Mälaren. Norr Mälarstrand. Photo by Thorbjörn Andersson.

period of the Stockholm School was the multi-talented Erik Glemme (1905–1959). He worked for Holger Blom at the parks department and was the chief designer for Norr Mälarstrand. To Glemme must be credited the delicate texture and continual variety experienced along the linear sweep of the shoreline.

Norr Mälarstrand contains, almost in miniature, the world of ideas of the Stockholm school. A walkway winds in soft curves from beginning to end, flows past sitting places, sunny spots, jetties, a look-out terrace, small pools, playgrounds, small patches of garden, sculptures, and a small café over the water. At one point, the natural line of the beach has been scooped out to create a small water inlet, only for the pleasure of bridging it and increase the sense of being close to water (Fig. 11).

When the park was laid out, in 1941–1943, Sweden was isolated from the world by the war. As a consequence, the park only built upon very regional and local features. As nothing could be imported, only plants that could be obtained in Sweden were planted. Many Lake Mälaren landscapes were recreated here, such as grazing land enclosed with birches, groves of hazel bushes, wetland with alders. Human influence on the landscape is represented by a courtyard surrounded with a dry stone wall, a small fisherman's cabin painted white, a Hop Hut, *Humlehyddan* (Fig. 12). It offers an example of the association of tradition and renewal: its intimate garden is framed by a low stable stone wall, with an airy complement of hop bines growing on a hut-shaped superstructure.[33] Norr Mälarstrand is still today a favorite spot among Stockholmers. In summertime, people bask in the sun, swim in the water, windsurf and sail on the lake, enjoy the view of the lake, have their lunch breaks at the little café. In the wintertime, the frozen surface of Lake Mälaren offers walking grounds with surprising perspectives of the city, but also skating and skiing possibilities. Erik Glemme regarded the surface of the lake as much a part of the active park domain as the lakeshore itself, only blue instead of green (Fig. 13).

Blom's genius resided in his ability to frame a new park ideology, and Erik Glemme was the designer who gave form to many of the parks. There are probably hundreds of environments in Stockholm that bear Glemme's artistic signature. Many

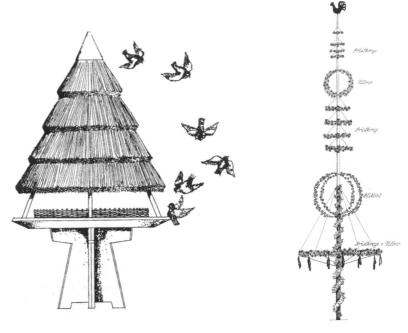

Fig. 14. Open air theatres for public life: concerts, meetings, theatre plays. Rålambshovsparken. Photo by Thorbjörn Andersson.

Fig. 15. Bird feeding table for non-migrant birds in wintertime. Sketch by Kalle Lodén.

Fig. 16. Midsummer pole, used at the traditional celebration of the longest day of the year. Sketch by Kalle Lodén.

new examples in the inner city were not built on virgin land but resulted from remodelling of older parks. This was done without sentimentality, in a way characteristic of the modernist movement. Among other cultural institutions generated by Blom's park program was the Park Theater, a group of performers sponsored by the city who travelled in the summertime from park to park presenting plays at no charge to the audience. The Park Theater still exists six decades later, performing from May until September, moving its stage sets every night to another park. A number of outdoor theaters were designed and built in the parks to provide audience seating (Fig. 14). The social program also offered, as previously mentioned, supervised play for children in day care centers open to all. Here, children could be left under the guidance of preschool teachers, or participate in the activities with their parents. The parks also presented, among other amenities, a public display of sculptures created by leading Swedish artists. They were sponsored by a special city authority; and set in appropriate landscape surroundings, improving the aesthetic qualities of the parks and the squares. Blom understood the need to employ able colleagues, and also had on payroll artists working as a team with the landscape designers. This cooperation resulted, for instance, in a sculptural climb and slide structure for park play, designed by Egon Möller Nielsen, a bird-feeding table to be used in the wintertime designed by Kalle Lodén, who also designed a mid-summer pole for the traditional Swedish mid-summer celebration (Fig. 15, 16). A designated graphic program was made for signs and messages in the parks, and the artists were also asked to design fences and railings, for instance to shelter staircases in the parks. The park theater and the public art program can be understood as

Fig. 17. The designers worked with seasonal change and wintertime recreation to make possible year-round use. Norr Mälarstrand. Photo by Thorbjörn Andersson.

Fig. 18. Aerial showing the inner city of Stockholm with parks built during the period highlighted. Photo by Stockholm Parks Department.

expressions of a deliberate political choice to make high-culture practices more democratic by moving them out of the theater salons or the art museums, places where working class people might feel ill at ease.

The construction of the park system in Stockholm was part of a bigger goal, ultimately building a democratic society with maximum happiness to all. However, the hegemonic ideology of this mid-century Utopia can only be received with some skepticism by a critical mind. Even if there is no doubt that the whole program was meant for the good of the people, it also implied and encouraged the exercise of wide authority by elected representatives. The unbroken unity with which Swedish society engaged in radical change during these years has surprised international observers, and displays what one could call Machiavellian tendencies, although carried out within the transparency of a democratic political system. The pursuit of a detailed blueprint for modern life, "as it was supposed to be" according to the social democratic vision, affected in many ways individual possibilities. Free will, a most human feature, was at times brushed aside. This may have later led to the development of leftist ideologies within the Social Democratic Party that precipitated the downfall of the Swedish Utopia triggered by the student revolt and related waves of change which rolled over the western world in the early 1970s.

The Stockholm School of Park Design under the directorship of Holger Blom pursued and, at the same time, developed a tradition of landscape design in the Stockholm parks (Fig. 17). It can be called its historical legacy. This can be seen as a paradox, since modernist architects repeatedly rejected any attachment to historical values. Maybe the Stockholm School proves its unique quality exactly here in combining past and future. It made form and function inseparable, driven in equal parts by political vision and social pathos. Design and content now followed a coordinated logic, achieving a genre of landscape architecture completely derived from societal conditions, rather than from either form or fashion as is often the case. Although Swedish society has gone through many changes over the last half century, the tradition of making parks for everyday life, drawing inspiration for their design from the essence of the local landscape, has in many ways been upheld in the parks of Stockholm. The park theater still tours parks in the summertime. The public art program lives on, adding new sculptures to the municipal parks. The staffed playgrounds still attract children from the surrounding multi family housings. And what is maybe the most important notion; Stockholmers continue using the parks in a relaxed mode as if these were shared living rooms; playing, celebrating, socializing in a way that gives Stockholm city life a special and quite original spirit (Fig. 18).

Bibliography

Andersson, Thorbjörn. "Erik Glemme and the Stockholm Park System." In *Modern Landscape_Architecture: A Critical Review*, edited by Marc Treib, Cambridge: The MIT Press, 1993.

Andersson, Thorbjörn. "To Erase the Garden: Modernity in the Swedish Garden and Landscape." In *The Architecture of Landscape 1940—1960*, edited by Marc Treib, Philadelphia: University of Pennsylvania Press, 2002.

Asplund, Gunnar, et al. *Acceptera*. Stockholm: Tidens förlag, 1931.

Blom, Holger: "Stockholms gröna ytor," *Byggmästaren* 16 (1946).

Henschen, Helena, ed. *Barn i stan*. Stockholm: Stockholms Stadsmuseum, 1991.

Hirdman, Yvonne: *Att lägga livet tillrätta*. Helsingborg: Carlssons förlag, 1989.

Myrdal, Alva, the archives of, letter collection 1930—1950.

Statens offentliga utredningar 1936:59 (Public Investigation Series). Stockholm, 1936.

Notes

[1] Andersson 2002, p. 2

[2] Henschen 1991, p 179

[3] Henschen 1991, p 229

[4] Henschen 1991, p. 229

[5] Henschen 1991, p. 93

[6] Henschen 1991, p. 235

[7] Alva Myrdal also received the Nobel Peace Prize in 1972 for her activities and writings on social matters, where she always saw the family as the fundamental unit.

[8] Hirdman 1989, p. 13

[9] Hirdman 1989, p. 106

[10] Here also must be pointed out that Swedish socialism happened and lived on within a completely democratic system.

[11] Hirdman 1989, p. 81

[12] Hirdman 1989, p. 16.

[13] Hirdman 1989, p. 93.

[14] Ibid.

[15] Alva Myrdal does not mention her friends by name, but it is not a far guess that they are the young economists in the so called Economist's Club as one group and the architects behind the Stockholm Exhibition and their written manifesto *Acceptera* (accept) as the other. These architects were Sven Wallander, Uno Åhrén, Gregor Paulsson and Gunnar Asplund. Apart from that, Sven Markelius was among the close architect friends; he designed the houses that the Myrdal family lived in.

[16] Myrdal letter collection.

[17] Several of these collective houses were built in Stockholm. The most well known, located on John Ericsson Street, is still structurally intact, although it no longer in content meets the vision.

[18] Hirdman 1989, p. 99.

[19] Ibid.

[20] Gunnar Myrdal was Minister of Trade in the Swedish government from 1945 to 47.

[21] Hirdman 1989, p. 131.

[22] SOU no 1936:59.

[23] Hirdman 1989, p.123.

[24] Hirdman 1989, p. 122.

[25] Asplund 1931, p. 72.

[26] Asplund 1931, p. 67.

[27] Andersson 2002, p. 4.

[28] Andersson 1998, p. 238.

[29] Andersson 1998, p. 227.

[30] Andersson 1998, p. 228.

[31] Andersson 2002, p. 22.

[32] Blom 1946, p.1 ff.

[33] Andersson 1993, p. 122.

Gardens, City Life and
Culture

Gardens, City Life and
Culture

Gardens, City Life and
Culture

Gardens, City Life and
Culture

Gardens, City Life and
Culture

Gardens, City Life and
Culture

CHAPTER 11

Cities in the Garden: American New Towns and Landscape Planning

Nicholas Dagen Bloom

Protected by a carefully designed street pattern which minimizes traffic and which provides pedestrian underpasses beneath even moderately busy streets, these boys and girls are free to explore their new city. There are streams to ford, woods to explore, bike paths to ride, formal playgrounds and swings and slides and completely unplanned fields and meadows in which to romp.

Columbia (Maryland) Public Relations (Rouse Company 1968, 4)

The leading American new towns of the 1960s, Columbia (Maryland), Reston (Virginia), and Irvine (California) pioneered large-scale environmental planning on a scale that has seldom been duplicated. Now largely complete, these three towns each contain thousands of acres of preserved open space, man-made lakes, nature centers, community gardens, extensive decorative plantings, and active-use park space. This abundant and multi-use open space can be traced not only to initial planning efforts, but also to persistent activism on the part of local citizens. With nearly fifty years of experience behind them these new towns are ideal laboratories for the study of long-term results of landscape planning. As this article shows, the conventional wisdom of what "good" landscape planning achieves in planned communities is only partly supported by a close examination of long-term results.

The American new town planners of the 1960s may have devised innovative landscape systems, but in other respects they simply returned to an earlier and mostly forgotten landscape tradition in American suburbs. America's first planned suburb, Llewellyn Park, New Jersey (1857), preserved and enhanced much of the natural landscape within its borders. Some of the more elite suburbs of the nineteenth and early twentieth century, such as Riverside, Illinois (1868) and Shaker Heights, Ohio (1912), also showed sensitivity to existing nature features. Most suburbs that followed, however, either did not have the luxury of large preserved lands or simply neglected nature preservation. Most twentieth century suburbs (into the 1960s) replaced natural areas with a highly cultivated landscape incorporating lawns, hedges, and trees. Manicured and private space served as a delightful setting for homes and few residents or developers placed an emphasis on natural landscapes. Even today in the United States suburban nature preservation is primarily found in wealthier suburbs that have the resources to remove land from the open market (Jackson 1985).

The designers of Reston, Columbia and Irvine could look back not only to the better American suburban traditions, but also the garden city or new town tradition as it had developed in Europe. From these towns came grander notions of landscape preservation including the idea of greenbelts. The early new towns such as Letchworth (1903) and Welwyn Garden City (1919) incorporated a mix of carefully landscaped parks and gardens for resident use with large areas of open space (including both natural areas and active farms). The incomplete American garden city Radburn (1929) influenced the modern American new town's adoption of grade separated pathways and superblock residential development (large green spaces and recreational facilities sited behind groups of houses). Post-World War II new towns in Europe including Tapiola (1951) and Harlow (1947) continued to set aside undeveloped areas while still providing extensive space for active and passive recreation. Scandinavian towns such as Tapiola garnered extensive attention for an effective integration of landscape and architecture.

American new town developers and planners knew a great deal about Radburn and many visited European new towns such as Tapiola during the early planning phases. In time, their plans directly reflected the established new town tradition of enhancing natural settings through careful landscaping and open space preservation. American new towns, however, were generally built at lower densities (more single-family homes) than their European counterparts (Bloom 2001).

Emphasis on nature preservation in the American new towns of the 1960s emerged in tandem with the rising power of the environmental movement. The pleasure that Americans, particularly the middle class, take in nature was a growing cultural phenomenon. Nature appreciated by city dwellers has its roots in nineteenth-century environmental efforts that led to the creation of city and national parks and national forests. Americans preserved and created these early parks as much for their cultural importance – a reminder of American greatness, the belief in the ability of nature to inspire citizens and artists,. and as a release from the pressures of urban living – as for their natural resources. The middle class of America, while responsible for its fair share of environmental destruction, has also provided much of the leadership in environmental preservation and education.

The 1960s and 1970s witnessed a new vitality in environmental efforts, spurred by the publication of Rachel Carson's *Silent Spring*, the growing counterculture, and the increasing popularity of tourism that brought more Americans into contact with nature (Rome 2001; Rosenzweig 1998; Marx 1999; Shabecoff 1993).

The burgeoning environmental ethic had an effect on new towns, and new towns attracted many Americans who valued the natural environment as a cultural resource. Developers promised that automobile use would be reduced through planning of transit alternatives, local employment opportunities, and convenient shopping. Developers also began to see nature preservation as a potential marketing tool to suburbanites. Enhanced profit in the future could be expected on the sale of reserve land if careful landscape planning created a superior "product" for high-income suburbanites.

Reston's Environmental Pioneers

The master plan for Reston of 1962 envisioned a bold new concept for American suburbia. The developer and planners pictured Reston as a sophisticated, adult-oriented suburban city housing nearly 75,000 residents on 6800 acres of Northern Virginia countryside (outside of Washington, D.C.). Planners, building on the new town tradition, aimed to give definition to the landscape through the use of high-density corridors of apartments and town houses rather than just single-family homes. Residents of these high-density complexes and those living in a limited number of single-family homes would be able to walk along grade separated wooded pathways or drive on landscaped parkways to convenient and attractive "village" centers. There they would find not only shopping but public space, theaters, galleries, recreational facilities and meeting halls. Each village was to have a theme, such as boating, horseback riding, or golf that would be emphasized through design. Early clusters of housing by notable architects best reflect the vision of these early years as well as the connection to the European new town movement (Fig. 1).

With some changes over the years (more single-family housing than originally envisioned, more conservative architecture, and the thematic village ideals abandoned), this early vision has been largely realized (2005). The approximately 56,000 citizens of Reston enjoy a great range of open spaces. Planners carefully preserved the natural beauty of the site as whole by placing higher density housing on ridgelines reserving valleys for open space and artificial lakes. Inhabitants of single-family houses have yards, but even those residents in townhouse and apartment complexes have access to private landscaped common areas maintained by local community or "cluster" associations. Adjoining these private landscaped areas is an extensive system of open spaces and recreational facilities maintained by the citizen-run Reston Association, the privately run local government of the community (Fig. 2).

Mature forest blanketed many of the thousands of acres the developer Robert Simon purchased in the 1960s and the Reston Association still looks after the forests, streams, lakes, fields, and wetlands in 1,100 acres of open space (Fig. 3). Grade separated pathways take walkers and runners into thickly planted river valleys and around lakes and golf courses (Fig. 4). Joseph Stowers, a longtime Reston activist,

Fig. 1. These images reflect the mix of landscape planning styles in Reston. The Lake Anne Village center (above), loosely modeled on Mediterranean ports, reflects the thematic hopes of the early developer. The lake landscape (below) is more typical of the soft edge of Reston lakes. Photo by the author.

and other members of the independent citizen group known as the Reston Community Association, fought to expand and connect the pedestrian/bike pathway system in Reston: a system that now includes fifty-five miles of paths, including grade separated underpasses and ninety-five bridges. The Reston Association has made space available for garden plots on open land, too, an innovation not part of the original plans. Alternative environmental management techniques are employed by the

Fig. 2. The pathway system deep in the woods of Reston (above). A meadow in a section of Reston's preserved lands (below). Photo by the author.

Fig. 3. Map reflecting the open lands of Reston. From the *Nature of Reston*.

association: carp are used to control aquatic weeds and wasps to attach gypsy moth eggs; nature's own processes are employed to help restore stream beds; and native plant species are encouraged (Reston Land 1989).

The community, with help from the developer, has attempted to understand and appreciate the natural landscape preserved around them. Reston, during the 1960s, developed an innovative environmental education program. Vernon Walker, hired by Simon to run a nature center, had been trained as a science educator and came to Reston from New York, where he had developed a relationship with L.B. Sharp, a pioneer in American outdoor education. Walker convinced Simon "that the best environmental teacher was the outdoors itself." Walker described Reston's open space philosophy in 1969: "What is the character of the open space [in Reston]? . . . We have learned to avoid building permanent structures on floodplains. There is hope! The land is used for walkways…bridle paths, tot lots, and other recreation"(Bloom 2001, 271). Walker helped create environmental management committees in the two existing villages to look after their respective open spaces and educated children through walks and other techniques. Walker ran the center for many years, but died in 1982 at the age of fifty (Rathburn 1987, 6).

The community created the Walker Nature Center in 1987. Seventy acres of trees, trails, streams and wildlife have been "dedicated to Vernon Walker's vision of Reston's open space as an all-season educational experience." The center includes trails, a picnic pavilion, wildflower garden, a meditation area, outdoor displays, and a demonstration natural meadow. In 1989, the Reston Environmental Education Foundation was formed to promote a broader range of programs, and with the support of the Reston Association, now offers on a yearly basis "200 programs and reaches 7,000 participants." Nature education activities include preschool and school programs, summer camps, teen programs, teacher workshops, service projects, family programs, lectures, and much more (Bloom 2001, 271).

Although the pathway system is lightly used, in light of Reston's large population, it is rarely empty of citizens. Occasional crimes have occurred on the secluded pathways (and many of the grade separated underpasses are dank and dark), but good weather finds numerous Restonians out walking and enjoying the attractive natural surroundings. Outside the natural areas, the traffic of Reston has worsened as residents and visitors (including tens of thousands working in local office parks) fight for space on roads and in parking lots. The internal bus system has not kept pace with community growth and barely manages to serve the different

Fig. 4. Modernist multi-family housing in an older village reflecting the meeting point between "cluster" association lands and community open space (above). An underpass in the older section of Reston with public art projects (below). Photo by the author.

commercial centers it links. Residents decline to use the walkway system as a daily commuting or shopping route, on either foot or bike, and drive to their nearby village centers and schools. Early hopes of altering resident behavior through design, particularly automobile dependence, have not reached fruition.

Columbia's Abundant Nature

The developer of Columbia, Maryland (1963), James Rouse, envisioned his community as a series of intimate small towns; the target population of 100,000 residents was to be divided into a number of 'villages' of approximately 12,000 residents. Each village was to have its own center that would combine in one location public spaces, stores, a high school or middle school, community center, churches, and recreational facilities. These villages were subdivided into a series of residential neighborhoods that included a range of housing types. Columbia was to be family oriented and emphasized schools and community facilities as the center of life and neighborhoods. Surrounding the housing and other community facilities, future residents would find a green canopy created by thousands of acres of open space including forests, fields and lakes. Pathways and landscaped parkways were to wind through these lands.

While changes have been made in the texture, scale and detail of the planning, to a remarkable extent the community's initial vision has been realized today. If Columbia has not been as widely lauded for its landscape planning as other communities it may be because the architectural idiom of the town was set more by speculative builders than professional architects; developers constructed standardized apartment and housing styles within the larger planning framework. Design and landscape was not as carefully integrated at the residential level as it was for the town as a whole (Fig. 5).

Planners of Columbia had little say over housing in the 1960s, but they showed genuine interest in environmental planning. They carefully surveyed the 14,000 acres assembled for the town and created a series of "overlay" maps to best preserve nature areas: "With deliberate disregard of land ownership, these overlays isolated for inventory such existing features as tree cover, waterways and watershed areas" that would be retained as part of the final site planning. The staff "was determined to preserve the general contour of the rolling farmland and to perpetuate wooded areas where practicable." By 1970, the planners had graduated to even more detailed environmental planning: "Instead of the 5 foot contour suitable for general planning, 1 foot contours are checked in the field; roads are walked before the final grades are set in order to minimize cuts or fill; trees to be saved are decided upon by size and species, and a road may bifurcate to save a 30-inch oak." The planners, in a nod to cultural preservation, even integrated older farm buildings into the planning of village centers and other community facilities (Fig. 6) (Tennenbaum 1965).

This careful attention to detail shifted planning ideals away from abstract concepts such as a garden city style greenbelt that would "protect" the town from sprawl. The proposed 3900-acre greenbelt was abandoned as planners decided that "nature had done a better planning job on the land with three stream valleys." The planners observed that "each of these valleys . . . gave the land a natural definition, and could give the village their definition." In addition, by the time the planners had made provisions for all of the low-density uses, including golf courses, lakes, parks, bridle paths and other recreational uses, the acreage to be set aside for the greenbelt had been used (Fig. 7) (Hamilton 1964).

Much of the impetus for the preservation came from the ideals of the developer, James Rouse, a leading figure in American urban affairs. He remembered in 1977 that after the purchase of the land "we said in the first communication we ever sent to the people of the county that we believed it was possible to build an urban community that could respect the land and preserve the stream valleys and the flood plains, while providing a human habitat." Rouse not only valued nature for itself, but he was a great believer in the positive effect of nature on the human heart: "How do you measure the value of seeing a muskrat swim across the lake? A whistling swan? You don't have to measure it to know that extraordinary things happen to the human soul and human heart and human mind when there is this natural association with nature." Rouse's belief in the effect of environment on character was unshakable (Rouse 1977).

Some of Columbia's open spaces today are manicured, while others are thickly wooded stream valleys and woods. Not only did the Rouse Company preserve thousands of trees, but it planted hundreds of thousands more, many of which are now nearing maturity. The beauty and the clarity of the streams and the thick foliage that still blankets the community are remarkable. The natural areas do much, especially in summer, to compensate for architectural blandness. The Columbia Association, the town's citizen-run, private version of local government, maintains the open spaces – 3,400 acres of open space and 93 miles of pathways (including man-made lakes, hundreds of footbridges, and a number of grade separated underpasses and overpasses). A large

Fig. 5. Typical housing in Columbia that reflects the conventional approach to design in most of the residential sections. Open land interweaves through these developments of multi-family housing (above) and single-family housing (below). Photo by the author.

proportion of Columbia residents claim to use the pathways at least once a year (a recent survey found that 75% had used one or more of them annually); nevertheless, the paths are primarily used for recreational purposes rather than the functional vision of the early planners (Kellner 2005). In terms of environmental management, the association uses minimal amounts of pesticides

Fig. 6. An adaptive reuse of an older barn structure in Columbia, now used as a religious facility. Photo by the author.

Fig. 7. A map from the early planning days reflecting the preservation of stream and river valleys in Columbia. From *Columbia: A New City*, Rouse Company, ca. 1969.

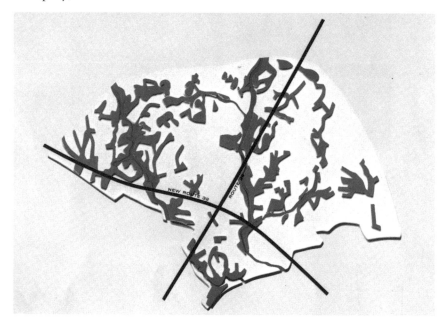

and fertilizers and mows smaller areas than originally planned (Winieweski 1978, 50). A full-time ecologist is responsible for the open-space areas and conducts regular environmental education programs for local groups. The association stocks the lakes (Fig. 8) with fish and tries to monitor water quality to ensure "that open spaces are habitable for birds and other wildlife" (Columbia Association 1998, 8–10).

Preservation of the environment has remained a priority of the association and residents during the last decades. A 1984 planning report prepared by the citizen led organization known as the Columbia Forum reflects the many efforts of residents and developer: "In terms of respect for the land, Columbia has set a high standard for other large scale developments. More than one third of Columbia's land is permanent open space; there is more wildlife and more trees than existed in the area prior to development. Most of the watercourses have been protected and add considerably to the beauty of the area. Through the Columbia Association and through other state and local organizations, including large numbers of volunteers, the open space, trees, and wildlife have been protected and made accessible to an appreciative population" (Columbia Forum 1984, 4). The Waterfowl and Habitat Advisory Committee, a resident organization, looks out for the open spaces in Columbia and makes sure the animals that live there are protected. The committee also organizes regular clean-ups at local lakes; members work to keep waste out of the open-space system. Local schools, scout groups, and environmental groups conduct their own programs. Although Columbia does not have the same level of environmental education as Reston, that will change in coming years, in large part because resident efforts have led to the creation of the Middle Patuxent Wildlife Area.

Residents lobbied hard for the creation of the wildlife area, one of the largest parcels of open space left in Howard County. Dr. Aelred Geis with other citizens led the effort to preserve 1,000 acres in Columbia's last village, River Hill. The parcel contains forests, meadows, wetlands, and a river, as well as abundant wildlife. The area has been well studied over the last thirty years, and eight reports by professionals and citizens have focused on its potential as open space. Originally, the valley was to be flooded and turned into a lakefront community, but Geis convinced Rouse that the land should be preserved because of its environmental richness. On a visit to the area in 1967, Rouse, "dressed in a suit…[lay down] on his stomach in a ditch to watch the [mating flight of the woodcock] and was so enchanted by the bird's towering flight that he declared the area off limits to the bulldozers." The establishment of the refuge did not occur until after Rouse's death, but the parcel has been preserved in its natural state, and plans call for trails and a nature center that will educate the community about the many habitats present there (Bloom 2001, 273).

Columbia developed the wild natural areas envisioned in the original plans. Natural spaces preserved on such a large scale, along with the high degree of environmental activism, made this community very different from the suburbs it sought to replace. There are a few deficiencies in the planning, however. The pathways winding through woods have occasionally been targets for criminality and have developed, in parts of the town, a dangerous reputation that may or may not be deserved. My impression is that the pathways are not heavily used in light of the town's growing population. Columbia's uniform green palette (and bland suburban architectural idiom) can be baffling and is

Fig. 8. Lakefront living in Columbia reflects the soft edges of the lake environments in Columbia and the integration of buildings and water (below). Many of these lakes have water quality issues. Photo by the author.

unvaried throughout the community. The reliance on the automobile and worsening traffic outside the preserved areas also threatens the community's quality of life. Columbia may have convenient schools, shopping, and recreation areas linked by pathways, but this has not necessarily led to a decrease in automobile use. There is no viable transit alternative, the internal bus system barely functions, and air pollution and noise from automobiles (of its 88,000 residents and thousands of employees from local office parks) is noticeable even from many of the preserved natural areas. Like Reston, the planning has failed to diminish the American love affair with the automobile.

An Irvine Paradise

Irvine, California's original planning has shifted more than that of Reston or Columbia, but these changes have actually enhanced the landscape planning. The original plan by the Irvine Company for the 90,000-acre Irvine Ranch from the early 1960s envisioned a college town of 100,000 residents, divided into neighborhoods, surrounding a new campus of the University of California. A more ambitious plan adopted in 1970 superceded this early concept and raised population targets to 400,000. Irvine incorporated as a city in 1970 in line with this more ambitious and urbane plan. This larger plan still divided the future population into discrete neighborhoods surrounding the university but now included a linear urban spine featuring commercial and community facilities. Irvine from the beginning was envisioned as a well-designed suburban city with options for play, work, and study; to a great extent, it has become that today for 175,000 satisfied residents.

The earliest residential neighborhoods featured narrow "greenbelts," single-family and attached upscale housing, extensive recreational facilities and a village concept—and set the pattern to come. Unlike Reston and Columbia, urban design techniques were used to distinguish one village from another. Planners of Irvine acknowledged a great debt to planning theorist Kevin Lynch who encouraged planners to focus on how people actually experience the city rather than adopting abstract ideals about urban form. Mixed-use village centers, for instance, may have been the heart of planning in Reston and Columbia but were much less important in Irvine. Village centers in Irvine were simply nicely designed shopping centers without the blend of functions envisioned at the other new towns. The villages of Irvine, however are much more thematically distinct in terms of landscaping, planning, and architecture.

Lynch's emphasis on "edges," "pathways," "neighborhoods," and "landmarks" are evident throughout Irvine. Some Irvine villages were oriented to the ocean, others to inland hills, and some to the university. Wider streets defined the borders of villages and most traffic was diverted around smaller neighborhoods. One village might be clothed in a Mediterranean style while another in Mission details. The Irvine Company also made a point of using architects for most of its projects rather than relying on speculative builders with standardized plans as was done in large areas of Reston and Columbia.

Plantings are also strategically used to give definition to the town: palm trees might give definition to a Mediterranean style area while plane trees grace another (Fig. 9). One of the town's leading planners admitted "landscape is more important than buildings" (Watson 1998). Designers employed manicured nature as a palette to add identity and beauty to villages, and although nature reserves were set aside under citizen pressure, they were not an integral part of residential planning. In Columbia and Reston, by contrast, sufficient natural vegetation and water existed to integrate developments with wild areas and the developers of the eastern new towns set aside larger parcels of open space for the pathways and surrounding landscape within neighborhoods.

Fig. 9. Two villages in Irvine distinguished from each other through thematic landscape planning. This contrasting style of planning (including landscape elements and architecture) provides for orientation within the city as a whole. Photo by the author.

The Irvine Company has, however, created attractive, pedestrian oriented greenbelts (narrow strips of open land) running through most residential areas. These are narrow open spaces in comparison to their Columbia and Reston counterparts, but they offer attractive views for residents and space for tot lots, walking, running, and rollerblading. Because they run through residential areas and because many houses have sight lines, the Irvine greenbelts are also more easily monitored by residents than the wooded paths of Reston and Columbia. The numerous plantings and grass of the Irvine greenbelts added luxuriant growth to an area that was essentially semiarid and have demanded extensive water use (Fig. 10). In the late 1970s, the Irvine Ranch Water District initiated a "'total water management program' under which all sewage effluent is recycled for use as irrigation water in greenbelts and croplands" (Scott and O'Donnel 1980, 11-36).

The ambitious urban plan of 1970 did make an attempt to unify some of the different villages and greenbelts through the creation of multiple-use urban corridors. This corridor, zoned for a mix of uses, followed the drainage canals that snaked through the city. Planners envisioned these corridors as the future equivalent of Venice's canals and would be used for "bridle trails, bicycle paths, pedestrian trails, and recreational activity centers." The activity corridor as constructed is today filled with a variety of uses including stores, community centers, schools, offices and churches, but the only unifying features are a bike path, drainage canal, and a linear road system; it does not meet the standards originally set nor does it reflect the attention to landscape in the rest of the town (Bloom 2001, 62). Since the 1970s the Irvine Company has, however, continued to add new villages. Irvine planners continue to use landscaping to distinguish new neighborhoods and have added easily monitored pathway systems, smaller parks, and plentiful recreational opportunities.

Irvine residents during the past three decades actually played a leading role in making natural space a much greater and more permanent part of their community. The company preserved open space for greenbelts and turned what was a dusty ranch into a lush environment, but it had not developed environmental preservation programs on the scale of either Columbia or Reston. Over time, however, the community and the company have come to an understanding. Slow-growth and environmental movements, with the often reluctant cooperation of the Irvine Company, have led a successful effort to preserve 45,000 acres of wilderness of the original 90,000 acres of the ranch. This radical change from the initial plans brings the environmental planning of Irvine into line with those of the other new towns – perhaps even exceeding them.

Fig. 10. Elaborate landscaping in an Irvine Village made possible by "grey" water recycling. Photo by the author.

Fig. 11. The linear urban corridor in Irvine that follows the drainage canals. Although it includes riding and walking paths, and a variety of urban uses, it has not equaled its original ambitions. Photo by the author.

Community members had started expanding the preservation of open land in the early 1970s by approving a bond issue to create parks and bike paths. The bike-path system, consisting of well-marked trails along roads and a few grade-separated pathways, covers the entire city. By 1988, the city had created more than 1,000 acres of park space and 900 acres of preserved open space. The city also opened a nature education program out of a center in Turtle Rock Park. Citizen activism also proved instrumental in adaptive reuse of a group of older agricultural buildings from the Ranch (City of Irvine 1998, 18).

In 1989, the city adopted a plan to preserve 9,500 undeveloped acres within and around Irvine while shifting development to other areas of the city. The Irvine Company, surrounding municipalities, and the city agreed to an extraordinary plan in which the city and surrounding municipalities gained extensive open space without paying for it, and the company gave up development in certain areas in exchange for higher-density residential and industrial expansion in others. The plan, now expanded to preserve an estimated 44,000 acres of the former ranch, includes major acreage in the northern foothills, and even "3.2 miles of beautiful Pacific Ocean shoreline" in Crystal Cove State Park. Much of the preserved land lies in an open space reserve split between the southern and northern sections of the ranch and is managed by both the Nature Conservancy and the state and local government. This management includes restoration of indigenous plant and animal species, long-term plans, and a schedule of hikes and tours of the properties. It remains to be seen how some areas will be reached, who will manage them, and what the exact nature of open space will be (Bloom 2001, 275).

Other areas of the reserved lands, such as Newport Back Bay, Crystal Cove State Park, Peters Canyon Regional Park, and Wilderness Park, are already part of the reserve system. Crystal Cove, for instance, is open to the public and contains a stunning beach, high cliffs, fields, and foothills. The reserves are an important resource for the communities that surround them because not only do they provide a respite and cultural edification, but they also offer a reminder of the arid, rugged landscape that has been replaced by the manicured development on the Irvine Ranch. Without these preserves, the landscape's earlier identity would have been completely lost.

Irvine has nature preserves and also traffic problems as serious, and perhaps worse, than the other new towns (Irvine's office parks form a major employment hub in Southern California). There is no internal bus system, as there is in Reston and Columbia, and Orange County buses are infrequent in the community. The convenient schools, shopping, and community facilities are primarily patronized by people arriving in cars. The bike-path system is extensive, but it is rare that people can be seen actually using it. Cars rule the road in Irvine. As at the other new towns, the environmental ethic has not transformed the daily lives of individuals in any appreciable manner.

Lessons from the New Towns

After almost fifty years of development, the new towns offer important planning lessons for those seeking to plan large areas of suburban or ex-urban land. In all these communities, nature is part of the cultural life of most residents. The new towns are notable for integrating traditional suburban characteristics in a well-wooded landscape. More active residents appreciate both the cultivated and wild areas of their communities, and many have sought to expand and improve upon them. Developers and residents have added to the suburban landscape an element usually reserved for distant parks and forests: a sense of wildness, free from the ordered system of gardening usually found in suburbia. The investment in open spaces and careful planning has netted impressive profits to developers as these have become very desirable towns.

From the perspective of landscape planning the new towns offer a number of simple but important lessons. The first is that open space provision *per se* is less important than the organization of particular landscapes. A single-minded focus on numbers of acres (beyond scientific habitat planning) is probably less important than how that land is preserved, maintained, and utilized by residents. This may seem to be an obvious point, but it still escapes many planners.

Residents of Irvine probably benefit more than many residents in Columbia and Reston from the open spaces in their neighborhoods. Open spaces near Irvine homes are carefully structured as safe recreational spaces. There is little fear associated with these narrow greenbelts that are landscaped as opposed to natural spaces. Sight lines from houses to open spaces allow a casual surveillance of the greenbelts. Irvine does have natural areas, but these are distinct from villages and are either state parks or regulated ecological zones. Landscape planning, and the application of varied landscape palettes, above all helps give identity to Irvine neighborhoods (covering vast areas) in order to distinguish one area from another.

The larger, secluded river valleys in Reston and Columbia, in a natural state, are important from an ecological point of view (and delightful for those seeking serenity), but can create dangerous situations and a reputation for crime. Open space usage is light in respect to population size and how closely natural space has been linked to housing complexes. Wild nature and the pastoral suburban landscape appear to be mismatched in the security obsessed American suburbia of today. A society less obsessed with crime, abduction, and juvenile delinquency might, however, find natural areas around the home less threatening.

Urban design has not aided the sense of security in Reston or Columbia. Grade separated and/or isolated pathways through thick green spaces may be desirable from a pedestrian safety point of view but in practice are unacceptable in lightly policed natural settings. Irvine has the fewest number of these underpasses and, again, the lack of these is probably a factor in the sense of safety. Pedestrian underpasses at Columbia and Reston are often dark and dank and represent a potential threat to personal safety. Even if attacks rarely occur on these pathways or underpasses, their structure can dissuade many citizens from venturing out. Designers in the future must find more creative means of separating pedestrians and automobiles. In light of how many residents live in these towns, and the cost of holding this land out of development, the path system in Reston or Columbia does not seem cost effective in increasing quality of life. Active recreation spaces such as playing fields, for instance, are much more heavily used.

Artificial lakes, although desirable for the enhanced value and beauty they bring, have been difficult to maintain at a high quality in Reston and Columbia. Silting and eutrophication has undermined water quality in these lakes and the expensive remediation demanded has been inadequate. Concerns have also been raised about dams undermining stream quality below the new lakes. It would be unwise, however, to avoid lakes in future towns. In all these new towns the most popular pathways of the new towns surround lakes irrespective of water quality. Bodies of water also provide a visual focus for neighborhoods and lakefront housing remains some of the most desirable. A legal mechanism within the community association bylaws upholding the association's responsibility to care for the lakes could have had a good effect. Another option is that undertaken by Irvine. Irvine's lake in Woodbridge is less "natural" and thus better maintained. With a hard, cement/stone border and no obvious ecology—really a large-scale swimming pool—it is more attractive as an amenity.

The importance of citizen involvement in maintenance and improvement of open space is a hallmark of all these communities and in different ways has helped preserve and expand open spaces. Organized clean-ups, nature education, and lobbying for improvements have made a major difference in preserving open space. Support from citizen run community associations, which in Reston and Columbia control the open space, has been equally influential. Irvine's city government and local community associations have shown close attention to park space and environmental issues.

To the degree citizens feel that open lands are their common property, the land will be maintained and even enhanced over time. An unexpected benefit of the common holding of property by community associations is the ability to preserve open space even during overheated real estate markets. Across the United States in the last decade homeowners have rudely awakened to the private ownership and development of lands they thought were forever wild or marginal. These towns do not have that problem.

Elitism can be considered the only major drawback of these open space plans. Because much of the land in these new towns are technically "private" spaces owned by the Community Associations they are not widely used or advertised to citizens from other towns (and signs occasionally appear stating that they are for the use of community residents only). This may account for the relatively light use compared to population density; on the other hand, lack of publicity about these areas has also helped preserve the ecological integrity.

Finally, planners hoped that the environmental ethic would spread beyond the natural areas and become part of a more ambitious reordering of American suburban life. In all the towns, the planners may have provided highways, shopping malls, cul-de-sacs, and parking lots, but they also tried to make shopping areas and schools within walking or biking distance on grade-separated walkways. Nature pathways were to become parts of daily routines for students, shoppers, and athletes. The developers even added their other innovations to foster alternative environmental practices. At Columbia, planners envisioned a shuttle bus moving rapidly through town on its very own road. Even when this system proved too expensive and was abandoned, the local community association kept an internal bus system running through decades of low ridership. Idealistic Reston residents developed their own internal transit system and commuter bus service that proved popular for many years. The Irvine city government created a remarkable system of bike paths that stretch across the city.

These innovations, however, have had a negligible effect on use of the automobile. In 1976, planners Burby and Weiss found that although bus use was higher among new-town residents than those living in conventional subdivisions, "community residents overwhelmingly use their cars to travel to work, and to convenience stores, supermarkets, and shopping centers." The only appreciable change in habits came in the children's use of pathways for walking to school (Burby and Weiss 1976, 28). The dominance of the car has only increased with time and has been confirmed in a recent study of commuter behavior (Forsyth 2005, 267-268). A minority of concerned citizens has tried to build on the work of the early planners by supporting pathway creation, mass transit, and mixed-use developments, but even they have failed to make an appreciable difference in driving habits. As in others parts of new town life, design and services did not invariably revolutionize behavior.

Bibliography

Bender, Thomas. *Toward an Urban Vision: Ideas and Institutions in Nineteenth Century America*. Baltimore: Johns Hopkins University Press, 1982.

Bloom, Nicholas. *Suburban Alchemy: 1960s New Towns and the Transformation of the American Dream*. Columbus. Ohio State University Press, 2001.

Bloom, Nicholas. *Merchant of Illusion: James Rouse, America's Salesman of the Businessman's Utopia*. Columbus: Ohio State University Press, 2004.

Burby, Raymond and Shirley Weiss. *New Communities, U.S.A.* Lexington, Massachusetts: Lexington Books, 1976

City of Irvine. "Irvine Community Services." 1998.

Columbia Association. "The Columbia Association." 1998, Columbia Archives.

Columbia Forum. "A Planning Process for Columbia." 1984, Columbia Archives.

Forsyth, Ann. *Reforming Suburbia*. Berkeley: University of California Press, 2005.

Hamilton, Wallace. "The Physical Plan," Howard Research and Development Company, 17 September 1964, Columbia Archive.

Jackson, Kenneth T. *Crabgrass Frontier: The Suburbanization of the United States*. New York: Oxford University Press, 1985.

Kellner, Barbara (Director, Columbia Archive). Interview by the author, 11 November 2005

Marx, Leo. *The Machine in the Garden: Technology and the Pastoral Ideal in America*. New York: Oxford University Press, 1999.

Olsen, Joshua, *Better Places, Better Lives: A Biography of James Rouse*. Washington, D.C., Urban Land Institute, 2004.

Rathburn, Robin. "Nature Center Opens in Reston." [Reston] *Connection*, 21 October 1987.

Reston Land Corporation, "Reston," ca. 1989, George Mason Special Collections.

Rome, Adam. *The Bulldozer in the Countryside: Suburban Sprawl and the Rise of American Environmentalism*, Cambridge: Cambridge University Press, 2001.

Roslenzweig, Roy and Elizabeth Blackmar. *The Park and the People*. Ithaca: Cornell University Press, 1998.

Rouse Company. "Youth in Columbia." *Columbia*, September 1968, Columbia Archive.

Rouse, James. "The Value of Wildlife as an Integral Part of the Urban Community," 18 June 1977, Columbia Archive.

Scott, Louise and Frank O'Donnel. "Irvine: Ten Years into a Fifty Year Plan." *New Worlds,* April 1980.

Shabecoff, Philip. *A Fierce Green Fire: The American Environmental Movement*. New York: Hill and Wang, 1993.

Tennenbaum, Robert. "Planning Determinants for Columbia." *Urban Land*, April 1965.

Watson, Raymond. Interview by the author, 18 November 1998.

Winieweski, Kay. "Water Quality in Columbia's Lakes: A $40,000 Question." *Columbia Flier*, 2 February 1978.

CHAPTER 12

Marrakech: An Ecological Miracle and its Wanton Destruction (1071–2000 A.D.)

Mohammed El Faïz

Translated from the French by Maryrica Ortiz Lottmann

For centuries Marrakech has been distinguished for its ingenious urban design and cultivation of water resources. But today the city's rich material and cultural heritage is threatened not only by negligence but by poverty, urbanization, and commercial real estate development.[1] From its founding in the eleventh century until the beginning of the twentieth century, the city of Marrakech epitomized the garden city. The urbanized core of the medina[2] was nestled in a circle of greenery formed by orchards and kitchen gardens. Beyond the walls lay the land reserved for the palm plantation, with its sixteen thousand hectares[3] of palm trees and various fruit trees, with crops interspersed among them. Successive circles of vegetation, including orchards and cultivated fields, led out to the N'Fis Wadi, which formed the city's western border (Fig. 1). In this essay we will present the characteristics of this model garden city, examine the impact of urbanization on its evolution, and pose some questions about its future.

An Urban Model Inspired by Garden Art

The city of Marrakech was founded in 1071 during the Almoravid dynasty (1061-1147). Until that time the plain had been overtaken by wild vegetation consisting of thorny jujube trees, dwarf pistachio trees, palm trees, and oleasters. The wadis of the Upper Atlas Mountains ended in marshy hollows before flowing into the Tensift River. The Almoravids chose to establish their settlement on this inhospitable site, and this decision proved to be a wise one, for the site transcended the limitations of the environment and topography. Marrakech stood far enough from the stagnant water near the Tensift River, yet close enough to the Issil Wadi, a natural conduit against flooding. The site also lay below the Upper Atlas Mountains, whose waters fed the wadis that supplied the city's water system. All of these advantages were not immediately apparent to the city founders of that era, but the developmental history of Haouz confirms the wisdom of the Almoravids' decision to choose a site where two huge aquifers meet.[4]

Over the course of nine hundred years the city of Marrakech built an impressively green heritage. In the twelfth century there appeared a new type of garden, the Almohad *agdal*, with its kiosks and pavilions (*menzah*), its high towered walls, its immense orchards and cultivated enclosures (paradises), and its fountains, reflecting pools, and huge reservoirs.[5] In the parched desert where birds "choked from thirst," the designers of these gardens created a rustic landscape and a substitute for

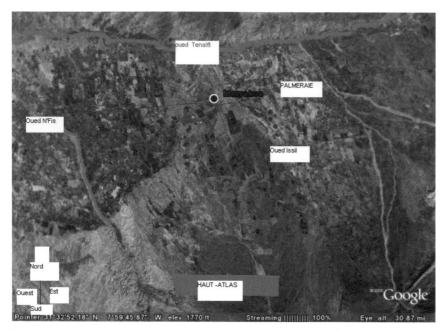

Fig. 1. Satellite photo
Fig. 2. Aerial photograph of the *Agdal*

Paradise (Fig. 2). For centuries the royal parks served as symbols of sovereignty, and Marrakech also produced other, less well known garden types (the *arsa*, the *jnân*, the *riyadh*). These gardens were even more refined and sophisticated than the *agdal* and utilized water, tiles, trees, and flowers to create elaborately decorated, private settings.

The architecture of Arab towns and metropolises used the garden as a key concept in their development. Historians describing these medieval cities extolled their promenades and orchards and the surrounding vegetation. The model of the garden city prevailed everywhere. From Damascus to Baghdad and from Cordoba to Marrakech, the houses resembled rectangles and cubes engulfed in a sea of greenery. The thirteenth-century geographer Al-Qazwînî (active around 1275) drew a diagram of the garden city based on Qazvin, his place of birth, now located in Iran. Here one sees three concentric circles and a nucleus of buildings surrounded by orchards and cultivated plots[6] (Fig. 3). The Arabs knew how to plan their cities around the construction of gardens, and in later periods this model migrated to India and came into full flower under the Mughol dynasty (1526-1857). There King Babur (1483-1530), author of a garden treatise, first planned his garden then oriented the city around it (Fig. 4). The art of gardens, one of the most valuable contributions of Arab civilization, accompanied the progress of urbanization and also inspired the design of the famous cities of Muslim Andalusia[7] and North Africa.

Today Marrakech can pride itself on the wealth and diversity of its many types of gardens. Elsewhere we have described the evolution of the garden styles known as the *agdal*, the *arsa*, the *jnân* and the *riyadh* and have discussed their significance for the world history of gardens.[8] The creation of this ecological heritage was possible only through the mastery of hydrological techniques. The development of aqueducts and of subterranean drainage galleries (*khettaras*)[9] permitted the increase in water supply that was needed to cultivate gardened enclosures in an arid land. The emergence of a strong political power and the need to showcase its ideology also contributed to the birth of the Almohad garden (Fig. 5).

All of the public works projects built during the medieval period (dams, bridges, aqueducts, mosques) are characterized by an identical aesthetic, one that emphasized power, restraint, and beauty. These works of art were meant to serve nature rather than control and straight-jacket it. Thanks to this philosophy, today we can still admire the historic bridge of Marrakech and other medieval works of architecture, which are so unobtrusive they seem to commune with the surrounding landscape. In 1913, while on a mission to Marrakech, Jean-Claude Nicolas Forestier (1861-1930) was surprised and enchanted by this garden city:

> Nothing is more startling than the spectacle set before your eyes when, while en route from Casablanca and still some kilometers from Marrakech, you suddenly see, in the middle of a great barren plain bordered on the south by the blue and white line of the snow-covered Atlas Mountains, the abundant and unexpected verdure, a greenery fresh and soothing, of an immense oasis within which the old Berber city is almost hidden. And after two hundred kilometers down a long

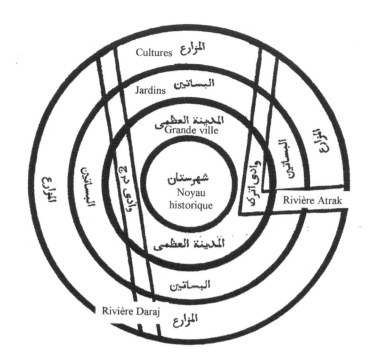

Qazwin (XIIIe s.)

Fig. 3. Qazvin by Al-Qazwînî
Fig. 4. Qazvin by Matrakçi (XVI c.)

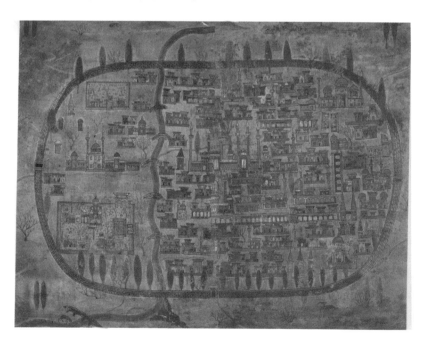

road through bare plains, it is an unexpected pleasure to approach the city by traversing a green palm plantation, though its trees are ravaged and scattered. It is likely that the measures already taken will make it possible to maintain this wonder. Truly it would be devastating if land speculation and private allotments were allowed to compromise this

Fig. 5. Aerial view of the Khettara
Fig. 6. Garden-city according to the Lambert plan

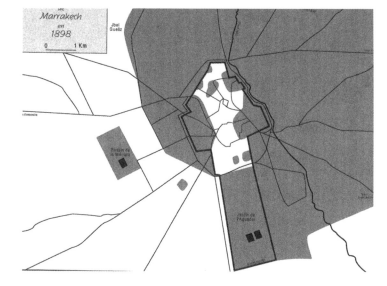

settlement, which, protected and developed, could exceed the beautiful palm trees and palm plantation of the famous Elche, in Spain.[10]

Though the decrees promulgated after 1929 succeeded in saving the palm plantation and the landscapes characteristic of the city, the urbanizing tendencies of the two last decades are dooming the ecological heritage. They have sapped the basis of Marrakech's ecosystem and threaten to destroy it in short order.

Ecological Heritage versus Urbanization

We when speak of the park spaces of the medina we mean all of the cultivated outdoor areas set aside for optimal enjoyment and relaxation. These green spaces can include large natural areas or even an isolated tree near an individual home or apartment building, and they also include all intermediate spaces such as public squares, large public parks, parks in the exurbs, and regional parks. In short, they involve all types of outdoor areas where vegetation is present. To give even a quick overview of the recent history of the medina it is necessary to examine the origins of the garden city and thereby understand its development and the causes of its decline. We must establish a precise diagnosis of the health of these park spaces then formulate measures to safeguard and even bolster the medina's ecological patrimony.

Three periods characterize the evolution of Marrakech's park space: the pre-colonial period (1071 to 1912), the colonial period (1913 to 1956) and the period of independence (1956 to the present).

The Era of the Garden City (1071 to 1912)

The pre-colonial period is characterized by the emergence of a garden city surrounded by green spaces that overflowed the city walls and also served as great centers of horticultural production. Though ecological change is inevitable, this fact should not mask the threats that urbanization sometimes imposes on wooded spaces. The construction of the Almohad *casbah*[11] in the twelfth century was undertaken as part of a vast garden called Al-Sāliha, and the extensions made by the Saadians in the sixteenth century encroached on the old orchards. But this urbanization was largely balanced by the development of royal parks and the extension of new gardens.

Until the beginning of the twentieth century Marrakech remained a park-like city. Its 65,000 inhabitants lived in an area two-thirds of which consisted of old orchards. Foreign travelers of the late nineteenth century confirmed the impression of a dense fabric of greenery,[12] and this density was not limited to the walled area of the medina (Fig. 6). Much of the city and its surroundings were the exclusive domain of the palm plantation, the royal gardens, the food-producing *jnānāt*,[13] and the large imperial olive grove called the Semlalia. All these green spaces, which were owned by the *habous* (religious institutions), the state, or influential members of society, gave the medina a "rustic aspect" (A. Mandleur).[14] The rural character of the city remained intact until the Protectorate established its colonial and urbanizing influence.

The Protectorate: Modern Parks Triumph over Traditional Green Spaces

The period of the Protectorate was marked by the creation of a new city outside the walls, while the medina was limited to its role as a traditional space. Though the colonial government may have intended to preserve the Morocco of yesterday, in fact its decrees led to a kind of socio-spacial segregation and demonstrated a laissez-faire attitude towards the traditional elite. Over time colonial rule proved detrimental to the ecological balance of the medina. The Great Depression and two world wars caused the scarce financial resources to be directed toward improvement of the European quarter, benefiting only the 10,000 people occupying this lightly populated space. Yet the soft urbanization of the new European quarter, known as Guéliz, was for the most part balanced by enlarging the gardens and parks that had been envisioned in the colonial plan for urbanization.

The medina served as a center of attraction for rural migrants who settled there in successive waves. From 1910 to 1930, the population grew to 60,000 inhabitants, and between 1912 and 1950, the Muslim population doubled. Rural migration reached its height between 1935 and 1945. The city had been designed to contain one million inhabitants, but within a span of fifty years it was forced to house more than twice that number, resulting in urban sprawl and the disappearance of the green spaces of the medina.[15]

In order to profit from the growing demand for housing, real estate promoters did not hesitate to divide the orchards and gardens into lots. Thus an irreversible movement began to take shape, and a few years of feverish speculation led to the asphyxiation of the medina and the destruction of numerous gardens. The harmony of the historic quarter was broken up for the sake of building a heterogenous collection of facades without regard for the allocation of space. During a quarter century the many housing tracts built to the north and east and all along the walls of the old city triumphed over the historic orchards that for the inhabitants of Marrakech had given a particular character to the promenade (*n'zâha*). Today there remain only the toponyms that testify to the character of the medina in past centuries: a space of beautiful vistas and *joie de vivre*.

The Decline of the Garden City Following Independence

After independence, park space was determined by population growth and by urbanization outside the city walls. From

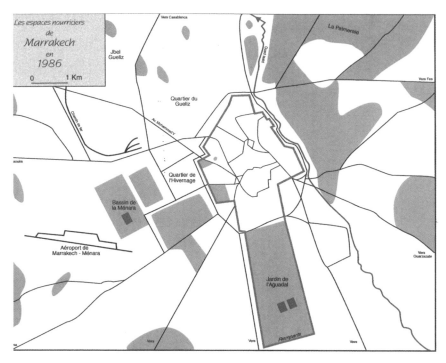

Fig. 7. The City decline after the Independence

1960 forward, Marrakech saw huge demographic changes. From 1960 to 1982, the population grew from 243,000 inhabitants to 440,000. City maps show the development of satellite towns to the southeast (Sidi Youssef Ben Ali), to the north (Mohammedia-Daoudiat City), to the west (Douar Laskar, Douar Iziki), and they also show the multiplication of outlying tent villages (*douars*).[16] In 2000, the population reached one million, and there was much more urban development. Given these powerful trends, one wonders about the fate reserved for the model garden city. On the 1953 city map of Marrakech the historic quarter of the medina appears densely urbanized, but some islands of greenery remain. In the east the Bahmad Agdal has survived, and so have portions of the Lāafiya Jnān, the Bousekri Jnān, the Al-Luck `Arsat, the Bouachrine `Arsat, and in the west a corridor of gardens formed by the Al-Mamounia `Arsat, the My Abdeslam `Arsat, the gardens of the Koutoubia, and the parks and orchards of City Hall (Fig. 7). To this list, which is not exhaustive, it is necessary to add the great Almohad Agdal whose orchards and olive groves extend southward. Outside the medina, a corridor of greenery occupies the entire width of the Avenue des Remparts (from Bāb Jdid to Bāb Nqob) and extends westward to embrace the Hivernage district, the Experimental Farm, and the historic Menara Garden. Only the buildings of the air base interrupt the flow of park space. The scattered spots of urbanization concentrated around Jbel Guéliz and along the Avenue of Casablanca seem to emerge from a sea of greenery. Though population growth and urban development inside the medina appear to have undermined its ecological inheritance, the European quarter seems more balanced and more open to its natural surroundings.

A major conclusion emerges from analyzing the city map of 1953: the destruction of landscaping in the old city destroyed its garden-city character, but this destruction worked to the benefit of its rival, the new city, which was transformed into a garden city and preserved that title until recently. By comparing the 1953 city map with that published in 1986, one can extrapolate the condition of the parks today.[17] Apart from the green space of the *agdal*, the My Abdeslam `Arsat and the small spots formed by the remnants of the City Hall and Koutoubia gardens, the medina has lost all the traditional park space of its historic legacy. The cartographers erroneously designated as green space the twenty hectares of the orchard of the Bahmad Agdal, for the small remaining piece of this garden is entirely in ruins. The same is true of the Bouachrine 'Arsat, where some remarkable trees still remain.

The above remarks based on cartographic evidence are confirmed by a statistical analysis of the green spaces in each district. The following table compares population growth to fluctuations in the amount of green space:[18]

Urban districts	Population	Park space in hectares	Ratio of park space in square meters per inhabitant
Médina	235,000	49.0	2.08
Guéliz	12,000	14.2	11.83
Hivernage	6,600	199.0	301.51
Mohammedia-Safi	58,000	2.0	0.34
Extension-ouest	29,000	2.5	0.86
Sidi Youssef b. Ali	77,000	———	———
Total	**417,600**	**266.7**	**316.62**

Source: M.El Faïz, *Jardins Historiques, op. cit.* p. 54.

On the basis of the international standard of ten square meters of green space per person, one can conclude that except for the Guéliz-Hivernage district, the other urban sectors (comprising 95% of the population) are overpopulated.[19] The situation is particularly alarming for the medina and for Sidi Youssef ben Ali, which concentrate more than two-thirds of their inhabitants in the urban center. These statistics, along with the cartographic analysis, illustrate the irreversible shrinkage of green space.

From this rapid historical review we can draw two important observations. During its long history, the medina of Marrakech underwent population growth and urbanization by maintaining a balance between vegetation and the built environment. Until the beginning of last century, the medina's inhabitants had at least sixty square meters of park space per person; that is to say, they possessed six times more green space than the standards imposed by modern town planning. A citizen of Marrakech had to walk only a few meters to enter the gardens and orchards and fully enjoy their many benefits.

Crisis of the Garden City and its Consequences

Judging by developments over the last fifty years, we can state the following facts:
- The balance between vegetation, the built environment, and demographic growth has been broken. For the first time in the history of the medina, urbanization works to the detriment of park space and it ignores the need to renew the inherited ecological capital. Consequently, today's citizens lack not only traditional private gardens and orchards but also must travel several kilometers to find a tranquil change of scene.
- Gardens within the walls of the old city (especially the *riyadhs* and gardened courtyards) have been paved over because of the continued increase in the price of water and interference with the medina's traditional water supply system, a system which was based on the *khettaras*. These actions have harmed the city's ecology.[20]
- The most recent administrative division (1997), limiting the Medina Prefecture to the area within the walls, has placed more pressure on open spaces. Often such decisions are made for the sake of parking, government buildings, or the tourist industry, and very seldom do they add more green space, for in this context park space is considered a less urgent need or a useless luxury.
- The paving of streets and plazas smothered root systems and caused many trees to die.

These elements are some of the many factors that diminished the medina's park space and they underscore the loss to urban

Fig. 8. The triumphant desert
Fig. 9. The time of vandalism

ecology in the historic center of Marrakech. The interpretation of the most recent aerial photographs and their digital reproduction accentuate the stress on vegetation (Fig. 8). They confirm the disappearance of gardened spaces that in the past formed a green belt within the city walls. Cruelly, the districts with the greatest population density suffer the most from the lack of parks (Fig. 9).[21]

Since the time of the Hanging Gardens of Babylon until our own day, countless gardened enclosures have been destroyed through human negligence, that is, through uncontrolled urbanization. To stop this degradation, each individual needs to view the whole planet as a garden and to act in harmony with nature and not against it. Though Marrakech may be wounded and attacked on every side, the city can still provide the opportunity to build the garden–planet of the future.[22] Its location, its potential, and its past as a garden city entitle it to play this role and even demand that it do so. At a minimum, the city must be given a chance to perform this function. In order to make this rebirth possible we must immediately begin a vast and daring program to protect and restore the historic gardens of Marrakech. Today this undertaking must be a priority. While poverty and unemployment are long-term problems, the loss of a cultural inheritance is irreversible. No remedy in the world can cure a ravaged national conscience or restore to a nation its lost garden art.

Bibliography

El Faïz, Mohammed. "Pour une histoire de longue durée des aménagements hydro-agricoles dans le Haouz." In M. Marié and A. Bencheikh, (collected works), *Grands appareillages hydrauliques et sociétés locales en Méditerranée*. Paris: Presses ENPC, 1994.

El Faïz, Mohammed. *Marrakech: patrimoine en péril*. Paris: Actes Sud/ EDDIF, 2002.

El Faïz, Mohammed. *Les Jardins de Marrakech,* Paris: édition Actes Sud, 2000.

Forestier, Jean-Claude Nicolas. *Grandes villes et systèmes de parcs*. Paris: Institut Français d'Architecture, 1997.

El Faïz, Mohammed, éd. *Les jardins historiques de Marrakech: mémoire écologique d'une ville impériale*. Florence: EDIFIR, 1996.

Anon. "Le rapport préliminaire du dernier Schéma Directeur de la ville de Marrakech." (SDAU) Report to the Municipality of Marrakesh, 1988.

Eveno, Claude and Gilles Clément eds. *Le jardin planétaire*. Chateauvallon: éditions de l'Aube, 1997.

Notes

[1] Marrakech is the only city in Morocco to be classified by UNESCO as a World Heritage site for both its physical environment (1985) and it cultural riches (2001).

[2] In Morocco and elsewhere in North Africa, the medina is the name given to the historically Muslim city as opposed to the European city built during the French protectorate (1912-1956).

[3] One hectare equals 2.47 acres.

[4] El Faïz, Mohammed. "Pour une histoire de longue durée des aménagements hydro-agricoles dans le Haouz." In Marié, M., Bencheikh, A., (collected works), *Grands appareillages hydrauliques et sociétés locales en Méditerranée*. Paris: Presses ENPC (1994): 28-29.

[5] The Almohad dynasty reigned from 1130 to 1269. During that time the Moroccan empire extended over much of Spain (Al-Andalus), North Africa, and the Sahara.

[6] El Faïz, Mohammed, *Marrakech: patrimoine en péril*. Paris: Actes Sud/ EDDIF, 2002, p. 86.

[7] The Arabs conquered Spain in the eighth century. Their territory, known in Arabic as Al-Andalus (Muslim Spain), endured until 1492, when the kingdom of Grenada fell to the Christians.

[8] El Faïz, Mohammed, *Les Jardins de Marrakech, Paris,* édition Actes Sud, 2000. *Agdal* is a term of Berber origin and refers to the great royal gardens of the thirteenth century, together with their immense reservoirs. The `arsa is smaller than the *agdal* and consists of pavilions and agricultural plantations. A *jnān* contains fruit and palm trees and is generally located outside the walls of the old city. *Riyahds* are gardened courtyards located inside the grand houses within the walls.

[9] The *khettaras* are drainage galleries that make it possible to utilize subterranean waters for agricultural and urban purposes. The technique originated in Persia and spread to the rest of the world in ancient times. *Khettaras* are found in the oasis of Tourfan and also in China.

[10] Forestier, Jean-Claude Nicolas, *Grandes villes et systèmes de parcs*, édition Norma. Paris: Institut Français d'Architecture (1997): 206-7.

[11] The term *casbah* denotes the fortified royal city that was home to the sultan and his court.

[12] El Faïz, Mohammed, éd. *Les jardins historiques de Marrakech: mémoire écologique d'une ville impériale*. Florence: EDIFIR, 1996.

[13] The word *jnānāt* is the plural of *jnān*.

[14] Ibid, p. 51.

[15] Ibidem.

[16] The *douars* are rural settlements inhabited by peasants and gardeners. Once integrated into the urban perimeter, they became shanty towns.

[17] Source: Ministry for Agriculture, Rabat.

[18] Table is based on "Le rapport préliminaire du dernier Schéma Directeur de la ville de Marrakech" (SDAU, 1988).

[19] The figures for the Guéliz and Hivernage districts should be revised downward, following their recent transformation into zones for the construction of buildings. From 2000 to 2005 the appearance of the famous European city completely changed with the increase of high-rise buildings.

[20] The paving over of the garden courtyards in the grand houses of the medina deprived the historic city of its garden heritage.

[21] These are the central, northern, and eastern districts.

[22] Eveno, Claude and Clément, Gilles, eds, *Le jardin planétaire,* Chateauvallon: éditions de l'Aube, 1997.

Gardens, City Life and Culture

Gardens, City Life and Culture

Gardens, City Life and Culture

Gardens, City Life and Culture

Gardens, City Life and Culture

Gardens, City Life and Culture

CHAPTER 13

Gardens as Cultural Memory in Suzhou, Eleventh to Nineteenth Centuries

Yinong Xu

Two interesting issues are implied by this title of the essay.[1] One centers on the attitudes towards the past in garden conservation over time in Suzhou, while the other concerns the possible ways of garden's contribution through conservation to urban culture and life. In this short essay I mainly focus on the diverse implications of different modes of intervention in garden conservation; to do this, I take Cang Lang Ting and the Garden of the Embroidered Valley as primary examples, followed by a fleeting analysis of a few other well-known gardens in Suzhou to widen the horizon of discussion. Since studies of garden culture in imperial China form an integral part of what we now call "the arts," and since its past, like the past of Jinling that Stephen Owen has observed, was one "in which a historical past and a literary past were inextricably woven together," (Owen 1990, 421) the reader will find that in the process of discussion the language, vocabulary, and sometimes methodology derived from the study of literary prose and poetry are constantly applied to gardens.[2] At the end of the essay, I briefly examine the issue of possible roles that these gardens may have played in Suzhou. The paucity of primary materials available to us, however, imposes a dual limitation on this discussion: (1) it is one of defining the question, rather than finding its affirmative answers; and (2) instead of a preferred diachronic analysis, a synchronic approach is adopted.

In his classic, *Jiangnan yuan lin zhi*, written in 1937 but first published in 1963, Tong Jun 童寯 offers us a fairly comprehensive mapping of gardens in the Jiangnan region. At a point in his account of a history of these gardens, Tong remarks: "If one desires to search those gardens in Jiangnan which were created in the Song period (960-1278), one will not find [even] one or two out of ten. But among those built in the Ming period (1368-1644), after changes of their ownership and in the wake of their restorations [*chong xiu* 重修], still quite a few have survived through the Qing period (1644-1912) to the present day. ... When talking about the gardens of the Jiangnan region in terms of their quality and quantity, no place surpasses Suzhou today." (Tong Jun 1984, 24, 27) Apart from the recognition of Suzhou's importance in studies of private gardens, a particular line of reasoning can be derived from Tong's remarks. Tong obviously acknowledges that in order for a garden to "survive" over time, it has to be "restored." "Restorations," however, do not necessarily guarantee the survival of these gardens; hence the survival of "still quite a few" rather than all of them. And for that reason any uncritical and undifferentiated use of the word "restoration" is prone to obscure the complex picture of the vicissitudes of gardens.

All these, however, are based on the assumption that some of the gardens from the Ming period or beyond *did* survive. On this point, Craig Clunas, for instance, thinks otherwise: "Despite continuity at the level of names, and in the face of our understandable wish to believe otherwise, the sad fact is that no garden landscape of the Ming period survives in anything like its original form, whether at Suzhou or anywhere else." (Clunas 1995, 40) The notions of "continuity" and "survival" employed here by Clunas are predicated upon a set of criteria that do not appear to coincide fully with the criteria used by many of garden essayists in late imperial China, even though questions of historicity and authenticity were a serious concern for men of letters from the Song period onward. If we are to approach the issue from the European perspective, the use of the inherently ambiguous term "form" by Clunas does not seem to lend any clarity to the point, as it means "shape" on the one hand and "idea" or "essence" on the other within Western thought,[3] and the crux of the matter in the study of gardens is as much of the physical changes themselves as of how people have conceived them. On the physical plane, Clunas's conclusion, as we will see in the following sections, may still have been reached a little too hastily and in too simplistic a manner, as he seems to have overlooked the fact that spatial disposition and configuration of a garden as a whole was in many cases taken as one of the crucial bases on which work of restoration or appropriation was executed, and conceptually it constituted a major, and perhaps defining, part of garden landscape and identity.

A number of gardens in Suzhou were conserved indeed, but the conservation was effected not only by "restoration" but through a range of interventional modes; on the other hand, the word "restoration" invites us to ask precisely what is meant to be restored in each event of intervention. For the convenience of discussion, I pay attention only to a number of selected events of garden building on the basis of old garden landscapes, by highlighting three characteristic modes: that of emphasizing "restoration" or even "building afresh" and thus delivering a keen sense of "continuity" of the garden through time, that of making a new garden by physically "appropriating" the old while tacitly acknowledging conceptual resonance between the new and the old, and that of completely "superseding" the old and thus foregrounding incongruity and disjunction. Imbued with interplays between physicality and conceptuality, these three highlighted modes represent a continuum of conceptions and practices on the terrain of garden conservation, and no clear and fast line can be drawn between them, either across different gardens or across different periods of a single garden's history.

The most prominent case of garden restoration for continuity is Cang Lang Ting 滄浪亭,[4] initially built by Su Shunqin 蘇舜欽 (1008-1048). Victimized by the opponents of the Qingli 慶歷 Reform of 1043-1045 and consequently deprived of his official status, Su Shunqin traveled south in the early spring of 1045 and sojourned in Suzhou. Probably about two years later, he purchased the site of a disused garden previously owned by the Wu-Yue dignitary Sun Chengyou 孙承祐 (936-985) in the south of the city. He then built a pavilion on the site by the stream, named it Cang Lang, wrote an essay entitled "Record of Cang Lang Ting," and throughout the following months composed a number of poems associated with the site.[5]

By the Northern Song (960-1126), the art of gardening had served a purpose in scholarly culture in the same way that literary composition had for centuries: self-cultivation and self-expression. Su Shunqin cultivated and then expressed himself with his Cang Lang Ting by coping with a set of fundamental relationships always present in the life of any literary men—the relationships of the self with heaven-and-earth and the myriad things (tian di wan mu 天地万物), with past human events, and with current society. His narration of these relationships in prose and poetry concerning Cang Lang Ting is a working out of the problems of self. These relationships are intertwined and centered on the problem of freedom from attachments. It is a problem that Su Shunqin has to tackle at this moment of crisis in his life.

It has often been mistaken that the naming of Su Shunqin's pavilion reveals his intention to retreat.[6] But the term *cang lang*, coming from the well-known line contained in both the *Mencius* and "Yu fu" of the *Chu ci* anthology, carries a meaning of profound polarity: "When the *cang lang* waters are clear, I can wash my hat strings in them;/When the *cang lang* waters are muddy, I can wash my feet in them."[7] It metaphorically defines a scholar's desired political stance in society: if government is righteous, a Confucian gentleman should seek official employment, signaled by the ribboned cap of official rank; but if government is corrupt, then a gentleman should retire to an idle existence and dangle his feet in a pond.[8] It is this situational oscillation between the two polar—mutually contrasting and complementary—approaches to life that provides the basis of Su Shunqin's frame of mind when he built Cang Lang Ting, and later attracts other scholar-officials' as well as the Qing emperors' attention to the site. Su Shunqin was not prepared to give up his political aspirations. He felt so distressed over his misfortune, he reasons, because of his desire for fame and wealth, the addictive attachment that he now deplores. The Cang Lang site helps him ponder over the vicissitudes of his past pursuits, find the 'true delight' of the freedom from attachments, reach a new level of understanding, and eventually overcome himself.[9] He turns passive escape into positive waiting: to him, although the political situation of the 1040s was turbid, it might not remain so; someday, government could be once more honest and upright.[10]

By erecting and naming his pavilion and then by writing about it, Su Shunqin transformed the meaning of the old garden. Garden construction is like literary composition, which articulates the builder's or owner's thinking, expresses his values and aspirations, and inspires others to write about it. Similarly, garden reconstruction recomposes what has been written, thus adding to it new ideas, altering its value, and enriching its meanings. What Su Shunqin did with the site by the time he wrote the "Record of Cang Lang Ting" was no more than erecting a pavilion,[11] but with the addition of this single structure to the existing garden site and the naming of it, he recomposed a work so that it now conveyed important messages that its predecessor had not. A fundamentally new garden was created, foregrounding a conceptual disjunction with the old site. In a reverse perspective, however, the splendid configurations of the ponds, hillocks, and foliage of the site offered him the luxury of tranquility and inspired his thinking and writing. The site therefore becomes both the setting and the subject for literary composition. A two-way working is in process here, simply because the site of the old garden lends itself to the referencing of all categories—nature, history, and society.

Su Shunqin's waiting met with some encouraging result—he was reinstated in his official status, and was appointed in 1048 to the position of Assistant Prefect of Huzhou 湖州. But before he went to his post, a sudden illness took his life in the twelfth month of that same year. After Su Shunqin's death, the ownership of the site frequently changed throughout the remaining years of the Northern Song and beyond, until the Yuan (1260-1368) period when it became occupied by a couple of Buddhist monasteries; and Su Shunqin's pavilion had long ceased to exist.

In 1546, a monk named Wenying 文瑛 erected a new pavilion by the side of his Dayun 大雲 monastery, and named it Cang Lang. Wenying then asked Gui Youguang 歸有光 (1506-1571) to write a "Record of Cang Lang Ting," noting this event (Gui Youguang, 15.20a-21a). Offering a delineation of a full circle of the processes in which first "Cang Lang Ting became Dayun monastery" and then "Dayun monastery [once again] became Cang Lang Ting," Gui Youguang's "Record," however, does not really *record* Wenying's act; through artful rhetoric, it effectively turns an allusion into an attribution, whereby the idea of the "restoration" of the pavilion comes into being. What Wenying says, as Gui Youguang tells us, is that

Fig. 1. Cang Lang Ting. Contained in Song Luo, *Cang Lang xiao zhi*, 1695.

he built a pavilion in the place where Su Shunqin's pavilion once stood. Alluding to Su Shunqin's story, Wenying created a Cang Lang pavilion in its own right and he asked Gui Youguang to record *his* reason for this act. Yet Gui Youguang insists that Wenying merely "restored" what was once there and his pavilion not only owes its existence to that of Su Shunqin but is really a continuation of the latter—Wenying's pavilion has to be attributed to Su Shunqin's.

The underlying driving force for the "restoration" of Cang Lang Ting, Gui Youguang reasons, comes from the everlasting quality of *ming*, "name" and "reputation" and its rightful bearers, the *shi*, literary men. Gui Youguang makes this point by citing, as well as *not* citing, historically prominent local figures in both the recent and remote past, who are not the kind of *shi* that Gui Youguang has in mind, and are therefore of little importance with regard to any enduring site. Thus the history of Cang Lang Ting is basically a literary one: the name of Su Shunqin can last forever because he is a literary man, and because there are latecomers who share his values and aspirations.[12] But to account for the fact that it is this Buddhist monk who "reconstructed" the pavilion and "restored" its name, Gui Youguang has to make a statement at the end of the essay about what kind of a person Wenying "really" is: "Wenying reads books and likes poetry. He associates with my circle, and we call him the Cang Lang monk." Somewhat condescendingly identifying Wenying with the *shi*, Gui Youguang seems to say to Wenying: "Should you wish your act of construction to be meaningful, and your pavilion to be worthy of a record, you have to be one of us, upholding this culture of ours."

The effect of Gui Youguang's textual intervention was not immediate but far reaching. In his "A Brief Note on Gardens," Yuan Hongdao 袁宏道 (1568-1610) does not regard Cang Lang Ting as restored:

The gardens and pavilions that were famed in the past, among which were the Qian family's South Garden, Su

Zimei's Cang Lang Pavilion, Zhu Changwen's [朱長文, 1041-1098] Pleasure Patch, and Fan Chengda's [范成大, 1126-1193] Shihu Old Retreat, all have become desolate and disused. What were said to be lofty ridges and limpid ponds, hidden hilltops and emerald-green bamboos, have turned into places where young herdsmen and firewood collectors reap straws and seek whetstones (Yuan Hongdao 1981, 180-81).

But both Wenying's and Gui Youguang's names enter every local gazetteer compiled thereafter, under the entry "Cang Lang Ting," and the wording is that "Wenying *re*-constructed Cang Lang Ting" and "Gui Youguang composed a *ji* record." The cultural continuity of Cang Lang Ting was invented.

The conversion of the site of Cang Lang Ting back to that of a garden happened in 1695 when Song Luo 宋犖 (1634-1713), in his capacity as the incumbent provincial governor of Jiangsu, built a pavilion on top of the hill and retained the name Cang Lang Ting for it. At the same time, he added to the site a number of structures all in close relation to Su Shunqin's literary work (Fig. 1). It is also from this time that Cang Lang Ting became a government property, and functioned as a government-owned guesthouse. The intensity of Song Luo's interest in Cang Lang Ting was such that, apart from having composed a number of poems associated with the site, he contributed part of his salary to the total cost of the construction work, which lasted six months. Then in 1696, he wrote the "Record of the Restoration of Cang Lang Ting" before he compiled his two-chapter *Short Historical Anthology of Cang Lang*. Two years later, he compiled the *Collected Works of Su Zimei* and wrote a preface to it.

Song Luo consciously delivers a strong sense of continuity in his "Record" that registers his own act: his work brings Cang Lang Ting back to its former outlook (*fu jiu guan* 復舊觀) (Song Luo 1884, B.1a-2b). Except at the level of the topographical disposition of the place, this sense of continuity does not dwell on the plane of its physical appearance, however: Su Shunqin's Cang Lang Ting was to Song Luo less a historical fact than a timeless image in association with Su's deeds and aspirations, and what had been restored were the values signified by the name of the pavilion. But why did Su Shunqin become such a special reference for Song Luo that he seems to have been obsessed with "rebuilding" Cang Lang Ting and "restoring" everything that was associated with Su Shunqin?

Su Shunqin's life is a classic example of the recurrent tragedy—"a worthy person did not meet his time," *bu yu shi* 不遇時. He was noted by his contemporaries for his literary talent, political insights and aspirations, and personal integrity—all the necessary qualities for a promising career—but such promise was shattered by his early death only four years after he was forced out of office. There was a widely shared sense of keen regret for Su Shunqin's fortune, and it was this sense of regret for unfulfilment that had borne upon Song Luo's acts of reconstructing Cang Lang Ting and writing about it. Moreover, the adversity that Su Shunqin suffered was not peculiar to Su himself, and no scholar official who aspired to long lasting fame in literature and government service was immune to it. The concern was therefore a generic one, from which Song Luo himself could not escape. In this sense, Song Luo's feeling towards Su Shunqin's misfortunes was more than just sympathy; it was empathy. And such empathy was turned into action with a vengeance.

Not only is part of Song Luo's narrative in his "Record of the Restoration of Cang Lang Ting" strikingly similar in style to that of Su Shunqin's "Record of Cang Lang Ting," but he deliberately repeats some of the specific features that appeared in the latter. All these, *prima facie*, make Song Luo's essay a simple pastiche. But it is not. What Song Luo did was to

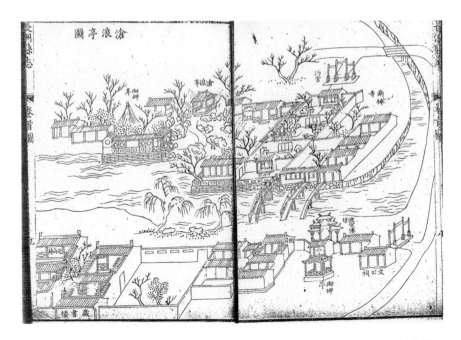

Fig. 2. Picture-map of Cang Lang Ting. Contained in Li Guangzuo 李光祚 (*jin shi* 1733), *Qianlong Changzhou xian zhi* 乾隆長洲縣志, edited by Gu Yilu 顧詒禄 et al. (Suzhou, 1753).

re-write the story, because something in the earlier version both attracted and disturbed him. By additions, deletions, and alterations, he redirected the story and emended the sources of his anxiety. He *re*-produced a scenario that would hopefully make things as they should be and should have been, thus establishing a continuity with an idealized past pointing to an idealized future. The acts of Song Luo were therefore not those of simple repetition, but those of rectification: the site for him should be rectified from a place for involuntarily dangling one's feet in the pond to one for positively washing one's hat strings.

Song Luo did not regard his "restoration" of Cang Lang Ting as a one-off work, but took its maintenance into consideration as well. Indeed, throughout the ensuing but the last two centuries of the imperial era, Cang Lang Ting was repaired or restored time and again (Fig. 2). Among minor repairs to the garden there were two major restorations, in 1827 and 1872-3, respectively by the incumbent governors of Jiangsu, Liang Zhangju 梁章鉅 (1775-1849) and Zhang Shusheng 張樹聲 (1824-1884). Liang Zhangju pursued the restoration of Cang Lang Ting in an age when the Suzhou region was still notably prosperous. Liang was inspired by Su Shunqin's story as much as by Song Luo's endeavors—he not only wrote an essay, bearing the same title as that by Song Luo, but also compiled a four-chapter work entitled *Historical Anthology of Cang Lang Ting* in the same year.[13] Even the narrative of part of his "Record of the Restoration of Cang Lang Ting" is similar to that of Song's.[14] Yet a closer reading of Liang Zhangju's "Record" reveals subtle variations in his emphasis. On the one hand, literary tradition alone is seen as having guaranteed the perpetuation of Cang Lang Ting, which "has nothing to do with fame, rank, power, and wealth." In this respect, Liang's reasoning resonates more with Gui Youguang's than with Song Luo's. On the other hand, by silently adding to the site a shrine of Liang Hong 梁鴻 (first century C.E.), who is noted for his personal integrity and great learning, as well as his aspiration for leading a reclusive life in the mountains,[15] Liang Zhangju somewhat tactfully counterbalances the meaning of Cang Lang Ting as emphasized by Song Luo, and projects to the site his own desire expressed in his later writings by picking up Su Shunqin's minor and superficial longing for retreat expressed in the latter man's early poetry. In other words, Liang Zhangju subtly and yet profoundly readjusted Song Luo's rewritten story of Su Shunqin's Cang Lang Ting.

The Cang Lang garden restored by Liang Zhangju lasted for less than thirty-five years until extensive damage was inflicted on the whole city of Suzhou during its fall to the Taiping rebels in 1860 and its recapture by the imperial army two years later. Suzhou's role as a regional metropolis was subsequently taken over by Shanghai. Zhang Shusheng's narratives in his

"Record of the Restoration of Cang Lang Ting" center on a new central theme—the theme of "returning" to the former splendor of the garden (Zhang Shusheng 1929, 2.4b-5b). By rearranging the principal structures on the site, he projects a "new" outlook of Cang Lang Ting (Fig. 3), an outlook that is in congruence, not with a remote past, but with the recent one. If Song Luo's and Liang Zhangju's "restorations" of Cang Lang Ting centered on reproducing scenarios that indicated what things should be and for that reason pointed to the future, Zhang Shusheng's work was oriented towards the past. Song Luo and Liang Zhangju certainly paid attention to the past, but the past they utilized was distant and thus easy to manipulate, allowing the present to pursue the future. By contrast, the past to which Zhang Shusheng referred was a recent one and for that reason was a *real* past to which returning could be seen as possible. This theme of returning, however, serves a grander vision: Cang Lang Ting was taken by Zhang Shusheng as an indicator of the fortunes of the whole city and the whole region, and its restoration this time as a sign of their recovery from the devastating war against the Taiping rebellion. And this particular garden is able to assume such a role largely because it was a local government property.[16] The social, economic, and political

Fig. 3. Picture-map of Cang Lang Ting. Engraved on stone in 1883.

turmoil inflicted on the Suzhou region by the Taiping rebellion is not perceived by Zhang Shusheng as incidental, but rather as inherent in the propensity of things, their life cycle in which progression and reversal alternate. The alternation does not happen fortuitously, but at its right time. Thus the foreboding of the recovery of the region by the restoration of Cang Lang Ting was not a forced one for Zhang Shusheng, but only a revealing of the ineluctable process of development in which all things work correlatively.

Each event of intervention, from the time of Monk Wenying down to that of Zhang Shusheng, is registered in the local gazetteers under the rubric 'Restoration,' which suggests a common understanding or expectation of the life cycle and cultural continuity of the garden. This common understanding is based on the continuity of assumed location of the site, on the continuity of its name that carries with it a wide range of implications, and on the continuity of the spatial disposition and topographical configuration, which is emphasized in nearly every text on Cang Lang Ting. Yet I have demonstrated the particular reasons compelling each individual to take on the task of restoration, and the specific agenda with which the individual accomplished the enterprise. With every restoration of the garden, new ideas regarding the meaning of the site accumulate. Su Shunqin's "writing" happens to both site and text, giving rise to the original story of Cang Lang Ting, and so does Gui Youguang's, Song Luo's, Liang Zhangju's, and Zhang Shusheng's "rewriting," which enriches the meaning of the story. The site provided illustrations for the texts, and the texts functioned as footnotes to the site. Text and site thus function correlatively, each requiring the other as a condition for its own meaningful existence. Ideas flow between the site and the texts, through the vehicle of the allusive names. As a result, Cang Lang Ting did not become a fixed form in either physical or referential terms; the central theme threads through its history, but different elements and interpretations add up time and again, all coming out of their particular social, political, and intellectual contexts. The physical site and literary works associated with it thus converge and form an integrated whole, "an ideational tumulus,"[17] that grows and enriches itself, rendering the act of remembrance more vivid and memorable (Figs. 4 and 5).

Fig. 4. Cang Lang Ting. View toward the southeast from the opposite of the stream.

Fig. 5. Cang Lang Ting. Rocks at the back of the Hall of the Luminous Way (Ming Dao Tang 明道堂).

★

Admittedly, the case of Cang Lang Ting was unique among the scholars' gardens in Suzhou, in that it was turned into a property owned by the local government in 1695. Probably for that reason the idea of "restoration"—either projected or perceived—for cultural continuity is particularly salient and sustained in the trajectory of its development. This does not mean, however, that the idea of garden restoration itself is unique to Cang Lang Ting. I have cited at the beginning of this essay Tong Jun's observation that each intervention in the history of a private garden usually happened right after a change of its ownership. The specific direction of intervention was then dependent on the new owner's social background, personal experience, and his line of thinking at the time of intervention. When any of these was in agreement with that of a previous owner of the garden, the condition for explicit "restoration" was likely to emerge. A notable example of this kind is the Garden of the Embroidered Valley (Xiu Gu Yuan 繡谷園).

In 1647, the local scholar Jiang Gai 蔣垓 purchased a small plot of land in the northwest of the city and built a garden. The garden did not gain its name, however, until an old stone was excavated in the garden, on which the two characters, *xiu gu*, were inscribed. Judging from the style of the calligraphy, Jiang Gai believed that they must have been written around the Northern Song period or even beyond. He marveled at the timely surfacing of the two stone-engraved characters as part of the causal conditions of things (*shu* 數) in the alternation of their concealment and appearance, Jiang Gai embedded the stone in the wall, took the two characters as the name of his garden, and in 1660 wrote an essay entitled "Record of Xiu Gu" (Jiang Gai 1970, 39A.40b). Three points made in his "Record" are worth specifying for the present discussion. First, the announced purpose of building a garden was to acquire a place for his father's reading and learning after his retirement, although the sense of a *garden* is clearly played down when this exalted purpose is specified. Second, Jiang Gai created the Garden of Xiu Gu, but the creation was made on the basis of an existing physical disposition of the place Jiang purchased, and its previous owner is not mentioned. Third, in the naming of the garden Jiang Gai takes the name's "fine" quality—including its respected literary origin,[18] its calligraphic character and its timely surfacing—as a priority, and its "correspondence" with the garden landscape as secondary. Jiang Gai thus effects a conceptual disjunction between his newly created garden and its predecessor by appropriating both a term that miraculously surfaced as the name of his garden, and a physical disposition from the place whose owner he made anonymous.

After Jiang Gai's death, the garden changed hands three times until his grandson, Jiang Shen 蔣深 (1668-1737), bought it back in the late seventeenth century. At Jiang Shen's request, Yan Yudun 嚴虞惇 (1650-1713), a distant relative of the Jiang family, wrote a "Record of the Restoration of the Garden of the Embroidered Valley" (Yan Yudun 1970, 39A.40b-41a). After retelling the story of Jiang Gai's finding of the name of the garden, Yan Yudun writes:

> After Xiaolian 孝廉 [i.e., Jiang Gai] passed away, to whom did the garden belong? The name Xiu Gu seemed to have died and vanished for about forty years. Xiaolian's primogenitary grandson named Shen, whose literary name being Shucun 樹存, is erudite and fond of what is ancient. He collected his grandfather's literary works, and discovered the "Record of the Embroidered Valley" previously written [by Jiang Gai]. … Regretting with deep feeling that the halls and structures had not been inherited [by the family], he restored it and moved back to it. Weeds were cut and wastes were removed; the precipitous [rockery] was heightened and deep [ponds] dredged; grown plants became more luxurious and paints fresher. Looking around the pavilions and verandas, he found that the old stone [on which the two characters, *xiu gu*, were inscribed] still existed along. Shucun thereupon said,

"Alas! This is my grandfather's bequeathed intent." He then had the "Record" written calligraphically, carved on a [different] stone, and embedded it along with the old stone in the wall.

The "restoration" of the garden is signaled foremost by the restoration of its name. Furthermore, Yan Yudun's hyperbolic enumeration of the physical activities of Jiang Shen's restoration work, such as weeds cutting and waste removal, reads very similarly to Jiang Gai's narration of his own; this reinforces a sense of repetition and thus continuity. But what Jiang Shen did to the Garden of the Embroidered Valley was expectedly more than making it afresh. From the "Record of the Belvedere of the West Cultivated Fields" written in 1729 by his grandnephew, Sun Tianyin 孫天寅, we know that he enlarged the site and added more garden features to it; later in the 1710s he built the Belvedere of the West Cultivated Fields (Xi Chou Ge 西疇閣) on the site.[19] In a similar vein to Song Luo's sense of continuity of Cang Lang Ting, Yan Yudun's understanding of continuity of the Garden of the Embroidered Valley is not predicated on the physicality of the garden, but elsewhere—his reading of the event of Jiang Shen's "restoration" of the garden is solidly grounded in the conservation of the family property, whereby the cultural import of the name of the garden is reduced merely to one of the signifier and thus entirely secondary. Yet Jiang Shen's restoration of the garden would have remained superficial to Yan Yudun if it had been construed merely under the category of "garden":

> Thereafter Shucun read books in it. Looking up, he recites the words of Yao and Shun; looking down he follows the path of Duke Zhou and Confucius. He exalts the pure and fine, and cherishes the lofty and upright. He then has restored the enterprise of the Jiang family.

Whether Jiang Shen's restoration work truly contributes to the continuity of the site depends on what kind of a person he is, and what kind of cultural life he is leading. Yet such continuity will not be sustained without the lasting medium, which Yan Yudun has to emphasize:

> Everything under Heaven has its time to evince or obscure itself, and has the causal conditions for its splendor and fading. The *xiu gu* stone had been obscured for hundreds of years, and Xiaolian obtained it; Xiaolian's garden had been disused for scores of years, and Shucun restored it. From these we know that nothing under Heaven can last long; only the written word will be passed down to infinity. Shucun keenly pursued the immortality of the "Record" [by Jiang Gai] and the [*xiu gu*] stone—so profound his thought was!

The newly restored garden, Yan Yudun seems to reason, will be transient after all; it functions as an enabling setup, from which Jiang Shen's filial piety is demonstrated, his family enterprise of learning is continued, and most important, the weight of the written word on the perpetuation of cultural memory is illustrated. To corroborate his argument, Yan Yudun mentions at the end of his essay one way in which the memory of the garden is to live on:

As Shucun asked honorable Wang Shigu 王石谷 (i.e., Wang Hui 王翬, 1632-1717) to present the garden on painting, scholars in the whole realm have all composed songs and poems on the event; the splendid scenes of the garden stays indistinctly before their eyes and in their mind. When I manage to escape someday from the net of the dust and return to my home place, free and unfettered on the zither and books, and on chatting with relatives about the past events, I can still poeticize the grass, plants, stream, and rocks in the garden on Shucun's behalf.

The Garden of the Embroidered Valley was indeed remembered well after the Jiang family lost its hold on the site, and accounts of it continued to appear until the late nineteenth century in a number of scholars' *bi ji* writings, notably in the works of Qian Yong 钱泳 (1759–1844), Liang Zhangju, and Huang Tifang黃體芳 (*fl.* 2nd of the nineteenth century).[20] What seems of particular interest is the incongruity between the perspectives of these later scholars and those of Yan Yudun and Sun Tianyin on the garden. The two parties certainly share a few features of interest, such as the surfacing of the engraved stone and Wang Hui's involvement in the history of the garden. There are also features that they naturally do not share—the account of some events that happened after Yan and Sun's time, including that the garden had changed hands from the Jiang family first to the Ye family between 1796 and 1820, then to the Xie family in the 1820s, and finally to the Wang family in the 1830s. Yet there is one piece of information that both Yan Yudun and Sun Tianyin could have provided in their essays but failed to do so, and on which by contrast the later scholars relish. It is the omission of this information by Yan Yudun and Sun Tianyin that is most telling.

In the year *ji mao* 己卯 (1699) of the Kangxi康熙 reign (1662–1722), Jiang Shen held a Party of Sending the Spring Off (*song chun hui*送春會), in which a number of men of fame attended, including You Tong 尤侗 (1618–1704), Zhu Yizun 朱彝尊 (1629–1709), Hui Shiqi 惠士奇 (1671–1741), and the then twenty-six-year old Shen Deqian 沈德潛 (1673–1769) who took the most inferior seat. Wang Hui and his pupil, Yang Jin 楊晉 (1644–1728), were invited to produce a painting on the event. Sixty years later, again in the year *ji mao* (1759) of the Qianlong乾隆 reign (1736–1795), Jiang Shen's son, Jiang Xiangen 蔣仙根, staged a second Party of Sending the Spring Off, and the now eighty-six-year old Shen Deqian, having retired from his ministerial office, this time was offered the most senior seat. Although Qian Yong, Liang Zhangju, and Huang Tifang each devotes space this time to the narration of the two events, no sense of garden restoration is conveyed by these scholars' texts. Considering the date range, Yan Yudun and, in particular, Sun Tianyin surely could have mentioned the 1699 event. In terms of cultural significance of the event, the absence of even a brief mention of it from their essays seems odd.

If we read the scenario from another angle, however, the discrepancies between the two sets of texts become fairly logical. For Yan Yudun and Sun Tianyin, both being relatives of the Jiang family, the theme of "restoration" of the garden has to be highlighted, in which the continuity of the site embodies the continuity of the family enterprise. The 1699 gathering, remarkable as it was for Suzhou culture, might distract Yan and Sun's focus of attention. Yet Qian Yong, Liang Zhangju, and Huang Tifang from an outsider's point of view place the garden in its larger context. The name of the garden persisted largely because of the character-engraved stone, but its neutrality seems to have facilitated the shifting of focal interest from the Jiang family to the local community. By noting, if not celebrating, the frequent change of ownership after the Jiang family, they attach importance, not to the fortunes of the site as a single family's property, but to the functioning of the site itself as a setting in which a fraction of local history unfolded. In the relentless cycles of nature are weaved the affective cycles of splendor and fading of human achievements.

Thus, we discern here two sets of cultural memories of the garden among scholars, each being grounded in a different perspective. Like the case of Cang Lang Ting, the name of the unaltered site of the Garden of the Embroidered Valley, the Jiang family's resumption of its ownership, and the constancy of its spatial disposition and scenic character warrant the embedment of Yan Yudun and Sun Tianyin's claim of its conceptual continuity along the family line in its physical continuity. Yet in a broader view, the frequent change of its ownership after the Jiang family and the neutrality of its name have facilitated the interpretative focus of the outside observers from the family enterprise to the interplay of human society and the natural world, whereby the memory of the site is enriched. This scenario contrasts with that of Cang Lang Ting, which remained a property of the local government that could be perceived as an unchanging entity, and whose name is strongly value-laden. In the latter case, the views of both the central protagonists and commentators follow a shared direction of thinking; yet it ramifies at different points, allowing the values of the site to be accumulated.[21]

The specificity of the cases of Cang Lang Ting and the Garden of the Embroidered Valley does not circumscribe the intellectual contour of garden conservation in Suzhou, but merely highlights a few of its salient features. Four crucial factors—the garden's name, site, ownership, and spatial disposition—operating in different ways have consistently contributed to their salience. However, to broaden our perspective of garden conservation in Suzhou, let us have a look at some vignettes extracted from the past events of a few other prominent gardens in Suzhou.

The first of such vignettes comes from the Art Patch (Yi Pu 藝圃, Fig. 6). By the end of the seventeenth century, the site of this garden had changed at least three times in both ownership and name, from Yuan Zugeng's 袁祖庚 (1519-1590) Mountain Grove in the City (Cheng Shi Shan Lin 城市山林) and Zui Ying 醉穎 Hall in the 1560s, to Wen Zhenmeng's 文震孟 (1574-1636) Medicine Patch (Yao Pu 藥圃) in the 1620s-1640s, to Jiang Cai's 姜埰 (1607-1673) Nurturing Patch (Yi Pu 頤圃) as well as Jingting Mountain Cottage (Jingting Shan Fang 敬亭山房) in the early Qing, and then after Jiang Cai's death, to the Art Patch of his second son, Jiang Shijie 姜實節 (1647-1709). Most of these names have the implication of the

alternative stance to entering government service; many of them adhere to the generic character "patch," and the name of Jiang Shijie's garden was made phonetically close to the name his father's. But the owners were of different personalities with diverse cultural experiences and social backgrounds. Throughout the nearly one and a half centuries structures in the garden had been altered as well, as Wang Wan's 汪琬 (1624-1691) enumeration of the main elements in the garden indicates that quite a few buildings were added to the site by the Jiang family (Wang Wan 1933a, 39A:26b).

Fig. 6. Art Patch. View of the rockery.

To thread these owners together as a chain of resonating events, so as to suggest a cultural continuity of the site, Gui Zhuang 歸莊 (1613-1673), Wei Xi 魏禧 (1624-1680), and Wang Wan, who were asked by Jiang Shijie each to write a record of the garden, apparently have taken different approaches. And yet their approaches turned out to reverberate with each other. Wang Wan emphasizes the long-lasting fame and singularity of the site despite the repeated change of its ownership, as compared to many other anonymous garden sites that merely provide pleasure and display wealth, but which will soon be "scattered in the cold wind and transformed into sprawling weeds." He does so by succinctly summarizing each owner's distinctive character of integrity in such a way that, by complementing each other, the different characters of these owners have converged in the history of the site, and the separate owners have become as if they were one (Wang Wan 1933b, 39A:26a-b). Thus the site becomes identified with this collective character.

Wei Xi, acknowledging the fine groves and water of the garden, similarly traces its history back to the 1560s, emphasizing that the three principal successive owners—Yuan Zugeng, Wen Zhenmeng, and Jiang Cai—were all "men of virtue"; then he makes an analogy: "I would compare this with Master Liu's congratulating his appreciative meeting with the rocky mound" (Wei Xi 1943, 33-34). In 809, Liu Zongyuan 柳宗元 (773-819) wrote one of the famous eight *ji* essays in Yongzhou 永州, in which he describes how he found and purchased a remarkable rocky mound by the side of Gumu 钴鉧 Pond in the Western Hills, making a point that the value of a thing can be appreciated only if it meets the right person in the right place (Liu Zongyuan 1979, 765-66). Wei Xi's rhetoric does not come to the effect that the garden's history can be sliced into periods of different ownership and alternating splendor-fading pattern—by alluding to Liu Zongyuan's story, time is suspended, whereby Yuan, Wen, and Jiang are made collectively a worthy owner of the garden and the garden is a worthy object of their liking.

Now we come to the two essays written by Gui Zhuang, Gui Youguang's grandson (Gui Zhuang 1984, 284, 360-61). In both texts Gui Zhuang insists that the garden landscape of Jiang's was no different from that of Wen's. But his argument gains particular force in the one that functions as a postscript to the lintel-inscription of "Mountain Grove in the City," the very phrase that the first owner of the garden, Yuan Zugeng, used for its name. Much similar to Gui Youguang's making of the relationship between Cang Lang Ting and Dayun Monastery, Gui Zhuang's project of the history of the Art Patch is one of a full circle: "The Mountain Grove in the City became the Medicine Patch; this happened at the point when the Ming was to decline. The Medicine Patch turned back to the Mountain Grove in the City; this happened long after the dynastic change." Yet this circle is delineated against the constructed contrast: "Although the world has undergone tremendous changes, the ponds, terraces, flowers, and bamboos of this place are still as they were in the past"—the garden landscape is thus portrayed to have remained the same in the midst of social and political upheavals. Cultural continuity of the site is established on the basis of both the suspension of time in the garden and the relentless transformation of the outside world.

Site, name, and spatial disposition are also central to our second vignette, from the Garden of the Master of the Net (Wang Shi Yuan 網師園, Figs. 7 and 8). Situated about 600 meters east of Cang Lang Ting, it was initially built and given its present name in the late 1750s by Song Zongyuan宋宗元 (1710-1779), but quickly fell into disrepair. In the 1790s, Qu Zhaokui瞿兆騤 (1741-1808) came in possession of the site and substantially rebuilt the garden. One of the essays recording the event, "Record of the Garden of the Master of the Net," was composed in 1795 by Qian Daxin 錢大昕 (1728-1804).[22] A point crucial to Qian Daxin is the continuity from Song Zongyuan's garden to that of Qu Zhaokui. The latter man, Qian

Fig. 7. Garden of the Master of the Net. View of the Veranda of Shoot the Duck (She Ya Lang 射鴨廊) from the opposite of the pond.
Fig. 8. Garden of the Master of the Net. View of the east bank of the pond.

Daxin writes, "by chance passing by this place, heaved a sigh at it, in fear that its disuse would lead to [the place being entirely covered with] rampant weeds." Qu Zhaokui then purchased the site, and

> Following the existing disposition of the garden, he built structures afresh. He piled up rocks and planted trees, and their composition was appropriate. He erected additional pavilions and kiosks, thus the old were replaced with the new. … The garden is certainly not the same as that in the past, but the name 'Master of the Net' is still retained. This is not to forget what was before.

Qu Zhaokui's intervention, therefore, was not one of "restoration" but the building of a new garden. Yet one can still claim its continuity from the past to the present, and hope for continuity to the future, if "the name 'Master of the Net' is still retained," for "this is not to forget what was before." Again, the former outlook of the garden relies less on the physical appearance of its buildings, rocks, and ponds, than on the meanings that its name carries; what was before will be conserved and thus will live on with this everlasting name. This does not suggest a total neglect of the physicality of the garden in the notion of continuity; something of it must be there: structures were built afresh by "following the existing disposition of the garden." In other words, for this garden to remain the Garden of the Master of the Net, the general configuration of the site had to continue to be recognizable, just as for Cang Lang Ting to last, the encircling water and the hillock had to continue to define the physical character of the site.

The existing physical disposition plays a similar role in the "restoration" of the Garden of the Artless Administration (Zhuo Zheng Yuan 拙政園, Fig. 9 and 10)—our third vignette—but its name causes notable uneasiness to the restorer.

Fig. 9. Garden of the Artless Administration. View of the Cave-Heaven of Another Kind (Bie You Dong Tian 別有洞天) and the Bao'en Temple Pagoda in distance.

Fig. 10. Garden of the Artless Administration. View of the pavilion of With Whom Do I Sit (Yu Shui Tong Zuo 與誰同坐).

Initially constructed in 1509 by Wang Xianchen 王獻臣 (*jin shi* degree, 1493) and given prominence by the literary and pictorial works associated with it by Wen Zhengming 文徵明 (1470-1559), the garden has undergone a complicated process of development.[23] Suffice it to note that by the first half of the seventeenth century, the garden had long become derelict. In 1631 Wang Xinyi 王心一 (1572-1645) bought a plot of land identified in modern scholarship as the eastern part of the former garden,[24] and built on it a new garden named "Garden-Residence for Returning to the Fields" (Gui tian yuan ju 歸田園居). One hundred years later, the central part of the former Garden of the Artless Administration was acquired by Jiang Qi 蔣棨, the incumbent prefect of Suzhou, who built his Garden of Returning (Fu Yuan 復園). In his essay written in 1747 recording the event of Jiang's work, Shen Deqian pays much attention to the naming of the garden:

> In between Lou and Qi Gates of the city of Suzhou there is a famous garden. The reason for the garden to take the character *fu* as its name is that Prefect Jiang made a garden by repairing an old site, and then named it as such.

> ... It had been a hundred years since then [in Wang Xianchen's time], and the garden had become disused and turned into a wasteland, which was overgrown with brambles and weeds, and where wild beasts took refuge. Our host found this place and then acquired it, remarking that extravagance may be curtailed, but a famous quarter must not be allowed to be abandoned. ... [Jiang Qi] then piled up rocks by following bulges [on the site], dredged pools by following the depressions.

  ... [The garden] had been brought back to its former outlook, and thus was named 'Returning.'

And after citing examples of famous gardens and residences of the remote past, Shen Deqian continues:

> Today, the restoration of it was made on the basis of the disused Garden of the Artless Administration. Our host takes [this garden] as an in-the-grove residence for his reclusive life, to which he attached his affections and by which he nurtures his spirit, ... and yet he did not intend to assign to it a name of his own, for fear that this, because of our generation, would lead to a quick disappearance of what was previously so exhaustively and whole-heartedly conceived and set out ... (Shen Deqian 1986, 81-82).

  The restoration work was executed by "building afresh" and yet "following the existing disposition." What precisely was restored, however? In the original text, the pronoun "it" takes the place of the object of the "restoration;" hence its ambiguity. We have to remember that the place was famous because of the famous people associated with it, of the famous artistic and literary works about it, and perhaps of its sheer age. Yet the baseline for its fame in Jiang Qi's view is the fact that it was once a *garden* site. For this reason, it would seem intolerable if the site were to be used for any other purpose than gardening. In this line of thinking, what was "restored" by Jiang Qi, as Shen Deqian perceives it, was a generic but decent garden; that is, the site was reinstated in its former condition, or "outlook," of a garden site, and for that very reason, the new garden was given the name *fu*, "returning." It is worth noting an interesting point pertinent to many of the gardens in Suzhou: the perceived natural cycle of splendor and fading, rise and fall, renders garden restorations multifarious: in a specific context, it could refer to continuity of the particular garden per se, to continuity of the site for a generic garden, or to continuity of the site of studied historical or cultural significance.

  The matter of naming the garden was considered by Jiang Qi, through Shen Deqian's writing, to be critical to the whole enterprise of construction, just as it was in Cang Lang Ting, the Garden of the Embroidered Valley, and the Garden of the Master of the Net. A common objective—assigning value to what was in the past and therefore conserving it—runs through all of them, but the reasoning behind Jiang Qi's choice is outstanding, and we are apprised here of an unsettled mind. Perhaps Jiang Qi understood well that his garden was no longer what it was before, or the site was only a third of that of before and thus could not be equated with it; he could not take the name of the previous garden. On the other hand, he may have felt that his was not a new, different garden either, but one that had just been "restored;" his garden consequently did not have an identity of its own. Thus he gave his garden a name, "returning," which for him was not really a name for a garden, probably because in this context it conveyed no other meaning than the one on the surface. Is it possible that Jiang took his new garden merely as a transient phase of the development of that overshadowing Garden of the Artless Administration in the natural cycle of its splendor and fading, or that he really intended to build a new garden in its own right and give it a name of unknown signification but his act was interpreted otherwise by Shen Deqian? What can be certain is that both Jiang Qi and Shen Deqian were well aware of the power of naming—it had the capacity to change, for better or worse, the perception of reality as well as the reality itself; and for that reason it plays a pivotal role in garden formation and transformation.

  On the other side of the eastern wall of Jiang Qi's Garden of Returning is our fourth vignette—the garden-residence built by Wang Xinyi from 1631 to 1634, which still remained in the hand of the Wang family. Set aside the remarkable duration of the latter garden as one single family's property,[25] its proclaimed initial creation stands out as a stark contrast to Jiang Qi's construction. Not only did Wang Xinyi assign his garden a new name, but neither the Garden of the Artless Administration nor any figure involved in its history is mentioned in his essay, "Record of the Garden-Residence for Returning to the Fields," written in 1642 (Wang Xinyi 1986, 75-77). After referring to the land he purchased as "derelict fields," *huang tian* 荒田, and thus implying the absence of any visible sign of a garden before his construction, he tells us how the spatial disposition and configuration of his garden was generated:

> On the ground ponds were dug where appropriate. Earth taken from the ponds was heaped up to form heights, and on the heights hills were made where appropriate. Over the ponds, in between the hills, buildings were made where appropriate.

If it could be solidly established that the site of this Garden was really the eastern part of Wang Xianchen's Garden of the Artless Administration, Wang Xinyi's enterprise should present to us an unequivocal case of creating a new garden that was claimed to have nothing to do with its predecessor.[26]

Such a proclaimed stance of Wang Xinyi to some extent resonates with that of Su Shunqin in the building of Cang Lang Ting. When Su Shunqin purchased the site, "an older conception of a garden was still present;" although in his "Record" Su Shunqin mentions the name of Sun Chengyou, his intention may well have been to bring out a strong disparity between himself as man of letter and Sun Chengyou as a royal dignitary. Similarly, Zhu Changwen explains to us in his "Record of the Pleasure Patch (Le Pu 樂圃)" that his garden-residence was built in the 1070s on the site of the Garden of the Golden Valley (Jin Gu Yuan 金谷園) owned by one of Qian Yuanliao's 錢元僚 (887-942) junior relatives; the contrasting image is thus projected between a noted local scholar and a warlord's underlings.[27] In other words, both Su Shunqin and Zhu Changwen, without any apology, make sure that their respective gardens supersede the existing ones, and their particular ways of mentioning the former owners in these cases bring benefit to their cultural enterprise at the expense of the latter. By contrast, leaving Wang Xianchen and the Garden of the Artless Administration out of his "Record," Wang Xinyi's approach is one of indifference to the past events of the site, so that his building of the garden would be read emphatically as an act of writing rather than rewriting on the landscape.

As Steven Knapp has reminded us, "the locus of authority is always in the present; we use, for promoting and reinforcing ethical and political dispositions, only those elements of the past that correspond to our sense of what presently compels us" (Knapp 1989, 131). The exquisiteness of choices made by these scholars in keeping memories of the past alive testifies that they did not slavishly follow what was before, but meticulously exercised their authority of utilizing the past in the service of the present; in other words, perpetuating collective memory on the part of these scholars was an ongoing process of creation. And the working together in different ways of the four crucial factors that they employed—name, site, disposition, and ownership—is made to contribute as much to cultural continuity as to disjunction in the development of a garden site.

At the end of his "Record of the Lingering Garden," Yu Yue 俞樾 (1821-1907) writes: "… I know that the name of the Lingering Garden will remain forever in the world. For that reason, I write this note to let those who later record the famous gardens in Suzhou to have something to investigate" (Yu Yue 1970, 39C.18a-b). The last sentence reads nearly verbatim as one of the last sentences of Song Luo's "Record of the Restoration of Cang Lang Ting." The purpose and intended readership of their writings are very clear: they were for further studies and their readers were expected to be those who had scholarly capabilities and interest in doing so. Their actual and potential readership was of course much broader than what they have stated; so was that of other scholars' writings on the gardens in Suzhou, including local gazetteers. But it was still extremely limited if the whole population of the region is considered. Thus, when we use the phrase "gardens as collective memory," we are begging the closely interrelated questions of the scope of collectivity on the one hand, and the specific content of memory on the other.

I have argued elsewhere that the collectiveness of reading the garden site of Cang Lang Ting should be defined in terms of social groups and its reception by the public was gained on the basis of diverse interpretations; and that most of the essayists were very conscious of such diversity, making clear distinctions in particular between those who were classically educated and those among the populace (Xu 2005, 43-50). The differentiation made in Song Luo's "Preface" to the *Collected Works of Su Zimei*, for instance, is largely representative of the views of those writers. After briefly telling us why and how he restored Cang Lang Ting, Song Luo writes:

> Moreover, the people of the Suzhou region, elegantly fond of anecdotes of the past, on fine spring or autumn days come in their walking shoes and gather here in crowds. The site thereupon has come to be one of the famed scenic sites of the prefecture. When my kind of people and I visit and ponder on the traces of what used to be, we pace around its site and then think about its person; thinking about its person, we will then surely contemplate and sigh over his life, and seek out his prose and verse. By doing so, we more or less come to know a fragment of what it was really like during his life. Perhaps the way of "going on further to make friends" is just like this (Su Shunqin 1961, 299).

The disparity emphasized here between the readings of Cang Lang Ting by the "crowds" and by Song Luo's "kind of people" is both revealing and misleading: the disparity was so significant as to be highlighted, and yet it misleads us into thinking that this is the only disparity within the complex readings of gardens.

Not only did all of those people whom Song Luo would identify as his kind have a solid background of classical education but they were judged as sharing closely profound knowledge of literary history and tradition. Yet even among these men of letters, the reading of gardens was multifarious. Depending on their social contexts and personal experiences, their perspectives ranged from a fondness of what was ancient and meditation on the past, aspirations to elegance as opposed to worldly vulgarity, and natural cycle of splendor and fading; to appraisals of personal integrity and the nurturing of the virtuous, admirations for the modes of lofty thinking behind the choice of retreat, and an appreciation of perceived filial piety. Their conceptions nevertheless usually tended to be specific to the individual gardens in question, while comprehending the significance of the specificity in the larger contexts of heaven-and-earth and the myriad things, past human events, and current society. Most of the gardens also provided them with desirable settings for numerous "elegant gatherings" (*ya ji* 雅集), such as the Parties of Sending the Spring Off held in the Garden of the Embroidered Valley. The importance of such gatherings attached to the gardens was such to Qian Daxin, for instance, that he has to proclaim in his "Preface to the Banquet Gathering at the Estate of Cold Emerald" that "I think the splendor of gardens and pavilions must have the aid of distinguished personages' drinking and poetry-chanting for it to last to immortality" (Qian Daxin 1998, 139). Once again the production and transmission of literary works were the repository of value of an event of this kind.

These "elegant gatherings" were very exclusive, of course. Those of modest educational background, who were not in the circle of the local cultural elite, would have little chance to participate in such events. Upon visiting the gardens, they might try to appreciate the literary works that had accumulated and been displayed in steles, couplets, and plaques, reflect on the interplay of this literature and the garden views, learn their past events and anecdotes, and enjoy their fine sceneries. But the vast majority of visitors were ordinary people, who received meager or no education, and who, in the eyes of scholars, would confuse Wang Xinyi's Garden-Residence for Returning to the Fields with the Garden of the Artless Administration, and would prefer the "Liu 劉 Garden" to the "Mountain Estate of Cold Emerald" for the name of the Lingering Garden (Wu Yifeng 1994, 7; Yu Yue 1970, 39C.18b). Their access to the gardens was very much tied to the local custom of seasonal outings, and to some other special events. The nineteenth century local scholar Xu Qi 許起 notes: "In our Suzhou, gardens are fully open on the fine spring and autumn days, inviting people to roam in them to sightsee; local gentry often lead their wives, concubines, sons and daughters to ramble in swarms of people" (Xu Qi 1939, 21). Qian Yong tells us that "[when the Mountain Estate of Cold Emerald] was open for the first time in the second year of the Daoguang 道光 reign [i.e., 1823], there was not a single day without visitors. That created a furor" (Qian Yong 1979, 529). Precisely what attracted the common people to the gardens, however? Qian Yong gives us a hint:

> [Gardens such as the Lion Grove (Shi Zi Lin 獅子林) and Garden of the Artless Administration] are all famous splendors in the prefecture. Every spring, in the second and third months, peach flowers all bloom, rape flowers also blossom. Men and women of the whole city would come out for excursions [in them], very much like that depicted in Zhang Zeduan's *Qingming shang he tu* (Qian Yong 1979, 523).

Yet perhaps the most telling sources are Gu Lu's 顧錄 (b. late 1790s) *Record of the Pure and the Fine*, published in 1830, and Yuan Xuelan's 袁學瀾 (b. 1804) *Record of the Sensuous Beauty of the Yearly Splendor of the Wu Prefecture*, written less than twenty years later. On the custom of spring outings, Gu Lu writes:

> In the spring warmth hundreds of blooms in gardens try to outdo each other. The gatekeepers, with an exaction of petty money for sweeping the fallen flowers, allow people to roam in them to sightsee. Men and women ramble in crowds, and fine gauze and silks are like clouds.

> In gardens rare birds and plants are raised, courtyards are cleaned and galleries are neatened; calligraphies and paintings by the famous and virtuous are hung [on the walls], and bronze ritual vessels and books from antiquity are displayed; furthermore, precious flowerers are planted, with cotton tents and reed screens to keep them from

the sun and rain. Pavilions, out-looking halls, terraces, and waterside kiosks are decorated afresh. Those seeking flowery fragrances and scenic views are most intent on lingering around [these gardens].

Everywhere are peddlers and petty vendors seizing upon the opportunity; fragrant sweets and fruity cakes are all palatable, and gimmicks and toys attract and please children—wherever they are, a market appears. ...

All over Northern and Southern Gardens rape flowers blossom; it is particularly magnificent in the Northern Garden: in the genial breezes they are gaily-colored in profusion, like gold spreading out to the limit of one's sight. Everywhere sheds were built with entwined and bound reeds, in which wine heaters and tea tables are set up to welcome the excursionists, with blue unlined upper garments and white lined jackets [i.e., waiters and waitresses] mingling with the guests; when the sun is setting at the hills, sounds of cheerful talks can still be heard ... (Gu Lu 1986, 73-74).[28]

Gu Lu also mentions Tiger Hill (Hu Qiu 虎丘) in the northwest suburb of the city, as well as Mt. Tianping 天平 and Mt. Lingyan 靈巖 to the west, as favorite places for excursions. What is presented here are scenes of spectacles and pleasure-enjoyment. The ordinary people were drawn to these gardens simply because they were, above all else, *gardens*; they were among the scenic places in the region but more easy to reach than the distant mountains and hills. They visit them for their fame, their fine sceneries of flowers, bamboos, rocks, ponds, and buildings. They might go to the Lion Grove for its "extraordinary rocks and deep and hidden caves" or the "five old pine trees that grow on the rocks," to the Garden of the Artless Administration for the "three or four pearl camellias entwining with each other, the flowers of which, when blooming, are large, resplendent, bright, and charming, while scattered in profusion and setting each other off—they are the only ones seen in the Jiangnan region," or to the Lingering Garden "where twelve extraordinary rocky peaks are gathered"[29] (Gu Lu 1986, 75-76). It seems likely that these visitors read the gardens as places where the customary seasonal outings (perhaps with a ritualistic tinge) were facilitated, and for them the value of the gardens thus lay in the provision of sensory pleasures, irrespective of whether they were significant cultural sites. On the other hand, the owners of some of the gardens seem to have attuned to the atmosphere created by these seasonal customary outings; the temporary display of precious plants and rare animals in their garden, the calligraphic works, paintings, ancient bronze vessels and books, were aimed more at contributing to the staging of tourist attractions and marvels than at adding to the cultural and literary significance of the gardens. In other words, the perceptions of gardens as places for pleasure-enjoyment momentarily subsided the readings of them as sites of cultural and literary significance. This observation does not have any negative implication, for as Marc Treib has argued in the context of contemporary debates on meaning in landscape design, "pleasure can be a valuable pursuit, as valid as the pursuit of meaning" (Treib 2002, 101).

Such considerable incongruity among receptions and readings of the gardens by different social groups and in different situations is hardly surprising. "Significance lies with the beholder and not alone in the place;" (Treib 2002, 99) in other words, value is not inherent in the garden site itself; it is given to the site in the process of interaction between the subject and the site. Garden history is fundamentally a literary one; any assignment of value to gardens thus demands literary education. Suzhou society in that respect was never homogeneous. Yet garden history is at the same time also a hedonistic one; hence the cyclical surfacing of the shared reading of gardens across diverse social groups. Moreover, since "significance is culturally circumscribed and, ultimately, personally determined," (Treib 2002, 97) the signification of gardens in Suzhou culture and life is bound to be complex; so is their conservation. The historical, cultural, and material richness of these sites lends themselves to the endowment of diverse values across the wide social spectrum. For the classically educated, the making and remaking of a garden might resonate with natural cycles of either rejuvenation or supersession; they might embody either cultural continuity or disjunction; they might either point to an idealistic future or an actual past. Thus, in their readings of the garden sites, memory and history were combined.[30] For the general populace, garden conservation ensured that the *gardens* they seasonally visited were made anew (*xin* 新), an image that could bear the sign of the present conditions of their life and the possible condition in the near future, and such an image in their memory would outlive the historical facts. It may therefore be appropriate for us to pluralize our subjects of discussion by referring to gardens in Suzhou as cultural memor*ies*.

Bibliography

Bai Juyi. *Bai Juyi ji*. Annotated and punctuated by Gu Xuejie. Beijing: Zhonghua shuju, 1979.

Cao Lindi. *Suzhou yuan lin bian er ying lian jian shang*. Enlarged ed. Beijing: Huaxia chubanshe, 1999.

Chen Congzhou. *Yuan lin tan cong*. Shanghai: Shanghai wenhua chubanshe, 1980.

Chen Congzhou. *Yuan yun*. Shanghai: Shanghai wenhua chubanshe, 1999.

Chen Qiyou. *Lü shi chun qiu jiao shi*. Shanghai: Xuelin chubanshe, 1994.

Chen Zhi and Zhang Gongchi, eds. *Zhongguo li dai ming yuan ji xuan zhu*. Hefei: Anhui kexue jishu chubanshe, 1983.

Clunas, Craig. "The Gift and the Garden." *Orientations* 26, no. 2 (1995): 38-45.

Fan Chengda. *Wujun zhi*. Nanjing: Jiangsu guji chubanshe, 1986.

Fan Ye范曄 (398-445). *Hou Han shu*. Beijing, Zhonghua shuju, 1965.

Forty, Adrian. *Words and Buildings: A Vocabulary of Modern Architecture*. London: Thames & Hudson, 2000.

Gu Gongxie. *Xiao xia xian ji zhai chao*. Preface 1785. *Hanfenlou mi ji* ed. Shanghai: Shangwu yinshuguan, 1917.

Gu Lu. *Qing jia lu*. Nanjing: Jiangsu guji chubanshe, 1986.

Gu Zhentao. *Wumen biao yin*. Nanjing: Jiangsu guji chubanshe, 1986.

Guan Chengjiao. *Gui Zhenchuan shi wen xuan*. Nanjing: Jiangsu guji chubanshe, 2002.

Gui Youguang. *Zhenchuan xian sheng ji*. *Si bu cong kan* ed.

Gui Zhuang. *Gui Zhuang ji*. Shanghai: Shanghai guji chubanshe, 1984.

Hawkes, David. *The Songs of the South: An Ancient Chinese Anthology of Poems by Qu Yuan and Other Poets*. Harmondsworth: Penguin Books, 1985.

Hong Xingzu 洪興祖 (1090-1155). *Chu ci bu zhu*. Punctuated and collated by Bai Huawen et al. Beijing: Zhonghua shuju, 1983.

Huang Tifang. *Zui xiang suo zhi*. Suzhou: Jiangsu shengli Suzhou tushuguan, 1940.

Jiang Gai. "Xiu Gu ji," in Wu Xiuzhi and Cao Yunyuan 1970, 39A.40b.

Jiang Hancheng 蔣瀚澄 (1897-1981), comp. *Cang Lang Ting xin zhi*. 1929.

Knapp, Steven. "Collective Memory and the Actual Past." *Representations* 26 (Spring 1989): 123-49.

LAU, D.C. *Lao Tsu, Tao te ching*. Harmondsworth: Penguin Books, 1963.

Liang Zhangju, comp. *Cang Lang Ting zhi*. 1827.

Liang Zhangju. *Gui tian suo ji*. Beijing: Zhonghua shuju, 1981a.

Liang Zhangju. *Lang ji xu tan*. Beijing: Zhonghua shuju, 1981b.

Liu Dunzhen. *Suzhou gu dian yuan lin*. Beijing: Zhongguo jianzhu gongye chubanshe, 1979.

Liu Zongyuan. *Liu Zongyuan ji*. Beijing: Zhonghua shuju, 1979.

Meng zi. *Shi san jing zhu shu* ed. Rpt. Beijing: Zhonghua shuju, 1980.

Mote, F.W. "A Millennium of Chinese Urban History: Form, Time, and Space Concepts in Soochow." *Rice University Studies* LIX, no. 4 (Fall 1973): 35-65.

Nora, Pierre. "Between Memory and History: *Les Lieux de Memoire*." *Representations* 26 (Spring 1989): 7-24.

Owen, Stephen. "Place: Meditation on the Past at Chin ling." *Harvard Journal of Asiatic Studies* 50, no. 2 (December 1990): 417-57.

Qian Daxin. "Han Bi Zhuang yan ji xu." In Zhou Zheng 1998, 139.

Qian Yi, comp. *Zhuo Zheng Yuan zhi gao*. Restricted circulation. Suzhou: 1986.

Qian Yong. *Lüyuan cong hua*. Beijing: Zhonghua shuju, 1979.

Shen Deqian. "Fu Yuan ji." In Qian Yi 1986, 81-82.

Song Luo, comp. *Cang Lang xiao zhi*. 1884 ed.

Strassberg, Richard. *Inscribed Landscapes: Travel Writing from Imperial China*. Berkeley, CA: University of California Press, 1994.

Su Shunqin. *Su Shunqin ji bian nian jiao zhu*. Collated and annotated by Fu Pingxiang and Hu Wentao. Chengdu: Bashu shushe, 1991.

Su Shunqin. *Su Shunqin ji*. Collated and punctuated by He Wenzhuo. Beijing: Zhonghua shuju, 1961.

Tong Jun. *Jiangnan yuan lin zhi*. 2nd ed. Beijing: Zhongguo jianzhu gongye chubanshe, 1984.

Treib, Marc. "Must Landscapes Mean?" In *Theory in Landscape Architecture: A Reader*. Edited by Simon Swaffield. Philadelphia, PA: University of Pennsylvania Press, 2002. This essay originally appeared in *Landscape Journal* 14, no. 1 (1995): 47-62.

Wang Wan. "Yi Pu hou ji." In Wu Xiuzhi and Cao Yunyuan 1933a, 39A:26b.

Wang Wan. "Yi Pu ji." In Wu Xiuzhi and Cao Yunyuan 1933b, 39A:26a-b.

Wang Xinyi. "Gui Tian Yuan Ju ji." In Qian Yi 1986, 75-77.

Wang Yi 王逸 (fl. 1st half of the 2nd century C.E.). *Chu ci zhang ju*. *Si bu cong kan* ed.

Wei Xi. "Jingting Shan Fang ji." In *Wuxia ming yuan ji* 1943, 33-34.

Wu Xiuzhi and Cao Yunyuan, comps. *Wuxian zhi*. 1933 ed. Rpt. Taibei: Chengwen chubanshe, 1970.

Wu Yifeng. *Deng chuang cong lu*. *Hanfenlou mi ji* ed. Shanghai: Shangwu yinshuguan, 1917.

Wu Yifeng. *Xunzhitang cong chao*. Beijing: Zhonghua shuju, 1994.

Wuxia ming yuan ji. Suzhou: Jiangsu sheng li Suzhou tushuguan, 1943.

Xu Qi. *Shan hu she diao tan zhai chao*. Preface 1883. Suzhou: Jiangsu shengli Suzhou tushuguan, 1939.

Xu Yinong. "Boundaries, Centres and Peripheries in Chinese Gardens: A Case of Suzhou in the Eleventh Century." *Studies in the History of Gardens and Designed Landscapes* 24, no. 1 (March 2004): 21-37.

Xu Yinong. "The Making and Remaking of Cang Lang Ting: Attitudes Towards the Past Evinced in the History of a Garden Site in Suzhou," in *Histories of Garden Conservation: Case-studies and Critical Debates*. Edited by Michel Conan, José Tito Rojo, and Luigi Zangheri. Firenze, Italy: Leo S. Olschki, 2005.

Yan Yudun. "Chong xiu Xiu Gu Yuan ji." In Wu Xiuzhi and Cao Yunyuan 1970, 39A.40b-41a.

Yu Yue. "Liu Yuan ji." In Wu Xiuzhi and Cao Yunyuan 1970, 39C.18a-b.

Yuan Hongdao. *Yuan Hongdao ji jian jiao*. Annotated and collated by Qian Bocheng 錢伯城. Shanghai: Shanghai guji chubanshe, 1981.

Yuan Xuelan. *Wujun fan hua ji li*. Nanjing: Jiangsu guji chubanshe, 1998.

Zhang Shusheng. "Chongxiu Cang Lang Ting ji," in Jiang Hancheng 1929, 2.4b-5b.

Zhao Yi. *Gai yu cong kao*. Beijing: Zhonghua shuju, 1963.

Zhou Zheng. *Liu Yuan*. Suzhou: Gu Wuxuan chubanshe, 1998.

Zhu Qianzhi. *Lao zi jiao shi*. Beijing: Zhonghua shuju, 1984.

NOTES

[1] I am indebted to Michel Conan and two anonymous referees for constructive comments on the draft of this essay.

[2] In fact, Chen Congzhou (1999, 200) has made it very clear that "studies of Chinese gardens should begin perhaps with studies of Chinese literature."

[3] For a summary of the development of the concept of "form" in Western architectural history, see Forty 2000, 149-172.

[4] The following discussion of Cang Lang Ting is extracted from Xu 2005, 3-63.

[5] Some modern scholars, on the basis of Su Shunqin's writings, hold that he constructed Cang Lang Ting in the summer of 1045 and took it as his place of abode. See, for instance, Chen Zhi and Zhang Gongchi 1983, 17; Su Shunqin 1991, 627. Yet both internal and external evidence strongly suggests that the building of Cang Lang Ting happened no earlier than the autumn of 1046 on the one hand, and Su Shunqin never resided at the place on the other. For Su Shunqin's "Record of Cang Lang Ting" or "Cang Lang Ting ji," see idem 1961, 183-84.

[6] See, for instance, Cao Lindi 1999, 2-3.

[7] *Meng zi* 1980, 7A.55; Hong Xingzu 1983, 180-81. Translation by Hawkes 1985, 206-7, with minor modifications.

[8] See, for instance, Wang Yi, 7.2b-3a.

[9] The term 'overcoming self,' *zi sheng* 自勝, appears in his "Record" and alludes to a sentence in the *Lao zi, Dao de jing*: "He who overcomes others has force;/He who overcomes himself is strong." See Zhu Qianzhi 1984, 134. Translation by Lau 1963, 92. This phrase also appears in the *Lü shi chun qiu*, in Chen Qiyou 1994, 145.

[10] Su Shunqin repeatedly emphasizes in his prose and verse that "there is something worth awaiting" 有待 for him; this is why he mildly criticises Bo Yi and Shu Qi for starving themselves to death even though "both did meet their time," and ridicules Qu Yuan for committing suicide "once exiled." See Su Shunqin 1961, 45-46, 102; cf. 132-3, 121-4, 257.

[11] Fu Pingxiang and Hu Wentao (Su Shunqin 1991, 300, note 1) speculate that Su Shunqin built quite a few structures on the site, but closer analyses of the texts in connection to our knowledge of the city in the eleventh century render such speculations tenuous.

[12] The names of Zhang Dun 章惇 (1035-1106) and Han Shizhong 韓世忠 (1089-1151), who owned the site respectively at points after Su Shunqin, were omitted by Gui Youguang, for instance. The hiatus made in the chain of ownership of the site renders the claim of cultural continuity more effective.

[13] Cf. Liang Zhangju 1827, and idem 1981a, 187.

[14] Cf. Liang Zhangju 1827, 5a-6b; Song Luo 1884, B.1a-2b.

[15] For Liang Hong's biography, see Fan Ye 1965, 83.2765-68.

[16] The symptomatic role of Cang Lang Ting may well have developed from a perceived correspondence between the collective fortune of the gardens of a region and the cycle of prosperity and decline of that region—a notion that was most emphatically put forward by the Northern Song scholar, Li Gefei 李格非 (ca. 1045-ca. 1105), in his *Record of Famous Gardens in Luoyang*, or *Luoyang ming yuan ji*, in Chen Zhi and Zhang Gongchi 1983, 54.

[17] This phrase is first used by Mote 1973, 53, referring to the city of Suzhou.

[18] Jiang Gai conjectures at the end of his "Record" that the term *xiu gu* may have come either from a line in one of Su Shi's 蘇軾 (1037-1101) poems; or from Bai Juyi's 白居易 (772-845) "Cao tang ji," in idem, *Bai Juyi ji* 1979, 933-35, and for an English translation of this text, see Strassberg 1994, 134-37.

[19] Sun Tianyin, "Xi Chou Ge ji," in ibid., 39A.41a.

[20] Cf. Qian Yong 1979, 525; Liang Zhangju 1981b, 221; Huang Tifang 1940, 5. The garden was utterly destroyed in the war of 1860.

[22] Compare, for instance, the views presented by Zhang Ruhu 張汝瑚, a seventeenth-century scholar, cited in Guan Chengjiao 2002, 129; by Zhao Yi 趙翼 (1727-1814) 1963, 909-10; by You Tong, in Song Luo 1884, "Preface"; and by Gui Youguang, Song Luo, Liang Zhangju, and Zhang Shusheng.

[23] Qian Daxin, "Wang Shi Yuan ji," in Chen Zhi and Zhang Gongchi 1983, 420-21. In order to add historical and literary weight to Song Zongyuan's building and Qu Zhaokui's rebuilding of the Garden of the Master of the Net, Qian Daxin through careful wording establishes its association in both location and name with Shi Zhengzhi's 史正志 (*jin shi* degree, 1151) Hall of Ten Thousand Volumes in the 1170s. For a fuller presentation of this point, see Xu 2005, 51-53.

[24] For an account of this garden's history, see Qian Yi, *Zhuo Zheng Yuan zhi gao* (Suzhou: restricted circulation, 1986), 2-4.

[25] See, for instance, Liu Dunzhen 1979, 53; Chen Congzhou 1980, 22; Qian Yi 1986, 3. No qualification is given for this identification in any of these works.

[26] It was to remain so until at least the first half of the nineteenth century.

[27] Wang Xinyi's view is shared by many other scholars, including Shen Deqian, the same scholar who wrote a "Record" on Jiang Qi's "Garden of Returning," emphasizing its conceptual and physical debts to the Garden of the Artless Administration. See Shen Deqian, "Lan Xue Tang ji," in ibid., 79-80. Cf. Wu Yifeng 1917, 5b and 1994, 7; Gu Zhentao 顧震濤 (b. 1750) 1986, 15; Gu Gongxie 1917, 23a-b; and Qian Yong 1979, 523-24.

[28] See Zhu Changwen, "Le Pu ji," in Fan Chengda 1986, 193-95. For a detailed discussion of this garden, see Xu 2004.

[29] Cf. Yuan Xuelan 1998, 92, 104-8, 124. According to Yuan Xuelan (104), the gardens would be open from the Qingming festival through the beginning of summer.

[30] Interestingly, in his enumeration of the places that people have been visiting, Gu Lu categorizes only two presently-recognized gardens within the city—Cang Lang Ting and the Garden of the Embroidered Valley—under the heading "Traces of the Past" (gu ji), whereas other well-known gardens are placed under the heading "Garden." (Ibid., 76-77) The categorization of Cang Lang Ting is understandably in line with Song Luo, Liang Zhangju, and Zhang Shusheng's reading of Cang Lang Ting—its very name did not signify the same kind of site as that of most private gardens in Suzhou. But in the case of the latter, is it possible that Gu Lu takes the import of its restoration in the late seventeenth century as an enterprise of the Jiang family, and consequently regards the Garden of the Embroidered Valley as having ceased to exist once its ownership changed to another family, even though it was still present in its physicality by the time Gu Lu wrote his book?

[31] I am using the concepts of history and memory suggested by Nora 1989.

Gardens, City Life and
Culture

Gardens, City Life and
Culture

Gardens, City Life and
Culture

Gardens, City Life and
Culture

Gardens, City Life and
Culture

Gardens, City Life and
Culture

CHAPTER 14

The Promenades and Public Parks of Tokyo: A Tradition Permanently Reinvented

Sylvie Brosseau

Throughout its history, Japanese culture has built in many ways a feeling and an awareness of its natural environment, merging local propensities and external contributions, first from China. This "nature" became a central impulse of numerous artistic expressions, particularly landscapes and gardens.

In Edo, the old name for Tokyo, natural surroundings (relief and water, vegetation and wild life), deeply wrought, were essential, since they contributed as much to the built environment as to social life. Landscaped nature and related social practices gave rise to some of the most elaborate aspects of urban culture in Edo, joining two features: diversity and large diffusion; and nature is still nowadays "the receptacle of the memory of a long past which sets up the present on a historical base"(Conan 2005, 67).

The Ancient System of the Walks of Edo: Construction and Social Functions

The Edo Period (1603-1867), ruled by the Tokugawa shogunate, was a long period of peace and stability (despite localized famine and unrest toward the end of the era) during which social order was strictly organized along a hierarchical scale and moral principles. The dominant class was the warriors, ahead of the peasants, the artisans, and last the merchants. To control the vassals, the shogunate instituted an alternate attendance system: the *daimyō*, powerful military lords, had to reside in Edo in alternate years and their wives and heirs had to stay there like hostages. The flood of people and wealth stimulated the development of a monetary-based economy. The production of crafts and urban consumption led to the strenghtening of a rich class of merchants, a powerful group also neutralized by the Tokugawa (at least that's what they thought) by sumptuary laws and social stratification.[1] These rules involved limitations on the things the rich commoners could use or have at their disposal, but quite the opposite, they entailed a lot of expense for the *daimyō*. After all, these constraints stimulated the imagination of the artisans and the city dwellers.

The growth of the city of Edo, the country's political and then economic capital, was exceptional, reaching a population estimated over one million inhabitants at the beginning of the eighteenth century. Most of the people, *bourgeois* and town dwellers, although bereft of all objective political powers, played a major role in the expansion of a specific type of urban culture which generated various spaces of "organized transgression" tolerated by the shogunate to maintain the social order.[2] This culture was based on a careful and detailed observation of the material world and the perception of the here and now by the senses. The appreciation of nature (that is an infinite number of natural elements and phenomena, and their permanent changes), occupied a preponderant place. Throughout the Edo era, these natural resources were woven into the city fabric as temples and sanctuaries were developed, private and public gardens created, trees planted along the roads, rivers, canals, and the sea. Even though public creations resulted from governmental decision, the people were at the origin of diverse modes of appropriation. The formation of the site of Ueno provides an example.

At the very beginning of the Edo Period, in 1624, the third Shogun Tokugawa Iemitsu settled, on the advice of a monk, to build a vast Buddhist temple to assure the protection of the city.[3] Around the pond and on the wooded hill of Ueno, many temples were constructed, cherry trees planted, accumulating references to numerous celebrated places around the imperial and historic capital Kyoto.[4] Ueno rapidly became the most famous place where to admire cherry blossoms, and an exemplary *meisho*, "a place with a name," that is a famous place. The creation of the Ueno landscape with its cherry trees and temples was clearly meant as a historic and symbolic transfer of substance and legitimacy to the new power in a city in full expansion. Before the first Shogun, Tokugawa Ieyasu, Edo was no more than a little fishing port, and by creating symbolic links between places rich in history in the ancient imperial and the new political capital, the shogunate sought to reinforce its power (following the principle of Nara or Heian rulers who had drawn on Chinese precedents).

Fig. 1. Ueno Kiyomizudō Shinobazunoike (View of Ueno with the pond Shinobazunoike and the temple Kiyomizudō), Hiroshige, Meisho Edo Hyakkei, (One Hundred Famous Views of Edo), 1856.

In Ueno, the people of Edo indulged in cherry blossoms in the spring (Fig. 1), lotus flowers on the pond in the summer, the full moon in the fall, and the snowy landscape in winter. Thus, these walkways were used throughout the year according to a calendar reflecting the rhythm of nature and its popular practices, not in deference to the shogunate as expected. Infatuation with visits to Ueno initiated the genuine popular celebration of *hanami,* which signifies "to contemplate flowers" and more specifically those of cherry trees. *Hanami* became a popular urban practice that grew with the unfolding of new urban landscapes. In the City of Edo melting pot, sacred rites of the countryside and aristocratic aesthetic culture merged into renewed popular practices, *hanami* offering the most significant model. *Hanami* was originally an agrarian ritual, then a ritual of the court, and it became a popular and collective celebration to which the people of Edo added a hedonistic sense. One participated in *hanami* to celebrate the spring renewal, the promise of a fertile year which is beginning, and also to enjoy the ephemeral beauty of flowers while remaining keenly aware of this world impermanence. It was an occasion for celebration not to be missed.

In the middle of the Edo Period (around 1716-1736), when city growth and construction intensity reached their peak, walks and places for enjoying landscape and nature became more and more numerous.[5] The list of natural elements or events that gave rise to social practices in a place is indeed long: admiring flower blossoms (of plum, cherry, or peach trees, azalea or iris in the spring, of wisteria or lotus in the summer), capturing fireflies, then dragonflies, or listening to the song of insects at the end of the summer, contemplating the full moon, then the reddening of leaves that marks in a spectacular manner the passage towards winter, standing in awe in front of the snow, etc. Having a meeting in a landscape in harmony with the season, drinking, eating, having a good time, enjoying diverse activities in a festive group atmosphere and sharing collective forms of emotion and excitement, bonded together time, space, and shared identities. *Hanami*, as well as many other rituals on the same model, gave rise to genuine group leisure practices without being emptied of either their symbolic content or their aesthetic value.

Fig. 2. Goten-Yama, Hanazakari (View of the Cherry Blossoms, Goten-Yama), Hiroshige, Meisho Edo Hyakkei, (One Hundred Famous Views of Edo), 1845. Goten-Yama was Shogun's private property open to the people.

These places for excursions and meetings were either developed within the enclosure of temples seeking to attract visitors by further cultivating seasonal themes rather than religious motivations, or they were officially opened by the shogunate to control urban development and folk activities,[6] and in some cases in private gardens or orchards. The fame of these beauty spots or famous locations called *meisho*, was spread by the publication of images and collections of woodblock prints some becoming similar to historical guidebooks (Fig. 2).

These sites present a number of recurrent features: a hill or an elevation with a view over the urban landscape and the distant background, luxuriant trees, and water (pond, river, canal, or ocean) that were conducive to the development of certain gaze and behaviors. References to historical events, and to real or imaginary figures created symbolic layers of narrative and added to the aura of each place. A city topography, at one and the same time concrete and symbolic, developed into a network of places and landscapes rich in evocations and meanings, appropriated by the people through active, varied and multi-sensory behaviors. Therefore, the beauty spots allowed cultural transmission and transformation, linking the constitution of new urban areas and landscapes and the spread of popular practices dispersed within the great city of Edo.

Daily life in Edo with its numerous visits to various temples, sanctuaries or other *meisho*, was structured according to the rhythm of the seasons. The people of Edo were immersed in a world where places and moments, nature and culture are deeply interconnected. This mutual embedding of space and time permeates the social calendar and dictates ritualized behaviors. Even today, in the heart of the megalopolis, the calendar reflects, guides and provides information about a variety of seasonal phenomena. It proposes social events that encourage rituals and active commitment, and not only contemplative attitudes towards nature.

Generally, the theater and the pleasure district are considered as the center of Edo's specific culture, the limited area where the merchant and artisan classes of Edo could feel free and show themselves. The walks, famous sights and the social practices taking place there, developed throughout the Edo Era, represent a different center of this culture, completely open to everyone, also to women, children or people without money.

Parks as Instruments of Cultural Change in the Meiji Era (1868-1912)

The Meiji Era was a time of rapid and important transformations of the political, economic and social structure of Japan. A feature of this period is its awareness of this process, instituted as a narration: the Meiji Era is a moment of rupture in which everybody is involved to reach a scope, the modernity and progress of the whole nation. However, at the beginning, struggles between different factions and different approaches of modernization created a source of instability. Deep social unrest led to a swift decrease, by half, of the population. After important upheavals during the two first decades of the Meiji Era, Japan devoted to set up a constitutional order, centered on the emperor, with an elected diet, and started a determined industrializing policy inserted in a capitalist economy. Intense programs of learning developed a policy of opening of Japan in order to modernize the country and assimilate Western concepts and techniques. Many Japanese traveled and studied abroad, sent by the government, and many foreign specialists were invited into Japan as experts and teachers.

In the city of Tokyo, many Edo famous places were beset by troubles and destroyed. Some Buddhist sites were destroyed, as a sign of rupture with the ancient system, and perhaps because their vast domains were rapidly used for other purposes. Then, the immense enterprise of modernization demanded a profound urban restructuring (the widening of roads, construction of transportation or technical networks); the ministries, mainly the Army and Education, requisitioned numerous plots of land to build military installations, universities and schools considered indispensable and having priority. Next, due to industrial turnover, numerous sites, such as the banks of the Sumida River, became ruined more or less rapidly and disappeared. Even though Japanese civilization derived a renewed cultural vigor from its rush for modernity, the transition did not go smoothly.

City planning of western cities provided the new urban model. In Europe after the 1840's public parks conceived as new amenities appeared first in England then were transplanted, with their specific appearances, functions and practices into all European cities and beyond. The Meiji government thought that the capital, to be on a par with Western cities, required such an "amenity" to express and contribute to its modernization. In 1873 (Meiji 6), the government instituted by decree the first administrative system of public parks in Tokyo. In fact, to compensate for lack of means since its priorities were industrialization and the establishment of a strong and modern army, the government designated five of the most famous and frequented *meisho* of Edo by a new word, *kōen* that means "public garden." This decree aimed at establishing a modern city with public parks on the European model (precisely London, Paris, Berlin and Vienna[7]), to provide secure places for recreation, and to preserve some remains of Edo city. It is also significant about the modernity expressing its existence before truly materializing itself (Gluck 1999, 9).

So, in spite of the Meiji government's will to break with the past, some continuities are visible: continuity of space because the new public parks were all famous places of Edo; continuity of practices; and also continuity in the decision making and control by a central authority. Like the Tokugawa shogunate government, the modern administration decided locations, names, and later on the design of new parks, in the same intent to control urban development and contain popular practices.

The Meiji Period did not break with the past but rather restricted prior opportunities. In spite of these limitations, most ritualized social practices with their power to mold a proper cultural conscience were maintained, and the sense of nature as a palimpsest of accumulative processes and memories partially survived.

In 1882, when the city recovered its population level prior to the Meiji restoration, the government promulgated a law about the renovation of Tokyo advocating the creation of forty-nine parks whose size and location were selected to emulate London and Paris. Seventy percent of them were Edo beauty spots, and half of them Shinto shrines. A few gardens attached to the ancient residences of *daimyō*, the vassal lords of Tokugawa, inscribed on this list of public parks were rapidly transformed into allotments and destroyed. Thus the Tokyo renovation law further contributed to the reuse and redefinition of ancient places for economic reasons and almost certainly because the bucolic character of Tokyo was still evident. However a genuine and important creation was set in motion: Hibiya Park, at the heart of the city and next to the imperial palace. This park was meant to reflect changes in lifestyles and town planning, rather than to satisfy a definite need for green space; to demonstrate the modernization of the downtown then under complete overhaul, and to demonstrate the new government capacity to bring projects to a successful conclusion.[8] The stakes were great.

The municipal commission in charge of the project faced a major challenge: defining a modern public park following Western ideas and yet suitable for Tokyo. As a consequence of many hesitations, work did not start until 1902, and the park was inaugurated in 1903. Honda Seiroku (1866-1952), a young agronomist who had spent two years at university in Germany (Dresden and Munich), was made responsible for the project in 1900. He was neither an architect, nor a landscape gardener, so in order to avoid criticism, he gathered different opinions and commissioned expert's reports from different specialists (botanists, gardeners, doctors, engineers, etc). He also availed himself of his own experience in Europe and of German works on the composition of gardens and public parks. He developed a consensus by combining varied elements to integrate them into numerous requirements and functions. He succeeded in his project, and created a whole out of diffeerent places open to innovation and renewal of urban practices. This park is a space of a new type, presenting Japanese and Western characteristics, but fundamentally original in its structure, resulting in the reconfiguration of landscape elements borrowed from various sources.

In nineteenth century Europe, public parks were more than urban ornaments or places for public recreation open to all. They also provided spaces where the higher classes tried to teach or advocate their own lifestyles, leisure activities, aesthetic values in support of *bourgeois* distinction. Park regulations were established to frame the expression of correct attitudes and conducts for common people to learn about more civilized behaviors and to become less ignorant of good urban manners. Moreover, at this time the nation offered a central moral theme in Europe, and particularly in Germany then fully engaged in the construction of its national unity. The parks offered spaces which allowed one to develop or maintain this sense of national identity, thanks to landscapes, statues, and spaces devoted to official events. Hibiya Park exemplifies the reception of the central theme of the nation in Japan during the Meiji Era, and the deliberate use by the state of landscape and its expressive potential to contribute to the foundation of the national modern identity.

The plan for Hibiya is divided into four main parts (Fig. 3): a large lawn and nearby a Japanese garden occupy the center of the park; the entrance with regular-shape flowerbeds is in the southwest angle; at the opposing northeast angle, remains of fortifications and moats of Edo castle subsist. Wide walks connect these different areas. The park's largest space is

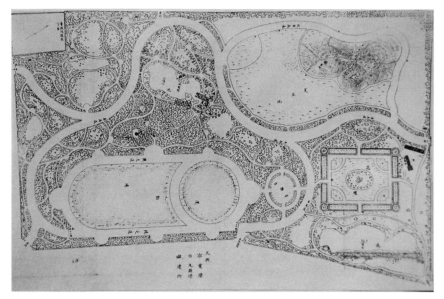

Fig. 3. Hibiya Park, Original Plan in 1900.

formed by the main lawn, named on the original plan *undōjō*, (sport ground), and Honda borrowed its shape directly from the plan of a municipal Prussian park.[9] This space was utilized at the time for all sorts of gatherings, for sport, and various celebrations or official parades. Very soon, the park played the role of an urban square at the center of the city used for official national events, but also for transgressions and more or less obliquely political actions.[10] Honda conceived this vast central lawn as a sign of modernity, but the city of Edo already had its empty sites and meadows. They had been used as training grounds for horsemanship by the samurais, but also as places for walks, games, collecting plants. It certainly made it easier for Honda, and later for the inhabitants of Tokyo, to introduce this kind of space and to adapt to its new functions. And ever since the creation of Hibiya Park, all large public parks possess a vast central grass field allowing for multiple collective or individual uses. The imported schemes resulted from a process of selection allowing the appreciation of preexisting amenities with a renewed meaning,[11] and introduced a new public vocabulary amenable to the construction of a modern Japanese identity.

The Japanese garden entrusted to a master gardener constitutes the other central and important pole of Hibiya Park. Its composition, in the style of a landscape garden follows the model of *daimyō* pleasure gardens of the Edo period. Features of this type of garden, *kaiyūshiki-teien*, are visible there: in the center a pond is circumscribed by a footpath; creeks and waterfalls, rock lanterns of stone, various pavements, well-built thickets, and groves follow each other along the path. Allusive landscapes (making reference to other gardens or famous *meisho* and to different *stimmung*) unfold around the pond, appear and disappear, and combine into an ensemble through the movement of the rambler.

The geometric flowerbed at the entrance is another Western borrowing. Honda was a forestry specialist, not particularly attracted to flowers, but he gave in to pressures to create an exotic flowerbed. At the public opening, it was this section of the park that most attracted the visitors' curiosity.[12]

In the opposite corner, a fortification wall of the Edo castle and the ditch forming a pond were preserved. The original idea did not come from Honda either, but the intention was to guard a trace of an important historic place in the modern city. At Hibiya, as in all *meisho*, links to an evocative past are present and as a matter of consequence it participates in the constitution of the cultural identity of the city and of its inhabitants.[13] The example of Hibiya shows that the introduction of modernity to Japan has not proceeded from a *tabula rasa*, but rather from a selective and accumulative process happening by trial and error.

Wide paths suitable for horse carriages or bicycles were supposed to reach the center of the park very quickly as a testimony of modernity. A luxurious Western-style restaurant was implanted there so as to allow elite Japanese to invite foreign visitors in an appropriate setting. It also offered an occasion to discover new table manners, new bodily attitudes. Even today, this restaurant (called "*Bois de Boulogne*"[14]) maintains its role as a more or less formal meeting place in the center of a business district. One can have a drink there on an outdoor terrace "as in France," a rarity in Tokyo.[15] Parks in Europe are mostly visited for the sake of being in nature, whereas the habitants of Tokyo come to Hibiya to "breathe the perfume of the city for cafes are found there, restaurants with bouquet on tables installed outside where one eats with knives and forks, and drinks coffee as abroad" (Suzuki and Sawada 1997, 91). In Hibiya, all these new uses spread rapidly and disseminated models of behavior, such as walking in the evening under the first electric lights, listening to Western music played at the kiosk (installed in 1905), and practicing tennis (in 1920, three courts were made accessible to women for the first time in Japan).

Hibiya, the first modern park of Japan, rapidly considered as a new *meisho*, became the public park archetype in the Japanese form. With its numerous fittings, its variety of landscapes and atmospheres, such a park was and still is an essential space to engage with past and new modes of perception: perception of physical realities, cultural representations, social

Fig. 4. *Hanami* enjoying the cherry blossoms nowadays in Ueno Park.
Fig. 5. *Hanami* enjoying the cherry blossoms nowadays in Jindaiji Park, a former military ground.

behaviors. A stroll allows any visitor to link up several possible routes, each of which forms part of a narrative of Japan's modern identity, and puts nature, history, traditional and innovative popular practices in contact with each other. The park provides support for public display of an ensemble of aesthetic values and meanings that condition the feeling of nature and have the power to evoke past and present memories.

By means of the example of Hibiya Park, it clearly appears that the cultural changes of the Meiji Era did not simply proceed by imitation of some western models. It appears that the "modernity" or the "tradition" were always composite and

Fig. 6. Enjoying the red leaves turning in fall in Jindaiji Park, a former military ground.

Fig. 7. Mizunomoto Park, a former military ground, in summer.

permanently redefined in large part by dynamic improvising.

The Parks from the Post-War Era: A Policy Development

At the end of the Second World War, most houses, buildings and infrastructures of Tokyo were in ruin. The parks were transformed into temporary cemeteries, homeless shelters, or agricultural land. Rapid reconstruction of the industry and its infrastructures, rather than quality of urban environment and public amenities was the priority.

Urban development accelerated after 1955, when the so-called "High economic growth" period began, and pollution intensified, while natural resources gradually disappeared. The inhabitants responded to these changes, since cultural engagements with nature, such as watching fireflies in June or fishing in the rivers, became more and more precarious, places where they could be performed became seen as markers of the quality of the environment. The degradation of the natural environment of the city that had been exceptionally rich until the war went on rapidly.[16] Today the ratio of green spaces per inhabitant in Tokyo stands among the smallest among industrialized cities.[17] Soon parks appeared indispensable to improve the quality of the environment, and to respond to public demands. In 1971, the governmental Agency for the Environment was created and multiplied plans for environmental improvement, nature protection, and greening again the city. In 1981, the General Plan for Tokyo Green Spaces presented the first commitments. The following year, the long-term plan for Tokyo set the ratio of six square meters of green space per inhabitant as a goal to be reached at the beginning of the twenty-first century; a new goal of seven square meters per inhabitant for 2015 was substituted in the 1997 long term plan, revised in 2000. As a result the area of parks and gardens in the metropolis of Tokyo has tripled during the last twenty-five years, yet still short of the goal. It will however be difficult since after a long period of decline, population growth in the central wards is expected. Yet, the Bureau of Tokyo's City Planning directly involved in global economy development and great cities trade pointed that: "Charming urban spaces beautified by water and greenery represent a precious social capital that symbolizes the prosperity of a city" (Bureau of City Planning 2002, 37). Today, the quality of the environment reflects a political and economic vision of the quality of life.

Beyond their quantitative aspects the plans and statistics also express qualitative concerns, not only about aesthetics but rather about quality of natural surroundings. There is a revival of appreciation of the presence of living nature inserted into the city fabric by the multifarious practices of daily life linked to concrete and particular manifestations of the natural cycles (Fig. 4).

First, in the 1970's, the metropolitan government of Tokyo undertook the development of large urban parks on disused ancient military grounds in peripheral wards[18] (Fig. 5, 6 and 7). Then, in the 1980s, the city became involved in the protection and development of wooded hillsides to the west of the metropolis. An inventory of woods, patches of remnant nature, was established and protection measures were put in place before

Fig. 8. Tama Shinrinkagakuen, (Tama Forest Park) in the western hill district, during the cherry blossoms.
Fig. 9. Sakuragaoka Park in the western hill district, in fall.

they were open to the general public (Fig. 8 & 9). In the center, alignments of exceptional trees, relics of the nature formerly enjoyed in the capital city, were studied, protected and inserted along circuits across the city. Coeval with these conservation projects of natural spaces mostly located in the west, restoration programs of natural areas were initiated mainly in the east of the city, with the creation of maritime parks in the Bay of Tokyo.

An Example of Social and Cultural Appropriation: The Maritime Parks of Tokyo

The port of Tokyo is at one and the same time ancient, since it played an essential role in the development of the city of Edo since the sixteenth century, and recent since it only obtained its status as an international harbor in 1941.[19] It is a central locus of the city history and formation; it has also been beset during several decades by all aspects of the rupture of balance between city life and economic growth, environmental pollution and urban development.

The situation was resented by the inhabitants of Tokyo. They found themselves completely cut off from the sea by the industrial development of the harbor in the bay. Huge landfills had began in the Edo Period and accelerated during the 1960s. Today, the total area reclaimed over the sea represents 4500 hectares of land in Tokyo, that is three central wards of the city.[20] Besides, a dam was constructed along the shore to protect the urbanized zones from flood, further isolating inhabitants from the inaccessible and even invisible sea. The sea was treated as a source of potential disasters, and no longer of advantages. The bay became a valuable space for construction, and no longer an amenity. The balance between the city and its harbor was broken.

The inhabitants denounced the landfills as causes of nuisances, proof that urban development was always geared towards economic development detrimental to the quality of life. The maritime landscapes had always been greatly appreciated, the coastal road offering remarkable scenic sites with plantings of pines and other trees. All along the coastline on the route leading from Edo to Kyoto numerous temples and sanctuaries offered fine panoramic views of the seascape, as well as cherry blossoms or autumn foliage. One could appreciate the sea from the coast or even better from a boat, having a tour or a banquet, by day- or moonlight. Other places of beauty, *meisho*, were famous sea bird watching spots. Especially during migration periods, ducks and other aquatic birds were numerous at river mouths where waders could be observed as they moved around sandy banks. Gathering shells on the beach was a good excuse for a day trip and group leisure in the spring. Then the sea assumed both an important aesthetic and recreational role, and an economic resource thanks to fishing and gathering shells or seaweeds.

We ought to acknowledge that since the Edo Period the Bay of Tokyo has always been used both for dumping liquid and solid waste, reclaiming land to develop harbor activities, commercial, industrial and residential activities, and leisure activities such as walks, picnics, fishing or collecting shells, pleasure boating and swimming. However, the intensity and number of encroachments, the scale of their impact on the environment and the landscapes, as much as the degree of conflict between economic and leisure activities have tremendously changed.

Public debate about the bay and its future began at the end of the 1960s. The Bay of Tokyo was one of the most diversified biotopes in the world. The destruction of shallow banks, modification of streams, eutrophication of waters came under severe attack. At the beginning of the 1970s, the imbalance between economic development, the increase of material riches and the quality of the urban and natural environment became public knowledge. However if industrial activities took up more than half of reclaimed land until into the 1970s, industry was in part eliminated from the maritime zone of Tokyo because of economic development and change.

Local associations and "resident movements" expressed their concerns about specific problems aiming at limited and precise results. These protests did not merge into powerful movements, but remained isolated and disseminated throughout the metropolis. Inhabitants mobilized against the industrial confiscation of the maritime domain, and called for the creation of parks as a means of re-appropriating the public domain along the sea, which had been for so long close and familiar. They seemed weak because of their size and dispersion, but their local impacts added up and influenced public choices.

In 1970, the metropolitan authorities decided to create maritime parks. A commission, from a synthesis of data on the state of places and various demands, proposed three directions in 1972: make the sea accessible in more places all along the maritime domain of Tokyo; to take into account the continuity of the maritime environment created by the sea, the bank and the land border, as much as from a point of view of ecological balance as from accessibility so as to allow varied recreational activities; and to integrate in a concrete fashion the participation of inhabitants, their knowledge and experiences, as much in the conception as in the administration of parks.

The maritime park project engages with two great preoccupations of the time: on the one hand, diversifying the uses of reclaimed lands in order to reconcile harbor and urban activities, taking advantage of the deindustralization; and on the other hand, regenerating the environment and creating parks. The commission in charge of maritime parks presented a program in 1975 and the first parks opened to the public at the beginning of the 1980s, but for lack of public transport, public use was not significant until ten years later. Today, forty-two parks have been completed by the Port Bureau Authority in the entire maritime domain of Tokyo, comprising

Fig. 10. Odaiba Marine Park, a picnic area.
Fig. 11. Kasai Marine Park, the seashore landscape.

310 hectares of land and 474 hectares of water domain, to which four metropolitan parks, comprising 170 hectares, administered by the Bureau of Tokyo's green spaces should be added.[21] The area of the ensemble represents therefore 480 hectares. Two-hundred hectares are still projected for a total of fifty seven sites (Fig. 10, 11 and 12). These "maritime parks" are classified into three types according to their layouts, positions, uses and landscape features: coastal parks, harbor gardens, and linear routes.

There are seven coastal parks, containing between seven and eighty-six hectares, meant to retrieve the coastline for leisure

Fig. 12. Odaiba Marine Park, the promenade along the seashore.

activities. Beaches have been recreated in three of them, and everywhere else various rough stone waterbreaks form accessible banks. These parks allow fishing, bird and aquatic life watching, making barbecues, or even camping. Public facilities allow numerous sports practice, such as windsurfing, sailing, and even golf on a fifty-four hectare course, at very little cost. There are nineteen harbor gardens, containing between a half and five hectares, meant to improve the urban environment quality and make the harbor more accessible to inhabitants. These are interstitial, buffer zones running alongside harbor installation, or even tree-lined wharves from which one can watch boat activities. These places offer a space of relaxation for harbor employees, and afford a window on the harbor for the inhabitants of the city.

There are sixteen linear walkways or tree-lined roads forming a pedestrian network meant to connect the different parks and gardens. Efforts at linking the city and the port highlight the goal of establishing a network of parks and green spaces. It is possible nowadays to go on foot or by bicycle across the entire maritime domain, and beyond the entire city, passing on leveled grounds or artificial islands through parks and tree-planted walkways. This has given rise to a new type of urban hiking.

Paradoxically, since the grounds of these parks have been created *ex nihilo*, the most artificial landscaping has made it possible to reach nature and contact with the sea again. It has allowed a renewal of ancient practices, like gathering shells, fishing, enjoying the maritime landscape, or the discovery of new seaside activities like windsurfing, and luxurious idleness on the beach, or even the revival of latent abilities. For example, the present infatuation with bird watching revives the ancient appreciation of migrations or nest building during the Edo Period. In the same way, present day barbecue parties reactivate and perpetuate deep-rooted practices and attitudes. In these parks, multiple routes intersect each other proposing diverse sporting or leisure activities, didactic or sensitive discovery of nature, cultural or historic promenades. Thus diverse concerns are brought together by these networks of landscapes and sceneries, ensuring the unity of nature protection and leisure activities. This originality, which satisfies modern concerns about the environment, ensures their success with town-dwellers.

The program of Tokyo maritime parks constitutes at one and the same time an environmental project and an urban project at the scale of the metropolis. It substitutes to the anarchic development of landfills according to private interests, the will to create a common public space for the entire urban community beyond a cosmetic intention only to improve the image of the city.

As we have seen earlier, the rituals of social life engage modes of perception and appreciation—collective and multi-sensory—of landscape and nature, which are rooted in Japanese culture, and they contribute to social integration. The Bay, which had been vital for the blossoming of Edo urban culture, has vanished forever out of existence. However, the creation of the maritime parks has sparked the development of new natural processes, biotopes are being regenerated and new and unprecedented balances between city and environment come into being. Natural phenomena and symbolic meanings mutually enrich one another; nature and culture recombine with each other indefinitely and create new landscapes.

Parks as Places of Expression of Modernity and Identity

Beyond the rupture of ancient balance and the apparent disorder of megalopolitan development, Tokyo demonstrates a capacity to regenerate itself from principles of engagement with space and nature issuing from a deep-rooted cultural matrix. These principles were born out of a long process of historic stratification, particularly rich in Tokyo since the city has a long history as a great city.

Public parks offer, at present, a favorable setting for the unfolding of multiple practices, following a temporal setting determined principally by the seasons. These numerous practices allow inhabitants throughout the year to share attitudes, values and emotions. Common cultural identity and social bonding reaffirm each other. Whereas other cities have monuments, the memory of the past in Tokyo does not reside within some built relics, but within practices that never stop evolving and yet always arouse the sense of memory and connect the present to a significant past for individuals and groups alike.

Even in a large city like Tokyo, these practices recreate local communities. They reveal values and fundamental questions of Japanese society, like integration and the desire to be together, the sense of nature and its aesthetic perception. Some critics claim that the feeling towards nature to Japan has become a fiction, and its celebration in preserved or restored places a simple illusion. However in the construction of this "fictional" nature, individuals are actors, they play a role and are not simply a passive audience. Popular culture does not allow itself to be completely manipulated by consumerism, but succeeds in re-asserting itself through its appropriation of new practices. The routes are not only "a course subtly but efficiently conceived in order to guide the masses along the same paths" (Pelletier 1998, 72).[22]

Social rituals that develop in the parks, simply put, enable groups of people to establish a dwelling place for themselves. This appropriation or re-appropriation of their environment by some local communities or diverse types of groups results from a fundamental renewal of sociability: people come together again, share food and drink in the open air, in landscaped nature, share emotions, pleasure, desires. The pleasurable landscape becomes a memorable place and a symbol of the reunited group. The local communities formed themselves into defense movements because the integrity of the landscape and the maritime milieu had been compromised. Thanks to the appropriation of their new territory, they are given the opportunity of rediscovering bodily attitudes, of reaching a multi-sensory understanding of the milieu, and of moving beyond the posture of passive spectator.

Japanese culture continues to value shared perception and appreciation of nature. In spite of urban vicissitudes, in the vast region of Tokyo, inhabitants maintain an intimacy with nature through all sorts of creative expressions. In the newly constructed and landscaped nature, living elements and natural changing phenomena are numerous and breathe life into space. The entire cycle of the seasons of nature is made sensitive in its most concrete aspects. The importance of this cultural change may seem paradoxical given the low ratio of green space per inhabitant, but it results from a century old conception and schematization of nature by Japanese people.

Besides, these practices introduce a resistance to consumerism and to the homogenization of time and space in the modern city, by contrasting with them a subtle calendar, insisting on variations of light, climate, season, sensibility, and possible uses. The parks, spaces of a rediscovered nature, and the behaviors they induce concern fundamental ways of being in the world and making sense of life.

Bibliography

Berque, Augustin. *Le sauvage et l'artifice*. Paris: Gallimard, 1986.

Berque, Augustin, Michel Conan, Pierre Donadieu, Bernard Lassus and Alain Roger. *Mouvance, cinquante mots pour le paysage*. Paris: Editions de la Villette, 1999.

Bureau of City Planning, ed. *Tokyo no toshikeikaku no hyakunen (100 years of city planning in Tokyo)*. Tokyo: Tokyo Metropolitan Government, 1996.

Bureau of City Planning, ed. *Planning of Tokyo*. Tokyo: Tokyo Metropolitan Government, 2002.

Bureau of Construction, ed. *Tôkyô no kôen-ryokuchi mappu (Map of Tokyo's parks and greenery)*. Tokyo: Tokyo Metropolitan Government, 2004.

Conan, Michel. "Les paysages de l'eau : pour une poétique de la présence." *Urbanisme* 343 (juillet/août 2005): 67-71.

Debié, Franck. *Jardins de capitales*. Paris: Editions du CNRS, 1992.

Edo Tokyo Museum, ed. *Ô-Edo Happyakuya chô (Great Edo hundred eight quarters)*. Tokyo : Edo Tokyo Museum, 2003.

Fiévé, Nicolas and Paul Waley ed. *Japanese Capitals in Historical Perspective*. London: Routledge Curzon, 2003.

Gluck, Carol. "Re-présenter Meiji." In *La nation en marche. Etudes sur le Japon impérial de Meiji*, edited by Jean-Jacques Tshudin and Claude Hamon, 9-39. Arles: Philippe Picquier, 1999.

Higuchi, Tadahirô. *Kôenzukuri wo kangaeru (Thinking about park planning)*. Tokyo: Gijôdô, 1996.

Hiwatashi, Tetsuya. *Tôkyô no minato to umi no kôen (The port of Tokyo and the marine parks)*. Tokyo: Tôkyôto kôen kyôkai, 1994.

Iinuma, Jirô and Shirahata Yôzaburô. *Nihon bunka toshite kôen (Parks as Japanese culture)*. Tokyo: Yazakashobô, 1994.

Kawazoe, Noboru. *Tôkyô no genfûkei, (Tokyo's original landscape)*. Tokyo: Nihon Hôsô Shuppankyôkai, 1983.

Kita, Sandy. "From Shadow to Substance. Redefining Ukiyo-e." In *The Floating World of Ukiyo-e: Shadows, Dreams, and Substance*, 27-79. New York: Abrams and the Library of Congress, 2001.

Ooms, Herman. "Forms and Norms in Edo Arts and Society." In *Edo, Art in Japan 1615-1868*, edited by Robert T. Singer, 23-47. Washington: National Gallery of Art, 1998.

Parutenon Tama Rekishi Museum, ed. *Kôgaikôrakuchi no Tanjô (Birth of tourist sites in the suburb)*. Tokyo: Historical Museum of Parutenon Tama, 2002.

Pelletier, Philippe. "Glocal Tokyo. Trois exemples d'évolution socio-spatiale à Tokyo." *Daruma* 3 (printemps 1998): 69-81.

Pons, Philippe. "La culture urbaine à l'époque Edo : une incubation de la modernité." In *Images du Monde flottant. Peintures et estampes japonaises XVIIe-XVIIIe siècles*, edited by Editions de la Réunion des Musées Nationaux, 30-39. Paris: Réunion des Musées Nationaux, 2004.

Pons, Philippe. "Un attachement sélectif à la nature." In *Les sentiments de la nature*, edited by Dominique Bourg, 31-46. Paris: La Découverte, 1993.

Rouvière, Christian. "La nature dans la ville et la qualité de l'environnement au Japon." In *La qualité de la ville*, edited by Augustin Berque, 150-157. Tokyo: Maison Franco-Japonaise, 1987.

Sawada, Seichirô and Suzuki Satoshi. *Kôen no hanashi (Narrations on parks)*. Tokyo: Gihôdô, 1997.

Shimizu, Makio. *Kasairinkai no kôen to suizokôen (Kasai marine park and its aquarium)*. Tokyo: Tôkyôto Kôen Kyôkai, 1996.

Short, Kevin. *Nature in Tokyo*. Tokyo, New York, London: Kodansha International, 2000.

Tanaka, Seidai. *Nihon no kôen (Public parks of Japan)*. Tokyo: Kashima Shuppankai, 1993.

Waley, Paul. *Tokyo, City of Stories*. New York: Weatherhill, 1991.

NOTES

[1] Of course during the long Edo period, the true content of the social stratification changed, even if the form lasted. The warriors became samurai without war nor glory (some of them felt passionately about gardening) and the great merchants controlled the wealth of the country, becoming increasingly powerful.

[2] The most well-known are the theater and the pleasure quarter, Yoshiwara, but a lot of *sakariba*, places of popular amusement and *meisho*, famous places, bloomed in the whole city.

[3] The site of Ueno was at the northeast limit of the city, called *kimon*, that is to say "the devil's gate", therefore considered as inauspicious. The first of the built edifices, Kan'ei-ji, became the guardian temple of the Tokugawa.

[4] These sites themselves, Lake Biwa and Mount Hiei, close to the imperial capital, in the Omi Province, referred to Chinese landscapes and poetic theme, *The Eight Views of the Hsiao and the Hsiang Rivers*. This initially Chinese theme, transmuted into *The Eight Views of Omi (Omi hakkei)*, spread in Japan from the 13th century and later became a popular theme of *Ukiyo-e*, Japanese prints.

[5] The popular habitat of Edo was made up of long buildings of wood built running along lanes, called *nagaya* like tenement housing. One family would make use of six *tatamis*, being 9.7 m² The *nagaya* areas occupied 16% of the urban territory, but they regrouped 600,000 inhabitants at the beginning of the 18th century, being more than half of the total population of its maximum. The concentration and this promiscuity no doubt explains in part the importance of open air public spaces for the people of Edo.

[6] During the shogunate of Tokugawa Yoshimune (1716-1745), the creation of recreational public places, *meisho* offering splendid views of the sea, Mount Fuji or Mount Tsukuba, resulted from a planned development. Yoshimune, eighth Shogun, permitted access to several of his hunting reserves, woods situated around Edo. Incidentally, as the fiscal pressure increased on townsmen and as he imposed sumptuary laws urging frugality, he opened to the public the garden of one of his properties to the south of the city, Goten-Yama, planted with cherry trees and maples with a view over the sea. It was planted with cherry trees along the Sumida River and willows along the Kanda River, in the eastern part of the city, in order to create walkways. To the west, a public garden with peach trees, Nakano Momozono, was realized. He also created a botanical garden adjoining a charitable hospital (Koishikawa Yôjôsho). Yoshimune was particularly involved in daily affairs of government and of Edo city.

[7] The new department in charge of Tokyo's parks precisely estimated surface areas, varied ratios and locations of the parks in these four cities to work out a project.

[8] The heart of the city was under complete renovation with the construction of several ministries, office buildings, and a luxurious residence for foreign guests called Rokumeikan (1883) where high society of the Meiji Era used to reunite and organize receptions. In front of the park, the Imperial Hotel, first western-style establishment in Japan, opened there in 1890, before being reconstructed by the American architect Frank Lloyd Wright in 1922. The central station of Tokyo added itself in 1914, with a large esplanade in front where official parades took place.

[9] The governments of the Meiji and Taisho Eras, (1912-1925) encouraged sporting practices such as hiking, mountain climbing, cycling, in Tokyo and in its nearby suburbs, in order to encourage the constitution of a healthy and vigorous national people, and afterwards good soldiers.

[10] For example, a riot broke out in 1905 (Meiji 35) against the peace treaty at the end of the Russo-Japanese war; student protest movements opposed the police during the 1960s and 1970s; syndicates organize every year a ritual gathering of the first of May there, and Hibiya remains the point of departure for all important protest marches.

[11] For example *hanami* today. First *hanami* has an important collective meaning, since it marks the start of the new (academic) year (in Japan, the year begins in April for schools and universities, enterprises, Parliament, new television programs, the baseball championship, etc.). Celebrating the cherry blossoms can take different forms: a solitary walk, celebration with one's family or with a group of friends. More specifically, new employees recruited during the preceding year and graduating in March, take their position on the first of April, and one of their first duties concerns the organization of *hanami* for the group of colleagues of their department. The new recruits go into a park, choose a good location, mark it with plastic sheets or cartons. While some of them protect the location all day while waiting for the arrival of all the colleagues, others buy drinks and food. In this case, this form of *hanami* becomes a ritual which marks the change of the new employees status and has an obvious role of social integration in the enterprise. So, an originally sacred and agrarian ritual has become a rite of passage integrated within the contemporary socio-economic system and taking place in the city.

[12] It is true that the use of the geometric garden introduces an irony, because it was part of an older social order in Europe, but in the imagination of Meiji, Western embodies civilization and modernity. Which just goes to show that modernism and its aesthetic expression state differently according to the

context (Gluck 1999, 11, 16).

[13] Honda participated in the safeguard of another vestige of the Edo Era. It concerned a tree of exceptional height, a *ginkgo biloba*, which was part of the garden of a *daimyô* residence comprised in the sector under renovation. The tree was on the right of way of a new road, and should therefore have been chopped down. Honda undertook to displace and transplant it in Hibiya Park, placing even his position at stake if the operation failed. The transplantation succeeded, Honda saved face, and the tree survived. At the tree foot, a plaque relates the anecdote adding to the narrative of place.

[14] A highly fashionable public forest landscaped in the second half of the nineteenth century in Paris.

[15] The first western style restaurant, serving French cuisine, opened in Ueno Park in 1872. The recertification into parks of five high places of Edo by the decree of 1873 had as a principal consequence the implantation of private concessions which developed in the bosom of parks, of luxury western restaurants. At the beginning, in Hibiya, it was forbidden to eat and drink in the park, seated on the ground, in the traditional manner. To eat was authorized only at the designated place, that is to say at the restaurant. Rapidly the habitual behaviors recaptured their rights, and the two ways to create co-habitation, and continue to create it.

[16] The population of Edo surpassed one million inhabitants but nature (vegetation, water and wild life) was very present. The residences of the *daimyô* with their vast gardens covered 60% of urban territory; the temples and sanctuaries provided planted courtyards or gardens, representing 15%, which made a total of three quarters of the surface of the city. And what's more, the woods, the steep banks planted with trees were numerous.

[17] The ration of m² green spaces per inhabitant provides a very clear classification: metropolis of Tokyo: 5,46 m²; Tokyo (23 wards only): 4,45 m²; Paris: 11,8 m²; Seoul: 17,4 m²; Los Angeles: 17,8 m²; Vancouver: 26,5 m²; Londres: 26,9 m²; Berlin: 27,4 m²; New York: 29,3 m². According to (Metropolis of Tokyo ed. 2004).

[18] These grounds were in fact the remains of a green belt constructed around Tokyo in the 1930s, at first to control its extension, moreover in the bounds of the anti-aerial defense.

[19] The Bay actually comprises five large ports: Tokyo (founded in 1590), Yokosuka naval base (1850), Yokohama (1859), Kawasaki (1927), Chiba (1954), Kisarazu (1955). In this paragraph, we refer uniquely to the maritime domain of the metropolis of Tokyo. All the coast of the Bay underwent the same intense modifications as those detailed for Tokyo, with the same type of recovery of the environment and of the landscapes today.

[20] A project for completely filling up the Bay had even been seriously proposed in 1958. A commission studied its feasibility, and the idea reemerged in the 1980s.

[21] The port of Tokyo, as elsewhere in Japan, is directly administered by the Metropolitan Government of the city, which facilitates the coordination of projects.

[22] Pelletier, a geograph, considers the present development on the landfills as only an extension of the center of the city (where the price of land is the highest), and a place producing a facile consensus (aesthetic, social and cultural). We don't completely agree with this univoque criticism of the ultraliberalism economy, not by naivety but because users are not "cultural idiots," and these maritime parks as a whole constitute a generous, free and open public space. The waterfront of Tokyo is not only "a space of consumption for consumers."

Gardens, City Life and
Culture

Gardens, City Life and
Culture

Gardens, City Life and
Culture

Gardens, City Life and
Culture

Gardens, City Life and
Culture

Gardens, City Life and
Culture

CHAPTER 15

Ecological and Socioeconomic Dimensions of Homegardens of Kerala, India

U.M. Chandrashekara[1] and S. Sankar

Kerala state, situated in the Southwestern part of India, lies between 8° 18' and 12° 48' N latitude and 74° 22' and 77° 22'E longitude. The state, with an extent of 38,863 square kilometers, has a population of over thirty-two million people and density of 819 persons per square kilometer. Here the per capita cultivable land is only 0.11 ha and over eighty percent of the total population is at least partly dependent on agriculture and over seventy percent of the agricultural holdings are below 0.2 ha (KSLUB, 1995). A factor peculiar to Kerala when compared with other states of India is its village system. In other states, in general, the dwelling houses are clustered together in a locality and the cultivable land stretches outside it. In Kerala, each farmer has his dwelling in his own plot; irrespective of landholding size. Thus in Kerala, homestead farming is the most prevalent type of landuse system covering about eighty-eight percent of the total landholding and about forty-one percent of the total cultivable area of the state. Depending on the nature and type of components, most homegardens in the state can be classified as agrosilvopastoral system, consisting of herbaceous crops, woody perennials and animals. Some homegardens represent agrisilvicultural systems consisting only of the first two components. In this chapter, size class distribution of homegardens, plant species distribution and diversity, socio-cultural and market and non-market values, including opportunity for gender equality in managing the systems, are highlighted.

Size of Homegardens

Like in several other tropical and subtropical regions, the average size of a homegarden in Kerala is much less than a hectare (0.5 ha; Nair and Sreedharan, 1986; Babu *et al.*, 1992; Kumar *et al.*, 1994; Sankar and Chandrashekara, 1997), indicating the subsistence of the practice. Furthermore, it is also reported that in the state, small homegardens (<0.4 ha) found to represent fifty-three percent, while medium homegardens (0.41-.12 ha) and large homegardens (>1.2 ha) represent twenty-eight percent and nineteen percent respectively (Sankar and Chandrashekara, 2002). It may be mentioned here that very often such small sized landuse systems with monocropping are not viable, particularly in the rural ecosystems (Jose and Shanmugaratnam, 1993). Thus multi-tiered and multi-species structure is essentially the major feature identified for its socioeconomic adaptability and stability, biological balance and resilience, and sustained productivity at a low-level equilibrium.

Horizontal Structure of Homegardens

The Kerala homegardens are thought to be at least 4000 years old (Kumar and Nair, 2004). The existence of homegardens in

Kerala has been recorded by foreign travelers for centuries. For instance, Ibn Batuta who visited Kerala in the fourteenth century has written that "we next came to the country of black pepper, Malabar. Its length is a journey of two months from Sindabar to Kawlam. The whole way by land lies under the shade of tree ...... And in all this space of two months journey, there is not a space free from cultivation. For every man has his own orchard with his house in the middle and a wooden fence around it" (Batuta, 1929). The practice of managing homegardens as a complex system with cultivated, semi-cultivated or retained plants, mainly perennials and semi-perennials is still a common phenomenon in the state. However, the horizontal arrangement of the components of homegardens seems to vary across garden size. Generally, the coconut (*Cocos nucifera*) trees form the architectural base of the homegardens around which the other components are orchestrated (Jose, 1991). One important feature of coconut is that it lends itself to intercropping due to its special growth form, canopy and root characteristics at different growth stages. Sufficient light reaches the understory of a coconut garden to permit the growth of intercrops except from about the eighth to the twentyfifth year of palm growth (Nair, 1983). The chances of overlapping of the root systems of the coconut palm and the intercrops are minimal as most of the palm roots are found near the bole. The coconut palms are planted at a spacing of 5 x 5 meters to 7.5 x 7.5 meters apart. However, small and medium farmers do not follow any specific spacing and planting is done according to availability of spaces. Both in coconut dominant homegardens and mixed species gardens, at a glance the arrangement seems haphazard, but a closer scrutiny would reveal that each ensemble occupies a specific niche. About half as many species including *Carica papaya, Achras sapota, Psidium guajava, Syzygium aromaticum, Moringa oleifera, Murraya konigii* etc., are planted only in the interior of the homegardens. Many medium and small-crowned fruit trees such as *Artocarpus incisa, Arotcarpus heterophyllus, Citrus aurantium, Mangifera indica, Spondias pinnata, Musa* sp. and herbaceous (non-seasonal) perennials and annuals such as *Curcuma amada, Curcuma longa, Zingiber officinale, Manihot esculenta* are grown both in the border and interior parts of the homegardens. The tall trees and bamboos with large canopy are often placed near the border of the homegardens. Trailing crops like *Piper nigrum, Diascorea alata, Vigna ungiculata* etc., are planted close to the trees so as to save production cost on additional trailing materials. However, small fruit trees like *Euginia jambosa, Averohoa carambola, Anona reticulata, Emblica officinalis* etc. are arranged close to the home. Ornamental plants are mostly confined to the courtyard, footpath and adjacent areas.

Species Composition and Diversity

The homegardens of Kerala are glorious examples of species diversity in cultivated and managed plant communities. Over 170 species were recorded (Appendix 1) from an inventory made in 228 randomly selected homegardens in the state (Sankar and Chandrashekara, 2002). Inventory of plants in the live fences alone of 60 homegardens registered 68 species (Chandrashekara *et al.*, 1997). Jose (1991) listed 179 species from 80 homegardens in a village. These include 71 tree species, 6 perennial herbaceous crops, 23 annual crop species, 18 medicinal plants and 61 ornamental plants. During a survey conducted in a homestead of about 1 ha in size in the central agroclimatic zone of the state, 124 plant species were encountered of which 60 were tree species (Chandrashekara, 1995). All these observations indicate that the homegardeners are perpetual 'experimentors' and are constantly trying and testing new species (Ninez, 1987). As observed elsewhere (Rico-Gray *et al.*, 1990; Yamamoto *et al.*, 1991), in Kerala there is no specific time of the year for planting or introducing new plant species into the gardens. A study indicated that in Kerala, the diversity index for homegardens ranged from 0.251 to 0.739 suggesting its floristic diversity as moderate to low compared to a value over 0.90 for the species-rich evergreen forests (KAU, 1994). However, when measuring the species diversity, sub-species and varieties of a given crop species are also considered separately, therefore species diversity values in the homegardens are often comparable to that in the evergreen and semi-evergreen forests located in the given agroclimatic zone (Chandrashekara, 1995). The density-based Shannon-index of diversity may vary in response to the size of the homegardens with more value in large homegardens (1.1187) followed by small (1.0469) and medium (1.0084) homegardens. This may be attributed to the fact that while the limited space forces people to accommodate many different species in relatively small plots, the large space provides the people to try to grow more numbers of species with an aim to optimize the crop yield and also obtain a diverse variety of crops from large plots. Jose (1991) reported that small homegardens in a village in Southern Kerala have high tree crop density compared to larger ones. Similar observation was made in the southern and northern agroclimatic zones of Kerala (Sankar and Chandrashekara, 2002). Thus it was concluded that small farmers, in spite of small holding size, go for high intensive cropping with a keen interest to increase yield to the maximum extent. However, there are instances where the tree density and basal area in small homegardens are lesser than those recorded in large size homegardens due to the importance given by small landholders for understory crops than for tree crops.

Horizontal Structure of Homegardens

The multi-species homegardens of Kerala are also multi-layered. The plants of different heights and architectural types, though not planted in any apparent orderly manner, perfectly occupy the available space both horizontally and vertically (Chandrashekara, 1997). In most all agroclimatic zones in the state, five canopy strata have been identified in the homegardens. The first layer lies within 2 meters from the ground and is constituted by vegetables, tuber crops, grasses and other herbaceous plants. The second and third layers (within 2 to 10 meters from the ground) are almost continuous and overlapping each other. Some of the common constituents of these layers are banana, nutmeg, papaya, mango, cocoa, young coconut palms and saplings of trees. The upper most canopy layer is formed by coconut palms, areca nut palms, teak, jack fruit tree, mahogany, and other tall trees at about 10 to 25 meters in height. However the choice of species is determined by the agroclimatic and farmers' socio-economic conditions. Analysis of area occupied by canopy cover of different constituents indicated that in traditional homegardens, not less than 40-45 years old, the crown area to land area ratio ranged from 210 to 888 percent (Sankar and Chandrashekara, 2002).

Species Inventory in Homegardens

Inventory of floristic diversity in homegardens in Kerala revealed that, in general, homegardens play a negligible role in conserving wild species diversity outside the protected areas. However, they are the informal experimental stations for transfer, trial and adaptation of domesticated species. Similarly, these homegardens represent a 'genetic backstop,' preserving species and varieties that are not economic in field production and are planted in small scale for reasons of taste preference, tradition, or availability of planting materials. It may be worth mentioning here that of the approximately 300 major vegetables favored today world over, 200 are produced in homegardens, while only twenty are used in field cultivation (Ninez, 1987). Such an analysis may also be extended specifically to homegardens of Kerala in order to appreciate the importance of homegarden agroforestry in conserving and utilizing biodiversity.

Role of Women in Homegarden Management

Women play an important role in introducing many crops, particularly in the nearest surroundings of homegardens. However, in general men have an upper hand over women in decision making in terms of introduction of cash crops and perennial trees. The role of women in homegarden management depends on factors like their occupation, size of the homegardens, opportunities for off-farm jobs and socioeconomic condition of the family. For instance, Sankar and Chandrashekara (2002) recorded that in about 60 percent of total number of small homegardens (<0.4 ha) women contribute significantly to the management of the system. They also reported that only in 22 percent and 12 percent respectively of total number of medium sized homegardens (0.41- 0.12ha) and large homegardens (>1.2ha) the role of women in garden management is significant. In general, women contribute more labour to homestead farms than men. It is estimated that about 94 percent of the total female labour days was constituted by family labor (Jose, 1991). This 94 percent of the female labor (family labor) forms 41 percent of the total labor employed in the homestead farm in a year. Since this is unpaid labor, it is not given due value, and is not included in any statistics and thus becomes invisible. The emerging agricultural scenario and the trends in Kerala's cropping pattern - the drastic transition from subsistence to cash crop monocultures - would increasingly marginalize women. Women's work would become more burdensome and less socially valued (Dunkelman and Davidson, 1988). The marginalization process would be accelerated where there is a desperate and pervasive need for cash to meet family needs. If those needs can only be supplied by the market, unpaid traditional roles would no longer evoke respect, thereby undercutting the authority of women (Huston, 1985).

Like in other regions, in Kerala the homegardens seldom meet the entire basic staple food needs of the family. However, they are complementary to other crop land. Thus homegardens are a component of the larger farming system of the household. Indeed, if the homegarden is the only land available to the household, food crops such as cassava will dominate the species composition of the garden (Kumar and Nair, 2004). It is estimated that about 50 percent of the total number of homegardens contribute less than 25 percent of the total income of the household (Sankar and Chandrashekara, 2002). On the other hand, about 32 percent and 20 percent of total number of homegardens studied contributed about 25 to 50 percent and greater than 50 percent of the household income respectively. However, the contribution of homegardens for the state economy of wood and bamboo is significant. For instance, according to Krishnankutty (1990), homesteads provide 74 to 84 percent of wood requirements in Kerala. Similarly the traditional homegardens constitute a principal source of bio-fuels for rural households. For example 51 percent of the fuel-wood collected in various geographical regions are derived from homegardens (Shanavas and Kumar, 2003). Analysis of supply and demand of bamboo in Kerala state indicated that during the year 1993-94 the estimated demand for bamboo was 169,000 metric tons. Of the total supply of bamboo in State, homegardens contributed 63 percent and forests the remaining 37 percent (Krishnankutty, 1998). Homegardens of Kerala are also recognized as repositories of non-timber products such as medicinal and aromatic plants, ornamentals, gums, resins, chemical extractives and green leaf manure. It may also be mentioned here that very often yield of a crop in a given homegarden may be more than the requirement for home consumption, and the excess quantity may not be enough to sell in the market. In such a situation, farmers exchange their crops among themselves or offer to those who do not have such items. In some parts of Kerala, it was also recorded that homegardeners who are having bamboo clumps in their gardens cut branches of bamboo during the months of December and January and use the thorny branches to fence their crop lands. They also offer the bamboo branches to their relatives and friends for the same purpose. In addition, several crops of homegardens in Kerala are often instrumental in linking heterogeneous communities in the village ecosystem. For instance, the bamboo weaving communities obtain suitable bamboo poles from the homegardens and weave items such as bamboo mats, baskets, fish nets etc. While some of these items are offered to those who supplied the raw materials, the rest will be sold by the weavers. Thus homestead bamboo, like many other crops, is one element in a complex system of rural relationships where human beings are the main actors.

Traditional Knowledge and Practices for Sustainable Management of Crop Diversity

It is a known fact that many traditional communities in tropical and subtropical countries have traditional knowledge and practices to conserve natural ecosystems and associated biodiversity (Chandrashekara and Sankar, 1998; Ramakrishnan *et.al.*, 2000). Similarly, many farming communities have such traditional knowledge and practices for managing crop diversity and using the bioresources sustainably. Homestead farming is not an exception to this. For instance, cultivation of bamboo as a crop component in homesteads of Kerala has a strong traditional ecological base. Certain traditional practices of homestead bamboo cultivation and their benefits to farmers (Chandrashekara, 1996) listed in Table 1 also explain the management of crop species diversity in the system.

Thus the traditional homegardens of Kerala represent a typical example for agroforestry systems. This farming system is rich with inherent ecological, social, economic and cultural strengths. In this context, farming practices associated with homegardens could also be adopted by the forest department and local communities, leading to ecodevelopment, ecosystem rehabilitation and ecosystem recovery. Rehabilitation efforts in degraded forests near tribal settlements, such as tree planting and associated activities, could not solve the problems of tribals in the long run. On the other hand, once the multi-species, multi-crop and multi-tier systems like that of homestead farming are adopted, there is every chance to ensure food security of the local tribal community, raise of their economic and social status and improve ecosystem health. Similarly, homegardens can be

Practice	Benefits
Cultivation of bamboo in corner of homestead	Freedom of movement for gardener within garden: more space available from other crops
Trenching around bamboo clump	Restriction of horizontal spread of bamboo roots thereby reducing competition with other crops
Mounding of soil around clump	Stimulation of production of new culms
Detopping of culms	Reduction of shading to other crops; formation of longer axillary branches useful for fencing
Intercropping with shade tolerant, short duration crops	Less impact of bamboo on yield of intercrops; crops can be harvested prior short duration crops to bamboo branch cutting season so avoiding the risks of damage caused in this process. These crops are also suitable for cultivation on raised beds, so reducing root competition with bamboo.

Table 1. Traditional practices of homestead bamboo cultivation and their benefits to farmers (based on Chandrashekara, 1996).

regarded as the model in developing integrated social forestry. By utilizing the farmers' skills in managing and sustainable use of plant diversity, and by using ecologically, socially and culturally accepted species for planting, it is possible to make the social forestry program more successful even in difficult areas.

Conclusions

It is clear that the traditional homegardens of Kerala help conserve crop diversity, reducing the pressure on local natural forests by being a source of food, timber, fuel wood, fodder, medicinal plants, etc. Crops derived from homegardens are one element in a complex system of rural relationships where human beings are the main actors. However, during the last few years a shift in the multiple cropping pattern of homegardens towards mono-cropping has been observed. With radical changes in time preferences there is a growing disinterest among farmers to deal with long gestation tree crops. There is a risk due to market instability and unresolved diseases like coconut wilt, quick wilt of pepper, phytophtora of arecanut, etc. Vagaries of the monsoonal rain also have long term ill effects. Further, most of the households earn income from other sources and relegate farming to the background. Population increase and consequent erosion in the family bondage has also been a problem leading to fragmentation of the family holding into bits of small plots, rendering the homegardens unsustainable. In this context, total community commitment is required to make the available land under homestead farming sustainable. It is also reasonable to expect positive government action, such as launching of agroforestry extension activities, education and training for farmers on agroforestry, and supply of quality plant propagules and technical know-how, to help farmers attain diverse varieties of crops in their homesteads. It may also be pointed out here that our primary and secondary and even higher institutions of learning do not have curricula on homegarden agroforestry systems. Lack of solid research data to highlight the importance of crop combinations in homestead farming is another constraint in revitalizing traditional homegarden agroforestry practices. Auto-ecological and syn-ecological properties of plant components, particularly trees, plant-plant interactions, economics of homestead farming, resources management and utilization and other aspects are yet to be studied systematically. This is possible only when priority is given to conducting research on homegardens at the same order of magnitude as given to controlling pests and diseases in cash crops and to breeding new varieties of rice.

Bibliography

Babu, K.S., D. Jose, and G. Gokulapalan. "Species Diversity in a Kerala Homegarden." *Agroforestry Today* 4 (1992): 15.

Batuta, Ibn. "Travels in Asia and Africa, 1325-1354." Translated by H.A.R. Gibb. *Broadway Travelers Series*. E. Denison Ross and Eileen Power, eds. Kelley, New York: 1929.

Chandrashekara, U.M. "Ecological and Economic Benefits of Tree Components in Homestead Farming Systems of Kerala." In *Understanding Ecologically Sustainable Economic Development*, edited by P.P. Pillai and R.P. Nair, 104-108. Institute of Planning and Applied Economic Research, Dr. John Mathai Centre, Thrissur, 1995.

Chandrashekara, U.M. "Strengths and Weaknesses of Traditional Systems of Bamboo Cultivation in Rural Kerala." *Agroforestry Forum* 7 (1996): 21-23.

Chandrashekara, U.M. "Growth and Architectural Analyses of Trees of Agroforestry Importance in Kerala." *Range Management & Agroforestry* 18 (1997): 151-163.

Chandrashekara, U.M. and S. Sankar. "Ecology and Management of Sacred Groves in Kerala, India." *Forest Ecology and Management* 112 (1998): 165-177.

Chandrashekara,U.M., S. Sankar, P.K. Shajahan, M.E. Blowfield, and E.R. Boa. "Fencing Patterns in Homegardens of Kerala, India: A Case Study." *Range Management & Agroforestry* 18 (1997): 41-53.

Dunkelman, I. and J. Davidson. "Women and Environment in the Third World: Alliance for the Future." London: Earthscan Publications Limited, 1998.

Huston, P. "Third World Women Speak Out." Asian Women's Research and Action Network. Davao City, Philippines: 1985.

Jose, D. *Homegardens of Kerala: Small and Marginal Farmers' Response to Change in Agrarian Structure and Environmental Constraints*. M.Sc. Thesis, Agricultural University of Norway, 1991.

Jose, D. and N. Shanmugaratnam. "Traditional Home Gardens of Kerala: A Sustainable Human Ecosystem." *Agroforestry Systems* 24 (1993): 203-213.

KAU (Kerala Agricultural University). *Research Report 1992-93*. Vellanikkara, Thrissur, Kerala, India: Kerala Agricultural University Press, 1994.

Krishankutty, C.N. 1990. "Demand and Supply of Wood in Kerala and Their Future Trends." *KFRI Research Report* 67.

Krishanankutty, C.N. "Socio-economic and Ecological Aspects of Developing Bamboo Resources in Homesteads of Kerala. Part 2. Economic and Management Aspects." *KFRI Research Report* 125, Peechi, Kerala: Kerala Forest Research Institute, 1998.

Kerala State Land Use Board (KSLUB). *Landuse Resources of Kerala State*. Thiruvananthapuram, Kerala, India: Kerala State Land Use Board, 1995.

Kumar, B.M. and P.K.R. Nair. "The Enigma of Tropical Homegardens." *Agroforestry Systems* 61 (2004): 135-152.

Kumar, B.M., S.J. George, and S. Chinnamani. "Diversity, Structure and Standing Stock of Wood in the Home Gardens of Kerala in Peninsular India." *Agroforestry Systems* 25 (1994): 243-262.

Nair, M.A and C. Sreedharan. "Agroforestry Farming System in the Homesteads of Kerala, Southern India." *Agroforestry Systems* 4 (1986): 339-363.

Nair, P.K.R. "Agroforestry with Coconuts and Other Tropical Plantation Crops." In *Plant Research and Agroforestry*, edited by P.A. Huxley, 80-102. Nairobi: International Council for Research in Agroforestry, 1983.

Ninez, V.K. "Household Gardens: Theoretical Considerations on an Old Survival Strategy." *Agricultural Systems* 23 (1987): 167–186.

Ramakrishnan, P.S., U.M. Chandrashekara, C. Elouard, C.Z. Guilmoto, R.K. Maikhuri, K.S. Rao, S. Sankar, and K.G. Saxena. "Mountain Biodiversity, Land Use Dynamics, and Traditional Ecological Knowledge." UNESCO, New Delhi, Oxford & IBH Publ.: New Delhi, 2000.

Rico-Gray, V., F.J.G. Garcia, A. Chemas, A. Puch, and P. Sima. "Species Composition, Similarity, and Structure of Mayan Homegardens in Tixpeual and Tixcacaltuyub, Yucatan, Mexico." *Economic Botany* 44 (1990): 470-487.

Sankar, S. and U.M. Chandrashekara. "Agroforestry Systems." In *The Natural Resources of Kerala*, edited by K. Balachandran Thampi, N.M. Nayar and C.N. Nair, 473-477. Kerala, India: WWF India, Kerala State Office, Thiruvananthapuram, 1997.

Sankar, S. and U.M. Chandrashekara. "Development and Testing of Sustainable Agroforestry Models in Different Agroclimatic Zones of Kerala with Emphasis on Socio-cultural, Economic, Technical and Institutional Factors Affecting the Sector." *KFRI Research Report* 234. Peechi, Kerala, India: Kerala Forest Research Institute, 2002.

Shanavas, A. and B.M. Kumar. "Fuelwood Characteristics of Tree Species in the Homegardens of Kerala, India." *Agroforestry Systems* 58 (2003):11-24.

Yamamoto, Y., N. Kubota, T and Priyono Ogo. "Changes in the Structure of Homegardens Under Different Climatic Conditions in Java Island." *Japanese Journal of Tropical Agriculture* 35 (1991): 104-117.

Note

[1] Address for correspondence: Dr. U.M. Chandrashekara, Scientist in charge, Kerala Forest Research Institute, Sub Centre, Nilambur, Chandakunnu-679342, Malappuram District, Kerala, India; E-mail: umchandra@rediffmail.com

Appendix 1. List of plant species recorded in the homegardens of Kerala, India.

Species	Family	Species	Family
Acacia auriculiformis	Fabaceae	*Aster sp.*	Asteraceae
Acalypha hispida	Euphorbiaceae	*Averrohoa bilimbi*	Oxalidaceae
Achras sapota	Sapotaceae	*Azadirachta indica*	Meliaceae
Adenanthera pavonina	Mimosaceae	*Bauhinia retusa*	Ceasalpiniaceae
Aegle marmelos	Rutaceae	*Begonia sp..*	Begoniaceae
Ailanthus excelsa	Simarubaceae	*Benincasa hispida*	Cucurbitaceae
Albizzia lebbeck	Caesalpiniaceae	*Bombax malabarica*	Bombacaceae
Allamanda cathartica	Apocynaceae	*Borassus flabellifer*	Arecaeae
Alocasia sp.	Araceae	*Bougainvillaea spectabilis*	Nyctaginaceae
Alstonia scholaris	Apocynaceae	*Butea frondosa*	Papilionaceae
Alternanthera sessilis	Amarantaceae	*Caesalpinia pulcherrima*	Caesalpiniaceae
Amaranthus sp.	Amarantaceae	*Caladium sp.*	Araceae
Amorphophallus companulatus	Araceae	*Calotropis gigantea*	Asclepiadaceae
Anacardium occidentale	Anacardiaceae	*Cananga odorata*	Anonaceae
Ananas comosus	Bromeliaceae	*Canna indica*	Cannaceae
Annona reticulata	Anonaceae	*Capsicum annum*	Solanaceae
Anthocephalus chinensis	Rubiaceae	*Carallia brachaiata*	Rhizophoraceae
Aporusa lindleyana	Euphorbiaceae	*Careya arborea*	Lecythidaceae
Areca catechu	Arecaceae	*Carica papaya*	Caricaceae
Aristolochia indica	Aristlochiaceae	*Caryota urens*	Arecaceae
Artocarpus heterophyllus	Moraceae	*Cassia fistula*	Caesalpiniaceae
Artocarpus hirsutus	Moraceae	*Casuarina equisetifolia*	Casuarinaceae
Artocarpus incisa	Moraceae	*Catharanthus roseus*	Apocynaceae
Asclepias curassavica	Asclepiadaceae	*Celosia cristata*	Amarantaceae
Asparagus recemosus	Liliaceae	*Chrysanthemum coronarium*	Asteraceae

Appendix 1. (cont.) List of plant species recorded in the homegardens of Kerala, India.

Species	Family	Species	Family
Cinnamomum zeylanicum	Lauraceae	Dillenia pentagyna	Dilleniaceae
Citrus aurantium	Rutaceae	Dioscorea alata	Dioscoreaceae
Citrus grandis	Rutaceae	Dracaena sp.	Liliaceae
Citrus limon	Rutaceae	Dracena sp.	Liliaceae
Citrus madraspatna	Rutaceae	Ecbolium linneanum	Acanthaceae
Coccinia indica	Cucurbitaceae	Eclipta alba	Asteraceae
Cocos nucifera	Arecaceae	Eichhornia crassipes	Pontederiaceae
Codeum variegata	Euphorbiaceae	Emblica officinalis	Euphorbiaceae
Coffea arabica	Rubiaceae	Erythrina indica	Fabaceae
Coleus amboinicus	Lamiaceae	Euenia jambos	Myrtaceae
Coleus aromaticus	Lamiaceae	Eugenia malaccensis	Myrtaceae
Colocasia esculenta	Araceae	Euoodia lunu-ankenda	Rutaceae
Cordyline terminalis	Liliaceae	Euphorbia pulcherrima	Euphorbiaceae
Corypha umbraculifera	Arecaeae	Ficus asperrima	Moraceae
Crossandra undulaefolia	Acanthaceae	Ficus elastica	Moraceae
Cucumis sativus	Cucurbitaceae	Flacourtia indica	Flacourtiaceae
Cucurbita moschata	Cucurbitaceae	Gardenia jasminoides	Rubiaceae
Curcuma amada	Zingiberaceae	Glyricidia maculata	Fabaceae
Curcuma longa	Zingiberaceae	Gomphrena globosa	Amaranthaceae
Cyclea peltata	Menispermaceae	Hedychium coronarium	Zingiberaceae
Dahlia sp.	Asteraceae	Hevea braziliensis	Euphorbiaceae
Dalbergia latifolia	Fabaceae	Hibiscus esculentus	Malvaceae
Delonix regia	Caesalpiniaceae	Hibiscus mutabilis	Malvaceae
Desmodium gangeticum	Fabaceae	Hibiscus rosa-sinensis	Malvaceae
Diffenbechia sp.	Araceae	Hydranchea sp.	Saxifragaceae

Appendix 1. (cont.) List of plant species recorded in the homegardens of Kerala, India

Species	Family	Species	Family
Impatiens balsamina	Balsaminaceae	*Oroxylon indicum*	Bignoniaceae
Impatiens sultanii	Balsaminaceae	*Pandanus sp.*	Pandanaceae
Ipomoea batatas	Convolvulaceae	*Pedilanthus tithymaloides*	Euphorbiaceae
Ixora sp.	Rubiaceae	*Peristeria elata*	Orchidaceae
Jasminum grandiflorum	Oleaceae	*Persea macrantha*	Lauraceae
Jasminum sambac	Oleaceae	*Phyllanthus acidus*	Euphorbiaceae
Jatropha curcas	Euphorbiaceae	*Phyllanthus niruri*	Euphorbiaceae
Lagenaria ciceraria	Cucurbitaceae	*Piper betle*	Piperaceae
Lannea coromandelica	Anacardiaceae	*Piper nigrum*	Piperaceae
Lantana camara	Verbenaceae	*Plumeria alba*	Apocynaceae
Lawsonia alba	Lythraceae	*Polyalthia longifolia*	Anonaceae
Leucaena leucocephala	Mimosaceae	*Pongamia pinnata*	Fabaceae
Mirabilis jalapa	Nyctaginaceae	*Portulaca oleracea*	Portulacaceae
Momordica charantia	Cucurbitaceae	*Prichardia pacifica*	Arecaceae
Morinda tinctoria	Rubiaceae	*Psidium guajava*	Myrtaceae
Moringa oleifera	Moringaceae	*Pterocarpus marsupium*	Papilionaceae
Morus alba	Moraceae	*Ricinus communis*	Euphorbiaceae
Murraya konigiii	Rutaceae	*Rosa indica*	Rosaceae
Musa sp.		Musaceae	*Sacharum officinarum*
Mussaenda sp.	Rubiaceae	*Salvia farinacea*	Lamiaceae
Myristica fragrans	Myristicaceae	*Sanseviera roxburghiana*	Liliaceae
Nerium odorum	Apocynaceae	*Saraca indica*	Ceasalpiniaceae
Nyctanthes arbor-tristis	Oleaceae	*Schumanianthus virgatus*	Marantaceae
Nympaea stellata	Nymphaeaceae	*Sida rhombifolia*	Malvaceae
Ocimum sanctum	Lamiaceae	*Solanum indicum*	Solanaceae

Appendix 1. (cont.) List of plant species recorded in the homegardens of Kerala, India

Species	Family	Species	Family
Solanum mamosum	Solanaceae	*Terminalia catappa*	Combretaceae
Solanum melongena	Solanaceae	*Terminalia crenulata*	Combretaceae
Solanum torvum	Solanaceae	*Terminalia paniculata*	Combretaceae
Spondias mangifera	Anacardiaceae	*Theobroma cacao*	Sterculiaceae
Swietenia mahogoni	Meliaceae	*Trichosanthus anguina*	Cucurbitaceae
Syzygium aromaticum	Myrtaceae	*Turnera sp.*	Turneraceae
Syzygium cumini	Myrtaceae	*Vanda roxburghii*	Orchidaceae
Tabernaemontana coronaria	Apocynaceae	*Vernonia sp.*	Asteraceae
Tagetus erecta	Asteraceae	*Vigna ungiculata*	Papilionaceae
Tamarindus indicas	Caesalpiniaceae	*Vitex negundo*	Verbenaceae
Tecoma stans	Bignoniaceae	*Zingiber officinale*	Zingiberaceae
Tectona grandis	Verbinaceae	*Zinnia elegans*	Asteraceae

Gardens, City Life and
Culture

Gardens, City Life and
Culture

Gardens, City Life and
Culture

Gardens, City Life and
Culture

Gardens, City Life and
Culture

Gardens, City Life and
Culture

Contributors

Thorbjörn Andersson is an elected member of the Royal Swedish Academy of Fine Arts who studied landscape architecture, architecture and art history in Sweden and the United States, and is currently professor at SLU Ultuna, Sweden in addition to his practice. His former teaching experience includes *Professeur invité* at EPFL-ENAC in Lausanne, Switzerland (2004) and at the Graduate School of Design at Harvard University, Boston, USA (2001). Thorbjörn Andersson has engaged in a wide range of projects but is probably best known for his work in planning and designing public spaces in the city. As one of Sweden's most prominent landscape architects, his work has won several prizes and been given international attention. A selection of his built projects was recently published in the book *Platser/Places*. He was the founder and editor of *Utblick Landskap* magazine and has been the author or co-author of a number of books, most currently *The Architecture of Landscape 1940-1960* (ed. M. Treib). A small selection of his recent work includes the Dania Park in Malmö (finalist for the European Rosa Barbara Award), the park and plaza of Hjalmar Branting in Gothenburg, the plaza and streetscape of Östra Boulevarden, Kristianstad, the sculpture center and park in Vinterviken, Stockholm, and the waterfront plaza Södertull in Malmö.

Nicholas Dagen Bloom received his Ph.D. from Brandeis University in 1999. He is an Assistant Professor of American History at the New York Institute of Technology and the author or editor of three previous books: *Suburban Alchemy* (2001), *Merchant of Illusion* (2004) and *Adventures into Mexico* (2006, ed.). He is currently writing a history of public housing in New York City for the University of Pennsylvania Press.

Sylvie Brosseau, after receiving her diploma in architecture and studying city planning in Paris, came to Tokyo, Japan in 1988 as a fellow of the Japanese Government at the Tokyo Institute of Technology, section of architecture. She continued her studies at Tokyo University, where she focused on the introduction of western urban models in Japan in the late nineteenth century and the renewal of urban spaces. Later she turned to the study of public parks, their conditions of creation and purposes, their layouts and specific features, role in city planning and social functions. This interest led to a historical research on the Japanese way of feeling nature, perceiving and building landscapes, developing particular relations between nature and urban space in present day Tokyo. She is an Associate Professor at Waseda University, School of Political Sciences and Economics where she teaches and conducts research.

Dr. U.M. Chandrashekara, Scientist in charge at The Kerala Forest Research Institute Sub Centre, Nilambur, is an ecologist working in the fields of land use and land cover charges, climate change, forests, community conserved biodiverse areas like sacred groves, agroforestry systems and impact assessment in different forest types. He has published over forty-five research papers and co-authored four books. He is currently studying the interrelation between above-ground and below-ground diversity in homegardens and other land use systems in the Nilgiri Biosphere Reserve of India.

Chen Wangheng is a Professor of Aesthetics at the Philosophy Department of Wuhan University, China. He is also Director of the Center of Landscape Culture Research of Wuhan University, a member of the International Association for Aesthetics and the Vice-president of International Advisory Council of International Institute of Applied Aesthetics (IIAA). Professor Chen is listed in the Dictionary of International Biography (23rd edition) and Asia Pacific Who's Who. He has won many research awards in the field of social science, and lectured at universities worldwide, including Dumbarton Oaks, on Chinese aesthetics of landscape and garden. Among his numerous publications are the following books: *History of Chinese Classical Aesthetics* (1998), *Ontology of Chinese Aesthetics in Twentieth Century* (2001) and *Chinese Bronzes: Ferocious Beauty* (2002). In 2005, Professor Chen started a new translation series on Contemporary Landscape Aesthetics.

Chen Zhehua is a postgraduate student studying in the College of Architecture and Urban Planning of Tongji University. She received her BA from the China Academy of Art for a thesis on *The Utilization of Montage and the Spatial Imagery of the Master-of-Nets Garden in SuZhou*. Her research interests concern traditional Chinese gardens, western influence on Shanghai private gardens during the latter Qing Dynasty, and the emergence and development of Shanghai parks, especially in the nineteenth to the twentieth century period.

Michel Conan, Director of Garden and Landscape Studies and Curator of the Contemporary Design Collections at Dumbarton Oaks, is a sociologist interested in the cultural history of garden design. He contributed to a renewal of garden history in France in the mid-1970s with the publication of several reprints. He recently published the *Dictionnaire Historique de L'Art des Jardins* (1997) and *L'Invention des Lieux* (1997), edited five Dumbarton Oaks symposia, *Perspectives on Garden Histories* (1999), *Environmentalism and Landscape Architecture* (December 2000), *Aristocrats and Bourgeois Cultural Encounters in Garden Art* (February 2002), *Landscape Design and the Experience of Motion* (May 2003), and *Baroque Garden Cultures, Emulation, Sublimation, Subversion* (December 2005). His most recent publications are: *The Quarries of Crazannes by Bernard Lassus, An Essay Analyzing the Creation of a Landscape*, Washington DC: Spacemaker Press, 2004; a reprint with an introductory study of Gabriel Thouin, *Les Plans raisonnés de toutes les espèces de jardins*, Paris: Bibliothèque des Introuvables, 2004; and *Essais de Poétique des Jardins*, Firenze: Daniele Olschki, 2004, which received the Grinzani Hanbury prize for the best garden book in Italy in 2005.

Mohammed El Faïz, economist and historian of Agronomy and Arab gardens, is currently researching and teaching at the Université Cadi Ayyad in Marrakech (Maroc). He is known worldwide for his contribution to the defense of the historic landscape of the city of Marrakech, and for the protection of its gardens and oasis landscapes. His publications range on a variety of topics concerning water, agronomy and gardens in the Arab-Muslim civilization. Most importantly: *Agronomie de la Mésopotamie antique: Analyse de l'Agriculture Nabatéenne de Qûtâmä*, édition J. Brill, Leiden-Köln-New-York, 1995; *Les jardins* *historiques de Marrakech: mémoire écologique d'une ville impériale*, édition Edifir, Florence, 1996; *Les jardins de Marrakech*, édition Actes Sud, Arles, 2000; Ibn al-Awwâm, *Livre de l'Agriculture (Kitâb al-Filâha),* édition revue et corrigée avec introduction de Mohammed El Faïz, édition Sindbad/Actes-Sud, 2000; *Marrakech: patrimoine en péril*, édition Actes-Sud/ Eddif, 2002; *Jardins du Maroc, d'Espagne et du Portugal: un art de vivre partagé (ouvrage collectif)* édition Malika/Actes Sud, Madrid, 2003; *Histoire de l'hydraulique arabe: conquêtes d'une école oubliée* Paris: édition Actes Sud, 2005.

Shirine Hamadeh, assistant professor of art history, completed her Ph.D. in the History, Theory and Criticism program at MIT in 1999. She spent the following two years developing her research on early modern Ottoman architecture and urban culture, first, as a post-doctoral fellow in Landscape Studies at Dumbarton Oaks in Washington, and then in Istanbul, as an NEH/ARIT research fellow. She taught at the American University of Beirut, her alma mater, before she joined the Department of Art History at Rice in January 2003. She has been published in *Muqarnas* and the *Journal of the Society of Architectural Historians,* and is currently revising her dissertation, *The City of Pleasures: Architectural Sensibility in Eighteenth-Century Istanbul*, which was awarded the 1999 Malcom Kerr Dissertation Award in the Humanities by the Middle East Studies Association, to be published as a book. Besides her research focus on Ottoman visual culture and processes of modernity, she is interested in and teaches courses on artistic exchanges between the Muslim world and Europe, nineteenth century colonial cities and orientalist painting and literature.

Ken Hammond is Associate Professor of History at New Mexico State University. He received his Ph.D. from Harvard University for a dissertation on *History and Literati Culture: Towards an Intellectual Biography of Wang Shizhen, 1526-90.* His research interests concern Late Imperial period Chinese cultural and intellectual history, especially the Ming dynasty (1368–1644). He is currently writing a biography of Yang Jisheng (1516-1555), which follows his career, arrest and execution, and posthumous career as a Confucian martyr. Dr. Hammond is also interested in Contemporary Chinese political culture, especially the revival of Confucian ritualism in the post-communist era.

Wilhelmina Jashemski received an M.A. in Ancient History at the University of Nebraska, and a Ph.D. in Ancient History at the University of Chicago in 1942. Her dissertation on *The Origins and History of the Proconsular and Propraetorian Imperium to 27 B.C.* was published in Chicago in 1950. She taught at the University of Maryland from 1946 until 1980. A first visit to Pompei in 1955 gave a new impetus to her career. She initiated a program of garden archaeology developing the practice of multi-disciplinary and international cooperation, and brought to life the lost gardens of Pompei. Her publications demonstrate the multiple contributions that garden archaeology can bring to the Humanities and the Sciences. Her first major work, *The Gardens of Pompeii, Herculaneum and the Villas Destroyed by Mt. Vesuvius,* photographs, drawings, and plans [by] Stanley A. Jashemski (New Rochelle, N.Y.: Caratzas Brothers, 1979-1993) has been followed by the *Natural History of Pompeii*, co-edited with Frederick G. Meyer (Cambridge; New York: Cambridge University Press, 2002), and *A Pompeian Herbal: Ancient and Modern Medicinal Plants*, plant portraits by Victoria I and Lillian Nicholson Meyer; photographs by Stanley A. Jashemski and others (Austin: University of Texas Press, 1999). She is presently finishing two edited volumes offering the first and most complete descriptions and interpretations available of the Gardens of the Roman Empire.

Lauro Magnani is a Professor of History of Modern Art at the University of Genoa. His research focuses on painting and sculpture between the sixteenth and eighteenth centuries and on garden architecture. His study of Genoese gardens and villas led to the publication of a monograph on the subject—*Il tempio di Venere. Giardino e villa nella cultura Genovese* (1987; 1988; 2005)—in which the gardens are analyzed in the context of the artistic and literary culture of their time. In *The Rise and Fall of Gardens in the Republic of Genoa, 1528 – 1797*, in *Bourgeois and Aristocratic Culture in Garden Art* (2002), he highlights the links between changes in garden art and issues of social mobility. He also published works on Genoese artistic production after the Council of Trento and on the sixteenth century painter Luca Cambiaso (1995).

Georges Métailié is a research worker (Directeur de recherche) at the CNRS (National Center for Scientific Research), member of the Centre Alexandre Koyré, Paris, France. He is conducting research on the history of the knowledge of plants and animals in China and Japan from an ethnobiological point of view. This work includes the history of botanical knowledge in ancient China, the formation of modern botany in China and Japan, the history of horticulture and its techniques, and the history of flowers in Chinese gardens. He is Honorary Associate of the Needham Research Institute (Cambridge, UK). His editorial board memberships include *Anthropozoologica* and *East Asian Science, Technology, and Medicine (EASTM)*. He is former president of the French association for Chinese studies and Founding Officer and former Treasurer of the International Society for the History of East Asian Science, Technology and Medicine. A list of recent publications can be found at: www.ehess.fr/centres/koyre/ Centre_A_KOYRE.html.

Robert Louis Rotenberg is Professor of Anthropology and Director of the International Studies Program at De Paul University in Chicago. His research interests focus on symbolic economies, that is, the exchange of objects for their non-utilitarian meanings, in modern urban societies, especially in Vienna, Prague, and Budapest. His major monographs include *Time and Order in Metropolitan Vienna: A Seizure of Schedules* (1992) and *Landscape and Power in Vienna* (1995). The latter work received awards from the American Association for the Advancement of Slavic Studies, the Society for Urban, National and Transnational Anthropology, and the Austrian Cultural Institute. Rotenberg is co-editor of and a contributor to *The Cultural Meaning of Urban Space* (1993), a collection of anthropological perspectives on urban landscapes. He is the editor of *Anthropology of East Europe Review: Central Europe, Eastern Europe and Eurasia*.

S. Sankar is a Senior Scientist at the Kerala Forest Research Institute in Peechi. His areas of research include soil quality assessment, management in natural forests and forest plantations, the development of criteria and indicators for sustainable plantation management and of agro-forestry models for different agroclimatic regions of Kerala and documentation of traditional knowledge and practices of the use of natural resources in different regions of Kerala.

David Schuyler is Arthur and Katherine Shadek Professor of the Humanities and Professor of American Studies at Franklin & Marshall College, where he has taught since 1979. A native of Newburgh, New York, Schuyler received his Ph.D. in history from Columbia University, where his dissertation was awarded the Richard B. Morris Prize. Professor Schuyler is author of *A City Transformed: Redevelopment, Race, and Suburbanization in Lancaster, Pennsylvania 1940-1980* (University Park: Penn State

University Press, 2002), *Apostle of Taste: Andrew Jackson Downing 1815-1852* (Baltimore and London: The Johns Hopkins University Press, 1996) and *The New Urban Landscape: The Redefinition of City Form in Nineteenth-Century America* (Johns Hopkins, 1986), co-editor of *From Garden City to Green City: The Legacy of Ebenezer Howard* (Johns Hopkins, 2002), and co-editor of three volumes of The Frederick Law Olmsted Papers, the most recent of which is *The Years of Olmsted, Vaux & Company, 1865-1874* (Johns Hopkins, 1992), as well as author of more than twenty articles in books and professional journals. Schuyler is advisory editor of the Creating the North American Landscape series at The Johns Hopkins University Press and a member of the editorial board of the Olmsted Papers publication project. He has served as chair of the Pennsylvania State Historic Preservation Board, is a member of the National Advisory Committee of Olana, the Frederic E. Church house and grounds, which is a New York State historic site, and is past president of the Society for American City and Regional Planning History. Schuyler is recipient of the Christian R. and Mary F. Lindback Foundation Award for distinguished teaching (1994), the Bradley R. Dewey Award for scholarship at Franklin & Marshall (2003), and the Lawrence C. Gerckens Award of the Society for American City and Regional Planning History for distinguished teaching (2003).

Yinong Xu is Senior Lecturer in Architecture at the University of New South Wales. Originally from Beijing, he obtained his Ph.D. in Architectural and Urban History from the University of Edinburgh. He is the author of *The Chinese City in Space and Time: The Development of Urban Form in Suzhou* (Hawaii University Press, 2000). His research has focused on urban history, garden history, and time and memory in the built environment.

Zhou Xiangpin is Associate Professor of Landscape Architecture at Tongji University, Shanghai, China. He received his Ph.D. from Tongji University for a dissertation on *Shaping the Urban Natural Environment*. His research interests concern Chinese classic culture and garden history, especially in the Ming and Qing dynasties. He is currently writing a book entitled *Prelude and Rudiment: Investigation of the Transitional Stage between Shanghai Private Gardens and Parks, 1868-1937*.

Index